The Cambridge Economic History of Modern Europe

Unlike most existing textbooks on the economic history of modern Europe, which offer a country-by-country approach, *The Cambridge Economic History of Modern Europe* rethinks Europe's economic history since 1700 as unified and pan-European, with the material organised by topic rather than by country. This first volume is centred on the transition to modern economic growth, which first occurred in Britain before spreading to other parts of western Europe by 1870. Each chapter is written by an international team of authors who cover the three major regions of northern Europe, southern Europe, and central and eastern Europe. The volume covers the major themes of modern economic history, including trade; urbanization; aggregate economic growth; the major sectors of agriculture, industry and services; and the development of living standards, including the distribution of income. The quantitative approach makes use of modern economic analysis in a way that is easy for students to understand.

Stephen Broadberry is Professor of Economic History at the University of Warwick and a Co-ordinator of the Economic History Initiative at the Centre for Economic Policy Research. His recent publications include *The Economics of World War I* (2005, as co-editor) and *Market Services and the Productivity Race, 1850–2000: Britain in International Perspective* (2006).

Kevin H. O'Rourke is Professor of Economics at Trinity College Dublin and a Co-ordinator of the Economic History Initiative at the Centre for Economic Policy Research. His recent publications include *The New Comparative Economic History: Essays in Honor of Jeffrey G. Williamson* (2007, as co-editor), and *Power and Plenty: Trade, War, and the World Economy in the Second Millennium* (2007, with Ronald Findlay).

The Cambridge Economic History of Modern Europe Volume 1

1700–1870

EDITED BY
Stephen Broadberry
and
Kevin H. O'Rourke

CAMBRIDGE
UNIVERSITY PRESS

CAMBRIDGE UNIVERSITY PRESS
Cambridge, New York, Melbourne, Madrid, Cape Town, Singapore, São Paulo, Delhi

Cambridge University Press
The Edinburgh Building, Cambridge CB2 8RU, UK

Published in the United States of America by Cambridge University Press, New York

www.cambridge.org
Information on this title: www.cambridge.org/9780521708388

© Cambridge University Press 2010

First published 2010

Printed in the United Kingdom at the University Press, Cambridge

A catalogue record for this publication is available from the British Library

Library of Congress Cataloguing in Publication data
Broadberry, S. N.
The Cambridge economic history of modern Europe / Stephen Broadberry, Kevin H. O'Rourke.
  p.   cm.
ISBN 978-0-521-88202-6
1. Europe – Economic history.   I. O'Rourke, Kevin H.   II. Title.
HC240.B6865   2010
330.94–dc22

2009050509

ISBN 978-0-521-88202-6 hardback
ISBN 978-0-521-70838-8 paperback

This book is dedicated to the memory of Larry Epstein.

Contents

Figures

Tables

Contributors

George Alter, Department of History, University of Michigan.

Dan Bogart, Department of Economics, University of California, Irvine.

Stephen Broadberry, Department of Economics, University of Warwick.

Gregory Clark, Department of Economics, University of California, Davis.

Lee Craig, Department of Economics, North Carolina State University.

Guillaume Daudin, Université Lille-I (Equippe) and OFCE, Sciences Po.

Tracy Dennison, Division of Humanities and Social Sciences, California Institute of Technology.

Mauricio Drelichman, Department of Economics, University of British Columbia and CIFAR.

Rainer Fremdling, Faculty of Economics, University of Groningen.

Concepción García-Iglesias, Department of Social Science History, University of Helsinki.

Oscar Gelderblom, Department of History, Utrecht University.

Regina Grafe, Department of History, Northwestern University.

Bishnupriya Gupta, Department of Economics, University of Warwick.

Debin Ma, Department of Economic History, London School of Economics.

Paolo Malanima, Institute of Mediterranean Societies, IISM-CNR, Naples.

Joel Mokyr, Departments of Economics and History, Northwestern University, and Eitan Berglas School of Economics, Tel Aviv University.

Larry Neal, Department of Economics, University of Illinois, Urbana-Champaign.

Kevin H. O'Rourke, Department of Economics, Trinity College Dublin.

Şevket Pamuk, Ataturk Institute for Modern Turkish History, Bogaziçi University, Istanbul, and European Institute, London School of Economics.

Leandro Prados de la Escosura, Department of Economic History and Institutions and Instituto Figuerola, Universidad Carlos III de Madrid.

Jean-Laurent Rosenthal, Division of Humanities and Social Sciences, California Institute of Technology.

James Simpson, Department of Economic History and Institutions, Universidad Carlos III de Madrid.

Peter Solar, Vesalius College, Vrije Universiteit Brussel, and Facultés Universitaires Saint-Louis.

Richard W. Unger, Department of History, University of British Columbia.

Hans-Joachim Voth, Department of Economics, Universitat Pompeu Fabra, Barcelona.

Jan-Luiten van Zanden, Department of History, Utrecht University.

Preface

It would be unthinkable for American undergraduates to be offered courses in the economic history of their own state, rather than the United States as a whole. In sharp contrast, most existing textbooks on European economic history are country-specific, implying the risk that students will misinterpret continent-wide phenomena as having been purely national in scope, and as having had purely national causes. The time has come for a textbook on European economic history that takes an explicitly pan-European approach, with the material organized by topic rather than by country.

This project thus aims to provide a unified economic history of modern Europe, explicitly modelled on the pathbreaking Cambridge *Economic History of Britain* (Floud and McCloskey, 1981). Each chapter has been written by two or three leading experts in the field, who between them were able to cover each of the three major European regions (northern Europe, southern Europe, and central and eastern Europe). Following the pattern established by Floud and McCloskey, we have broken down the project into two volumes, covering the periods 1700–1870 and 1870–2000 respectively. Each volume contains chapters based on the dominant themes of modern economic history: aggregate growth and cycles, sectoral analysis, and living standards. The approach is quantitative and makes explicit use of economic analysis, but in a manner that is accessible to undergraduates.

This is a project that would have been simply unthinkable two decades ago. That there has always been a tradition of pan-European economic history is evident from a glance at the earlier volumes of the *Cambridge Economic History of Europe*, and many of the giants in the discipline represented there have provided us with sweeping accounts of the economic development of the continent as a whole. It is striking, however, that the later volumes in that series, from the Industrial Revolution onwards, tend to comprise a series of national histories, with a highly selective coverage of both countries and topics. Meanwhile, the quantitative economic history that was beginning to be written in European economics departments from the 1970s onwards was more often than not purely national in scope – which was perhaps inevitable, as economic historians started using their own country's national statistics to quantify economic growth over the long run. Furthermore, the number of cliometricians working outside the British Isles remained comparatively small. The result was a European economic history profession that was both small and fragmented, especially when compared with our colleagues in North America.

How things have changed. A crucially important turning point came with the founding of the European Historical Economics Society in 1991, which aimed to bring together quantitative economic historians from across Europe working in both economics and history departments. In 1997, the society launched the *European Economic History Review*, which has provided a common forum for economic historians across the continent. Another major breakthrough was the launching in 2003 of an Economic History Initiative at the Centre for Economic Policy Research in London, Europe's largest economics research network. In combination with European Union funding for pan-European research initiatives, the result has been the development of a vibrant economic history profession in Europe which can genuinely describe itself as "European."

We put our contributors through two gruelling conferences at which we discussed chapter drafts, in Lund in 2006, and at the CEPR in 2007. We are naturally extremely grateful to the local organizers of both events. We would also like to thank all the contributors for the enthusiasm and stamina which they displayed on both occasions, and also for delivering their chapters in a timely fashion.

This project is an outgrowth of the EU-funded Marie Curie Research Training Network "Unifying the European Experience: Historical Lessons of pan-European Development," Contract no. MRTN-CT-2004–512439. It goes without saying that we are extremely grateful to the European Commission for their very generous financial support, without which this project could never have gotten off the ground. We are also grateful to the CEPR staff who provided such expert assistance in applying for the grant and administering this project. Much of the work on this book took place while O'Rourke was a Government of Ireland Senior Research Fellow, and he thanks the Irish Research Council for the Humanities and Social Sciences for their generous support.

Our training network was struck by tragedy in 2007, when one of our most respected and well-liked members, Stephan (Larry) Epstein died suddenly, at the age of just 46. Larry is an enormous loss to our profession, and we shall miss him greatly. These volumes are dedicated to him.

Stephen N. Broadberry
Kevin H. O'Rourke

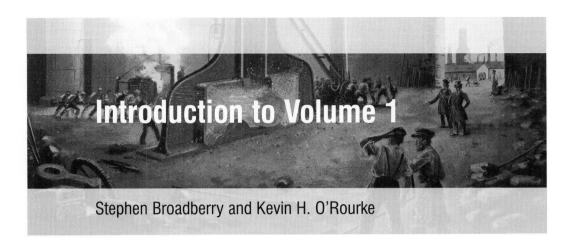

Introduction to Volume 1

Stephen Broadberry and Kevin H. O'Rourke

Volume 1 of this new economic history of modern Europe is centered on the transition to modern economic growth, which Kuznets (1974) defined in terms of the following six characteristics: (i) high rates of growth of per capita product and population; (ii) a high rate of growth of output per unit of all inputs – that is, total factor productivity; (iii) high rates of structural transformation from agriculture to industry and services, and from personal enterprise to large-scale impersonal organization of firms; (iv) changes in the structure of society and its ideology, including urbanization and secularization; (v) opening up of international communications, or globalization; and (vi) the limited spread of growth, leading to the divergence of living standards between "developed" and "underdeveloped" nations. The transition to modern economic growth occurred in Europe between 1700 and 1870, beginning in Britain, but spreading quite rapidly to other parts of western Europe.

Viewed in the grand sweep of history, this change was undoubtedly radical, and must be ranked alongside other epoch-making changes such as the change from hunting and gathering to settled agriculture. In recent decades, however, as it has proved increasingly possible to reconstruct the path of economic development at this time, it has become clear that the changes were more gradual and spread more widely across the economy than earlier generations had thought, thus calling into question the use of the term "Industrial Revolution." We have nevertheless retained the term, partly because it has become firmly embedded in the popular consciousness as well as the professional literature. However, perhaps more importantly, it should also be borne in mind that although the growth rate was slower than once thought, the economic changes of this period were nevertheless revolutionary in the sense that they proved irreversible and became an ideal type (de Vries, 2001). This is the true meaning of the attachment of the term "French Revolution" to the events of 1789, rather than the fact that the storming of the Bastille happened in a short space of time. Furthermore, it

Table I.1 GDP per capita in European countries, 1500–1870: growth rates and comparative levels

A Growth rates of GDP per capita (% per annum)

	1500–1700	1700–1750	1750–1820	1820–1870
UK	0.12	0.35	0.20	1.25
Netherlands	0.24	0.00	−0.02	0.83
Belgium	0.09	0.19	0.02	1.44
France	n.a.	n.a.	n.a.	0.85
Italy	−0.08	0.14	−0.22	0.61
Spain	−0.02	−0.10	0.10	0.27
Sweden	0.02	0.03	0.06	0.65
Poland	−0.13	−0.24	0.21	0.59
Russia	n.a.	n.a.	n.a.	0.64
Turkey	n.a.	0.16	0.07	0.52

B Comparative levels of GDP per capita (United Kingdom in 1820 = 100)

	c.1500	c.1700	c.1750	1820	1870
UK	57	73	87	100	187
Netherlands	67	109	109	107	162
Belgium	58	69	76	77	158
France	n.a.	n.a.	n.a.	72	110
Italy	83	71	76	65	88
Spain	63	61	58	62	71
Sweden	64	66	67	70	97
Poland	50–54	38–42	34–37	41	55
Russia	n.a.	n.a.	n.a.	40	55
Turkey	n.a.	35	38	40	52

Sources: Derived from van Zanden, 2001; Maddison, 2001; Pamuk, 2006; Álvarez-Nogal and Prados de la Escosura, 2007.

remains true that industry came to play a greater role in the economy as the modernizing economies shifted resources away from agriculture (Crafts, 1985a).

How rapidly did Europe grow between 1700 and 1850, and how much of a radical break with the past was this growth performance? In recent years, economic historians of Europe have made dramatic progress in quantifying the process of economic growth, and Table I.1 sets out the basic data for annual growth rates and comparative levels of gross domestic product (GDP) per capita. The systematic monitoring of comparative levels of per capita income is a relatively recent development, and helps to provide a consistency check on the growth rates for particular countries, which have normally been derived on an individual country basis.

The first thing that is apparent from Table I.1 is that the growth rate was much higher during the period 1820–1870 than during the early modern period 1500–1700. Indeed, during the early modern period, information on the parts of southern and eastern Europe for which we have data suggests declining living standards, in contrast to the slowly rising incomes of northwestern Europe, particularly Britain and the Low Countries. This is part of the well-known reversal of fortunes within Europe following the opening of new trade routes to the East via the Cape of Good Hope and the discovery of the Americas. The accompanying shift of per capita income leadership from the Mediterranean region to the Atlantic-facing economies of northwestern Europe has recently been termed the Little Divergence, to distinguish it from the Great Divergence of living standards between Europe and Asia which occurred after 1800 (Pomeranz, 2000; Allen, 2001; Broadberry, 2007).

The second result which is apparent from Table I.1 is that the transition to modern economic growth was a long-drawn-out process. Even in the lead country, the United Kingdom, the annual growth rate of per capita income remained less than 0.5 percent until well into the nineteenth century. Only after 1820 were rates of growth above 1 percent per annum seen, and then only in a handful of countries. The third conclusion which can be drawn from Table I.1 is that although its origins were British, modern economic growth transferred relatively easily to the rest of Europe, and indeed to the European settler colonies of the New World. All European countries in Table I.1 show an increase in per capita income growth after 1820, and this led to the Great Divergence of living standards between Europe and Asia.

The organization of this volume reflects our belief in the centrality of this transition to modern economic growth to understanding European economic history between 1700 and 1870. Part I focuses on aggregate developments, including shorter run business cycle fluctuations in Chapter 5 as well as longer run economic growth in Chapter 1. The inclusion of a separate Chapter 2 on population as well as a chapter on economic growth reflects the distinction that Kuznets made between modern economic growth and pre-industrial growth. As Malthus (1798) famously argued, rising living standards were typically only short-lived in the pre-industrial period, as population growth almost literally ate away any temporary gain in real wages. The Industrial Revolution period, by contrast, was marked by the coexistence of rapid population growth and rising per capita incomes, before Europe entered a demographic transition to a regime of lower population growth accompanied by sustained per capita income growth. Chapter 4, on trade and empire, reflects Kuznets's emphasis on globalization, as well as addressing the long-running debate on whether the West grew rich by exploiting the periphery. For a long time now, economic historians have established that the scale of the interaction between Europe and the wider world was not large enough on its own to explain the rise of the West (O'Brien, 1982). The alternative way of understanding the "European Miracle" is through institutional change, allowing Europe to achieve modern economic growth through the establishment of a system of incentives embedded deeply in the institutional framework of society. This is considered in Chapter 3, on state and private institutions.

Part II then provides a more detailed sectoral breakdown, examining developments in agriculture in Chapter 6 and in services in Chapter 8, as well as industry in Chapter 7. These three chapters focus on the issues of output and productivity growth as well as the changes in structure and organization that Kuznets emphasized. Part III then considers the upshot for living standards. In this section, as well as Chapter 9 on real wages and other indicators of the standard of living, we have included Chapter 10 on urbanization. This is one of the structural changes emphasized by Kuznets, which clearly also had a major impact on living standards. Finally, we address the issues of globalization and the divergence of living standards through Chapter 11 on Europe in an Asian mirror.

PART

I **Aggregate growth and cycles**

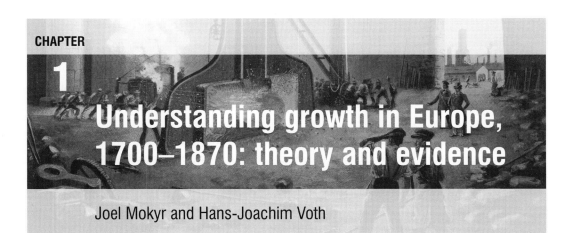

Understanding growth in Europe, 1700–1870: theory and evidence

Joel Mokyr and Hans-Joachim Voth

Contents

Incomes of ordinary citizens in developed countries today dwarf those enjoyed even by the wealthy elite during most of mankind's history. John Maynard Keynes, with slight incredulity, observed in 1930 that the economic problem of mankind (in Europe and North America at least) had been solved (Keynes, 1930). People no longer go hungry. Clean clothes, shelter, and warmth have gone from luxuries to necessities. By 1870, developments that would eventually deliver this full complement of riches were already in full swing. This chapter summarizes recent research by growth economists on how mankind escaped from a life that was, in the words of Thomas Hobbes, "nasty, brutish, and short." It contrasts these interpretations with the existing historical evidence and recent findings of economic historians. Four areas are of particular concern – demography, institutions, human capital, and technology. We conclude with suggestions for future research.

Theoretical approaches

In the late 1980s and early 1990s, macroeconomists began to turn their attention from business cycles to the determinants of long-run economic growth. Papers in the endogenous growth literature sought to explain why some countries had grown more rapidly than others. The main period of interest to which these models were applied was the post-war era. They returned to Kuznets's classic argument that current growth rates, when extrapolated backward, implied absurdly low incomes in early modern times and before. Therefore there must have been a long period of stagnation before modern growth started. But what was the source of the phase transition from a world of very low or zero rates of growth to a modern world of rapid and sustained growth?

From the 1990s onwards, scholars started to search for an overarching theory that could encompass both slow growth and the transition to rapidly increasing per capita incomes – a "unified growth model." The field has flourished since. A number of themes stand out – demography, the influence of institutions, human capital and culture, and the role of technology. We first summarize some of the most prominent contributions in the theoretical literature. In the main part of the chapter, we compare the theorists' predictions with the main facts unearthed by economic historians. Our conclusion offers some suggestions on how progress can be made.

Early models in unified growth theory, such as Kremer's (1993) paper, modelled the transition from stagnation to growth as one long, gradual acceleration of growth rates. As in some other papers in the endogenous growth literature, Kremer's model assumes that more people spell faster technological change, since the probability of a person having a bright idea is more or less constant. Because ideas are non-rivalrous, growth accelerates. Kremer showed that some of the basic predictions derived from such a simple growth model hold both over time and in cross-sections. Since 1,000,000 B.C., growth rates of population can be predicted from the current size of the population. Also, geographically separated economic units with greater surface areas produced bigger populations and higher densities. As population size and technology increase jointly, there is no steady state in Kremer's model. To avoid all variables showing explosive behavior, a demographic transition is necessary, so that fertility responds negatively to higher incomes above some threshold level.

In contrast, in exogenous growth models, technology "just happens," and adoption decisions are not explicit. Size itself does not affect technology or productivity change. In one application of exogenous growth to the transition to self-sustaining growth, Hansen and Prescott (2002) model the transition "from Malthus to Solow" by assuming that technological change in both the land-using (diminishing returns) and the non-land-using modes of production is exogenously given and constant. Initially, only the Malthus technology is used. In every generation, each lasting thirty-five years, productivity in their model increases by 3.2 percent in the "Malthus sector" (i.e. agriculture, where labor is subject to declining marginal returns) and by 52 percent in the "Solow sector" (where all factors of production are reproducible). Eventually, as the productivity of the unused technology increases exponentially, the Solow technology becomes competitive and is adopted. In this setup, an Industrial Revolution is inevitable, and does not depend on anything other than the differential growth rates of productivity used in the calibration.

A second class of models in which size matters also takes technological change to be exogenous. Here, the focus is on the conditions under which new techniques will be adopted. Early models in the tradition of Murphy, Shleifer and Vishny (1989) relied on demand effects, and hence the size of economies, to explain when a "big push" might occur. By "big push," authors in the tradition of Rosenstein-Rodan mean the simultaneous adoption of advanced technologies in many sectors. In order to pay the fixed cost necessary for adopting modern production, demand needs to be sufficiently high. This will often be the case only if a whole range of industries industrializes. The chances of this occurring increase with total output. One implication of these models is that industrialization might have been feasible long before it got under way – if only everybody had decided to invest earlier in fixed-cost technology, profits would have been high enough to justify the expense. Advances in technological knowledge themselves need not translate into greater output. Coordination failure can thus undermine the transition to modern technology.

High fixed costs and indivisibility also play a crucial role in models that put risk diversification at the heart of adoption decisions. Acemoglu and Zilibotti (1997) present a model with a tension between production requirements and household investment. Productive projects using new technology require substantial set-up costs. At the same time, households want to diversify their investments to minimize risks. Because of this, investment in the new, productive technology is initially very low, and so is output. This changes as households become richer – their savings become sufficiently large, relative to the capital requirements of new technologies, to avoid "putting all their eggs in one basket." Industrialization, once under way, generates the means with which to sustain itself. A number of lucky draws can get it started. Two identical economies may end up on very different paths, depending on whether they get lucky in the first round or not. Acemoglu's and Zilibotti's model also has the feature that households do not take into account the effect of their investment decisions on aggregate productivity. Industrialization may not occur, while being feasible. The model incorporates a stochastic component – industrialization may partly be the result of chance. One implication is that not every aspect of actual industrial transformations is fraught with meaning – and the country that actually went first may simply have been lucky.[1]

Many unified growth models link human capital accumulation with technology and the ideas-producing properties of population growth. These papers have argued that the transition to modern growth is accompanied by a growing importance of human capital (Becker and Barro, 1988; Lucas, 2002; Becker, Murphy, and Tamura, 1990). Galor and Weil (2000) made the nexus between human capital and technological change a cornerstone of the transition to rapid growth. They argue that the escape from stagnation took place in two steps – a transition from the Malthusian to a post-Malthusian state, and then to a modern-growth regime. Galor and Weil's key assumption is that, as technological change accelerates, human capital becomes more valuable: it allows people to cope with a rapidly changing workplace. Technological change accelerates as more people produce more ideas during the long Malthusian period. Because of a delay in the response of population to income growth, per capita incomes grow, if very slowly. Eventually, parents invest more in the human capital of their offspring. This in turn accelerates the growth of knowledge. Higher incomes make it easier for parents to have more children. At the same time, a growing value of human capital produces incentives to increase the quality of one's offspring, reducing quantity. Initially, after the start of

---

[1] Following Crafts's (1977) original contribution, this idea has been the subject of substantial debate among economic historians.

modern growth, the income effect dominated, leading to more births; later, the substitution effect became more important, and fertility declined.

Cervellati and Sunde (2005) as well as de la Croix (2008) alter this setup by arguing that life expectancy rose quickly with productivity. This in turn encouraged investment in human capital, as payback horizons lengthened. Even if technological change is only slightly skill-biased, a self-reinforcing cycle of better technology, greater life expectancy, and higher investment in human capital can get started. Boucekkine, de la Croix and Peeters (2007) show how rising population density may encourage higher literacy, through the cheaper provision of schooling services. Jones (2001) combines the population-ideas mechanism with a property rights regime that reserves a share of output for innovators. Based on his calibrations, Jones concludes that the single most important factor leading to a take-off in growth after the nineteenth century was more effective enforcement of intellectual property rights, which created the necessary incentives for the sector that produced the ideas.

Some observations from economic history

The population–idea nexus is key in many unified growth models. How does this square with the historical record? As Crafts (1995) has pointed out, the implications for the cross-section of growth in Europe and around the world are simply not borne out by the facts – bigger countries did not grow faster.[2] Modern data reinforce this conclusion: country size is either negatively related to GDP per capita, or has no effect at all. The negative finding seems plausible, as one of the most reliable correlates of economic growth, the rule of law (Hansson and Olsson, 2006), declines with country size. Even if we substitute "population" with more relevant concepts like market size, which might have influenced the demand for new products, the contrasting growth records of Britain and France are hard to square with endogenous growth models emphasizing size.[3] Moreover, it is disconcerting for these models that in 1750, on the eve of the Industrial Revolution, Britain had just experienced half a century of virtual demographic stagnation. One could also point out that if population size

---

[2] It is indeed striking that prior to the coming to the fore of the British economy, Europe's most successful economies tended to be city states (Hicks, 1969, p. 42). These, with high density but relatively small populations, had an advantage in solving the problems of setting up effective institutions of commerce and finance. Market size was less of a problem, in part because the fixed costs of setting up these institutions were not all that high, and because they tended to be open economies. The main source of economies of scale was not economic but military. Military power depended on total income and population.

[3] Some later models in the spirit of Kremer, such as Jones (2001), attempt to provide a solution to this problem by assuming increasing returns in the production of goods, and by allowing the number of new ideas to be a function of the existing stock of ideas.

is critical, China's early modern record is a puzzle. Its population rose from 130 million in 1650 to 420 million in 1850, yet no Industrial Revolution occurred. An interesting argument is made by Lin (1995). Lin argues that the relationship between population size and technological change depends on the source of innovation. In a world in which new technology is based entirely on learning by doing, greater size would imply more innovation, assuming that the advances were disseminated effectively over the larger unit. Once progress begins to depend more on experimentation and theory, such advantages disappear. Lin maintains that the success of China in the Song period (960–1279), as opposed to its relative stagnation in the seventeenth century and beyond, reflects a change in the source of innovation.

Even if "size mattered" in the data, it would not be clear what the relevant channel was. A larger population (without a collapse in per capita incomes) may be accompanied by positive externalities of a different kind. Regardless of whether size mattered to the generation or adoption of new technology, as the endogenous growth models suggest, greater size could simply have enhanced the division of labor. This in itself could have contributed to an acceleration of output growth. Kelly (1997) presents a model of "Smithian growth," where trade integration is promoted by improvements in transport infrastructure, leading to an acceleration of growth. He applies this model to Song-dynasty China. Similarly, in Europe, higher population density may have generated the scope for positive externalities, partly through improvements in turnpikes and canals, partly through long-distance trade (Bogart, 2005a, 2005b; Daudin, 2007). In this sense, it becomes easier to rationalize the commercial successes of the medium-sized, but densely populated and internationally integrated Dutch Republic in the seventeenth and eighteenth centuries.

Models in the "big push" tradition run into problems similar to population-based endogenous growth; the European experience after 1700 does not suggest that the absolute size of economies is a good predictor of the timing of industrialization. The size of most industrialization projects was small – even the largest textile mills, had they been financed by a single person, hardly constituted a large concentration of risk. Before the late nineteenth century, fixed costs in manufacturing were limited. Much diversification, moreover, could take place *within* the existing business structure of Britain during the Industrial Revolution.[4] When it comes to production technology with high fixed costs, adoption decisions *after* 1870 could possibly be explained by the

---

[4] Pearson and Richardson (2001) show that the typical entrepreneur in the Industrial Revolution was heavily diversified. Rather than describing the entrepreneur as a single-minded owner-manager who spent his entire life on the one business, they show the extent to which early entrepreneurs were involved in non-core ventures. Cotton masters and other textile producers in Manchester, Leeds, and Liverpool, for example, could be found as directors of insurance companies, canal and turnpike companies, gas companies, banks, and companies in other sectors.

big-push framework. Yet by that point in time, international trade was already doing much to break down the link between the size of the domestic economy and the possibility of technology adoption. If there were large fixed costs before 1870, they were in infrastructure, not in manufacturing. In Britain, these infrastructure investments – canals, turnpikes, harbors – do not appear to have suffered a great deal from capital scarcity. This is despite the numerous shortcomings of the British financial system, which ranged from the Bubble Act to usury laws that squeezed private credit, and the relentless borrowing by the Crown for much of the eighteenth century (Temin and Voth, 2008). On the whole, infrastructure projects were apparently financed without too much difficulty, mainly through local notables (Michie, 2000).

Finally, unified growth models that emphasize differences in productivity growth between the agricultural ("traditional") and industrial ("modern") sectors, such as Hansen and Prescott (2002), also encounter substantial empirical difficulties. At the point in time when overall growth rates began to accelerate, both the land-using sector as well as the industrial sector became more productive – according to some measures, at relatively similar rates (Crafts, 1985a). By definition, the Hansen–Prescott model has little to say about which country industrialized first, and why – the entire world is its unit of observation.

These observations are not meant as final verdicts on the merits or otherwise of unified growth models. They explain why we believe that theorists, applied economists, and economic historians should dig deeper – especially into the interactions between fertility, human capital, institutions, and technology. This is what the following sections attempt to do.

Malthus vanishing

Populations grew in most parts of Europe during the early modern period. In some parts, they surpassed the levels seen before the Black Death. Demographic growth accelerated decisively in many European countries in the late eighteenth century. There was substantial variation in timing, with Britain and Ireland leading the way, and France avoiding a major jump altogether. During the period 1500–1870, the economic impact of demographic factors changed. It went from being a crucial determinant of per capita incomes in most parts of Europe to a factor of declining importance as technological change accelerated after 1800. Growth theorists often refer to the period before 1750 as the Malthusian epoch. We first describe the Malthusian model and key changes in demographic–economic interactions after 1800. We then review the evidence and summarize what we know about how population pressure eventually fell away as a key economic variable.

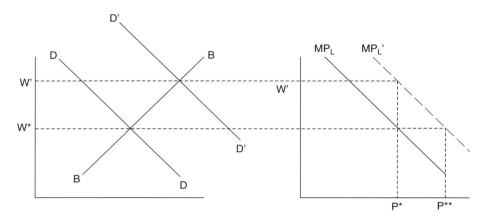

Figure 1.1 The Malthusian model

The Malthusian model relies on two main assumptions: first, that population growth responded positively to per capita incomes. As wages or per capita income fell, fertility declined (the "preventive check") and death rates increased (the "positive check"), as indicated by the upward sloping fertility schedule BB, and the downward sloping mortality schedule DD, in Figure 1.1. The second assumption is that income per capita was negatively related to population size due to diminishing returns to labor, illustrated by the downward sloping marginal product of labor curve, MP_L, whose position reflects *inter alia* the level of technology in the economy. A widely cited example illustrating the trade-off between incomes and population size is the Black Death. As European populations fell by approximately one-third to one-half of their pre-crisis levels, wages everywhere surged. Living standards in fourteenth-century England, conventionally measured, reached a high not seen again until the nineteenth century.

Together, the two assumptions underlying the Malthusian model imply that whatever advances in incomes occur will inevitably be frittered away through more babies. In Figure 1.1, birth and death schedules intersect at a wage W^*. The technology schedule in the right-hand panel then translates this into a feasible population size P^*. If a temporary technological shock moves the MP_L curve to the right, to MP_L', and thus drives the wage up to W', death rates fall and population starts to grow. Eventually, because of declining marginal returns, this will force wages down to their previous level (at population level P^{**}). As H. G. Wells put it, mankind "spent the great gifts of science as rapidly as it got them in a mere insensate multiplication of the common life" (Wells, 2005).[5]

---

[5] Galor and Weil (2000) assume that the response of fertility to incomes is delayed. Hence a one-period acceleration in technological change can generate higher incomes in the subsequent period, and a sequence of positive shocks can lead to sustained growth. While this solves the problem in a technical sense, it is unlikely to explain why fertility responses did not erode real wage gains over hundreds of years.

Clark (2007a) even goes as far as to argue that the average English person in 1800 was no better off than their ancestors on the African plains millennia before.

Higher death rates (depicted by a rightward shift of the mortality schedule from DD to D'D') imply higher per capita living standards. Unhygienic conditions and a deterioration in the microbial environment, for example, will boost incomes as they reduce the number of surviving children. Lower fertility rates can achieve the same effect. Welfare is not necessarily any higher, but the incomes of those who live will be. Europeans in the early modern period also reduced population pressure by ensuring that a high proportion of women never gave birth at all. The rest postponed marriage, further reducing fertility rates. This pattern is unique to Europe, and only occurred west of a line from St. Petersburg to Trieste (Hajnal, 1965). Other parts of the world, such as China, used infanticide for the same purpose, but with less effectiveness.

There are two variants of the Malthusian model. The model in its strongest form has its roots in the classic "iron law of wages." Without shifting mortality and fertility schedules, it predicts stagnant real wages. Without technological change or other supply shocks, population size will stagnate. The weaker version emphasizes equilibrating mechanisms, not outcomes. The positive and preventive checks identified by Malthus influence demographic growth. Only if these responses are sufficiently large, and only without further perturbations to the system, does the weak version lead *in the limit* to a return to a subsistence wage.

It is clear that the strong version – with stagnant wages at the subsistence level – can claim little empirical support. Stock variables like population size are invariably slow-moving. Shifts in mortality schedules (possibly as a result of urbanization) could produce new equilibria, but our chances of observing them will depend on the relative magnitudes of short-term and enduring shifts. For England, the real-wage data computed by Clark (2005, p. 1311) replace the traditional wage series computed by Phelps-Brown and Hopkins. They are based on a broad array of commodities and a comprehensive set of nominal wages. Both the Clark and the Phelps-Brown series show the same, surprising sharp decline in wages in Tudor England between 1495 and 1575. This decline is puzzling, since it was accompanied by a stable and then rising population, as well as by unusually long life expectancy. Recent calculations by Allen (2001) and others show that, in the long term, wages in Europe followed divergent trajectories. Northwestern Europe saw marked rises in wages, often at the same time as population increased. This would contradict the strong version if both north and south were subject to Malthusian forces.[6] Furthermore, some of the

---

[6] Real wages may not reflect changes in welfare, because some of the wage premia available in towns only compensated for higher mortality risk. We are also not sure how much payments in kind varied over time, and if higher payments in cash compensated for declining payments in wheat, etc.

debate regarding the outcome of Malthusian processes conflates real wages with real per capita GDP or income. This is problematic because participation rates and hours worked may have changed, leading to considerable changes in incomes per capita and per family even at more or less constant wages. Indeed, rising participation rates could, all other things being equal, lead to real wages and real income per capita moving in *opposite* directions. The rise of cottage industries in the countryside after 1650, the famed "proto-industrialization" phenomenon, would do exactly that. There is also reasonable evidence to believe that labor input was rising in the century before the Industrial Revolution (De Vries, 1994, 2008; Voth, 1998, 2001a, 2001b).

Confronting the model's predictions in its weaker form – with an emphasis on equilibrating mechanisms – is less demanding. We can observe flow variables such as births and deaths at high frequencies, and relate them to food prices and real wages. Over the short run, movements in population before 1750 seem to offer some limited support for a Malthusian response.[7] Mortality and nuptiality can adjust even over the short run. High-frequency events such as famines, wars, and epidemics had much smaller long-term effects than has often been assumed: a sharp decline in population was normally followed by higher wages. Within a few years, unusually high birth and low death rates would compensate for the initial decline in population (Watkins and Menken, 1985; Watkins and van de Walle, 1985). Lee's original work on the Wrigley–Schofield population data showed nuptiality responding (weakly, and with a lag that stretches credulity) to wages, but life expectancy to be largely independent of the wage.

In testing both the weak and the strong version of the Malthusian model, endogeneity is a major challenge. Wages influence population size and vice versa (Lee and Anderson, 2002). One potential way forward is to use an exogenous source of identification. Recent work by Kelly (2005) suggests that weather is a useful instrument for wages – the part of real wage variation that is driven by it is not the result of a feedback from population. Estimated in this way, there is strong evidence that Malthusian restrictions bound in England before 1650, with marriage rates reacting strongly (and positively) and death rates strongly (and negatively) to wage changes. Kelly's findings suggest that passing real-wage fluctuations had a larger effect on nuptiality than on mortality. This implies that, in the short run, the preventive check was stronger than the positive one, but both were significant.

Vector autoregressions offer an alternative method. Nicolini (2007) and Crafts and Mills (2009) use them to model the dynamic feedback

---

[7] See e.g. Galor (2005, pp. 183–84) for some graphs that indicate that in pre-industrial Britain population and real wages moved roughly in opposite directions, and that crude birth rates and crude death rates were negatively correlated.

between fertility, mortality, and the real wage in England. In this way, they examine the strength of the preventive and the positive checks. Both papers find much stronger evidence in favor of Malthusian checks and balances for the period up to the middle of the seventeenth century than for later decades. The fertility channel is particularly potent, while the mortality channel appears weaker. After 1650, the fertility channel declines in strength. Nicolini (2007) concludes that "perhaps the world before Malthus was not so Malthusian." As is the case with all negative results, it is not always clear if it is lack of power in the statistical procedures used, a shortage of identifying variation in the data, or the true absence of a causal link that is responsible. Overall, the IV-procedure used by Kelly appears more promising as a way to pin down causality and the strength of interactions.

Some progress has thus been made in terms of analyzing short-term responses. However, the precise contribution of demographic factors to divergent per capita incomes in early modern Europe remains largely unclear. Golden-age Holland had exceptionally high wages compared with the rest of Europe, and a stagnant population. It is not clear what particular feature of fertility behavior or of death schedules (if any) accounts for this beyond the high levels of urbanization. The Dutch example suggests that, while Malthusian adjustment mechanisms may have operated in the short run, many interesting shifts were caused by other factors. Since the late Middle Ages, there were throughout Europe regions and towns in which incomes exceeded subsistence levels, traditionally defined, without a concomitant rise in population size. Some unified growth models (Galor, 2005; Jones, 2001) predict (modestly) rising per capita incomes before the Industrial Revolution. This is on the whole confirmed: living standards drifted up, albeit slowly, in some parts of Europe in the centuries before 1800. The reason proposed – a delayed population response to technological advances – is not altogether persuasive: total fertility rates for females in many pre-modern populations (and especially European ones) were substantially below their biological maximum. Birth rates rebounded vigorously after each famine. This suggests that they could respond to rising living standards. One important question, then, is why Europeans curtailed their fertility, and why they did so in a peculiar way that involved delayed marriages for some women, and a life of celibacy for others. What social institutions underpinned the "European marriage pattern"? One interesting hypothesis links the emergence of fertility restrictions to the high price of labor after the Black Death (van Zanden and de Moor, 2010), which made female workers more valuable. This would have made it beneficial to keep them in the workforce as long as possible, and to delay motherhood. But why did this mechanism work in the Netherlands and not, say, in Italy, China, or India? This question is particularly relevant, since all these areas suffered plague outbreaks.

One way of linking the persistence of high wages with specific European features involves interactions between cities and death schedules. European cities were veritable death traps, with far higher mortality rates than the countryside. In contrast, in China and Japan urban and rural mortality rates were broadly similar (Woods, 2003). Different cultural practices, such as the regular removal of excrement from Far Eastern cities for use as fertilizer in the countryside, may have played an important role. Not only were European cities far more unhealthy places to live in under normal conditions (due to congestion and poor sanitation), but they were especially sensitive to contagious epidemics and military disasters such as sieges and plunder. Hence the DD curve in the graph, which is a composite of rural and urban demographic behavior, could slope upwards *over some part of the w-D space* because of a composition effect. There could then be multiple equilibria: societies could move from one state, where population was large, wages were low, cities small, and aggregate death rates low, to another, where wages were higher, cities larger, death rates higher, and the population smaller. A major shock, such as the Black Death, could push the economy from one equilibrium to another.[8]

Cities mattered for reasons other than excess mortality. They were the loci of much international trade, and of private-order institutions that supported the operation of markets in goods, capital, and labor. They were also centers of inventive activity. Urban activities produced a higher likelihood of inventing new techniques with a large economic impact: technology itself could have improved as a result of urbanization (Clark and Hamilton, 2006; Voigtländer and Voth, 2006). City growth may therefore have gone hand in hand with a slow, gradual outward shift of the technology schedule, making higher wages compatible with bigger populations. What this means is that, at any level of population, income would be higher with a larger urban sector, which would go some distance to explain the Dutch "anomaly." This means that far from being simply an *indicator* of productivity, urbanization itself could become a driving force increasing output per head. In this case, Malthusian forces could still dominate short-run changes, but the key *explanandum* would no longer follow from its basic tenets.

At some point, in the majority of European countries, population growth accelerated in an important way. Often, a rise in fertility and/or a decline in mortality signalled the end of the previous regime. Eventually, fertility rates followed the downward trend of mortality – completing the "demographic transition."[9] The latest revisions of the Wrigley–Schofield English population estimates (Wrigley et al., 1997) show that fertility increases dominated as a cause of more rapid growth; mortality played a role, but it was responsible for

---

[8] Such a model is developed in Voigtländer and Voth (2008).

[9] A good summary is Chesnais (1992). The concept goes back to the work of Warren Thompson in the 1920s.

only about one-third of the acceleration.[10] It seems that by 1750 the old demographic regime was breaking down. The work of Patrick Galloway (1988) shows that in the middle of the eighteenth century the short-term behavior of British vital rates was no longer responsive to changes in prices.

While some of the population explosion in Europe after 1800 derived for a while from higher fertility, declining mortality eventually became more important. Fertility followed the downward trend, in many cases with a delay measured in decades (Lee, 2003; Coale and Watkins, 1986). Most of this fertility decline was concentrated in a few decades, starting in 1870 and accelerating after 1890. In some countries, such as the United Kingdom, Germany, Sweden, the Netherlands, Finland, and Belgium, there were sustained and sometimes marked increases in fertility before decline set in. For example, the average number of children per woman rose from 4.5 to 5.5 in the Netherlands between 1850 and 1880. By 1900, it had returned to its earlier level. In most European countries the first significant reductions in fertility occurred after the 1880s, long after industrial change had started to take hold on the continent. Some countries saw large reductions in infant mortality before fertility started to decline (Sweden, Belgium, Denmark); in others, both series show a concurrent downward movement (France, Germany, Netherlands) (Chesnais, 1992).

Finding an economic reason for fertility decline has not been easy, and there is currently no consensus on the principal contributing factors (Alter, 1992). Variations both across Europe and over time present challenges of interpretation. The biggest comparative project on the fertility transition, the Princeton European Fertility Project (EFP), concluded that there was no clear link between socioeconomic factors and fertility change. Instead, ethnic, religious, linguistic, and cultural factors appeared to be dominant (Coale and Watkins, 1986). Woods (2000) reached a similar conclusion for Britain, attributing the Victorian decline in fertility to changing ideology, primarily "the desire or willingness to limit family size from the 1860s on" (p. 150), and suggests, more provocatively, that "the very question 'how many children should we have' was new to most Victorians" (p. 169). The leading explanation for fertility change is the "diffusion model," where knowledge about prophylactic techniques spread along linguistic lines. The principal reason why scholars have accepted the findings of the EFP is the remarkable similarity in the timing of the transition, and its spread along linguistic lines.[11]

---

[10] Wrigley (1983) showed that without mortality decline, eighteenth-century growth would have accelerated by 1.25 percent; without fertility change, growth would have improved by 0.5 percent. This implies that over 70 percent of the acceleration was driven by changes in fertility. Wrigley et al. (1997) qualify these conclusions to some extent, finding a faster decline in mortality, but the relative rankings are unlikely to change significantly.

[11] As Cleland and Wilson (1987) argue, "the simultaneity and speed of the European transition makes it highly doubtful that any economic force could be found which was powerful enough to offer a reasonable explanation."

Studies that go beyond the broad aggregates and look at regional data sometimes reach different conclusions. For example, in Bavaria the opportunity cost of women's time, religion, and political affiliations appear to have played a big role (Brown and Guinnane, 2002). Furthermore, the statistical basis for some of the EFP's conclusions may be less robust than had previously been assumed.[12] The simultaneity of the drop in reproduction rates across Europe in the decades before 1914 makes it unlikely that economic factors can account for the fertility decline all by themselves. Exogenous, non-economic factors probably dominated in the great decline of European fertility. This need not present a challenge to all growth models. Yet for the more ambitious class of structural models in the unified growth tradition, the apparent incapacity of economic factors to have a clear bearing on fertility outcomes represents a challenge.

In many models of long-term growth, the fertility transition plays a crucial role, and the timing of fertility decline is central to many theories explaining the transition to self-sustaining growth. The decline is normally modelled as a response to changing economic incentives. Leading interpretations by Becker and Barro (1988) and Lucas (2002) emphasize the quantity–quality trade-off facing parents in a context of faster technological change and higher returns to human capital. The standard arguments are that (i) skill premia surged, often because of technological change; and (ii) parents limited fertility as a response to this change in the trade-off between child quantity and quality. This is not unproblematic. Returns to human capital, conventionally measured, probably did not increase significantly before 1870. Models that link population dynamics to technological progress itself, such as Galor and Weil (2000), run into timing problems in the case of Britain, because demographic growth accelerated there in the mid-eighteenth century, *before* any serious impact of technological change on output per capita can be discerned. Furthermore, since the economic benefits of formal education were probably minor for working-class employment, any model of parental fertility choice based on quality–quantity trade-offs faces problems, explaining at best the demographic behavior of a minority group.

Definitive evidence for a quantity–quality trade-off is lacking. What is more plausible is to argue that the net *costs* of child quantity increased in the second half of the nineteenth century. An alternative interpretation thus emphasizes the importance of government intervention through compulsory schooling laws and child labor regulations. Doepke (2004) argues that the latter were

---

[12] A much larger research project on German fertility decline is now under way (Sheilagh Ogilvie, Timothy Guinnane, and Richard Smith, with Markus Küpker and Janine Maegraith, Economy, Gender, and Social Capital in the German Demographic Transition, available at www.hpss.geog.cam.ac.uk/research/projects/germandemography/2005), using that country's extraordinarily rich data sources.

crucial, and further argues that other government policies (such as education subsidies) could not have had a similar influence. If the importance of government intervention is confirmed, examining the economic and other factors behind the adoption of child labor laws or educational reforms becomes crucial (Doepke and Zilibotti, 2005). Galor and Moav (2006) emphasize the Balfour Act, which introduced compulsory schooling. In their view, support for the reform by capital owners, who needed more skilled labor, was critical.[13]

Yet we do not know with certainty that government intervention was crucial in moving children out of the factories and into the classrooms. For the United States, state schooling laws may only have had a small influence on child labor (Moehling, 1999). At the same time, data problems bias any estimate of such an effect towards zero. In the United Kingdom, Nardinelli (1980) and Kirby (1999) argue that child labor laws came in at the same time as technological changes made the employment of children less useful. There is therefore considerable tension between the views of theorists, who emphasize either rapid, skill-using technological change or effective government intervention, and the assessment of economic historians, who largely reject the former and find limited evidence of the latter.

Some data constraints will be hard to overcome. We have little information on what determined completed fertility rates, educational investment, age at marriage, and the like in the industrializing cities throughout Europe. There are no cohort-specific studies of fertility behavior at the micro level that would unambiguously identify the impact of discontinuous changes in schooling laws and the like. Wrigley and Schofield's famous *Population History of England* is based on family reconstitutions that focus on rural parishes, and their data end in 1837. Everywhere in Europe, family reconstitutions are harder to construct for the nineteenth century than for earlier periods because mobility increased. Future research should aim to improve our understanding of fertility behavior, and of the relevant costs of child-rearing. More detailed demographic analysis of the fertility choices of the working class – combined with information on rates of school attendance, the economics of apprenticeships and the like prior to and after the introduction of compulsory schooling laws – could do much to further our understanding of the demographic transition.

Institutions, good and bad

A good part of the modern debate about growth centers on the relative importance of institutions versus human capital (Acemoglu and Johnson, 2005; Rodrik,

---

[13] The failure of skill premia to rise (which we shall describe in more detail below) could then be explained by this supply shock.

Subramanian, and Trebbi, 2004; Glaeser et al., 2004). In cross-sections of countries from the late twentieth century, constraints on the executive tend to be positively correlated with higher per capita output. Because of the potential for reverse causation – with higher income per capita improving institutional quality – work on modern data has principally focused on finding an exogenous factor that affect institutions, but not economic outcomes, and so can be used to instrument for institutions. One such factor that has been used with great success is historical settler mortality. In a series of pathbreaking papers, Acemoglu, Johnson, and Robinson show that countries in which European settlers survived easily also ended up with more desirable institutional arrangements (e.g. Acemoglu, Johnson, and Robinson, 2001). They are markedly richer today, making it more likely that the link between institutions and efficiency is causal.

How much can institutional interpretations help us understand growth in Europe before 1870? What is the role of institutional change in the transition to self-sustaining growth? Any analysis of institutions in a historical setting needs to look beyond the role of the state and constraints on the executive. We do not know nearly enough about how institutions worked in Europe between 1500 and 1870 to pass judgement on their overall contribution to economic growth. In particular, we need to learn much more about legal processes, the role of "state building" and the importance of informal institutional arrangements.

Possibly the single best-known statement in the institutional tradition was formulated by North and Weingast (1989). They conclude that the Glorious Revolution and the Bill of Rights in England in 1688–89 did more than just put government finances on a firmer footing. Because of the boost to the role of Parliament and the greater influence of the common-law courts, the English monarch's power had been curtailed. Crucially, it was widely viewed as such because of credible commitment. High-handed breaking of contracts and seizure of property came to an end.[14] North and Weingast argue that, once property rights and constraints on the executive had been firmly established, risk premia fell. Capital accumulation accelerated, and investing in new ideas became much more profitable. Eventually, Britain's growth rate took off.[15]

Most institutional interpretations of the early modern period similarly focus on capricious despotic rule falling away. DeLong and Shleifer (1993) return to Montesquieu's famous argument that growth is more vigorous in republican states because they suffer fewer arbitrary interventions by the authorities.[16]

---

[14] These had previously been possible both through the legal system – namely the Star Chamber – and brute force (such as in the raid on the Tower of London, when the precious metals of goldsmiths were seized).

[15] North and Weingast are cautious not to link the events of 1688 directly to the Industrial Revolution, which began about seventy years later. Others have not been so prudent (e.g. Dam, 2005, p. 84).

[16] "An opinion of greater certainty as to the possession of property in these [republican] states makes [merchants] undertake everything … [T]hinking themselves sure of what they have already acquired, they boldly expose it in order to acquire more."

They argue that absolutist rule was harmful for three reasons – states run by ambitious, powerful princes fought more wars, taxed more comprehensively, and respected property rights less. Autocratic states also happened, on average, to be further away from the new trade routes to the Americas and Asia. It should be noted that only one of these channels is directly associated with the institutional interpretation in its narrow form, and DeLong and Shleifer cannot show that it is particularly potent.

A more recent paper by Acemoglu, Cantoni, Johnson, and Robinson (2005) argues that two of the channels identified by Delong and Shleifer interacted in a particular fashion to strengthen institutions. Countries that had opportunities for Atlantic trade experienced a gradual strengthening of bourgeois forces in society. Hence, "constraints on the executive" in Britain and the Dutch Republic grew, according to their estimates. Acemoglu et al. demonstrate that this improvement in the quality of institutions mattered for growth – urbanization rates surged wherever geographically determined "exposure" to Atlantic trade was high.

Institutional interpretations of the Industrial Revolution and its aftermath have emphasized the role of political economy. For the case of Britain after 1800, Acemoglu, Johnson, and Robinson (2005) and Acemoglu and Robinson (2006) have argued that political power mattered in large part because it made the redistribution of income possible. They distinguish between *de iure* power, that is, the power to pass formal laws and statutes, and *de facto* power, which includes the physical ability to overthrow the regime if those who have it do not find the policies to their taste. While by 1720 Parliament had concentrated a great deal of *de iure* power and thus elevated itself to the status of a meta-institution, it still needed to be concerned with the *de facto* power of the large masses of middle-class people who accumulated increasing economic wealth, and yet were to a great extent disenfranchised until the reforms of 1832 and 1867. Acemoglu et al. (2006) argue that the French Revolution acted as an exogenous shock to the political system of neighboring states. Defeat at the hands of Napoleon's armies prodded rulers in Prussia and Austria into major reforms. Elsewhere, conquest by the French swept away old political and social institutions in their entirety. Combined with the rising tide of technological change after 1850, the authors argue, the improved institutions of the set of countries ringing France accelerated growth in the early nineteenth century in an important way.

Institutions have thus gained a great deal of credence in the modern growth literature (Rodrik et al., 2004; North, 2005). Yet interpretations of Europe's growth record that rely primarily on institutions face numerous challenges. To start with, few scholars agree what institutions are, and how the concept should be applied to the past. North defined them as "a set of rules, compliance procedures, and moral and ethical behavioral norms designed to *constrain* the behavior of individuals in the interests of maximizing the wealth or utility of principals" (North, 1981, emphasis added). Greif (2006) includes other modes of behavior that create historical regularities. In Greif's model, beliefs and ideology act as "deep" parameters that determine the efficacy with which societies set up rules making exchange and investment possible. Yet there are few good theories that explain in detail how institutions change and why some economies end up with "better" ones than others. Standard measures in the literature such as the (perceived) risk of expropriation, government effectiveness, and constraints on the executive, can all easily reflect choices by governments, and may change quickly. For any model that implies that better institutions work wonders through capital accumulation or technological progress, this would be problematic. Glaeser et al. (2004) show that all three standard measures of institutions often change after a single election. Presumably, property rights that are simply protected because of a ruler's whim are not worth a great deal. The volatility of these measures over time makes it less likely that they identify some structural parameter of the political system. Other, more obvious variables, such as judicial independence, proportional representation, and constitutional review, vary much less and are more likely to proxy for the structural constraints on governments that North had in mind. Yet in modern-day data, the effect of these variables is small and insignificant. What would be needed to settle the matter is a "deep" parameter of a country's political constitution that does not change quickly, and that is not simply a reflection of current economic and political conditions.

For the period 1500–1800, the "constraints on the executive" variable, as compiled by Acemoglu et al., successfully predicts urbanization rates. The same is true of Delong and Shleifer's absolutism indicator. Yet both concepts are troubling for the early modern period. Data problems abound, and coding variables based on the complex institutional arrangements in place in many European states before 1800 is not a challenge for the faint-hearted. The Habsburgs ruling Spain, coded as perfectly absolutist by Acemoglu et al. for the sixteenth century, often failed to get tax or other concessions from the Cortes of Castile. In their other kingdoms, such as Aragon, many medieval "freedoms" and the assemblies that protected them curtailed the monarch's powers. For instance, even for that epitome of absolutist rule, the Sun King of France, Louis XIV (and coded as a perfectly unconstrained "1" by Acemoglu et al.), there are important question marks. Historians have largely rejected the idea that his rule can meaningfully be described as implementing a successful, far-reaching absolutist agenda. For a generation, a new consensus inspired by the works of, *inter alia*, Georges Pagès and of Roland Mousnier (1970) has emphasized how much French kings at the height of absolutism still governed through social compromise and consensus, maintaining the stability of a traditional society and the influence of old elites for much of the time. It seems doubtful that the currently available classification schemes capture enough of what is directly relevant to the argument that institutions and restrictions on the executive caused economic growth before 1800.[17]

States with extensive checks and balances, such as Venice, the Holy Roman Empire, and Poland, constrained their rulers' freedom of action. Yet they did not become hothouses of economic dynamism. This may be because fettering the prince was neither unambiguously good nor bad in economic terms before the rise of modern, centralized states with clearly defined and stable borders. The late S. R. Epstein (2000) has emphasized the advantages conveyed by a powerful state that could curb local rent-seeking and resolve coordination problems. Most "constraints on the executive" took the form of rent-seeking groups ensuring that their share of the pie remained constant. Unsurprisingly, large parts of Europe's early modern history read like one long tale of gridlock, with interest groups from local lords and merchant lobbies to the Church and the guilds squabbling over the distribution of output. One particularly striking example of the inefficiencies produced in French agriculture is provided by Rosenthal (1992). None of the groups that offered resistance to the centralizing agendas of rulers in France, Spain, Russia, Sweden, and elsewhere were interested in growth. Where they won, they did not push through sensible, long-term policies. They often replaced arbitrary taxation by the ruler with arbitrary exactions by local monopolies.[18]

In the early modern period, states with good institutions were often weak. The cut-throat nature of international politics undermined the viability of good governance. The League of Cambrai (1516) laid Venetian power low, and contributed to the eventual decline of Venice's prosperity. Today, constraints on the executive go hand in hand with lower probabilities of military conflict, as democracies are unlikely to go to war with each other (and tend to win in wars against non-democratic powers). In the early modern period, the correlation probably had the opposite sign. Political entities with highly effective constraints on the executive quickly became victims of outside powers whose rulers operated without being hamstrung by domestic opponents. Thus in early modern Europe less-developed but large and militarily strong political units, such as the young nation-states of Philip II, Gustavus Adolphus, and Louis XIV,

---

[17] For a recent critique of the revisionist argument, cf. Beik (2005).

[18] The case of Venice is instructive. In terms of its institutional setup, it is hard to think of a political entity that would more closely approximate the modern ideal. Property rights were well protected. The high bourgeoisie controlled politics and the courts. Doges were elected officials, theoretically for life but in reality subject to good performance. A patent system was in place as early as the fifteenth century. Yet despite its early riches and success as a sea power, Venice declined both militarily and economically.

threatened the richer but smaller city states in Italy, Germany, and the Low Countries. Economically successful but compact units were frequently destroyed by superior military forces or by the costs of having to maintain an army disproportionate to their tax base.[19] The only two areas that escaped this fate enjoyed unusual geographical advantages for repelling foreign invasions – Britain and the northern Netherlands. Even these economies were burdened by high taxation, the cost of surviving in a mercantilist world based on the notion that the economic game between nations was zero-sum, and that foreign trade was a servant of political and dynastic interests.

A fundamental trade-off was thus created: a powerful central government was more effective in protecting an economy from foreign marauders, but at the same time the least amenable to internal checks and balances. Carried to the Polish extreme, strict constraints on the executive were not conducive to economic development – not least because they could contribute to the disappearance of the state itself at the end of a sequence of gruelling military defeats. Rather than a weak or strong government, the most important institutional feature of a society might have been institutional agility, the capacity for institutions to adapt to changing circumstances with a minimum of pain and friction.

Two observations to summarize the importance of institutions in the post-1750 transformation of Europe are in order. One is that throughout western Europe we observe after 1750 a rising tide against the rent-seeking institutions that were associated with the mercantilist *ancien régime* (Mokyr, 2006). The roots of this development involve some combination of the changing political influence of economic elites and the influence of a more liberal ideology. Second, change often occurred by force (e.g. in the United States and France). The main exception is Britain, where the existence of a meta-institution (i.e. Parliament) permitted adaptation to changing circumstances and beliefs, and reform of the system without major upheavals (Mokyr and Nye, 2007). Yet even here it could be argued that the settlement following the Glorious Revolution would not have been possible without the bloodshed of the Civil War.

The literature on institutions in Europe, 1500–1870, has primarily focused on the state and formal institutions. Non-governmental institutions, both formal and informal, have received much less attention (but see Mokyr, 2008). This is striking since work on the medieval period has given prominence to these arrangements (Greif, 2006). If, as the institutions literature argues at a fundamental level, respect for property rights and recourse to due legal process are key for economic development, then we need to construct variables that

---

[19] In modern data, there is a robust, negative correlation between military conflict and political instability on the one hand, and growth on the other (Alesina et al., 1996).

more closely capture this dimension.[20] A more comprehensive and historically meaningful set of indicators should measure effective legal or customs-based constraints on the actions of the executive or of local power groups – anything that makes it harder for might to be right without due recourse to the law. In addition, opportunistic behavior leading to Pareto-dominated equilibria could be overcome by a host of mechanisms (besides the standard of third-party enforcement) in which members of select groups were able to establish their trustworthiness through a variety of costly signals (Greif, 2006) and play cooperatively. The modern literature on institutions has shown that such arrangements may still have a fair amount of explanatory power today (Ellickson, 1991; Posner, 2000). They need to be investigated for periods not covered by Greif, and their significance relative to that of formal institutions such as Parliament explored.

Eighteenth-century Britain is a case in point. In a recent paper Mokyr (2008) has argued that informal arrangements and cultural change had effects similar to public institutions, facilitating the operation of markets. Within a larger group of people, a stable equilibrium emerged that allowed signalling of trustworthiness. Middle-class people adopted certain virtues associated with gentlemanly behavior; since gentlemen were supposedly not greedy, they could be expected to cooperate in one-shot Prisoner's Dilemma games (Clark, 2000). Moreover, Britain in the eighteenth century experienced an enormous growth in formal and informal social networks, through the growth of friendly societies, masonic lodges, and eating clubs, with an estimated membership of 600,000 in 1800. The effect of this growth was to make reputational mechanisms more effective, since reports of non-cooperative behavior would soon be disseminated. This may have mitigated free-riding behavior in the private provision of public goods in eighteenth-century Britain, which included local administration, overhead projects, education, and health. It can be argued that such informal institutions not only supported markets, but also helped Britain take the technological lead, because the success of these informal institutions made its apprenticeship system particularly effective (Humphries, 2003). The apprenticeship contract was particularly vulnerable to opportunistic behavior, and in Britain the guild system that enforced it elsewhere was weak – yet it functioned well in Britain. As a consequence Britain could count on a large number of highly skilled craftsmen and mechanics, whose role in the Industrial Revolution may well have been critical.

Power-sharing arrangements between nobility and the rich bourgeoisie after 1830 underpinned some of the smooth functioning of institutions in Britain, as

---

[20] Acemoglu and Johnson (2005) argue that institutions protecting property are crucial, and that "contracting institutions" only influence the type of financial intermediation one ends up with.

Acemoglu and Robinson have emphasized. Workers may not have had *de iure* power, but their implicit ability to rebel gave them *de facto* power. Analysis based on "realpolitik" overlooks the growing influence of Enlightenment ideology on political institutions; analyses of what *de facto* power consisted of are still incomplete. The British military suppressed popular unrest in the 1790s as well as the Luddite riots very effectively, and the Chartist movement remained a mostly non-violent movement, its few more threatening outbursts readily suppressed. It may thus be that *de iure* and *de facto* power coincided to a great extent. Perhaps this was the key to the success of Britain's political model. It is striking, nonetheless, that while those who had political power did use it at times to redistribute income to themselves (most blatantly by the reformulation of the Corn Laws in 1815), the tendency to do so lessened as the nineteenth century wore on, and by 1860 rent-seeking in Britain was at a historical nadir.

Human capital and culture

In many models of long-run growth, the transition to self-sustaining growth is almost synonymous with rising returns to education, and a rapid acceleration in skill formation. Becker, Murphy, and Tamura (1990) model an economy without a fixed factor of production. Improvements in human capital directly feed into higher output. Human capital is produced, it is assumed, by investments of parental time. Parents maximize their own utility, derived by their own consumption, the number of children they have, and their quality. When parents start to invest massively in the education of their offspring, growth rates rise. Once incomes are high enough, fertility falls, leading to yet more investment in child quality. In this model, human capital and growth are almost identical. Lucas (2002) extends the approach of Becker et al. by adding a land-using sector with diminishing returns, and a modern sector where human capital enters linearly. Many unified growth models have followed in the same direction, adding interactions with the rate of technological change.

Developments during the Industrial Revolution in Britain appear largely at variance with these predictions. Most evidence is still based on the ability to sign one's name, arguably a low standard of literacy (Schofield, 1973). British literacy rates during the Industrial Revolution were relatively low and largely stagnant. This is especially true if we take into account the fact that Britain was relatively rich before the Industrial Revolution, and that demand for literacy rises with income (Mitch, 1999). Britain's ability or willingness to educate its young did not appreciably improve during the years of the Industrial Revolution. School enrollment rates did not increase much before the 1870s (Flora, Kraus, and Pfenning, 1983).

Models in the Lucas tradition often predict an increase in the demand for human capital during the transition to self-sustaining growth. Also, technological change should be heavily skill-biased. This is historically problematic. Our knowledge of the behavior of the skill premium over time is incomplete, because estimates are based on a few skilled occupations, which may not be representative. Moreover, the skill premium is a reduced form measure, and changes in it could reflect any combination of changing supply and/or demand factors. There is little firm evidence of an increase in the returns to education in the eighteenth or nineteenth century. Williamson (1985) claimed to show that the skill premium surged between 1750 and 1850 in Britain, and declined thereafter. The consensus view amongst economic historians does not accept the Williamson interpretation. As Feinstein (1988) convincingly demonstrated, there is no clear evidence that skill premia changed at all over time.[21]

It is doubtful that the main developments in manufacturing during the Industrial Revolution, or even developments in its aftermath, depended on an increase in human capital. Possibly, some administrative tasks became more important. The rise in pay rates for highly literate workers observed by Boot (1999) suggests that there were some (small) parts of the economy where formal education may have paid off. Yet technological change itself was probably not skill-biased. As the machine-breaking Luddite riots highlighted, it may well be that de-skilling accompanied the first Industrial Revolution.[22] This would present an important challenge to the dominant economic models of long-run development. In the textile industry, the cotton mules, spinning jennies, and Arkwright frames replaced skilled labor with a mixture of capital and unskilled labor. For more traditional sectors, the evidence is much more mixed. Clark (2007a) examined the ratio of craftsmen to laborer wages in England, 1700–1850. His evidence shows a decline from a premium of 65 percent to 50 percent. Of course, the building trade experienced limited technological change. If the sector is nonetheless indicative of broader trends in the economy, then one would have to conclude that mild de-skilling occurred in the one and a half centuries before 1850. Perhaps focusing on the *average* level of human capital in industrializing societies is less useful than changes in its distribution. The technological changes of the nineteenth century created a demand for highly skilled mechanics and engineers in the upper tail of the distribution, while possibly reducing the need for skills among manual laborers. The failure of traditionally measured skill premia to show a rise may well mask an increasing polarization within the workforce, with

---

[21] See also van Zanden (2009).

[22] Adam Ferguson, Adam Smith's contemporary, noted in 1767 that "Many mechanical arts require no capacity … ignorance is the mother of industry as well as superstition … Manufactures, accordingly, prosper most where the mind is least consulted." For a recent model emphasizing the role of de-skilling, see O'Rourke, Rahman, and Taylor (2008).

industrialization raising the returns to supervisory and advanced mechanical skills, and reducing those for standard ones (such as blacksmithing, carpentry, and weaving).

Also, for the time being the jury appears to be out on whether increased human capital formation from the middle of the nineteenth century onwards was an endogenous response to changes in factor prices and other economic incentives, whether it was a result of higher real incomes (education for one's children being a normal consumption good), or whether it was the result of "exogenous" shifts in the supply of education, such as the long-delayed effect of the Enlightenment, of nineteenth-century nationalism and nation-building, or attempts to strengthen social control over the lower classes.[23]

There is little evidence to support unified growth models if we identify human capital with formal education only, and the break with the preindustrial period as occurring in Britain after 1750. The main conclusion appears to be that, while human-capital-based approaches hold some attractions for the period after 1850, few growth models have much to say about the first escape from low growth. Models that endogenize the transition from skill-replacing to skill-using technological change are just beginning to appear (O'Rourke, Rahman and Taylor, 2008). Our verdict changes somewhat as we widen our focus. As we turn from the particular case of England to trends in Europe as a whole, analyze the longer period 1500–1870, and include broader definitions of human capital to include factors such as numeracy and discipline, as well as informal education such as apprenticeship, the fit between theory and history increases.

There is no doubt that some forms of human capital (such as literacy and numeracy) were on the rise in Europe long before the Industrial Revolution. In part this was due to the Reformation, in part due to slowly rising incomes, and possibly to a rising demand for literacy in the service sector during an age in which commerce and finance were growing rapidly. Measuring literacy rates in a consistent and comparable fashion is no minor matter, especially with the kind of pre-1800 sources available. A recent literature survey, focusing on the ability to sign one's name in and around 1800, rates this proportion at about 60 percent for British males and 40 percent for females, more or less at a par with Belgium, slightly better than France, but worse than the Netherlands and Germany (Reis, 2005, p. 202). Baten and van Zanden (2008) examine book production in early modern Europe. They find a veritable explosion of output per capita after the invention of moveable type, with production increasing between 10- and

---

[23] The latter effect would be in the spirit of Acemoglu and Robinson's (2000) paper, which sees the extension of the franchise as a reaction to revolutionary threats. A similar argument could possibly be made about the introduction of compulsory schooling.

100-fold. The Netherlands and the United Kingdom are far ahead of other countries – the richest areas consumed the largest number of books.[24]

One additional measure of human capital is numeracy. The ability to make sense of numbers, to remember them correctly, and to perform minor transformations is a crucial skill in many commercial transactions. Measurement in a historical setting can be achieved via a shortcut. As suggested by Mokyr (1985), we can use age-heaping as an indicator of numeracy. Many historical sources show a tendency for ages to be reported in multiples of five, while the true distribution should be smooth. A'Hearn, Baten, and Crayen (2009) compile a comprehensive database for the last two millennia. They find some evidence that numeracy was trending upwards in Europe from the sixteenth century onwards. Britain's experience after 1800 suggests stagnant literacy, despite sweeping changes in the economy. The more evidence we can collect on areas outside Europe, and the closer they can be linked to data on income differences as a result of higher numeracy, the more potent tests of models in the Becker and Lucas tradition become.

If we are to make progress, historians and economists need to broaden their conception of skills. They were not yet, as a rule, acquired at schools or similar formal institutions. Rather, they were mainly transmitted through personal contracts. Apprenticeship was the main form of training. Trainees would be "indentured" to a master. The contract involved a commitment by the trainee to work during his learning period, an obligation to teach for the master, and at times cash payments by parents (Humphries, 2003). New technology was put in place, made operational, and maintained by a small army of highly skilled men. They were clock- and instrument makers, woodworkers, toymakers, glasscutters, and similar specialists, who could accurately produce the parts, using the correct dimensions and materials, who could read blueprints and compute velocities, understood tolerance, resistance, friction, and the interdependence of mechanical parts. These anonymous but capable workers were an essential complement to inventors and engineers, and comprised perhaps 5 to 10 percent of the labor force. They turned models and designs into working machinery, operated and repaired it, and produced a rising tide of small, incremental, but cumulatively indispensable microinventions. Without them, Britain could not have become the "workshop of the world."

Most of the skills that the workers' elite of skilled craftsmen brought to the factories were the culmination of a century-long accumulation of expertise in traditional crafts. If the rise of new technology, and the high complementarity of their skills with the adoption of more productive machinery, made their human capital more valuable, we should find changes in the wage premium for this

---

[24] The authors argue that their indicator of human capital accumulation is a good predictor of subsequent growth (Baten and van Zanden, 2008).

group. Collapsing wages of handloom weavers might have been compensated for by the growing demand for the highly skilled craftsmen who erected the new spinning and weaving machinery in Lancashire. While evidence is fragmentary, there is some indication that employers scrambled to find glass-cutters, mill-wrights or fine mechanics in eighteenth-century England (Musson and Robinson 1960). One conceptually appealing test of human-capital based models of the Industrial Revolution would focus on movements in the pay rate of this labor aristocracy compared with the rest, and on the supply response that these differences in pay engendered.

We may have to widen our definition of the relevant human capital yet further. The rise of the factory system required general skills that were not necessarily transmitted through formal schooling – discipline, punctuality, and respect, in addition to literacy and numeracy. Recent work in labor economics has highlighted the importance of non-cognitive skills (Heckman and Rubinstein, 2001). The equipment and materials used by workers belonged to the capitalist and were costly. Factory owners needed to instill in workers a culture of loyalty and sobriety, and a willingness to take instructions from and cooperate with other workers. While similar to the discipline exerted by masters over apprentices, it was reinforced by the expensive equipment in factories.[25] Beyond that, the more complex technology and finer division of labor created interdependencies between workers that required coordination between them that would have been hard to enforce unless workers were willing and cooperative. Wage premia for *disciplined* work in the factories were high vis-à-vis other, more self-determined forms of employment, and the factory system's profitability relied crucially on work intensity (Pollard, 1965; Clark 1994). In addition, steep experience-based earnings profiles in the textile industry offered high returns to those who could stand the habituation to factory work. During their early years, when unskilled workers such as brick-makers were better paid, skilled workers were effectively investing in their own human capital; by age 35, they could look forward to earning 2.3 times the wages of a brickmaker, and more than a coal miner (Boot 1995).[26]

For similar reasons, monitoring workers was an important task. If "discipline capital" mattered more for the first Industrial Revolution than education as conventionally measured, economic historians should compile more compre-hensive wage measures that capture the rewards for workers who successfully

[25] This insight is hardly indebted to modern theory: Marx, in a famous passage, cites an industrialist telling the economist Nassau Senior that "if a labourer lays down his spade, he renders useless, for that period, a capital worth 18 pence. When one of our people leaves the mill, he renders useless a capital that has cost £100,000" (Marx, 1967, I, pp. 405–06).

[26] Coal miners are arguably a better standard of comparison, since the wage of textile operatives will also reflect differences in the harshness of working conditions – and since those in coal mines were probably worse than in textile factories, skill accumulation is a good explanation.

internalized the demands of the machine age. Also, if the returns to disciplining workers were large, we should find high and rising pay premia for outstanding foremen and other members of the evolving hierarchies that ensured the smooth running of nineteenth-century factories. The most obvious testable implication of this idea is that early factory owners should have had a preference for the employment of comparatively more pliable workers, even if they were of low skill – that is, women and children. This was very much the case in the early stages of the textile mills. Similarly, one valid test of the human-capital approach would focus on highly skilled workers such as the textile operatives examined by Boot (1995) and Leunig (2001), and ask whether they received greater rewards for investing in their skills (by accepting years of poorly paid on-the-job training) than, say, apprentices in traditional sectors.

These observations suggest that non-cognitive skills and informal education may have mattered more in explaining the transition to self-sustaining growth in Europe than formal schooling and traditional reading and writing skills. In this sense, distinctions between education and human capital on the one hand, and culture on the other become increasingly artificial. Since Max Weber's work on the spirit of capitalism, culture is one of the "usual suspects" that may determine wealth and productivity, and modern scholars (e.g. Jones, 2006, pp. 126–32; Temin 1997) have concurred. There is now increasing evidence that its impact can be demonstrated in modern-day data. This suggests that economic historians may want to revisit the issue. Guiso, Sapienza, and Zingales (2006) show an exogenous effect from culture to income. Culture also has a lot of persistence (see also Tabellini, 2006). Here, culture is defined above all in terms of the values and beliefs of individuals. While trying to control as much as possible for endogeneity, these studies show that when people trust one another, believe that if they work hard they will get ahead in the world, and that on the whole the formal institutions of power in the country are not threatening them, economic progress will ensue. We have no record, of course, of such poll-based data for historical times, and so there is no easy way that such findings can be reproduced. But the importance of private-order institutions in many early modern European societies is striking. These normally involved cultural beliefs that made people keep their promises and behave in an honorable way because opportunistic behavior was not a dominant strategy in a setting that ensured repeated interactions. Reputations became an asset to be managed carefully. In this interpretation, the middle classes of commercial societies adopted a more cooperative mode of behavior, leading to Pareto improvements. The focal point in such equilibria may well have been what middle-class people perceived as "gentlemanly behavioral codes." These signalled that one was uninterested in money, and hence would care more about honor than personal gain. This reduced the risk of cheating

(Mokyr, 2008). It may well be that such social norms were far more important than third-party enforcement of laws and contracts in the support of European markets, especially credit and labor markets.

But whence such middle class values? In an innovative paper, Doepke and Zilibotti (2008) emphasize the differences between aristocratic and middle-class behavior. Doepke and Zilibotti offer a model of class formation through endogenous, inheritable preferences. They argue that the rise of a bourgeois elite in industrializing Britain should be seen as a surprise. Before the transformation got under way, aristocrats had all the odds stacked in their favor – available funds, political connections, access to education. Yet few members of the old political elite actually got rich in manufacturing after 1750. Doepke and Zilibotti argue that this is because other groups in society – the middle classes – had accumulated a larger stock of "patience capital." A host of cultural practices and norms made them delay gratification. Artisans needed to acquire this skill, since it takes a long time to complete the training needed to become a craftsman. On the other hand, the old aristocracy taught their children how to enjoy leisure. It therefore provided them with a culture that worked against both hard work and investment. Through centuries of careful saving and educating their young, the middle class built up both financial capital and valuable cultural traits. As the new technologies of the Industrial Revolution suddenly offered greater returns to patience, the groups best placed to exploit them were not the elite but those with plenty of patience. Doepke and Zilibotti argue that it is this kind of culture that played a central role in the subsequent development of capitalist industrialism. In their account, the *absence* of well-functioning credit markets was key for the rise of the middle classes – only when financial markets are segmented do returns to patience differ across groups.

The concept of patience capital holds considerable promise. It may be no accident that the "nation of shopkeepers," as Adam Smith called Britain, became the first to industrialize. It offered an environment in which bourgeois values and practices flourished and gained in relative importance. If Europe saw a rise in bourgeois values prior to the Industrial Revolution, this was complemented by a rise in work intensity and the length of the working day for the lower classes, and a growing orientation towards the market at the expense of self-sufficiency. De Vries (1994) termed this change the "industrious revolution." By the eighteenth century, even Catholic rulers were abolishing holy days to boost labor input in their economies (de Vries, 2008). Clark (1987) found evidence that work intensity in the most economically advanced parts of Europe was much higher than elsewhere. Voth (1998, 2001a) argues that the work-year in Britain was already long in 1750, and that it lengthened further because of a decline in festivals, holy days, and the practice of taking Mondays off ("St. Monday"). Such changes are consistent with the model proposed by

Doepke and Zilibotti (2008), in which those with relatively limited "leisure skills" eventually became the dominant classes.

In recent years there has been growing interest in Darwinian selection models as an explanation of cultural change. Galor and Moav (2002) offer a model in which the crucial state variable that changed during the pre-industrial period is not just population size, but "human quality" (genetic or behavioral). Households endowed with more desirable human characteristics (education, the right genes, economically beneficial attitudes) produce more surviving offspring and gradually but ineluctably change the composition of the population. Therefore the quality of the human population drifted up prior to the Industrial Revolution. The Galor–Moav approach has recently received some qualified empirical support. Clark and Hamilton (2006) find that the rich and literate in early modern England fathered more surviving children. Clark's and Hamilton's result that wealthier Englishmen had more surviving children may suggest that, instead of leading to an upward drift in some unmeasured, unnamed indicator of human quality, this simply enlarged the proportion of those who had learned to save (and invest), and those who passed such values on to their offspring. Given that European living standards far exceeded subsistence levels during the early modern period, many more children could have been born. Constraints on fertility behavior were mostly social and cultural (working through nuptiality rates). Such a change in population composition could also have contributed to the decline in English interest rates since the Middle Ages (Clark, 1988), from 10–11 percent in the thirteenth century to 4 percent by the eighteenth. A gradual increase in savings, caused by compositional effects attained through the increase in the relative number of those who were more patient, would be an alternative to theories that attribute the rise in savings to the "Calvinist ethic." Compositional change may also help us to understand evolving demographic behavior. Fertility rates and age at first marriage often differ across subgroups, as both historians and economists have found.[27]

That natural selection improved in some definable dimension the quality of the population in the countries about to break out of the Malthusian model before the 1700s is still far from an established fact. Disentangling "inherent quality" changes from responses to new incentives seems a formidable challenge. Given that humans normally only start to reproduce in their late teens or early twenties, any process that relies on natural selection requires a very long time span – or strongly divergent fertility rates.[28] We know far too little about

---

[27] In addition to Clark and Hamilton (2006), one should mention the work by Herlihy (1997, pp. 56–57) and Galor and Moav (2002).

[28] Given that the earliest data are from the sixteenth century, there were only approximately five to six generations over which we can be reasonably certain that this selection effect might have worked – not a great length, given the modest reproductive advantage. All the same, recent genetic research has suggested that "evolutionary changes in the genome could explain cultural traits that last over many generations as societies adapted to different pressures" (*New York Times*, March 7 and 12, 2006).

the relative differences in reproductive behavior (as manifested, for example, in different marriage ages) and economic success in early modern Europe. Compositional change may have played a role, but at the current stage it is hard to tell. Grander claims about the prevalence of "survival of the richest" in Europe, and its absence in the Far East (Clark 2007a) rest on shakier foundations. What is needed is more evidence along the lines of the material gathered by Clark and Hamilton documenting differential fertility and survival over the long run, and in different parts of the globe.

Scholars in the field of cultural evolution such as Boyd and Richerson (1985, 2005) point to the fact that culture changes only in small part due to the compositional effects of natural selection. Instead, they point to learning and imitation as sources of cultural change. People receive part of their culture from their parents, whether through genes or education, but they are exposed throughout their life to other influences that may make them different from their parents. Such "biases" may have different forms, but here perhaps the most interesting is what they call "model-based bias" in which individuals observe certain other persons who have an attribute they regard as desirable (e.g. social status or wealth), and thus choose this other person as their role model. In a highly stratified yet mobile society such as Britain, the incentives to imitate the behavior of others viewed as higher-up in the hierarchy were strong. This would make the most successful workers and artisans try to imitate the bourgeoisie, by mimicking their behavior. The growth of a middle class would thus be far faster than differential reproduction would predict.

Technology

Technological change has remained the backbone of modern economic growth, simply because all other potential sources of productivity growth tend to run into diminishing returns. Capital accumulation, improved allocation of resources, gains from trade, better institutions, and economies of scale will increase output, but they are eventually subject to diminishing returns. No historically accurate picture of modern growth can be formed without understanding the connection between science and technology in the Industrial Revolution and beyond. Historical scholarship has bifurcated into a minority view, which continues to view science and scientific culture as crucial to the Industrial Revolution (Musson and Robinson, 1969; Rostow, 1975; Jacob, 1997; Lipsey, Carlaw, and Bekar, 2005), and a majority, which has dismissed the role of science as epiphenomenal and marginal (Landes, 1969; Mathias, 1979; Hall, 1974; Gillispie, 1980). Examples of the importance of science and mathematics to some of the inventions of the Industrial Revolution can certainly be amassed. It is equally true, however, that many of the most prominent breakthroughs in manufacturing, especially in the mechanical processing of textiles, were not based on much more science than Archimedes knew. In other areas of progress, such as steam power, pottery, and animal breeding, advances occurred primarily on the basis of trial and error, not a deep understanding of the underlying physical and biological processes.

The debate between those who feel that science played a pivotal role in the Industrial Revolution and their opponents is more than just a dispute about whether a glass is half full or half empty. The glass started from almost empty and slowly filled in the century and a half after 1750. Scientists and science (not quite the same thing) had a few spectacular successes in developing new production techniques, above all the chlorine bleaching technique, the soda-making process, and the inventions made by such natural philosophers as Franklin, Priestley, Davy, and Rumford. While the Industrial Revolution in its classical form might well have occurred, with a few exceptions, without much progress in science, it is hard to argue that it would have transformed into a continent-wide process of continuing growth without a growing body of useful knowledge on which inventors and technicians could draw. It is not possible to "date" the time at which this kind of collaboration began. In some areas it can already be discerned in the mid-eighteenth century. In crucial "new" areas of technology in the post-1820 years, scientific knowledge became increasingly important to the development of new technology. Two of the most remarkable developments of the era, the electric telegraph and the growing understanding of the chemistry of fatty acids used in soap and candle manufacturing, took place in the final decades of the classical Industrial Revolution. Trial and error, serendipity, and sheer intuition never quite disappeared from the scene, but improved knowledge about how and why a technique works made it far easier to refine and debug a new technique quickly, adapt it to other uses, and design variations and recombinations that would not have occurred otherwise. In chemicals, steel, electricity, food processing, power engineering, agriculture, and shipbuilding technology, the ties between formally educated people who tried to understand the natural phenomena and regularities they observed, and the people whose livelihood depended on putting such insights to good use, became tighter and closer after 1750, and continued to do so (Mokyr, 2002).

The underlying institutions that made this growing collaboration possible have been investigated at length. Although intellectual property rights were of some importance, they cannot possibly explain the entire process. Jones (2001) is the only growth paper to date that models time-varying institutional parameters directly. They turn out to play a pivotal role in his model regarding whether the Industrial Revolution was "inevitable."[29] Jones's parameter π_t, which is the proportion of total consumption allocated to people employed in the ideas-generating sector, is computed to match the data. Broadly speaking, the rise of resource-intensive research and development is captured correctly. At higher frequencies, the series displays a bizarre history (Jones, 2001, p. 24), falling from 0.44 percent to zero between the sixteenth and the eighteenth century, rising sharply in the eighteenth century, then falling to half that value in the nineteenth century, before leaping, by a factor of 12, to 5 percent in the twentieth century. Nothing in Jones's model allows for the complex motivation that propelled the ideas sector in earlier history, when many natural philosophers and inventors were as much interested in signalling as in financial gains, much like a modern open-source technology (Lerner and Tirole, 2004). Models that purport to explain the growth of technology in this age must recognize the different ways of assigning property rights in the two separate segments of the "ideas sector." Whereas prescriptive knowledge, that is, techniques, could be patented and thus be allocated at least some form of property rights, this was never done with propositional knowledge in which priority credit assigned to the owner did not include exclusionary rights. Yet it is hard to understand the growth of technology during the Industrial Revolution and after without explicitly recognizing the feedback between these two forms of knowledge (Mokyr, 2002; see also Dasgupta and David, 1994). Scientists in the pre-1850 period were rarely interested in reaping the material gains that their findings could generate, insisting on credit rather than profit. As "gentlemen-philosophers" they refused to make a living from their discoveries and were suspicious of anyone who did (Bowler and Morus, 2005, pp. 320–21).

It is also worth noting that a recent attempt to estimate the value of inventions accruing to the inventors for modern America has found that only about 2.2 percent of the value of an innovation is captured by the inventor him- or herself (Nordhaus, 2004). That the number was higher during the Industrial Revolution seems unlikely. The patent system is central to this story, but its effect on the process of technological progress during the Industrial Revolution is still very much in dispute. The operation of the patent system awarded monopolies to inventors, yet infringements and other failures of the system implied that first-mover advantages and old-fashioned government and private-sector prizes were as important as the rents earned by inventors.[30] The British patent system was far from user-friendly: it was costly to file a patent and often hard to defend patents against infringers (Khan and

---

[29] The parameter π in Jones's model defines the proportion of total income that accrues to those who are employed in the "ideas sector," and in equilibrium equals the fraction of labor in the economy allocated to producing new ideas.

[30] The literature on the operation of the patent system in Britain is quite large; for an introduction see Dutton (1984), MacLeod (1988) and MacLeod and Nuvolari (2007).

Sokoloff, 1998; Dutton, 1984). The patent laws were widely condemned as ineffective in protecting the vast majority of inventors, and did so at a high cost (MacLeod and Nuvolari, 2007). Most inventions, even the most successful ones, were not patented (Moser, 2005). The fact that Britain's system was thus less likely to encourage potential inventors than the corresponding US system does not seem to have affected British technological leadership before 1850. Charles Babbage, never one to mince words, denounced the patent law as "a fraudulent lottery which gives its blanks to genius and its prizes to knaves" (1830, pp. 333, 321). Inducement prizes for inventions, such as those offered by Parliament, may have been at least as effective in generating new ideas as protection by the patent system (Brunt, Lerner and Nicholas, 2008). The best we can say about the patent system is that it provided an *ex ante* belief that successful invention *could* pay off to a few lucky people, and thus provided a positive incentive.

Instead, a deeper and more encompassing social phenomenon was at play here, namely growing flows of information and improving interaction between people who made things (entrepreneurs and engineers) and people who knew things (natural philosophers). Not only did this interaction mean that what useful knowledge had to offer was accessible to those who could make best use of it; it also meant that the agenda of science was increasingly biased toward the practical needs of the economy. The bridges between *savants* and *fabricants* took many forms, from written technical manuals and treatises to academies and scientific societies, where they rubbed shoulders and exchanged ideas. By the closing decades of the eighteenth century it was normal for scientists to be consulted by manufacturers and farmers looking for improved bleaches, more efficient engines, or improved fertilizers.

By 1815, the need for this kind of collaboration had become a consensus, and European economies competed with one another in encouraging it. In Britain, the Society of Arts, established in 1754, the Royal Institution, founded in 1799, and the Mechanics Institutes (first established by George Birkbeck in 1804) were examples of how private initiatives could carry out this task in the land where people believed above all in private initiatives. Less formal institutions abounded, the most famous of all being the Birmingham Lunar Society, which brought together the top scientists with some of its most prominent entrepreneurs and engineers. Less well known but equally significant were the Spitalfields Mathematical Society, founded in 1717, and the London Chapter Coffee House, the favorite of the fellows of the Royal Society in the 1780s, where learned men discussed at great length the mundane issues of steam and chemistry (Levere and Turner, 2002). In France, Germany, and the Low Countries, government took a more active role in bringing this about (see, e.g., Lenoir, 1998). Not all of those efforts were unqualified successes: the engineers of the Paris École Polytechnique were often too abstract and formal in their research to yield immediate results. In Germany, the university system was on the whole rather conservative and resisted the practical applications that governments expected of them. New and more effective institutions were established, however, and the old ones eventually reformed.[31] The decades after 1815, then, were the ultimate triumph of the Baconian vision, which had formed the basis for the founding of the Royal Society in 1660. To achieve this triumph Europe had to undergo changes in its institutional set-up for the accumulation and dissemination of useful knowledge, yet these institutions were based on the scaffolds (to use North's term) of an Enlightenment ideology that firmly believed in material progress and advocated concrete programs as to how to bring this about.

Modelling the production of "new ideas" is a key challenge for growth models, and endogenous growth models have had to simplify away much of the historical richness. Thus the literature has not dealt effectively with the high riskiness of the inventive process, in which investing in the "ideas-producing" sector is more akin to purchasing a lottery ticket than to choosing an occupation.[32] While some models refer explicitly to "the number of ideas produced," such a concept is of course highly problematic, not only because ideas fail to meet the rules of arithmetic, but also because so many ideas generated were simply dead-ends, mistakes, or even pure fantasy. On the other hand, much of the new technology was the result of minor but cumulative improvements resulting from the experience and learning-by-doing of skilled craftsmen, rather than some kind of cognitive flash. While such artisanal advances were not all there was to technological change during the Industrial Revolution, their importance has been rightly stressed by historians (Berg, 2007).

Conclusion: progress out of misunderstandings

Theorists and economic historians interested in the transition to self-sustaining growth often appear as distinct tribes, separated by a common object of study. This has hampered progress in understanding how the switch from "Malthus to Solow" occurred. We highlight a few particular sources of misunderstanding, and offer suggestions for future research that should do much to reconcile the tribes and augment intellectual gains from trade.

---

[31] In Germany, universities had increasingly to compete with the technical colleges or *technische Hochschule*, the first of which was set up in Karlsruhe in 1825. In France new *grandes écoles* were set up to provide more practical education, such as the Arts et Métiers.

[32] Indeed, this aspect of technological progress may well be better analyzed by behavioral economists and decision theorists, who deal with models in which people systematically overestimate their own chances at succeeding. This was already understood by Adam Smith, who noted, "Their absurd presumption of their own good fortune is … still more universal [than people's overestimating their own abilities] … the chance of gain is by every man more or less over-valued, and the chance of loss … undervalued" (Smith, 1976 [1776], p. 120).

Economic theorists writing on long-run growth often apply their models to industrializing Britain, the classic, first case of an Industrial Revolution. This forces them to ignore or to play down inconvenient facts about economic history "wie es wirklich gewesen ist." Jones (2001), for example, produces a model in which working hours have to fall during the transition, while they probably rose in actual fact. Models in the Lucas and Becker tradition emphasize the increasing demand for and returns to human capital, when we find little evidence of this. Acemoglu, Johnson, and Robinson underline the importance of constraints on the executive in early modern Europe, when it is far from clear that the groups producing serious restraints had anything to offer for growth. The list could be extended, but it is mainly meant to be illustrative.

Economic historians have been quick to point out the most glaring contradictions, pointing out that the "Industrial Revolution in most growth models shares few similarities with the economic events unfolding in England in the 18th century" (Voth, 2003). We believe that the discussion should not stop here. The logic of many unified growth models makes them less than well suited as an explanatory toolkit for the classic British Industrial Revolution, despite the tendency of growth theorists to apply their models to that case (Galor, 2005; Hansen and Prescott, 2002; Lucas, 2002). When applied to the early modern period as a whole, unified growth models have much more to offer. Conversely, economic historians have been too narrow in many of their criticisms. Once we lengthen the period during which demographic changes are analyzed, examine human capital accumulation over the very long run, and broaden the relevant set of skills beyond literacy, as traditionally emphasized, many of the apparent contradictions are diminished. The Malthusian regime slowly broke down during the years 1500–1800, and many relevant changes in human capital probably began after the Reformation. In the same vein, once economic historians and theorists focus more on non-cognitive skills and cultural features such as patience, prudence, and discipline, it will be easier to build models that are broadly consistent with the historical record. In this light, unified growth theories have substantial explanatory power – especially those that emphasize a transition to modern growth in two phases (such as Galor and Moav, 2002), with Malthusian constraints declining first, and human capital becoming more important later.

The time period under consideration is not the only important source of misunderstanding. As the German philosophers Rickert and Windelband emphasized, history is 'ideographic' – seeking to explain what is unique. Theorists are, of necessity, 'nomothetic' – in search of covering laws. While the discussion of the British Industrial Revolution in, for example, Hansen and Prescott (2002) is meant as an illustration of a model that could apply to Europe (or, indeed, the world) as a whole, historians have often focused on empirical accuracy in individual cases. Equally problematic is the tendency to examine the logic of historical papers from a cross-sectional perspective. Economic historians have rarely resisted the temptation to demand predictive power for our own time's distribution of economic development from models designed for the crucial question of explaining "why Britain came first," and not France or China (Crafts, 1995; Broadberry, 2007). The models in Kremer (1993) and Galor and Weil (2000) apply to the world as a whole. Nonetheless, economic historians have criticized endogenous growth models because they fail to offer convincing explanations for income divergence between countries. This is clearly a case of hunting rhino with sharpened kiwis.

However, and by the same token, theorists have not given much attention to the important implications of cross-sectional differences in the timing of growth spurts.[33] For example, Hall and Jones (1999) document large differences in output per capita between rich and poor countries. They conclude that neither capital nor human capital can explain these differences; total factor productivity and "social capacity" must be responsible. The underlying models only make sense if we assume that economies have reached their steady state, or that they should have the means to converge to it rapidly. Most papers in the growth literature using the Summers-Heston dataset share this assumption. Yet when we examine the broad sweep of history, one of the most striking observations is the sheer time scale necessary for the escape from the Malthusian world. Even over the last 200 years the "take-off" into self-sustaining growth (some sad reversals such as Argentina apart) has occurred at different points in time in different countries. These differences in timing have proven hard to explain. A delayed start to economic growth will lead to an inverse U-shaped pattern of productivity differences over time. Relaxing the assumption that economies are in steady state, and focusing on what allows economies to enter the phase of rapid, self-sustaining growth, resolves some key puzzles in the current growth literature (Ngai, 2004). Relatively small inefficiencies can produce large differences in output per head if they *delay* the onset of modern growth. What is needed, then, is a set of theories modelling dynamics: what was behind phenomena such as timing, lags, and the long historical delays between prior historical changes and the onset of modern growth. This implies that theorists may continue to rely on cross-sectional evidence about divergent growth paths as inspiration for their models, but that economic history offers far greater riches. A closer collaboration between those who want to discern general laws and those who have studied the historical facts and data closely may have a high payoff. Only when we understand which inefficiencies and delaying influences produce the time pattern of "take-offs" that we observe during the last two centuries can we begin to claim that our understanding is as complete as the term "unified growth" theory suggests.

---

[33] One exception is recent work by Voigtländer and Voth (2006, 2008), who offer models designed to explain part of the "First Great Divergence" between Europe and China.

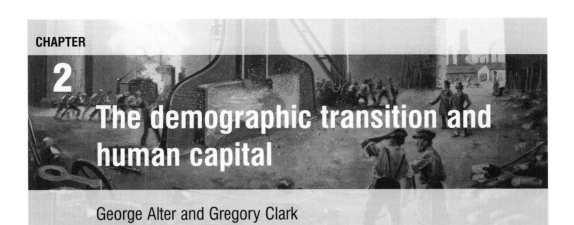

The demographic transition and human capital

George Alter and Gregory Clark

Contents

In 1700 four features characterized all of Europe: high fertility, modest educational attainment, the dominance of physical over human capital, and low rates of economic growth. By 1870 in much of Europe modern economic growth was under way. Fertility levels had begun their decline to modern levels, education levels were rising, and human capital was becoming an important income source. These conjunctions suggest that there must be a connection between modern economic growth, fertility decline, and rising human capital. The nature of that connection, however, is disputed. What triggered the switch to the modern demographic regime, with few children despite high incomes? Was this another independent innovation, as significant as the Industrial Revolution? Or was it just a delayed echo of the Industrial Revolution?

The Industrial Revolution and the demographic transition are the two great forces that explain the upward march of modern incomes. So far they have stood independently, the Industrial Revolution preceding the decline in fertility in Europe by more than 100 years. Our instincts suggest that there is some underlying connection. The difficulty is to connect them in a way that also explains fertility differences across countries in the pre-industrial world, the transition period, and the modern world.

The pre-industrial demographic regime

All European societies had high fertility in 1700, but matched by high mortality so that population growth rates remained modest. The average population growth rate in Europe in 1700–50 was 3.1 percent, ranging between 0.3 percent in the Netherlands and 8.9 percent in Russia (Livi Bacci, 2000, table 2.1). Figure 2.1, for example, shows two measures of fertility for England, 1540–2000. The first is the gross reproduction rate (GRR), the average number of daughters born per woman who lived through the full reproductive span, by decade. Such a woman would have given birth to nearly five children (daughters plus sons), all the way from the 1540s to the 1890s. Since in England 10–15 percent of each female cohort remained celibate, for married women the average number of births was nearly six.

The demographic transition to modern fertility rates began only in the 1870s in England, as in most of Europe, but then progressed rapidly. By 2000, English women gave birth on average to fewer than two children. The English experience was similar in timing to a whole range of western European economies.

The second measure of fertility is the net reproduction rate (NRR), the average number of daughters that would be born though their lifetime by the average female born in each decade. If the NRR is one, then each female just replaces herself over the course of a lifetime. Net reproduction rates fell much less between the pre-industrial and modern eras.

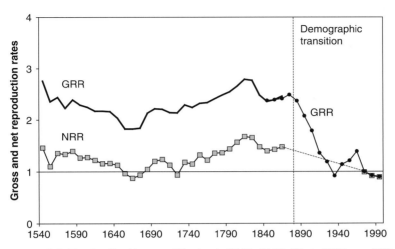

Figure 2.1 The fertility history of England, 1540–2000 (Clark 2007a, p. 290, fig. 14.6)

The mechanism that we believe kept population growth rates in line with resources before the Industrial Revolution was the Malthusian Trap. This depends on just three assumptions:

1. The *birth rate*, births per year per thousand persons, was constant or rising in real incomes. The birth rate at a given income varied across societies depending on social conventions on reproduction.
2. The *death rate*, deaths per year per thousand persons, declined as material living standards increased. Again, the death rate differed across societies depending on climate and lifestyles.
3. *Material living standards* declined as population increased.

Figure 2.2 shows these assumptions. In the upper panel birth and death rates are on the vertical axis, material income per capita on the horizontal axis. The first two Malthusian assumptions imply that there was only one level of real incomes at which birth rates equaled death rates, denoted as y^*. And this constituted a stable equilibrium. Thus y^* is called the 'subsistence income' of the society: it is the income at which the population barely subsisted, in the sense of just reproducing itself. This subsistence income was determined independent of the production technology. It depended only on the factors which set birth and death rates. These factors alone determined the subsistence income.

An implication of the Malthusian model is that in the pre-industrial world high fertility rates produced high death rates, low life expectancies, and low incomes. A society could raise incomes and life expectancy only through reducing the births at any given income. A second implication is that, unlike in the modern world, high-income groups within a society would have higher

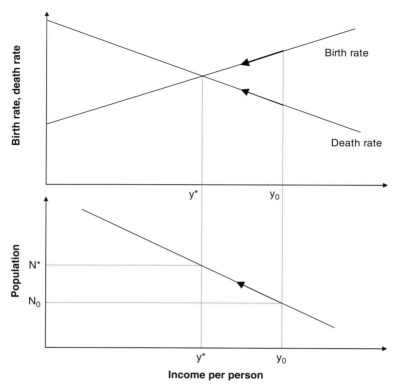

Figure 2.2 The Malthusian regime

net fertility. Thus the demographic transition must have involved greater changes in behavior among the rich than among the poor.

The bottom panel of Figure 2.2 illustrates the third assumption. The panel has on the vertical axis the population, N, and on the horizontal axis material income. As population increased material income per person by assumption declined. Figure 2.2 also shows how an equilibrium birth rate, death rate, population level, and real income were arrived at in the long run in a pre-industrial economy. Suppose we start at an arbitrary initial population N_0 in the diagram, lower than N^*. This generates an income y_0, above the subsistence income. At this income the birth rate exceeds the death rate, so population grows until income falls to y^* and population equals N^*.

Since the time of Malthus's second edition of the *Essay on the Principle of Population* it was believed that northwestern Europe was comparatively rich in the eighteenth century. It had a unique pre-industrial system of fertility limitation, and economic growth allowed some relief from the Malthusian constraints. From the earliest records fertility rates in northwestern Europe were well below biological possibilities. In England in the 1650s, for example, when fertility was at its pre-industrial minimum, the birth rate was 27 per 1000, less than half the biological maximum. The average woman then gave birth to only 3.6 children (Wrigley et al., 1997).

This northwestern European fertility limitation was the product of a unique pre-industrial social pattern of late marriage by women, combined with a large percentage never marrying, known as the European Marriage Pattern (Hajnal, 1965). Malthus himself argued that northwest European prosperity was based on its exercise of the *preventive check* on population growth through marriage choices. It was also thought that fertility limitation in northwestern Europe reflected a more individualistic, rational society where people realized the costs of fertility and took steps to limit it. Europe's eventual experience of the Industrial Revolution was thus foreshadowed hundreds of years earlier by its adoption of a modern marital pattern and family structure, a structure emphasizing individual choice and restraint (Macfarlane, 1979, 1987).

More recent research, however, suggests that perhaps most societies before 1800 limited fertility by as much as in northwestern Europe, though by different mechanisms. Eastern Europe, with very high fertility, was more the exception to pre-industrial norms than was northwestern Europe. This research also suggests that fertility limitation in northwestern Europe had little to do with rational individual calculation and much more to do with social customs.

Fertility limitation within Europe

The European Marriage Pattern, which kept fertility in northwestern Europe well below the biological possibilities, was a curious mechanism, for there is no sign in most of these countries that contraceptive practices were consciously employed before 1800.[1] Fertility levels within marriage were always high. Table 2.1, for example, shows marital fertility for a variety of countries in northwestern Europe before 1790 compared with the Hutterite standard. The Hutterites are communal Anabaptists of German origin, now mainly located in Canada, with good health, but early marriage and no fertility limitation within marriage. They thus provide a reference on the possibilities of unrestricted fertility.

Marital birth rates were lower than for the Hutterites, but by differing amounts across countries. But these deviations from Hutterite levels mostly stemmed from health and nutrition differences, and adherence to different social practices, such as weaning ages, without any sign of individual targeting of fertility.

---

[1] Only late-eighteenth-century France shows signs of widespread family limitation. There are also examples of fertility control among a few elites, such as the Geneva bourgeoisie, earlier in the eighteenth century (Henry, 1956).

Table 2.1 Births per woman per year, married women, northwest Europe before 1790

Country or group	20–4	25–9	30–4	35–9	40–4	All births (20–44)
Hutterites	.55	.50	.45	.41	.22	10.6
Belgium	.48	.45	.38	.32	.20	9.1
France	.48	.45	.40	.32	.16	9.1
Germany	.45	.43	.37	.30	.16	8.6
Italy	.43	.41	.38	.31	.16	8.5
Switzerland	.45	.38	.34	.22	.16	7.8
Scandinavia	.43	.39	.32	.26	.14	7.7
England	.43	.39	.32	.24	.15	7.6

Sources: Clark, 2007a, p. 73, table 4.1; Livi Bacci, 2000, p. 110, table 5.3.

Part of the evidence against conscious contraceptive practices is the lack of patterns in fertility that might be found where there was conscious control of fertility. With such control older married women would be more likely to have achieved their target fertility, and be avoiding further births. In this case, absent confounding factors, European marital fertility should have fallen further below the Hutterite standard for older women. As Table 2.1 shows, the relative birth rate in early Europe compared with Hutterite rates is instead independent of age.

Similarly, if there were a target number of children then we might observe that women with many children by a given age would show lower fertility at that age.[2] Or with targets, the death of a child would increase the chances of a birth in the following years, since now the family was falling further behind its target. Such targeting patterns do not occur within European marriages, with the exception of France, before 1800.

Yet, despite the apparent absence of contraceptive practices, the European Marriage Pattern kept births in northwest European populations low, at only thirty–forty per thousand. This marriage pattern had four features.

1. A late average age of first marriage for women, typically 24–26.
2. High fertility within marriage.
3. Many women, typically 10–25 percent, never married.
4. Low illegitimacy rates, typically 3–4 percent of births.

More than half of possible births were averted by this marriage pattern. The average woman completed a third of her childbearing years before she married. Women who never married reduced the number of births by another 10 to 25 percent. Thus fertility was reduced by a third to a half by the marriage pattern.

---

[2] Both these tests unfortunately run into the problem that people would have different targets for family size. The ones who want lots of children may then marry earlier and so still have high fertility levels at later ages.

Table 2.2 Total fertility rates before 1790 and in 1870

Country or group	Mean age at first marriage	Births per married women	Total fertility rate (TFR)	TFR 1870
Belgium	24.9	6.8	6.2	–
France	25.3	6.5	5.8	2.8
Germany	26.6	5.6	5.1	5.3
England	25.2	5.4	4.9	4.9
Netherlands	26.5	5.4	4.9	5.2
Scandinavia	26.1	5.1	4.5	4.6

Sources: Clark, 2007a, p. 76, table 4.2; Livi Bacci, 2000, p. 136.

Table 2.3 Total fertility rates in different pre-industrial societies

Country or group	Mean age at first marriage	% never married	Total fertility rate
Northwest Europe	26	12	5.0
Russia	16	1	7.3
China	19	1	5.0
Japan	19	1	5.2
Forager Societies	17	1	4.6

Sources: Clark, 2007a, pp. 71–90; Mironov and Eklof, 2000, pp. 57, 67, 73.

Table 2.2 shows how the European Marriage Pattern kept total fertility rates well below the biological possibilities in northwestern Europe. Interestingly, as the last column of the table shows, except for France these total fertility rates were still largely unchanged in 1870, long after the onset of the Industrial Revolution.

But limitation of fertility in northwestern Europe turns out to be not as unique as was once thought. Forager societies have limitations on fertility that are just as strong, but the mechanism is longer spacing between births. Recent research suggests equally strong fertility limitation in Japan and China in the eighteenth century, despite early and universal marriage. East Asian fertility was reduced by longer birth spacing and by infanticide (Lee and Campbell, 1997; Skinner, 1997; Smith et al., 1977).

As Hajnal famously observed, the European Marriage Pattern was found only in Europe to the west of a line drawn from St. Petersburg to Trieste. To the east, before 1800 marriage was early and universal, with again no fertility limitation within marriage. Thus fertility rates were very high: close to the biological maximum. Table 2.3 shows that eastern Europe, rather than the northwest, had an unusual level of fertility for pre-industrial societies.

The decline of fertility after 1870 seemingly has two possible drivers. The first is the rise in incomes consequent on the Industrial Revolution, the second a

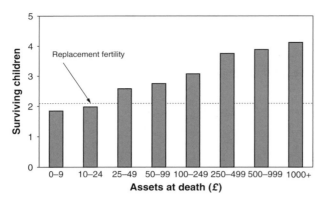

Figure 2.3 Wealth and surviving children, England, 1585–1640 (Clark, 2007a, p. 116, fig. 6.2)

general rise in human capital investments in children, stemming from a desire for "quality" as opposed to "quantity." But the evidence from the period before 1800 is that those with the highest incomes and the greatest investments in the human capital of their children also had the largest numbers of surviving children.

The clearest evidence we get of this is from pre-industrial England. Men's wills reveal both their surviving children and their assets at a time close to their death. Figure 2.3 shows the numbers of surviving children per man for eight bequest classes from wills of the early seventeenth century. There is a powerful connection between assets and surviving children. A man with less than £25 in bequests averaged fewer than two children. Someone with £1,000 or more averaged more than four children. Since wealthier men were more likely to be literate, net fertility was also positively associated with literacy. Those likely to have invested more in children's human capital also had more surviving children. Interestingly, the evidence is that this effect mainly operated from higher marital fertility rates among the rich (Clark and Hamilton, 2006, p. 730).

Evidence from rural Sweden in the mid-nineteenth century, and for eighteenth-century France, suggests a similar pattern of greater reproductive success by the more prosperous. In France, Dérouet (1980) found that crises had much greater effects on the demography of the poor than of the rich. The mortality of the poor rose and their fertility fell, widening the reproduction gap between rich and poor. Mironov, however, gives data for Russia in the 1840s and 1850s suggesting that net fertility varied little by social class, with birth rates high for all social classes – landed nobility to peasants – and mortality rates similar (Mironov and Eklof, 2000).

This suggests that at least in the areas dominated by the European Marriage Pattern there was a positive association between net fertility, income, and education which somehow changed into a negative correlation after 1870.

The Malthusian balance in eastern and Mediterranean Europe

The demographic regimes in eastern and southern Europe were very different from the northwest. In the northwest couples were expected to form economically independent households on marriage (Laslett, 1977). In contrast, households in eastern and Mediterranean Europe were often large and complex (Laslett and Wall, 1974; Wall et al., 1982). It has been argued that the much higher fertility of these regions stems from these differences in family structure. Complex households were often linked to land tenure systems that favored large families. Russian lords are accused of encouraging early marriage among their serfs to maximize labor on their estates (Hoch, 1982; Czap, 1978). Land allocations within peasant communes favored large households even after emancipation (Mironov and Eklof, 2000). Similarly, sharecropping systems in central Italy favored larger households. Landlords preferred sharecroppers with more adult labor (Doveri, 2000).

Earlier marriage increased fertility in eastern and Mediterranean Europe. But mortality was higher also, and life expectancy thus shorter (Berelowitch et al., 1997). Ethnically Russian communities suffered from high infant mortality rates, compared even with Jewish or Kazakh families living nearby (Ransel, 2000). Observers attributed this to early weaning, poor hygiene, and a belief that hardship in infancy produced robust adults (Ransel, 2000; Mironov and Eklof, 2000).

The effectiveness of Malthusian adjustments

Malthus described a world in which population adjusted to resources in ways that limited population growth and returned real wages to a subsistence standard. How strong were these adjustment mechanisms? Was pre-industrial Europe a self-equilibrating (homeostatic) system?

Ronald Lee concluded that European populations were "weakly homeostatic." But, as he nicely put it,

It is essential to realize, however, that as long as there is any trace at all of density dependence, no matter how weak, this tug, by its systematic persistence, comes to dominate human population dynamics over the long run, if not the short. (Lee, 1987, 452)

The strongest homeostatic mechanism was the decline in real wages when population rose. For Europe as a whole the elasticity of real wages with respect to population size was about –1.6. This implies that a 10 percent increase in population reduced real wages by 16 percent. Thus the Malthusian Trap.

Population responses to changes in real wages, the positive and preventive checks, were considerably weaker. Lee and others (Bengtsson and Reher, 1998; Galloway, 1988; Lee, 1981) found strong short-term mortality and fertility responses to real income shocks. High food prices in the wake of a harvest failure increased death rates and reduced birth rates. After five years, however, the net effects of these changes were modest. Lee and Anderson (2002) estimate that it took 107 years for the English population to offset only half of the effect of a shock to population size, such as a major epidemic. These slow adjustments kept wages near subsistence over a span of centuries, but were not enough to prevent significant wage changes in the medium run of generations. The wide swings in population size and real wages in Europe between the twelfth and the nineteenth centuries were primarily caused by external shocks, like the plague epidemics that reached Europe from Asia between 1240 and 1720.

This also suggests that the Malthusian positive checks would not contain population growth if there were a sustained decrease in the average mortality level, as Europe experienced by 1800. As a consequence Europe entered an unprecedented period of population growth.

The Malthusian regime in disequilibrium, 1750–1870

As others have observed, Malthus published his description of the demographic system of pre-industrial Europe at exactly the time when it ceased to exist. After 1720 mortality fell as first plague was defeated and then smallpox, the latter through vaccination. There were epidemics after 1800, like cholera and even a reprise of smallpox in 1871, but none was strong enough to raise mortality rates to earlier levels. Consequently populations all across Europe expanded rapidly.

As Table 2.4 shows, population growth occurred everywhere in Europe. Annual rates of growth were between 0.4 percent and 1.3 percent, except for France and Ireland. Europe's population more than doubled in 1800–1900, compared with increases of 32 percent in 1500–1600, 13 percent in 1600–1700, and 56 percent in 1700–1800 (Livi Bacci, 2000).

But population growth did not result in declining living standards, as had been the earlier experience in 1200–1315, 1500–1650, and 1700–1800. Food supply outpaced population growth after 1800. The Agricultural Revolution kept pace with population increase even before cheap grain from North

Table 2.4 Growth rates and rate of natural increase, selected countries, 1750–1900

Country	Rate of growth (persons per thousand per year)			Rate of natural increase 1850–1900
	1750–1800	1800–1850	1850–1900	
England	7.9	13.2	12.1	12.8
Norway	6.4	9.4	9.3	13.9
Finland		8.9	9.4	10.1
Russia	8.9	8.6	12.1	
Denmark		8.6	10.5	12.2
Romania		8.1	9.3	
Sweden	5.6	7.9	7.8	11.5
Europe	5.8	7.8	7.6	
Netherlands	2.0	7.8	10.0	13.0
Belgium		7.6	8.5	9.0
Greece		7.4	11.1	7.5
Germany	7.3	7.4	9.3	11.3
Spain	4.2	6.7	4.6	6.0
Serbia		6.6	13.8	
Switzerland		6.3	6.5	7.2
Austria-Hungary		6.1	7.4	8.1
Italy	2.9	6.0	6.3	8.9
Ireland	10.1	4.4	−7.7	6.9
France	3.5	4.3	2.2	2.0
Bulgaria		4.1	6.5	
Portugal		4.1	7.1	9.6

Sources: Livi Bacci, 2000, table 1.1; Sundbärg, 1968, table 11; Rothenbacher, 2002, CD-ROM, table 8.

America flooded markets in the late nineteenth century. This does not mean that there were no crises with demographic consequences, such as the "potato famine" of 1846, but the link between harvests and mortality disappeared as incomes rose.

Surprisingly, this common population growth occurred in a variety of demographic and economic regimes in northwestern, eastern and Mediterranean Europe. Figure 2.4 shows that population growth was, at best, weakly associated with economic development. There is only the weakest association between GDP per capita in 1850 and the rate of natural increase (birth rate minus death rate) 1850–1900. The fastest growth was in England, the industrial leader. But Belgium, another early industrializer, grew more slowly than rural Scandinavia and eastern Europe. France, with middling GDP per capita, had by far the lowest population growth.

In northwestern Europe nineteenth-century population growth followed a classic trajectory known as the demographic transition, which is illustrated for

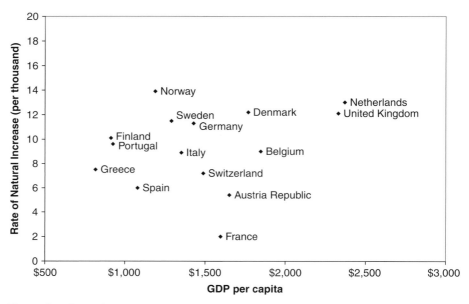

Figure 2.4 Rate of natural increase (1850–1900) by GDP per capita in 1850 (GDP from Maddison, 2003a; RNI from Rothenbacher, 2002)

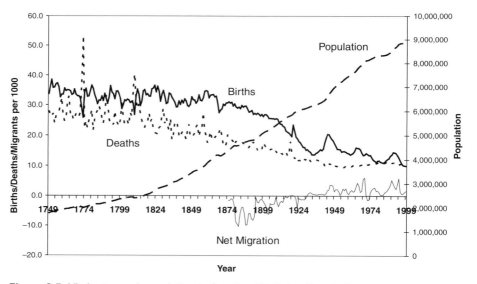

Figure 2.5 Vital rates and population in Sweden (Statistics Sweden)

Sweden in Figure 2.5. The crude death rate (deaths per thousand) began to decrease in the mid-eighteenth century. The crude birth rate (births per thousand), however, remained nearly constant until the 1870s. As the gap between birth and death rates widened, Swedish population growth accelerated. By the end of the twentieth century, falling birth rates closed the gap between births and deaths, ending population growth. The primary cause of population

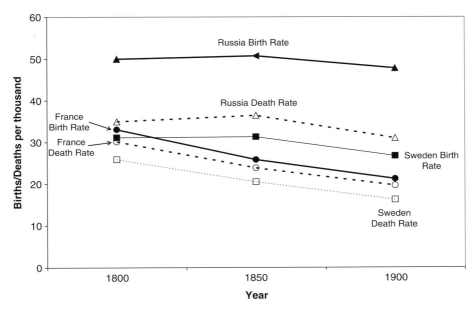

Figure 2.6 Crude birth and death rates for France, Russia, and Sweden for selected dates (Livi Bacci, 2000, table 6.3; Statistics Sweden; Mironov and Eklof, 2000, pp. 80–94)

growth in nineteenth-century Sweden and most of northwestern Europe was falling death rates.

In the Russian empire and much of eastern Europe population growth must be explained in a different way. Mortality, especially for infants, remained extremely high in eastern Europe. Blum and Troitskaja (1996) estimate that life expectancy at birth in the Moscow region at mid-century was about twenty-four years, compared with life expectancies of around forty years in western Europe. Birth rates in eastern Europe were also much higher than in the west. In Russia, early marriage resulted in a crude birth rate of around 50 per thousand (Mironov and Eklof, 2000).

The French case is unique. In France birth control became widespread at the end of the eighteenth century, resulting in an early decline in birth rates. Since decreasing fertility paralleled decreasing mortality, French population growth rates were low. While the European population more than doubled in 1800–1900, France grew by 65 percent, from 29 million to 41 million. In the same period England and Wales grew from under 9 million to over 30 million, and Germany grew from about 25 million to 56 million.

The three different demographic patterns are illustrated in Figure 2.6, which gives estimates of crude birth and death rates for Sweden, Russia, and France around 1800, 1850, and 1900. As we have seen, death rates were already falling by 1800 in Sweden, but the birth rate did not begin to fall until the 1870s. The estimated birth and death rates for Russia are much higher than those for either Sweden or France, but there were signs of decline in both by 1900.

What caused the mortality decline?

In an influential article and later book, Thomas McKeown argued that better nutrition caused by rising incomes was the main cause of the mortality decline 1800–1870 (McKeown, 1976; McKeown and Record, 1962). Subsequent research has challenged McKeown's conclusion. Instead of his emphasis on the direct impact of rising incomes through better nutrition, the current wisdom is that indirect connections between economic development and mortality were the most important: advances in knowledge, greater government effectiveness, and the growing integration of goods and information markets.

McKeown's nutrition argument rested primarily on discrediting other explanations of mortality decline, and he provided little direct evidence linking nutrition or the standard of living to lower mortality. In particular, he argued that decreasing rates of airborne diseases, especially tuberculosis, cannot be attributed to other explanations than improved resistance through better nutrition. Livi Bacci in dissent pointed to research suggesting that mortality only rose with severe malnutrition (Livi Bacci, 1991, 2000). Since this was uncommon except in famines, he argues that diet improvements had little effect on long-term mortality trends.

Medical knowledge

Most accounts of the mortality decline discount the role of medical science. It is supposed that doctors could not effectively treat or prevent disease before accepting the germ theory. James Riley argues to the contrary that even mistaken eighteenth-century medical ideas, by drawing attention to environmental factors ("filth theory"), led to measures that combated disease (Riley 1986a, 2001). Since the feared "miasmas" became associated with dead and rotting material, Europeans drained swamps, cleared refuse, and distanced themselves from graveyards, abattoirs, and waste. Riley credits this movement in particular with progress against malaria.

Vaccination against smallpox removed another major epidemic disease. In the eighteenth century, smallpox returned approximately every seven years in rural areas, and the disease was endemic in cities. Vaccination campaigns dramatically reduced the incidence of smallpox after 1800.

New ideas about child care also had an impact in some places. Infant mortality was particularly high in areas, like Bavaria, that practiced early weaning. Very young infants cannot digest non-human milk, and they receive protection against disease as well as nutrition from breastfeeding. In some places, mothers traditionally withheld colostrum, which is produced in the first few days after delivery and is particularly rich in nutrients and antibodies.

By the eighteenth century, medical opinion favored breastfeeding. In the mid-eighteenth century, Sweden began licensing midwives and training them to promote breastfeeding, and infant mortality fell after 1800 (Brändström, 1997). Ólöf Garðarsdóttir describes how a young physician halved infant mortality on the island of Vestmannaeyjar by teaching mothers to care for the umbilical stump (Garðarsdóttir, 2002).

Public health measures

The early public health movement also owed much to environmental theories of disease. These theories created an interest in clean water, closed sewers, and better ventilation even before germ theory was accepted. Advocates, like Chadwick in England, promoted waste removal, water and sewage systems, and more light and air in rapidly growing urban slums. Even though the environmentalists were often reluctant to accept the germ theory of disease, they promoted major infrastructure projects that finally ended the "urban penalty."

Simon Szreter argues that public health measures were much more effective than McKeown estimates. Szreter (1988) reinterprets McKeown's evidence to show that waterborne diseases played a larger role than McKeown acknowledged in mortality trends. The largest improvements in mortality occurred in the third quarter of the nineteenth century, when the implications of the germ theory could finally be incorporated in urban infrastructure. Hamburg, for example, which resisted measures based on the germ theory, suffered a devastating cholera epidemic in 1892, while the neighboring city of Altona, which had installed a more effective water filtration system, was much less affected (Evans, 2005).

Many of the measures that were initially successful in western Europe spread to eastern Europe. Mirinov describes an expansion of medical services in Russia and the proliferation of organizations dedicated to reducing infant mortality (Mironov and Eklof, 2000).

Epidemic controls

The major cycles of population growth and decline in Europe from the thirteenth to the eighteenth century were heavily influenced by severe epidemics, especially bubonic plague. Plague usually disappeared from Europe between epidemics, but was reintroduced by trade with Asia, where plague was endemic in animal populations.

A wide variety of explanations have been offered for the disappearance of plague, including viral mutations, competition between rat species, and new building materials. Recent authors highlight the increasing effectiveness of government interventions and communication (Bourdelais, 2006; Livi Bacci,

2000). By 1720, when the last epidemic of plague broke out in Marseille, the French government was able to impose a more effective cordon sanitaire on land, and shipping quarantines were more rigorously enforced.

Transport improvements

Epidemics in pre-industrial Europe were often triggered by other events, such as war and famine. In times of distress, refugees carried infections with them. For example, typhus epidemics followed Napoleon's defeat at Waterloo. Transport improvements reduced such refugee flows by creating broader food markets that were less affected by local crop failures.

Marriage

The history of nuptiality in nineteenth-century Europe is in many ways a story of the dog that did not bark. Pre-industrial marriage patterns were maintained, in spite of dramatic changes in economic and mortality conditions. The "preventive restraints" of late marriage and permanent celibacy did not erase the growing gap between births and deaths. Nor did the mass of new industrial workers liberate themselves from parental control to marry at younger ages, as many contemporaries feared. Differences between marriage patterns in western and eastern Europe also persisted.

Table 2.5 presents I_m, an index of the proportion married, showing the effect of marriage on fertility from the European Fertility Project (Coale and Watkins, 1986). Estimates in the table are sorted in descending order by their values in 1900. The results reproduce Hajnal's generalization about east and west. The highest values of I_m were in eastern Europe, the lowest values were in north-western Europe. Mediterranean countries tended to be in between. The two countries that are most out of place in Table 2.5 are France and Ireland. We saw in Table 2.4 that these countries also had unusually low population growth rates. But here we find that they earned that distinction in different ways. France falls between Spain and Italy, with the highest proportion of women married of any country in northwestern Europe. Ireland had the lowest proportion married in all of Europe in 1900. Population growth was slow in France, because of very low marital fertility resulting from the early adoption of birth control. In Ireland, marital fertility remained high, but marriage was extremely late, and permanent celibacy was common.

In eastern Europe marriage remained much earlier than in the west, but there were some initial movements toward later marriage. Marriage was earlier in areas with more land per capita, and marriage ages were higher in industrial areas (Berelowitch et al., 1997).

Table 2.5 Index of proportion married (I_m) for European countries, 1850–1900

	1850	1860	1870	1880	1890	1900
Serbia						0.804
Romania						0.735
European Russia			0.609			0.684
Hungary				0.688	0.712	0.676
Greece						0.637
Poland						0.634
Spain					0.591	0.573
France	0.533	0.539	0.542	0.550	0.555	0.557
Italy		0.551	0.558	0.533	0.530	0.527
Germany			0.462	0.498	0.493	0.505
Finland				0.496	0.490	0.487
Denmark	0.440	0.474	0.455	0.462	0.475	0.480
England and Wales	0.482	0.499	0.504	0.496	0.471	0.468
Portugal		0.441		0.459	0.462	0.466
Belgium				0.427	0.425	0.464
Luxembourg						0.461
Austria					0.458	0.457
Netherlands		0.407	0.440	0.468	0.449	0.454
Switzerland		0.375	0.411	0.444	0.428	0.438
Norway				0.410	0.424	0.425
Sweden				0.419		0.422
Scotland		0.399	0.399	0.400	0.380	0.384
Iceland	0.357	0.385	0.357	0.294	0.332	0.383
Ireland			0.399	0.364	0.330	0.316

Source: Coale and Watkins, 1986.

Migration

The rapidly growing populations of nineteenth-century Europe would have faced a grim Malthusian future if agricultural productivity had not risen, and if emigration to the New World had not helped relieve population pressures. The population of Europe in 1815 was 223 million. By 1913, 40 million people had emigrated to the New World. Emigration to the Americas occurred in two phases. Before 1880, most emigrants came from northwestern Europe, especially Britain and Germany. After 1880, the "new migration", from Scandinavia, Italy, and eastern Europe, was added to, and soon exceeded, the "old migration" (Poussou, 1997). By 1900, more than a million people a year were emigrating to the United States, the primary destination for most Europeans. As the costs of transatlantic travel went down, a growing proportion of migrants came to the New World to work rather than to settle (Moch, 1992). More than half of some nationalities returned to Europe from the United States, but there were also groups, notably the Irish and eastern European Jews, who overwhelmingly remained (Willcox, 1929, pp. 206–07).

Internally there was substantial migration of population from country to city as incomes rose. From 1815 to 1913 the rural population grew from 197 to 319 million. But the urban population expanded from 26 million in 1815 to about 162 million in 1913 (Bairoch, 1997).

Migration was not a new phenomenon in the nineteenth century. Early-modern cities depended upon migration, because death rates exceeded birth rates in most urban areas until late in the nineteenth century. Most migration involved short distance movements to nearby towns, and this pattern continued into and after the nineteenth century. With the simultaneous developments of population growth and the Industrial Revolution, however, the level of migration increased dramatically (Poussou, 1997).

The demographic transition

In the 1870s, birth rates began decreasing in most of western Europe, closing the gap between birth and death rates. Southern and eastern Europe joined this movement a few decades later, although fertility remained high in some places until after 1945. The gap between births and deaths was not completely closed until the twentieth century. But the movement toward smaller families began well before 1870 in a few places. Birth control has been identified among some elite groups in the early eighteenth century, and the turning point for France was in the 1780s, resulting in its distinctively low rates of population growth in the nineteenth century.

Figure 2.7 was constructed by the European Fertility Project, which used censuses and vital registration to estimate fertility by province in Europe (Coale and Watkins, 1986). On this map, provinces are shaded by the earliest decade in which an index of fertility decreased by at least 10 percent. The early fertility decline in France stands out. Birth rates began falling before 1830 in almost all regions of France except for the northwest. In contrast, fertility declines began more than fifty years later in England and Belgium, the most industrial countries in Europe. Parts of Hungary, indeed, began to change before some industrial provinces in the west. By 1900 most of western and central Europe had joined the movement to lower birth rates, and there are only a few areas in Spain and Italy that waited until after 1930.

The provincial-level data presented in Figure 2.7 is not the full story of fertility decline. Within regions, fertility usually fell earlier in urban than in rural areas, as Brown and Guinnane (2007) recently emphasized. Thus birth rates went down earlier in urban than in rural Bavaria. But this does not help us

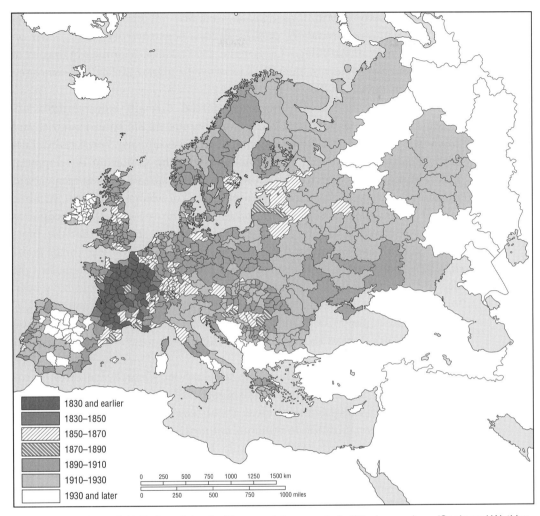

Figure 2.7 Earliest date of a 10 percent decrease in fertility, by province (Coale and Watkins, 1986)

to explain why the change occurred so much earlier in rural France than in urban Belgium.

Researchers involved in the European Fertility Project noticed a distinctive feature of the geography of the fertility transition. In Spain, for example, regional differences in fertility followed the boundaries between areas that spoke dialects of Spanish or different languages, such as Basque or Catalan (Leasure, 1963). In France fertility decline was later in Breton-speaking *départements*. Belgium, divided into Flemish- and French- speaking regions, shows most clearly the importance of linguistic borders. Lesthaeghe (1977) studied seventy Walloon villages matched to neighboring Flemish villages with identical economic conditions. Fertility fell first in the Walloon village in sixty-two of the pairs, and the fertility decline began twenty years earlier on average in the Walloon village (Lesthaeghe, 1977). Flemish couples in the city of Leuven were more likely to have small families if a migrant from Wallonia lived nearby (Van Bavel, 2004).

This suggests that family limitation spread through cultural diffusion. Linguistic boundaries mattered because they hindered the spread of ideas and information. It is unclear, however, what ideas were diffusing. Some researchers in the European Fertility Project concluded that the important development undermining opposition to birth control was the spread of new ideas about science, reason, and human agency, rather than knowledge about specific birth control techniques. What was important was the willingness of people to consider controlling family size. Since the evidence suggests that the most common birth control method during the fertility transition was *coitus inter-ruptus* (withdrawal), the means to reduce fertility were always available. But the idea of intervening in the "natural" process of reproduction could have been "*impensable*" (unthinkable) or "outside the calculus of conscious choice" (Ariès, 1960; Coale, 1973). This view implies that most Europeans *circa* 1800 had more children than they wanted, but were religiously or culturally unwilling to use birth control.

Christian doctrine, especially within the Catholic Church, has strong pro-natalist themes, and even Malthus dismissed the possibility of birth control within marriage. Enlightenment ideas about reason and humankind's role in nature, as well as opposition to religious authorities, made birth control within marriage ethically and socially acceptable. In support of this view Lesthaeghe showed a strong association between secular attitudes and fertility decline. In Belgium, fertility fell earlier in areas that voted for liberal or socialist parties rather than parties associated with the Catholic Church. Although nominally Catholic, these areas also showed independence from Church doctrine by violating rules that prohibited marriage in Lent and Advent (Lesthaeghe, 1991). In nineteenth-century France, fertility decline was later in places where priests refused to swear allegiance to the revolutionary constitution in 1791 (Lesthaeghe, 1992).

If new religious ideas played a role in the fertility transition, they constituted only one factor. Lesthaeghe and Wilson (1986) argue that both religion and modes of production affected the timing of fertility decline. Family limitation was slower to develop where production was organized in labor-intensive family units, like family farms and proto-industrial workshops, in which parents retained greater control over the work of their children. Economic development played a role in the transition to small families, but the relationship between income and fertility underwent a dramatic transformation.

Income and fertility

Economic models of fertility face a fundamental challenge. All plausible models of population regulation for the pre-industrial world depend on a positive association between net fertility and income. This positive correlation of fertility and income became negative in Europe in the period of the demographic transition after 1870, and there seems to be no association between income and fertility in high-income–low-fertility societies today. The numbers of children present in the households of married women aged 30–42 in both 1980 and 2000 were largely uncorrelated with income in Canada, Finland, Germany, Sweden, the United Kingdom, and the United States (Dickmann, 2003, table 2). This suggests that the income–fertility relationship within societies changed dramatically over time.

At the national level, the relationship between wealth and family size changed from positive to negative in late nineteenth-century Europe. This transformation is evident in Figure 2.8, which compares I_g, an index of marital fertility developed for the European Fertility Project, to per capita GDP in 1870 and 1930. In 1870, fertility correlated positively, but weakly, with national income. Fertility in England, the wealthiest nation in the world, was near the European average. The Netherlands, prosperous and predominantly

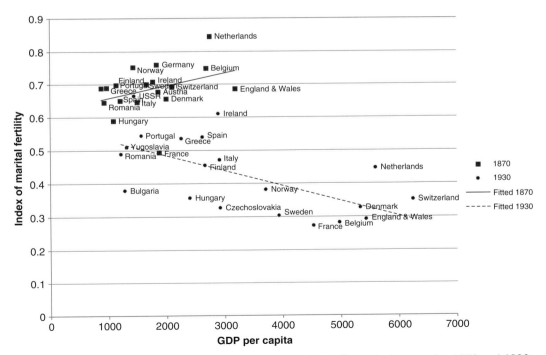

Figure 2.8 Index of marital fertility by gross domestic product per capita, 1870 and 1930 (Coale and Watkins, 1986; Maddison, 2003a)

Protestant, had high fertility. France, Catholic and rural, was the only country far below the European average in 1870. By 1930, a strong negative relationship between fertility and national income had developed. Fertility fell in every country, but it fell most in the most developed countries.

There have been many attempts to resolve this paradox. One such attempt argues that parents faced new choices. Falling average family size among the wealthy in the late nineteenth century was often blamed on the growing taste for "luxury" among wealthy women. Such women, it was argued, were becoming too attracted to parties, theaters, and fancy dress. They had become unwilling to bear children, who would hinder their pursuit of these pleasures. By the 1930s, this argument had been formulated in a less accusatory form with clearer economic implications. New products and new lifestyles in the growing metropolitan societies created by the Industrial Revolution expanded choices. Wealthy families responded by consuming more of these new products and services instead of producing children. This "phase change" type of explanation can also potentially explain why, once everyone had made the transition to the new regime, the income–fertility relationship stopped being strongly negative within high-income countries (but continued to be negative across countries at different income levels).

Most historians agree that attitudes about children changed by the nineteenth century. Europeans developed a more romantic view of childhood and of domestic life in general. Educational theorists like Froebel and Pestalozzi emphasized that early childhood is a special time in which play stimulates learning. Women were expected to stay at home to create a refuge for children from the competition and conflict of the world of work. There is evidence that middle-class women became less involved in their husbands' businesses in the nineteenth century than they had been before (Smith, 1981). The "bread-winner family" even became a common aim of trade union activism by 1900 (Humphries, 2007; Maynes, 2002).

In a famous 1960 paper, Gary Becker proposed that children should be analyzed as "consumer durables." Children, Becker observed, are more like automobiles and refrigerators than like gasoline or food. The benefits derived from children last a long time, and parents do not need to purchase new ones as these benefits are consumed. People do spend more on consumer durables as their incomes rise, but they spend their money on additional features that enhance the quality of these products rather than buying more of them. For example, they buy one Mercedes Benz rather than buying five Hyundais. Rich parents also spend more money on children than poor parents, but they do this by investing in high "quality" children rather than increasing the "quantity" of children in their family. Moreover, parents' preferences may change systematically as their incomes rise, so that the demand for child quality increases faster with rising income than the demand for child quantity, resulting in lower family sizes among the rich than among the poor (Sanderson, 1976).

Becker (1965) and others also point out that raising children is a time-consuming activity, and people switch their consumption towards less time-intensive goods when incomes go up. As wage rates rise, each hour spent on leisure involves giving up a larger quantity of goods, which could have been purchased by working an additional hour. High-income parents want to spend brief but intense "quality time" with a small number of children. This argument on its own would seem to rule out the positive association of income and fertility before 1870, but we may explain the large families of high-income parents in the pre-industrial world by looking at their sources of income. High incomes in the past came predominantly from ownership of non-human assets, while modern high incomes are usually derived from human capital. The incomes of the idle rich were scarcely affected by spending more time on their children, but the opportunity costs of large families are greater for individuals who are well paid for their skills and education.

As Becker (1960) emphasizes, his argument should not be confused with the common but misleading statement that children became more expensive over time. The prices of goods necessary to raise children in the nineteenth century – housing, food, and clothing – were not rising relative to incomes. If children became more expensive, it was because of changes in parents' preferences, not changes in prices. Children were perceived as being more expensive, because parents wanted them to have more comfortable lives and continue their educations rather than going to work (Szreter, 1996, 445).

Education and fertility

Education looks like a promising variable to explain fertility behavior before and after the Industrial Revolution. Education, however, can operate in two very different ways in reducing fertility. It could do so by changing parents' desires and aspirations. Malthus himself shared this view. In later editions of his *Essay on the Principle of Population* he argued that education teaches prudence and foresight and the desire to provide a better life for one's children. Education, especially female education, is the best predictor of family limitation today, although we shall see that it was not as easily correlated with fertility declines in the nineteenth century.

Alternatively, education could operate by raising the costs of children. In this story formal education became more closely tied to incomes after the Industrial Revolution, encouraging more investment in education per child and so fewer children. In most settled pre-industrial economies the bulk of labor demand was for agricultural work, where levels of human capital were low. Agricultural laborers in nineteenth-century England, for example, typically achieved their maximum wage by age 20. After this, earnings were flat until they declined after age 60 (Burnette, 2006). In this kind of economy, it is argued, parents would favor "quantity" over "quality" in children (Galor and Weil, 1996; Becker et al., 1990).

In the early nineteenth century, the demand for education in expanding industries remained weak. Most of the jobs transformed by the first stage of the Industrial Revolution (textiles, iron, and coal) did not require education or even literacy (Mitch, 1991). Estimates for England around the middle of the nineteenth century suggest that returns to education were positive but not large (Long, 2006; Mitch, 1991). Middle-class writers typically emphasized that schools taught morality and regular work habits, rather than economically valuable skills (Mitch, 1984). Both England and Belgium, the leaders of the First Industrial Revolution, had undistinguished records of providing mass education, compared with other western European countries.

Leadership in providing education was usually associated with religious and ideological motivations, rather than expected economic benefits (see Table 2.6). Literacy was generally higher in Protestant countries, where every individual was expected to read the Bible, than in Catholic countries. During the nineteenth century the Catholic Church invested heavily in the provision of schools,

Table 2.6 Primary school students per thousand children aged 5–14, 1870–1930

	1870	1900	1930
France	736.6	859.2	802.8
Germany	732.0	767.8	
Scotland	697.4	764.8	675.4
England and Wales	608.6	741.5	755.2
Switzerland	759.2*	726.5*	701.3*
Denmark		717.5	673.7
Sweden	588.6*	688.8*	779.4*
Austria	425.9	670.3	838.8
Norway	658.0	668.0*	716.3*
Netherlands	638.7	663.4	779.7
Belgium	582.3	592.4	700.8
Hungary	334.2	541.6	494.5
Ireland	384.0	525.5	750.8
Spain	401.4	475.3	717.0
Italy	286.3	382.0	594.1
Bulgaria		331.8	471.9
Greece	252.8	323.9	616.6
Romania		255.8*	588.4*
Portugal	131.6*	194.2*	300.4*
Finland		188.3*	582.2
Russia		148.6	

*Public schools only.
Source: Lindert, 2004.

but conflict between liberal and Catholic political parties for control over the curriculum delayed the provision of state support for education in some places (Soysal and Strang, 1989). Rulers, such as Frederick IV in Prussia and Napoleon in France, recognized the potential of education for promoting national integration, and schooling was used to create citizens loyal to the nation-state (Ramirez and Boli, 1987). Peter Lindert, however, argues that the way in which schools were financed was also critically important. In his account, the early development of schools in Prussia owed more to local control of finances than to exhortations from the royal government (Lindert, 2004).

The connection between economic growth and formal education became stronger later in the nineteenth century (Easterlin, 1981; Sandberg, 1979). As economies grew and became richer and less rural, science and engineering became more important. But bureaucratic systems in industry and government were also elaborated, multiplying the demands for clerks, accountants, and managers. Skills of all types – formal education but also artisanal skills and services – were more in demand.

Does the rising importance of human capital, however created, explain the fertility transition? Increased demand for education could reduce fertility by raising the relative value of quality (educated) children, and so leading to a substitution of quality for quantity. There is clear evidence, however, that such a direct link between modern low fertility and high education levels did not operate. As Figure 2.9 shows, this would imply a rise in the premium paid in the

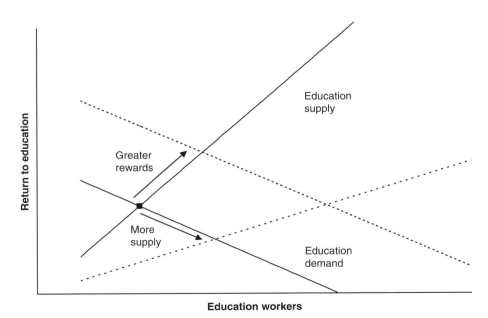

Figure 2.9 Effects of demand and supply changes for education

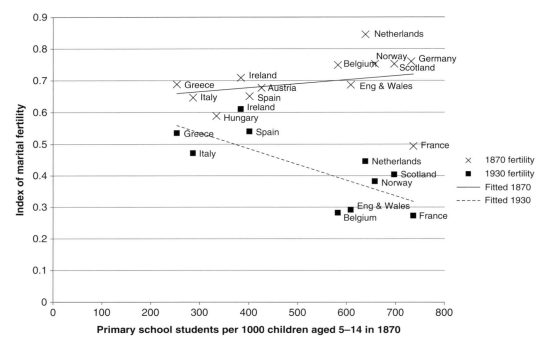

Figure 2.10 Marital fertility for 1870 and 1930 by school enrollment in 1870 (Coale and Watkins, 1986; Lindert, 2004)

labor market for skills after 1870. There is not a lot of evidence on the premium paid for formal education over this long period, but what there is for England suggests a decline (Williamson, 1982). There is plenty of evidence on the premium paid for artisanal skills for England and elsewhere in Europe, and again in this period the premium was declining (Clark, 2007a). The labor market evidence thus suggests that increases in the supply of education and skills were even greater than increases in demand. Parents in late-nineteenth-century Europe chose to supply ever greater levels of education to their children without large increases in the wage premium paid to educated workers.

The increasing supply of skills in European economies was achieved initially without any decline in quantity of children. Figure 2.10 shows the association between marital fertility in 1870 and 1930 and school enrollments in 1870. In 1870, the correlation between marital fertility and current school enrollments was still slightly positive. The correlation between fertility in 1930 and education in 1930 (not shown in Figure 2.10) was only slightly negative, partly because enrollment rates were converging across Europe, as Table 2.6 shows.

As Figure 2.10 reveals, however, the correlation between marital fertility in 1930 and school enrollment in 1870 was strongly negative. This implies that education affected fertility, not by increasing the cost of raising the current generation of children, in which case the effect would be immediate, but by changing the values of the next generation of parents.

Conclusion

The Industrial Revolution and the Demographic Transition were the vital elements that created the steady rise in modern living standards. Yet the Industrial Revolution preceded the Demographic Transition by three generations. It is hard to believe that these events are not related. They must be facets of some underlying process of social or economic change. But, as this chapter has illustrated, most of the theories that attempt to connect them fail to predict cross-sectional differences in fertility before, during and after the Industrial Revolution.

State and private institutions

Dan Bogart, Mauricio Drelichman, Oscar Gelderblom,
and Jean-Laurent Rosenthal

Contents

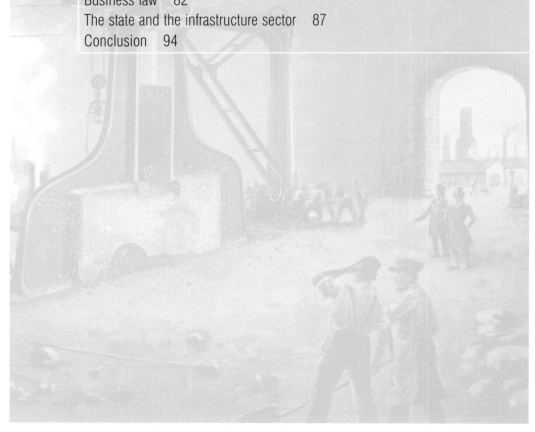

Economic growth depends upon institutions (rules that constrain human behavior and their enforcement mechanisms: North, 1981; Greif, 2006). Some of these rules arise by means of a public process, while others are privately adopted; some are explicit (written down as laws or contracts) and others implicit. Their enforcement can rely on public coercion, private third parties, or even reputation. We focus here on those institutions that are formal and publicly enforced. This is not because informal institutions waned with modernization, but rather because the formal institutions were the ones that underwent the most dramatic transformation during the period we are considering. Many polities adopted written constitutions and formal legislative organizations, and recast their laws. Even Britain, where no formal constitution was set down, saw electoral reform and an explosion of legislative activity.

Economic historians have long emphasized the role of institutions in ensuring prosperity; after a hiatus, development economics has come to similar conclusions (see, e.g., Acemoglu et al., 2001; Engerman and Sokoloff, 1997; Banerjee and Iyer, 2005). Scholars have particularly highlighted the benefits of secure property rights. In this light, England's early economic leadership sprang from the Glorious Revolution's institutional settlement (North and Weingast, 1989). The great variety of political and economic, public and private institutions that prevailed in Europe offers tempting ground for testing this largely inductive argument based on Britain. Although the variation in institutions is extensive, and well documented in the archival record, it raises its own problems: institutions, archaic or modern, are chosen. Furthermore, in the long run all institutions are sub-optimal; only change can allow growth to go forward. Given that Britain was the most successful economy in the period it seems natural to use it as a benchmark. One should bear in mind, however, that the earlier successes of Italian city-states and Dutch provinces and Germany's later catch-up proceeded with institutions that were hardly British. Finally, economists have focused heavily on national output, neglecting regional variation. The British institutions associated with the Industrial Revolution are equally connected to the Irish economy and the potato famine. Thus we tread gingerly.

It is also important to note that, if by 1870 the notions of state and nation had become interchangeable, this was not so in 1700. Sovereign states have long existed, but for most of European history they did not coincide with nations (some were multi-cultural and spatially dispersed, others tiny). The process of competition over territory was extraordinarily prolonged and violent. States faced the perils of external rivals and the resistance of provinces to any attempt at centralization. Moreover, although political boundaries west of the Alps and the Rhine changed relatively little after 1700, that was not the case to the east. The recombination of territories in eastern and central Europe poses obvious problems for us. While we try to consider the whole of Europe, this is not always possible.

While economic historians have often written the economic history of Europe as growth springing from the people's liberation from oppressive rulers, in many places growth arose from the elimination of geographic fragmentation and local privileges and practices (Epstein, 2000). These local privileges endured because they served as bulwarks against rulers' fiscal rapacity. In England, such protections were essentially inoperative because it was a small country that from 1066 enjoyed the costs and benefits of a very centralized and unified set of institutions. This chapter thus explores two questions: (i) how important were problems of sovereign expropriation relative to problems of fragmented authority? and (ii) to what extent did different parts of Europe adopt different institutions to solve similar problems in terms of property rights, infrastructure investment, and business law?

Our analysis puts far greater emphasis on international relations (i.e. war) than has been the case hitherto. Consider Alexander Gerschenkron's (1962) classic, *Economic Backwardness in Historical Perspective*. There, economic innovation pushes public and private institutions to evolve while domestic political struggles may hold them back. That narrative is appealing for central Europe and Russia, where reform and industrialization came late. Even in this region, however, institutional change issued from the crucible of war (from French intervention in Italy in 1857 all the way to the war that raged at the time of the October Revolution in Russia). In the west, institutional change owes more to Napoleon's legions than to industrialization.

An account of institutional change cannot leave aside the exchange of bullets and cannonballs any more than it can ignore the flow of ideas about political and economic institutions. Yet the interconnection of European polities did not bring about institutional convergence. Although in most countries reform led to more representation, higher taxes, legal innovation, and infrastructure investment, the mechanisms used to achieve these goals varied considerably. To some extent this is evidence of path dependence, but it was also the result of the desire of politicians to forge a national identity and thus to preserve differences between their institutions and those of their international rivals. We begin with a very broad issue, namely the evolution of political institutions. We then move through a more focused set of problems: taxation, commercial law, and infrastructure investment. While obviously incomplete, these topics allow us to highlight the key analytical issues in European institutional development between 1700 and 1870.

Political institutions

Between 1700 and 1870 European political units underwent complex, profound, and often locally specific transformations. We focus on three broad trends: (i) absolutism's continued rise from the sixteenth through the eighteenth century; (ii) its complex replacement by constitutional regimes in the nineteenth century; and (iii) the ascendance of the national state over both territorial empires and confederations of small sovereign units.

In empires a ruler or a state deploys its political and military control over multiple territorial entities, imposing different combinations of legal, economic, and cultural uniformity. Between the Roman period and World War I, there was at least one empire in Europe, and most kings aimed at becoming rulers of empires. For millennia empires were the dominant polities around the globe. Yet in Europe they succumbed to a tide of national states, which one could see rising after the Peace of Westphalia in 1648. The Habsburg and Holy Roman empires survived, but their control over territories other than their traditional bases waned. The Ottomans' sway over their European lands also slipped, even though they maintained a stronger grip over their Asian territories. Certainly by the outbreak of the War of the Spanish Succession in 1702, national states were gaining the upper hand in Europe.

Charles Tilly (1992) traces the success of national states to their absorption of the fiscal extraction system and military organizations into administrative units. Early modern European polities had largely relied on indirect (decentralized) rule for their coercion and extraction needs. While centralization was known to be more efficient, it was also much costlier. Gonzalez de Lara, Greif, and Jah (2008) argue that medieval potentates chose indirect rule because it was cheap, and their organizational choice proved persistent. Decentralized administration also constrained the capacity of European rulers to extract resources from their subjects, wage war, and control large territories. By the turn of the eighteenth century the tide was turning. Rulers increasingly brought fiscal and military structures into their administrative structures, thereby shedding the layers of intermediaries on which they had relied to negotiate with the elites. Sitting representative assemblies, quite common in the preceding five centuries, became rare; fiscal operations were wrestled from private control and subjected to central oversight; state finance ministries increasingly substituted for bankers and capitalists to whom kings had often outsourced their borrowing needs; and professional mercenaries were replaced by standing armies, composed almost exclusively of nationals of the states they belonged to (Drelichman and Voth, 2008).

While not doing justice to the wide variety of European polities, this rough characterization illustrates what set the new states apart from the political structures they came to replace. The fate of the countries that did not implement such reforms reveals their importance. The agrarian-based nobility of the Polish-Lithuanian Commonwealth based its power on the *liberum veto*, which allowed any member of parliament to nullify its acts and end the current session. As a result there was not much of a state in Poland by 1700. The reforms begun in 1764 came too late: Poland was divided between Russia, Austria, and Prussia. A similar system in Hungary had resulted in its absorption by the Ottoman Empire in the sixteenth century. As a rule, small states incapable of fielding standing armies and dominated by traditional elites were absorbed by the greater powers, Venice's loss of its 1,000-year independence to Napoleon being the iconic example of the fate that befell commercial and aristocratic city-states across Europe. Slightly larger states like the German principalities were enfolded in the fiscal–military machines of their more powerful neighbors. The Swiss Confederation, a collection of patriciate-ruled cantons, was overrun by the Napoleonic armies, although after the Congress of Vienna it managed to re-emerge in enlarged form and having acquired a government that could call itself central in some measure. Despite its loose organization, the Swiss Confederation managed to remain independent amidst the tug of war between France and Austria, illustrating the diminishing returns to the imperial model in Europe.

Two polities stood at the vanguard of change. Britain distinguished itself from the European norm with the construct of the Crown-in-Parliament and the other institutional innovations of the Glorious Revolution. The grand bargain of 1689 began a process whereby the kingdom acquired a representative assembly, a strong executive, a professional bureaucracy, and financial institutions designed to cater to the needs of the state; these "sinews of power" proved to be remarkably efficient in the consolidation of the state and the projection of military power (North and Weingast, 1989; Brewer, 1989). Many of these innovations were in fact imported or adapted from the Netherlands, the most successful of the handful of republics that survived in Europe. In the Dutch case, however, the process of change stalled, and fiscal centralization, though long debated, did not become a reality until the French forced changes after 1795.

While representative bodies with actual power survived, most polities shifted to direct absolute rule. One of the main dimensions along which absolute monarchies can be classified is their elimination of alternative political forces – especially the Church, the nobility, tax farmers, local and regional courts, and assemblies consenting to taxes (Finer, 1997). Traditional stakeholders' loss of power varied widely, and was by no means irreversible. The elimination of intermediaries, a part of the Enlightenment program, took root with the most vigor in Prussia, Russia, and Austria. These three countries were still in the early stages of state-building when they became absolute monarchies, and their central governments encountered relatively little resistance. Reforming rulers also prevailed in Spain (Charles III and his minister Campomanes), Portugal (with the reforms pushed forward by chief minister Pombal), and Sweden (Gustav III).

Their reforms, however, were largely reversed by their successors. France made some strides under Louis XIV, who succeeded in co-opting the nobility and reducing the power of the *parlements* to block royal edicts. The venal French system, however, blocked deeper reform. Offices were not only private and, by the eighteenth century, largely hereditary property; they also constituted one of the main forms of government debt. Reform was impossible without an alternative source of finance. In the face of the resistance of the nobility to accept new taxes, France lacked the means to issue new debt. This handicap eventually determined its mounting losses on the battlefields, and prompted the search for more radical reforms (Bordo and White, 1991; Brewer, 1989; Ertman, 1997).

The French *Ancien Régime* was the classic example of what Ertman (1997) has called "patrimonial absolutism," where the different bodies that constitute the state are the private property of individual elites. After Louis XIV's death the elites used their control of state institutions, most notably the *parlements*, to defend their special interests against the several attempts at enlightened reform. The confrontation between the Crown and the elites over the distribution of the tax burden would eventually lead to the French Revolution and radical change in political and fiscal institutions.

History has witnessed few moments of creative destruction so encompassing as the French Revolution. From its very outset the National Assembly sought to eliminate the intermediary bodies of the *Ancien Régime*. *Parlements* were dismissed; local assemblies (Etats) were abolished along with all feudal privilege; the Church was dispossessed of its wealth; and almost all guilds were dissolved. The National Assembly's plan for improving administration focused on central bureaucracies staffed by civil servants. The revolutionaries, however, were soon fighting for their lives, and their reforming zeal waxed and waned with the fortunes of French armies. The forces that had so completely wiped out all vestiges of the patrimonial regime eventually found themselves unable to give France a stable political order, a task that fell to Napoleon and that involved the reemergence of an autocratic empire in Europe.

Napoleon's most lasting institutional innovation was the codification of civil law. Reform was necessary to uphold the Revolution's commitment to centralization and to fill the void created by the elimination of provincial and local legal privileges. Carried by French armies across Europe, codified law was also the Revolution's most significant export (to which we shall return below). While restoration returned most of their power to the absolute monarchs who had been deposed by Napoleon, only the most recalcitrant ones, such as Ferdinand VII of Spain, went to the trouble of completely reversing the legal innovations brought on by the French.

Napoleon was, above all, a brilliant military commander who harnessed the power of citizen armies. These human tidal waves were almost immediately embraced by all the major powers. The diffusion of conscription on a large scale completed the state's integration of the military. As with many military innovations, citizen armies came at a price and eventually forced bureaucracies and administrations to evolve. The new type of conflict also carried a much larger cost in terms of lives. The Napoleonic wars caused almost as many deaths as the Thirty Years War in less than half the time; if the casualties of the French revolutionary war are added to the tally, the dead mount to two and a half million, one third of the lives lost in World War I (Tilly, 1992, pp. 165–166).

Citizens who laid their lives at the feet of the state needed good reason to do so. Pension systems for the maimed and the families of the dead thus had to be set up, and rulers could not turn a completely deaf ear to increasing demands for representation in government. The second and third quarters of the nineteenth century were thus characterized by what Finer (1997) has called the "constitutionalization" of Europe. Constitutions that survived more than a few years were overwhelmingly granted by sovereigns rather than proclaimed by revolutionary assemblies. Sweden led the way in 1809 (although, strictly speaking, it was reviving the 1772 charter of Gustav III), followed by Norway and a handful of German states in 1814–19 and 1830–34. After the fall of Napoleon new restrictive constitutions were enacted in France and the Netherlands. Following the revolutions of 1848, many countries enacted liberal constitutions; most were later revoked or modified to reduce popular representation.

S. E. Finer characterizes four types of constitutions. Neo-absolutist charters left most of the power in the hands of the ruler, although some maintained rump legislatures, often tilted towards the nobility and the landed elites. Spain (with the exception of its liberal periods), Holland under William I, Naples, Greece between 1843 and 1848, and a number of German states all fall under this category. The two other important types were constitutional monarchies, in which power was delegated to ministers answerable to the king (e.g. Austria, Piedmont); and parliamentary monarchies, where ministers responded to elected legislatures (e.g. Britain). The dividing line here is less defined, as most states started as constitutional monarchies and later morphed into parliamentary monarchies. For example, Austria was ruled with an iron hand by Metternich, who answered to the emperor alone; the revolutions of 1848 fatally weakened this system and eventually resulted in the introduction of a parliamentary system in 1867. France oscillated between the two systems, with parliamentary rule between 1830 and 1848, reverting to authoritarianism under the Second Empire, increasing again the role of the legislature towards the end of the 1860s, and finally becoming a parliamentary republic, the fourth type of constitutional state. By 1870 only Russia and the Ottoman Empire maintained absolute governments without constitutions.

European polities also provided a wide array of political and economic freedoms. While long before 1700 there were many polities where some (male) residents had political rights, nearly everywhere much of the population was not only disenfranchised but also bound in either slavery, serfdom, or other labor arrangements that severely limited its freedom to accumulate wealth or migrate. By 1870 all areas of Europe save the Ottoman Empire had abolished slavery and serfdom, even where the political franchise remained non-existent or very constricted (Bush, 1996). The increase in economic freedom, however, should not be overstated, because for several decades after emancipation workers in many parts of the economy had their mobility restricted by systems of passports that gave much bargaining power to employers. The evolution of individual freedoms resulted from the diverse interactions of constitutional processes, centralized states, and the emergence of citizen armies. Out of the tensions between the individual and the public sphere the phenomenon of nationalism in its myriad forms emerged, to play a defining role in the fortunes of the continent to this day.

Fiscal institutions

In the eighteenth century European states raised revenue to fight wars. Whether they wanted to expand their dominion, or merely defend them, rulers had to pay for their military (Brewer, 1989; Hoffman and Rosenthal, 1997). Europe's most powerful states – France, England, Prussia, and Austria in particular – funded either large standing armies or navies and sometimes both. They did so through a combination of taxation, wartime borrowing, and an ever growing public debt. Poor governments could only ally themselves to the great powers or pursue neutrality instead. Thus Spain and the Dutch Republic had to settle for playing second fiddle in European politics for lack of financial might (van Zanden and van Riel, 2004; Tortella and Comín, 2001).

Rulers knew that international competition was expensive, and that in turn colored all domestic political processes. In summer 1764 the French foreign minister, the Duke of Praslin, queried his ambassadors for information about the fiscal system in the countries where they were serving (Hartmann, 1979). At the same time Jean-Louis Moreau, Seigneur de Beaumont, Intendant des Finances, drafted a report on taxation in France. These reports, combined with data collected by modern historians, reveal the enormous differences in government revenues among mid-eighteenth-century European countries.

Table 3.1 underscores the overwhelming financial strength of the two great powers, England and France, in the middle of the eighteenth century. The incomes of the Habsburg monarchy, Spain, and Prussia were two to four times

Table 3.1 Annual public revenue of European states around 1765, in pounds sterling, and estimated share of direct taxes in total fiscal revenue in 1770

Country	Annual revenue (c. 1765)	% share of direct taxes (c. 1770)
France	12,350,000	49
Great Britain	9,702,172	24
Habsburg monarchy	3,972,749	51
Spain	3,944,000	10
Holland	2,417,807	43
Prussia	2,104,077	32
Sweden	1,734,108	n.a.
Denmark	1,029,918	49
Bavaria	476,667	46
Austrian Netherlands	244,141	0
Hamburg	184,223	30
Dutch Republic	117,700	0

Sources: Hartmann, 1979; Tortella and Comín, 2001, p. 156 (Spain); Coppens, 1992, p. 293 (Austrian Netherlands 1760–1769); Fritschy and Liesker, 2004, (Holland 1760–1769); Dormans, 1991, p. 158 (Dutch Republic 1762–1768). Exchange rates are approximate values for 1766 from McCusker, 1978.

smaller. Holland, often lauded for its ability to tax citizens, was a distant fifth. This ranking reflects the political reality of eighteenth-century Europe, with France and England vying for leadership. It also shows that size mattered. For example, tax revenues per capita in the imperial city of Hamburg were as high as in England. But its tiny population prevented it, or any other independent city from playing any role in European politics: total revenue is what mattered for military and political leadership.

Yet, precisely because of the differences in size, the revenues reported in 1765 cannot serve as a measure of fiscal intensity. When measured relative to GDP, England's extractive success shines relative to its major rival France (Mathias and O'Brien, 1976). Between 1665 and 1800 total revenue in England rose from 3.4 percent of GDP to at least 12.9 percent. In France, meanwhile, taxes slipped from 9.4 percent in the early eighteenth century to only 6.8 percent in 1788 (White, 2001). In terms of fiscal institutions, this put France in the lesser set of nations where, as in Sweden for instance, central government revenues came to between 5 and 10 percent of GDP (Fregert and Gustafsson, 2005). The truly exceptional fiscal regime was Holland's: in the early 1740s government revenues amounted to at least 14 percent of provincial income (Fritschy and Liesker, 2004; de Vries and van der Woude, 1997).

The divergent fiscal success of eighteenth-century states is confirmed by their respective per capita tax burden measured in daily wages of unskilled laborers.

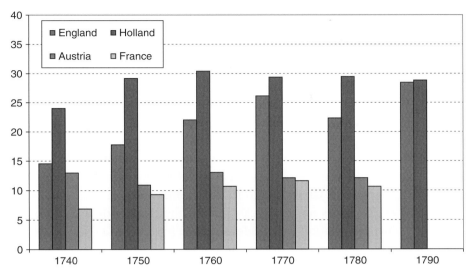

Figure 3.1 Tax pressure in various European countries, expressed as the number of (silver) day wages per capita, 1740–1790 (Fritschy, 1988, p. 54; Hoffman, 1994, p. 238; Dickson, 1987, I, pp. 36, 40; II, pp. 369–70, 380; Prak and van Zanden, 2006, p. 130)

The available data for the period 1740–1790 once again shows Holland as the fiscal champion, with England catching up after 1780 (Figure 3.1). In both countries in the 1790s the average person paid up to the equivalent of one month's daily wages in taxes per year. France's performance improved between 1740 and 1770, but it trailed far behind England and Holland until the Revolution. The same was true for the Habsburg lands of Austria, Hungary, and Bohemia, where inhabitants never paid more than the equivalent of thirteen days' unskilled wages to the central government per year.

One possible explanation for these differences is the substitution of indirect taxes like customs duties and excises for direct taxes on real estate, revenues from royal domains, or the sale of monopoly rights. England is the cherished paragon here: by 1765 land taxes brought in less than a quarter of public income, the rest coming from import and export duties and taxes on consumer goods. Holland is the other obvious example, but here direct taxes on land, real estate, financial assets, and income still represented 43 percent of total revenues. France's direct taxes brought in roughly half of revenues at mid-century (Riley, 1986b, pp. 55–65). Countries like Prussia and the Habsburg monarchy, on the other hand, relied even more heavily on domain revenues, land taxes, and the sales of monopolies. In 1765 the rulers of the Habsburg lands (16 percent), the Austrian Netherlands (16 percent), and Prussia (31 percent) still drew a considerable part of their income from their own possessions (Hartmann, 1979, p. 318). Spain also conforms to this image; over one-third of its revenue came from customs and excises, but the remainder stemmed from colonial remittances, monopolies, and land taxes (Tortella and Comín, 2001).

But if indirect taxation was so much better, why did other countries fail to emulate England or Holland? Surely it was not for lack of trying. European rulers knew their competitors' financial policies well, and they strove to ameliorate their own fiscal systems (Bonney, 1995, pp. 428–30). By 1720 most rulers accepted the detrimental effects of currency debasement. At the same time the major players, and many of the minor ones, instituted central bodies to monitor tax revenues, improved the registration of wealth holdings, and appointed specialists to consider tax reforms (Fritschy and Liesker, 2004; Capra, 1995; Irigoin and Grafe, 2006). In the seventeenth century, most states had levied excise duties on some scale, and in the eighteenth century experiments with income taxation were widespread (O'Brien, 1988a; White, 2001; Tortella and Comín, 2001; de Vries and van der Woude, 1997, p. 112).

The actual collection of taxes may not have been the problem, either. The vast majority of European rulers farmed out the collection of a large part of their taxes. Tax farming offered both short-term credit and a steady stream of income. The downside to tax farming was its overhead cost. In seventeenth-century Spain some 40 percent of revenues may have stuck to the fingers of the farmers (Tortella and Comín, 2001). Tax collection by government officials could be much cheaper. In Holland, for example, direct collection after 1750 cost between 8 and 9 percent of total revenue (Fritschy and Liesker, 2004, pp. 57–62). Yet it would seem unlikely that rulers settled for too high a deadweight loss. Indeed, the cost of tax collection in late-eighteenth-century France may have been as low as that of England (Norberg, 1994; Lindert, 2004).

Following Peter Dickson's seminal work on England's public finance, many economic historians today stress the value of representative government. The Glorious Revolution of 1688 consolidated Parliament's right to control the Crown's purse; in return it voted ever higher taxes. Parliament's ascendancy ran counter to the general gutting of representative assemblies that occurred in Spain and France and eastern Europe. Here the Dutch Republic would seem to be the odd one out, for despite its representative government and high levels of indirect taxation, it could not raise enough money to continue the struggle for military primacy after 1715.

But the financially less successful states did not just lack parliamentary control of taxation and expenditure. These were also composite monarchies, amalgamates of numerous territories with their own traditional liberties, political structures, and fiscal systems. In France, Spain, and the Habsburg lands the central government tried to, but could not, overhaul history's legacy of institutional barriers (Dickson, 1987; Irigoin and Grafe, 2006). For instance, the inhabitants of the *généralités* of Paris, Lyon, and Rouen always contributed far more money per capita than the population of Brittany, Burgundy, or Provence (White, 2001). Even the most successful fiscal regimes suffered from this kind of fragmentation. Britain had to settle for very low revenues from remote Scotland (O'Brien, 1988a). The central government of the Dutch Republic was engaged in perpetual negotiation about tax transfers from its seven provinces.

A related problem was that of local particularism. Traditional liberties allowed towns and provinces to administer taxation and keep much of the income (O'Brien, 2001; Dincecco, 2007). In France, for example, provincial authorities made it difficult to change land tax rates and raise total revenue. Besides, there were fixed tax quotas between towns and regions. The loss of income to the central government was particularly important when local economies were thriving, such as the towns of Flanders and Brabant in the Austrian Netherlands, the urban republics of the Swiss Confederation, or the ports of Catalunya. Urban autonomy added another irreducible constraint on monarchies. In Holland a major political crisis (imminent defeat in the face of Spanish troops in the early 1570s) was required before towns would hand over two-thirds of local revenues to the central government. Finally, in many regions noblemen, clergy, and sometimes even larger sections of the population, benefited from tax exemptions. On the whole old privileges sapped the tax base of *ancien régime* governments. In order to maintain their standing in Europe, the rulers of France and Austria reverted to ad hoc fiscal policies which complicated rather than simplified the management of public finance (Dickson, 1987; Bonney, 1999). This was not just costly in terms of administration; the arbitrary nature of many emergency measures also reduced tax compliance.

Fiscal centralization would have solved these problems, but achieving it required a major redistribution of political power in all European states except England (Dincecco, 2007). This is why the French Revolution and the subsequent Napoleonic wars were so important. France had to raise taxes and loans to finance its conquest of Europe. Then it relied on contributions from dependent territories. England, as the only remaining opposition, had to fund an unprecedented military campaign. The first reaction of rulers was to levy additional taxes on wealth and income. In England, Pitt the Younger introduced the first income taxes. The Dutch Republic also reverted to income taxation to cover expenses in the late eighteenth century (Fritschy, 1988). Napoleon's conquests also forced the governments of Prussia, Spain, and the Dutch Republic to centralize their fiscal systems (Poell, 2008).

As we saw earlier, the political reconfiguration brought about by the Congress of Vienna after Napoleon's defeat in 1815 reversed part of these changes. Fiscal centralization failed in the Netherlands before the liberal 'revolution' of 1848 because the absolutist constitution of William I sidestepped parliamentary control over public finance (van Zanden and van Riel, 2004). In Spain, several decades of internal strife between absolutists, reactionaries, and liberals preceded the unification of the fiscal system in 1845 (Tortella and Comín, 2001). The English stopped income taxes and reverted to excises and customs – where they managed to bring collection costs below 5 percent (Lindert, 2004). The problems with fiscal centralization in most countries are reflected in the share of indirect taxes in total revenues. In 1870 central government typically raised only between 20 and 40 percent of their revenue through taxes on wealth or income. The remainder came from customs and, especially after the liberalization of trade in the 1850s and 1860s, excise duties (Flora, 1983; Mitchell, 2003).

Thus it comes as no surprise that central government revenues grew modestly at best. In most countries the tax burden was often no higher in 1870 than it had been a century earlier. Most central governments' taxes still amounted to less than 10 percent of GDP. In France taxes actually fell from 10.4 percent in 1820 to 6.9 percent of GDP in 1870. In the Dutch Republic central government expenditure dropped from 14 percent in 1840 to less than 8 percent in 1870 (van Zanden and van Riel, 2004). This decline is partly explained by the expansion of these economies – absolute revenues were increasing because GDP was growing faster after 1815 than it had before 1789. Hence in northwestern Europe state coffers were relatively flush. To be sure, in southern and central Europe the picture was not so rosy, with GDP growth being slower there.

The moderation of the tax burden also reflected the reduction in European warfare. England, France, and Spain continued their struggle for empire beyond Europe, but these colonial wars were much less costly – or were lost early on, as in the case of Spain. At the same time governments were unable, or unwilling, to offer anything beyond armies in exchange for the taxes they levied. In that sense really very little changed in Europe between 1700 and 1870. Central governments were perfectly capable of designing fiscal institutions to raise money, but they used these revenues only to fight wars, or service the resulting debts. They did not consider tax increases for a more generous provision of public goods. In this respect it is telling that most nineteenth-century governments preferred to pass on the burden or benefits of infrastructural works to local governments or the private sector.

Business law

The political and fiscal changes discussed above coincided with legal reform. For economic historians, in advanced economies technological rather than political change drove the law. In more "backward" economies, growth was held hostage to legal conservatism – in particular restrictions on incorporation (Landes, 1969, Freedeman, 1979). More recently economists have argued that common law countries' institutions (in Europe, Ireland and the United Kingdom) are the most responsive to economic forces (La Porta et al., 1997). Countries that derive their law from Roman and later French codes have institutions that are the least responsive (these include all the countries on the Mediterranean and most of those carved out of the Ottoman Empire). Germanic and Scandinavian traditions fall somewhere in between.

Neither argument is very satisfactory. Indeed, the first business corporations were formed around 1600, while general incorporation laws were passed mostly after 1850, *after* industrialization had begun. The second argument takes as fixed the existence of institutions (law) that evolved ceaselessly. Although codes may have mattered they were short, and much was left to the interpretation of judges and revisions by legislators. Judges in common law countries had an obligation to follow both precedent and statute. On the Continent, it seems that the same was true in practice. Everywhere, European commercial law depended on accumulated legal expertise that reached back centuries (Hilaire, 1986). We thus turn to the legacy of the past before confronting the breaks of the French Revolution and general incorporation laws.

Although canon law was not initially friendly to credit, the legal problems of debts had been solved before 1700. Individuals in commerce could issue and endorse letters of exchange and commercial notes everywhere, including the Christian and Jewish communities of the Ottoman Empire. More generally, private individuals could borrow by mortgaging land and other assets or just signing private obligations. The matter of equity was more complex. Before 1800 multi-owner firms were typically partnerships. There were exceptions, such as in shipping and mining, where joint stock enterprise forms had arisen early on (Harris, 2000). In these firms, equity could be traded and investors had limited liability, but in other ways they resembled partnerships because the 'market' for the equity was extremely restricted – either to individuals engaged in the venture or to residents of the same town. In the case of partnerships, liability was unlimited and equity could not be traded. Business law in this sense was quite primitive. Even in silent partnership contracts (legal only in parts of Europe) equity was personal and very difficult to trade. As late as 1700 the few corporations that existed were intimately involved with the business of the state.

During the eighteenth century change was limited by the legacy of the financial crises of 1720–21. In Britain, though the crisis was successfully resolved and a consolidated tradable public debt emerged, the Bubble Act of 1720 severely constrained the development of new forms of equity claims. The French and Dutch governments adopted an equally restrictive stance towards privileged corporations, but they failed to consolidate the public debt into publicly traded instruments. Nevertheless, reform started under the Old Regime, most famously with the French *Code de Commerce* in 1673 (Hilaire, 1986, ch. 2).

In law, as elsewhere, the French Revolution was a watershed. Reforms were extensive and culminated in a series of codes (most famously civil, penal, and commercial). French battlefield successes ensured that laws enacted in Paris were diffused widely across Europe. But the push for reform had local origins. Before 1789 many of France's provinces had charters recognizing their specific legal heritage and fiscal autonomy.[1] Most provinces had a special appeals court (*parlement*) which vetted new royal laws for conformity with local custom and precedents. In 1789 there remained considerable variation in property, credit, inheritance, and, to a lesser extent, in business laws. The Revolution could not accept such a mess. The unifying codes were enacted under Napoleon and have often been portrayed as giving too much power to the executive. The codes also reflect the desire to break with the past. Because the *Ancien Régime* was aristocratic, with male primogeniture and privileges based on birthright, residence, occupation, or even wealth, the civil code attempted to provide family and property law that was blind to these distinctions.

Legislators strove to limit the reach of powerful individuals, and their provisions protected those that were perceived as weak. The civil code's rules for the division of estates limited testators' capacity to favor any particular heir. There were also quite specific rules for the administration of the property of minors and incompetents, and for protecting women's dowries against their husbands' creditors and the rights of debtors over creditors.[2] The code mandated simple rules for the rental and sale of property. At the same time the reforms provided essential elements of a property rights regime that was designed to secure both real property and private debt claims through title and lien registries. In a move that was perhaps less modern, notaries retained their role as mediators of family affairs. Although rarely required, the intervention of notaries in civil matters was pervasive (Hoffman et al., 2000). The Revolution had tried to make them strictly civil servants, but that attempt failed and the Consulate quietly sanctioned a return to a regulated market for notarial positions. Notarized contracts retained a critical advantage over purely private transactions: anyone who contested the execution of a notarized contract bore the burden of proof (Woloch, 1994).

The codes were short and perforce incomplete. The nineteenth century thus saw a steady stream of legislative action and a torrent of appellate decisions, both of which served to complete the French codes (even though they were not

---

[1] The regional specificity of law was an attribute of nearly all but the smallest European sovereignties, including the United Kingdom, as the example of Scottish banking bears out.

[2] In these matters it largely reprised Roman law, but keeping with tradition was as much a choice as was the break that created equal division of estates.

revised). Although appellate decisions were not published in full, as they are in common law countries, they were abundantly referenced in legal manuals that were the key companions to the codes and laws of the nation.

Trade and industry (henceforth commerce) were seen as needing different rules than those of the stolid civil code; these needs brought forth the commercial code of 1807. If the civil code was debtor-friendly and procedurally slow, the commercial code was creditor-friendly and emphasized speedy resolution. Where the civil code limited side contracts, the commercial code left business people considerable leeway to devise rules to govern their interactions. The civil code's reliance on government officials (notaries and judges) gave way to special courts staffed by commercial people who relied heavily on arbitration by experts.

The codes diffused swiftly because Napoleon ruled over much of Europe. They were adopted in Belgium, Italy, the Netherlands, parts of Germany, Spain, and Switzerland. Between 1815 and 1860, most of these countries wrote their own codes, with sometimes substantial alterations. For instance, only France had separate commercial courts, and no other country gave such an extensive role to notaries in private contracts. Even where the codes themselves were not imposed, such as in Prussia, Austria, or Portugal, reforms occurred. In Prussia, the monarchy allied itself with modernists and produced its own set of codes.

Table 3.2 Business law reform in Europe

Country	Codes via French occupation or annexation	Date commercial code adopted	Date general incorporation enacted
Austria-Hungary	No	1811	1899
Belgium	Yes	1851	1873
Ireland	No	None	1857
Italy	Yes	1865	1883
France	n.a.	1807	1867
Germany	Parts	1861	1870
Greece	No	1827	n.a.
Netherlands	Yes	1838	1863
Prussia	No	1807	1870
Portugal	n.a.	1833	1888
Russia	No	1836	Not before 1917
Spain	Yes	1830	1869
Serbia	No	n.a.	n.a.
Sweden	No	n.a.	1895
Switzerland	Yes	n.a.	n.a.
United Kingdom	No	None	1857

Note: For the regions that were occupied during the Napoleonic era, the date the commercial code was adopted is the date an 'indigenous' code was enacted.
Source: Lescoeur, 1877; Harris, 2000; Hecksher, 1954; Jonker, 1996; Owen, 1991; Cameron, 1967.

Conflicts between agrarian East Prussia and the more commercial West may explain some of the variation from the French version. Later, the need to conciliate those parts of Germany not under Prussian rule also dampened the capacity of the German code to set up a simple set of unique institutions.

Scandinavian countries also carried out large-scale legislative reform – but without codes. Russia and the Ottoman Empire escaped the early-nineteenth-century spread of civil and commercial law reform associated with codes. It is important to note, however, that the new central European countries all adopted some form of code. Some wanted to forsake their Ottoman, Russian, or Austrian past. When they did so, it became increasingly unlikely that they would base their codes on the French originals. Indeed, the French codes were never revised in the nineteenth century, and it was better to start from the newer Spanish or Italian ones.

Recently, scholars have emphasized the executive's capacity on the Continent to intrude in judicial proceedings relative to common law countries. Codes indubitably massively increased centralization and uniformity, but critics of this change should bear in mind the lack of regional institutional diversity within England. Evidence that the codes' inefficiencies slowed the Continent's industrialization is thin, not to say nonexistent. It is also true that another hypothesis needs greater investigation, namely that the codes and the failure to separate the judiciary from the executive branch of government laid the ground work for institutional change in the twentieth century that was less favorable to market-based economic change.

The corporation is the emblem of public–private institutional collaborations during early industrialization, and success or failure at deploying corporations has been a frequent explanatory trope in economic history (Landes, 1969; Chandler, 1977; Freedeman, 1979). Before 1850, each corporation was created as a specific grant by the sovereign or the legislature to a group of individuals (Mousnier, 1974; Epstein, 2000). A corporation's purpose could include local administration (municipalities or provincial governments) or the provision of public services (royal administrators were often grouped in corporations as were penitent societies). It could also include collecting the crown's taxes, as in the famous corporation of general farms in France. These organizations provided valuable antecedents to business corporations, because they created impersonal associations with secular purposes. From our perspective corporations have three important attributes: legal personhood (they could sue and be sued in court), a lifespan independent of that of its initial membership, and delegated management; but they rarely if ever had limited liability. From the Middle Ages corporations and material gain had often been linked, but that gain had come as reward for providing some public service. The great discoveries changed all that, because in many cases Europe's pursuit of empire and treasure depended on corporations (Harris, 2000).

Two obstacles prevented the expansion of corporations after 1700. Most rulers could not afford to liberalize rules about the creation of corporations without a serious drain on their treasury – they collected handsome fees for authorizing new ones or taxing their monopoly profits. The other obstacle was the foul reputation of equity claims after the collapse of the financial bubbles of 1719–21 in Amsterdam, London, and Paris. Nevertheless, by the 1770s corporations were making a comeback. That movement had its roots in two completely different set of endeavors: public utilities (canals and other improvements) and financial enterprises (insurance companies and investment funds). In both cases the corporation was a desirable organization relative to the alternatives because it allowed the spreading of risk (relative to a sole proprietorship), the earning of a return by principals (relative to a trust), and protection from dissolution in case of the death of a principal (relative to a partnership). Purely industrial enterprises, however, did not gain easy access to the corporation's advantages.

The French writers of the commercial code followed common practice by requiring state permission before a corporation could be formed. Facing demands for a joint stock enterprise form they allowed the free creation of limited partnerships with shares (*commandites par actions*). Silent partners enjoyed limited liability and tradable equity but managing partners had to take on full liability. While meetings of the shareholders (silent and general) could wield considerable authority, between meetings the general partner had the run of the firm. This form of enterprise was popular in France, the Netherlands, and Germany. It must have reduced the demand for corporations, but the history of its take-up in Europe has yet to be written.

Between 1800 and 1850 the general rule was that some corporations were formed in every country but not very many, except in Belgium (where nearly as many were formed as in France). In the 1840s and 1850s the rules for creating corporations were liberalized. Britain acted first. In part because common law did not allow silent partnerships, it faced a greater demand for a new joint stock form of enterprise than the Continent. Britain allowed for corporations with full liability in 1825, then double liability in 1844, and finally without liability in 1855. The Continent followed in dispersed order (see Table 3.2). The next century would face the difficult problem of regulating and governing corporations.

The state and the infrastructure sector

Infrastructure is the most specific area of our exposition, and serves as a crucible where political, fiscal, and legal change come together. Political and fiscal structures dictated the extent of public or private provision of infrastructure, while legal institutions shaped whether and how local entities or private investors stepped in when the central state declined to do so. Thus this sector is fertile ground for the study of the ways in which institutions influenced economic development. We provide a brief overview of policies towards roads, waterways, and railroads across Europe. One key theme is that restraints on sovereign expropriation and the degree of political fragmentation help to explain the patterns of state intervention and infrastructure development. Countries were also spurred to reform their infrastructure policies in response to their neighbors' efforts.

Roads

In 1700, most European road networks were maintained by local authorities (e.g. villages, cities, manors, churches). Some local authorities conscripted labor (known as the *corvée* in France and statute labor in England), while others collected tolls. Local authorities faced little oversight and had few fiscal devices, thus roads were not maintained and new investment was rare.

Many European states took steps to improve their road network. One of the unique aspects of English road policies was the mixture of local initiative and parliamentary oversight. A local group would petition Parliament for permission to form a "turnpike trust," levy tolls, and improve a stretch of road. By 1840 there were over 30,000 km of turnpike roads in England and Wales. Most were well maintained, permitting the use of large wagons and fast coaches (see Bogart, 2005a).

The Southern Netherlands also had an extensive turnpike network. It operated similarly to the English system, by combining local initiative with oversight from the Austrian government. The tolls were abolished by French authorities during the early 1800s but they were reinstated in 1814 (Milward and Saul, 1973, p. 441). Over the next few decades, the network grew to comprise 3,000 km of roads in Flanders, Brabant, and Hainaut (Ville, 1990, p. 16).

Spain and France had a different approach. In the eighteenth century, the crown designated some highways as royal roads and left others as local. The royal government funded its roads and established an administration (in France the Ponts-et-Chaussées) to build and maintain them. Secondary roads were the responsibility of municipalities, often through *corvée* labor. By 1800 France had 43,000 km of roads, over half of which were royal routes (Price, 1983, p. 37).

Napoleon accomplished little in the way of roads. After 1814, however, the French government increased its funding of national routes, and the primary network increased from 25,700 km to 34,000 by 1840. There were also changes in the funding and organization of secondary roads. An 1836 law expanded

Table 3.3 Road policies, 1700–1840

Country	Summary of road policy	Road km per capita (000s) c. 1840	Road km per sq km c. 1840
England and Wales	Mixture of local and turnpike network	1.98 turnpike 7.54 local	0.13 turnpike 0.49 local
Southern Netherlands/Belgium	Mixture of local and turnpike network	1.22 turnpike local n.a.	0.17 turnpike local n.a.
France	Mixture of local and state financing	1.0 royal 0.88 local	0.05 royal 0.05 local
Spain	Mixture of local and state financing	0.6 royal local n.a.	0.015 royal local n.a.

Sources: England and Wales (31,500 km turnpike roads and 120,000 km parish roads), British Parliamentary Papers, *Report on Roads*, 1841, XXVII, p. 79; Southern Netherlands (3,000–5,000 km, mostly turnpike roads), Ville, 1990, p. 16; France (34,200 km royal roads and about 30,000 km secondary roads), Price, 1983; Spain (5000–7500 km royal roads), Ville, 1990, p. 17. Population data from Mitchell, 1975.

municipalities' fiscal authority and allowed departmental councils to raise taxes for regional roads. The law appears to have been quite successful, in that spending on local French roads increased by nearly 50 percent between 1837 and 1850 (Price, 1983, pp. 37–41).

How did state policies affect road infrastructure? Performance can be measured according to several dimensions, including network size, quality, and cost of travel. Here we focus on network size, because it stands in for investment. Table 3.3 shows the number of kilometers of road per capita and per square kilometer in four countries. England and the Southern Netherlands had significantly higher road kilometers per capita and per square kilometer than did France or Spain. The data raise the question of whether France and Spain would have had a larger road network with turnpikes rather than royal roads. It is not possible to address such a counterfactual here; however, the adoption of turnpikes in France or Spain would probably have had a smaller impact than elsewhere. English turnpike trusts made road investments in a context where property rights to levy tolls were relatively secure. It is not clear that the French or Spanish crown could ensure such security, and thus private investors may have been hesitant about making such investments.

Political fragmentation also stifled investments in road networks. It was difficult for a turnpike road to pass through multiple jurisdictions, because each governing authority would be tempted to set a higher toll than the others. A large absolutist state, like France or Spain, could conceivably solve this problem, but in many cases the crown did not have the political will or the resources to control all of its sub-units. It is no surprise that transcontinental or transnational highways were rare before 1800.

Waterways

Waterway improvements included widening or diverting the path of rivers and the building of canals. Some areas were fortunate in having many navigable rivers before 1700. The Dutch Republic led the way. The network of navigable waterways was financed and owned by municipalities such as Utrecht, Amsterdam, and Harlem, which received rights from provincial estates, like Holland. Provincial estates issued *octrooi*, which specified rights of way and what fees municipalities could charge. The canal network expanded rapidly in the seventeenth century along with commerce and urbanization. By 1700 the Dutch had the most extensive waterway network in Europe, including over 650 km of canals (de Vries, 1978).

England tried to emulate the Dutch Republic in the early seventeenth century, but was hampered by competition between king and parliament over who could issue rights to improve river navigation. Both king and parliament repudiated the rights issued by the other as power shifted in their favor. Only after the end of political strife in the late 1690s did companies and cities begin making major investments in river navigation and later in canals. By 1840, England had over 7,000 km of navigable waterways, rivalling the Dutch as having the most extensive waterway network in Europe (Willan, 1964).

Canals were built in France during the seventeenth and eighteenth centuries, but the waterway network was not as dense. Many early canals were begun by private parties through privileges granted by the king or provincial assemblies. However, few projects were completed and the state began financing some canals in the second half of the eighteenth century. The French Revolution slowed improvement and by 1814 little progress had been made. In the 1820s, François Becquay proposed a network of waterways, to be built through concession contracts. Becquay clearly had the English model in mind when he devised his scheme, but investors were scarce (Geiger, 1994).

The French government wanted the waterways to be built and so it devised 'public–private partnerships' to implement Becquay's plan. The state borrowed from private investors, mostly Parisian financiers, and agreed to split the profits once the debt was repaid. Relations with investors were often confrontational, especially regarding the tolls and the return paid on the bonds. The French state eventually, in the 1870s, bought out the companies' interests and began financing many of its own canals (Geiger, 1994). By 1880, the French waterway network was largely government-owned (Ville, 1990, p. 38).

Belgian waterway policies were heavily influenced by the Dutch and the French. There was substantial investment in the 1820s when Belgium was under Dutch rule. Provincial authorities owned and financed half of all waterway projects, and another substantial portion was owned by private

Table 3.4 Waterway policies, 1700–1870

Country	Summary	Waterway km per capita (000s) c. 1850	Waterway km per sq km c. 1850
England and Wales	Private river and canal network	0.40	0.029
Dutch Republic/Netherlands	Municipal financing and ownership	0.53 (1830)	0.04 (1830)
France	Mixture of public and private participation	0.23	0.006
Belgium	Initially mixture of provincial and private ownership, later state-owned	0.36	0.05
Germany	State-owned network	0.07	0.005
Russia	Mostly state-owned network	0.01	0.0001

Sources: Ville, 1990, p. 31: England – 7,200 km; Dutch Republic – 1400 km in 1830); France – 4,170 km; Germany – around 2,500 km; Russia – 500 km. For Belgium the Waterways Association (1913) figure of 1,600 km was used.

concessions (Waterways Association, 1913, p. 47). In the 1860s, the state began purchasing private canals and assumed control over many provincial canals. Maintenance and construction were administered by the Ponts-et-Chaussées, which operated similarly to its French counterpart.

Germany and Russia made relatively few improvements to their waterways before 1870. Principalities initiated and financed most German improvements. For example, in Russia, Peter the Great had financed and built most canals, such as those linking Moscow with St. Petersburg (Fink, 1991). King Ludwig of Bavaria built the Ludwig canal to connect the Rhine and the Danube (Ville, 1990, p. 33). State ownership and financing increased after 1870 as imperial authorities undertook a number of waterway projects.

The comparison of waterway development across countries in Table 3.4 shows that networks were largest in England, the Dutch Republic, and Belgium, where private or municipal authorities had substantial control, and they were smaller in France, Germany, and Russia, where the state dominated. Would waterways have been more extensive if French, German, and Russian authorities had adopted the waterway policies of the English, Dutch, and Belgians? Reid Geiger (1994, p. 250) argues that profits on French canals were too low, because of low levels of urbanization and commercialization, to attract private investors. As a result, the state was left to finance the network. An alternative explanation for the slow development of French waterways was the state's inability to protect the property rights of companies, for instance when the French state reduced canal tolls without regard to the original concession contract (Geiger, 1994, p. 249).

Political fragmentation also stifled waterway development, but for different reasons. Rights of way were especially important for canals because they cut through farmland. In eighteenth-century France, canal promoters had difficulties negotiating with landowners in multiple jurisdictions. In theory, the crown could force landowners to sell their property, but local groups could appeal rights-of-way grants in court (Rosenthal, 1992). Political decentralization could also cause problems in approving projects that crossed boundaries. In the Dutch Republic, estates could not issue an *octrooi* for projects outside their province. Moreover, some projects were delayed because any city in the estates of Holland could veto an *octrooi*, including any which disproportionately benefited their rivals (de Vries 1978, pp. 31–32).

Railroad policies

Railroads were the most important infrastructure investment in many European countries, particularly in the east. Every European state quickly realized the importance of railroads for economic development, military security, and political unification. As before, the state could leave railroad planning, construction, and operation to private companies, but many states decided that subsidies or direct ownership was necessary (or more desirable) for railroad development.

Three types of policy patterns appear before 1870. One group of countries opted for private ownership combined with state subsidies, planning, or construction (France, Spain, Portugal, Austria-Hungary, Russia, and Italy). A second group started with private involvement but shifted to greater state involvement (Netherlands, Denmark, and Norway). The third group had a mixture of state and private participation from the beginning (Germany, Sweden, and Belgium).

Up to 1870 the United Kingdom and France had the highest degree of private ownership. Both, however, followed their policy model for waterways. In the United Kingdom, Parliament passed acts giving companies rights of way and the authority to levy fees. The companies made substantial investments without any subsidies from Parliament. There were complaints, however, about overbuilding, the lack of coordination between companies, and high fees. In France, the Ponts-et-Chaussées did the planning and engineering. The state gave companies leases on their lines for ninety-nine years and guaranteed dividends on securities issued for new construction. Out of this system emerged six large railroad companies that owned most of the French railroad network. The policy was fairly successful; Paris was connected by rail with all the regions of France.

Table 3.5 Railroad policies, 1825–1870

Country	Summary of railroad policies	Railroad km per capita (000s) c. 1870	Railroad km per sq km c. 1870
United Kingdom	Private ownership with no subsidies.	0.80	0.081
France	Private ownership with subsidies.	0.46	0.080
Spain	Private ownership with subsidies.	0.32	0.011
Portugal	Private ownership with subsidies.	0.16	0.008
Austria-Hungary	Private ownership with subsidies.	0.27	0.015
Russia	Mostly private ownership with state subsidies. Companies own 90% of track km.	0.17	0.002
Italy	Mostly private ownership with state subsidies. Companies own 90% of track km.	0.22	0.020
Netherlands	Shift from private to state ownership Companies own 43% of track km.	0.25	0.027
Denmark	Shift from private to state. After 1860 the companies own 36% of track km.	0.42	0.020
Norway	Shift from private to state ownership. Companies own 19% of track km.	0.20	0.001
Germany	Mixture of state and private from the start. Companies own 56% of track km.	0.47	0.035
Sweden	Mixture of state and private from the start. Companies own 61% of track.	0.69	0.006
Belgium	Mixture of state and private from the start. Companies own 69% of track km.	0.55	0.095

Railroads (UK Board of Trade, 1913): United Kingdom: 25,400 km, Netherlands: 900 km, France: 16,700 km, Belgium: 2,800 km, Germany: 19,100 km, Spain: 5,400 km; Norway 367 km; Italy: 6,000 km; Portugal: 694 km; Austria-Hungary 9,500 km; Russia: 11,200 km; Denmark: 750 km; Sweden: 2,860 km Ownership figures are from Bogart (2009).

Spain, Portugal, Austria-Hungary, Russia, and Italy also guaranteed interest or dividends for private railroad companies. Guarantees became common in Europe after the 1860s and, indeed, throughout the world. They are often viewed as a "give-away" to foreign investors, but they might have provided the necessary profits to compensate for the risks of lower than expected demand or arbitrary changes in regulation.

States could also build their own railroad networks rather than subsidize private companies with guarantees. The Netherlands, Denmark, and Norway began with a greater degree of private ownership, but then turned to direct state-financing and ownership in the 1860s. In several cases, politicians argued that state ownership was preferable to interest guarantees for private companies (Veenendaal, 1995, p. 191).

States also increased their ownership of railroads because they believed that this would increase military effectiveness and solidify their political power (Millward, 2005). The state focused on building the trunk lines connecting capital cities with their provinces and strategic borders. In Belgium, state ownership was part of a broader strategy to maintain independence from the Netherlands (Veenendaal, 1995, p. 191). In Germany, state-owned railroads were intimately linked with the political ambitions of Prussian leaders like Bismarck. The strategy was successful in that state-owned railroads helped Germany to unify and to gain territory from France in the Franco-Prussian war.

The comparisons in Table 3.5 suggest that railroad kilometers per capita or railroad kilometers per square kilometer were similar in countries with more private ownership versus countries with relatively more state ownership (e.g. Belgium and France). Therefore it does not appear that greater reliance on either private or state ownership influenced network development, at least by 1870. The impact on other aspects of performance, such as efficiency of operation, has yet to be determined.

As a final note, the years after 1870 witnessed new directions in the ownership and regulation of railroads. Railroads were nationalized in many European countries because they were a key asset in military operations and they offered new sources of government revenue (Bogart, 2008). Many states also increased their regulation of railroad fares and began to impose safety standards. These policies were a harbinger of the state's approach to European industry in the twentieth century.

Conclusion

We set out to evaluate the relative importance of problems of sovereign expropriation to problems of institutional stalemate associated with fragmented authority in Europe between 1700 and 1870. We found a dramatic increase in the involvement of central authorities in social and economic institutions. Provincial autonomy declined everywhere, as did that of local, sectoral, or class organizations. The center's power rose, but, contrary to North and Weingast (1989), in most places centralization did not lead to an increase in expropriation. More power seems to have allowed central governments to promote economic change and market integration, even if specific policies often relied upon local governments or the private sector. In this light, the link between restraints on the executive's power and economic performance, famously argued for England after the Glorious Revolution, seems to have few lessons for the Continent. There the institutional path traveled after 1700 largely consisted of expanding those powers. The reason for this alternative route lies in the oppressive political and economic fragmentation of Europe in 1700. Certainly until 1800, expanding the market (and thus reducing fragmentation) was widely seen as the principal policy for fostering economic growth. The means to achieve this – military operations as well as the implementation of tax reforms, legal changes, and infrastructure investments – all required a strong executive.

Beyond this broad trend, which can be observed in most parts of Europe, there was dramatic variation in the public and private institutions used to meet the challenges of international competition and industrialization. The changes in political structure, taxation, business law, and infrastructure realized by different polities depended on the historical antecedents of individual countries and on the extent to which large political events such as the French Revolution forced change. Evidence that economic logic produced the institutional variation we observe is scant – the public and private institutions in place by 1870 may well have been efficacious, but it would be foolhardy to presume that they were efficient.

The last lesson that emerges from this examination of public and private institutions relates directly to the title of this volume, that juxtaposes unification and European experience. Between 1700 and 1870 Europeans shared many experiences (war in particular). States, however, responded to the challenge of political and economic fragmentation in many different ways. Thus by 1870 institutions were more different across Europe than they had been in 1700. Suffrage where it existed in 1700 was generally quite restricted. By 1870 there were democracies with universal male suffrage, while other polities had no representation whatsoever. In 1700 public finance was an arcane art and taxation an opaque process nearly everywhere. By 1870 the western half of Europe had adopted many modern principles of taxation, while in the east reforms were very slow. In business law some countries had modernized their laws and opened access to incorporation, while others would wait until after World War I. Finally, the extent of infrastructure investment varied dramatically, because it depended on changes in political franchise, fiscal regime, and business law, and because it was facilitated by more general economic growth.

After 1870, public and private institutions would face new challenges; these would be met in a political and legal environment framed by the institutions devised in the nineteenth century. And even though the twentieth century finally ushered in institutions on a European scale, it has also seen the revival of regional politics. The problems of scale and unification faced by European rulers in the eighteenth century are still with us.

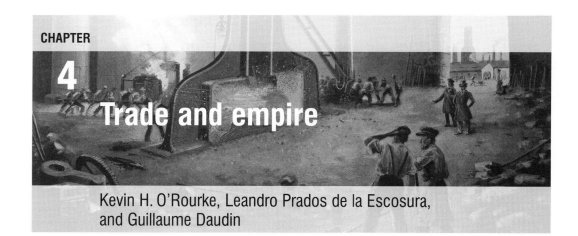

Trade and empire

Kevin H. O'Rourke, Leandro Prados de la Escosura,
and Guillaume Daudin

Contents

Introduction: the rise and fall of European mercantilism

At the start of the first millennium, western Europe was the most peripheral region in Eurasia. Like Africa, its exports largely consisted of forest products and slaves, and it had direct economic links with just two other Eurasian regions – eastern Europe and the Islamic world. By contrast, the Islamic world had direct economic contacts with all the regions of the then known world: eastern and western Europe, sub-Saharan Africa, the steppe societies of central Asia, and the highly developed civilizations of south Asia, southeast Asia, and east Asia (Findlay and O'Rourke, 2007).

By the eighteenth century, western Europe was no longer a peripheral appendage of the Eurasian landmass, but had become geographically and politically central. It was now in direct contact with all other regions of Eurasia, as well as with sub-Saharan Africa, but more importantly it controlled both North and South America, which were fully integrated into the world economy, importing slaves from Africa, exporting a variety of colonial goods to Europe, and exporting silver both to Europe and to Asia via the Philippines. As for eastern Europe, it was now in direct contact not just with central Asia and the Muslim world, but with east Asia and North America as well, as a result of Russia's Siberian conquests, which would prove to be the most enduring of all the European imperialisms of that time.

In contrast to China, which was relatively self-sufficient, European merchants and states had a strong interest in seeking out direct routes to sub-Saharan gold deposits, thus bypassing the Muslim middlemen who controlled the trans-Saharan trade; purchasing African slaves and using these on the sugar plantations of newly discovered offshore African islands; and ultimately in circumnavigating Africa, reaching Asian spice markets directly, and again cutting out Muslim (and Venetian) middlemen. Once Columbus stumbled upon the Americas, Europeans had every incentive to exploit the vast resources of this New World as fully as possible. All of these activities were extremely lucrative, and the mutual dependence of Power and Plenty (Viner, 1948) meant that states as well as merchants had a powerful motive to pursue them. Trade profited merchants, but also yielded revenues to the state; while the state needed revenues to secure trading opportunities for its merchants, by force if necessary. Trade and empire were thus inextricably linked in the minds of European statesman during the early modern period, which explains the incessant mercantilist warfare of the time.

The eighteenth century saw the gradual rise to preeminence of Britain in this struggle for power and plenty in the west, while Russia became dominant in the east. The Iberians continued their hold on Latin America, but the seventeenth century saw Portugal being replaced in the Indian Ocean and southeast Asia by

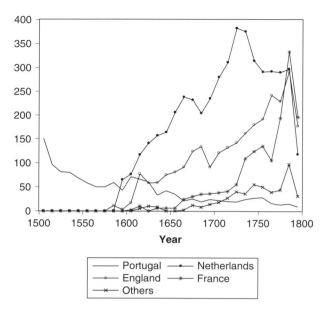

Figure 4.1 Number of ships sailing to Asia, per decade (de Vries, 2003)

the Dutch. 1648 was an important turning point, marking the end of the long-standing war between the Netherlands and Spain. This freed up silver and soldiers, two essential "inputs" for the Dutch East India Company's activities in Asia, and facilitated a series of conquests – in Ceylon, on the Malabar coast, and in the East Indies. By the late seventeenth century, the Dutch had succeeded in controlling the supply of spices such as cloves, leading to a dramatic reduction in their exports, and an end to southeast Asia's "Age of Commerce." As Figure 4.1 shows, the Dutch maintained their dominant position in European–Asian seaborne trade until the end of the eighteenth century. Meanwhile, the British found in India an abundant supply of several commodities, notably cotton textiles, which they exported not only to Europe, but to Africa and the Americas as well. By the third quarter of the eighteenth century, and after military victories at Plassey in 1757 and Buxar in 1764, the English East India Company was embarked on a path which would ultimately lead to dominion over the entire subcontinent. After the Bengal mutiny of 1857, India formally became part of the British Empire.

In western Europe, the triangular struggle for domination between the Netherlands, France, and England became a bilateral struggle between the latter two powers following William of Orange's takeover of the British throne in 1688–1689. England and France fought during the Nine Years War (1689–1697), the War of the Spanish Succession (1701–1713), and the

War of the Austrian Succession (1740–1748). The Seven Years War (1756–1763) was an important victory for Britain, which gained control of France's North American possessions as well as several islands and ports in the Caribbean and along the African and Indian coasts. In eastern Europe, Russia under Peter the Great and Catherine the Great was strengthening its position as a great European power, defeating Sweden in the Great Northern War, absorbing the former Grand Duchy of Lithuania and much of Poland, and expanding to the south at the expense of the Tartar khanates and the Ottoman Empire. Russia had already expanded eastwards as far as the Pacific by the middle of the seventeenth century; it now had secure footholds on both the Baltic and Black Sea coasts.

All these European powers pursued a variety of mercantilist policies, designed to enrich both the state and the local merchant class. These included protecting local industries against foreign competition, protecting the local shipping industry by preventing foreign merchants from trading with either the mother country or its colonies, and putting in place a variety of policies designed to extract as much profit as possible from those colonies. Empires yielded financial benefits by providing control over precious metal supplies (in Latin America); giving access to abundant supplies of slaves (Africa); allowing the cultivation of warm-climate crops such as tobacco and cotton, or trapping furs in colder climates, and selling these on to consumers in Europe (the Americas and north Asia); or allowing control over trade routes or, better yet, the sources of supply of scarce commodities such as spices (Asia).

Such considerations were also present at the time of the Ottoman expansion into central and eastern Europe, although the desire to spread Islam was another motivation, just as spreading Christianity was a concern of the early Iberian explorers. Booty, control over trade routes, and (in the fourteenth and fifteenth centuries) access to the silver mines of Serbia and Macedonia were all important motives for the Turks, and indeed the prospect of plunder can help to explain why many Christians fought on the Ottoman side. Furthermore, the Ottomans actively intervened to prevent the Portuguese from obtaining a monopoly of the spice trade in the Indian Ocean, fighting the interlopers both directly along the Persian Gulf and indirectly via their support for the sultan of Acheh, from where pepper continued to be exported to Ottoman-held territory, and from there to Venice. This allowed the Ottomans to continue enjoying the rents from the transit trade until the appearance of the Dutch and English in the Indian Ocean in the seventeenth century. The Ottomans were not mercantilists, in that they were not concerned with the interests of domestic merchants or producers, and correctly understood that imports were desirable, and that the fewer exports were needed to pay for these imports the better. However, they were also sensitive to the mutual dependence of Power and

Plenty, which was a general feature of the Eurasian geopolitical landscape at a time when the Military Revolution was making warfare more expensive, and reducing the number of states that were militarily viable at any given time.

This mercantilist system was swept away in the early nineteenth century as a result of technological and geopolitical change. Paradoxically, partly at least as a result of British successes there, the beginning of the end occurred in North America. As a number of observers predicted following the end of the Seven Years War, without a French presence threatening the British colonists there, those colonists would now find it easier to press for independence from the mother country. The fiscal crisis to which the conflict gave rise provided one trigger for the American Revolution, which ended with the Peace of Paris in 1783. French involvement was crucial for the rebellion's success, but this in turn led to a fiscal crisis in France which again was one of the triggers leading to revolution there. When war between Britain and France broke out yet again in 1793, it now had an additional ideological dimension adding to the severity and duration of the conflict, which only finally ended with the French defeat at Waterloo in 1815. By that time, Napoleon's invasion of Iberia in 1807 had been followed by a series of revolutions in Latin America, and by the 1820s independent republics (or an empire in the case of Brazil) had been established across Central and South America. Apart from Spanish Cuba and Puerto Rico, and British Canada, virtually nothing remained of Europe's New World empires. While these newly independent states adopted highly protectionist policies during the nineteenth century, those tariffs would be imposed in the context of a broadly multilateral international trading system, in which there were no more bilateral mercantilist restrictions on trade.

Several other factors promoted globalization between 1815 and 1870. The post-war settlement, ushered in by the Congress of Vienna, led to a remarkably durable peace in Europe. Despite the Crimean War, the Franco-Prussian war, and a number of smaller conflicts, and despite the fact that the period ended with the disaster of the Great War, the century after Waterloo was a peaceful one by European standards. The new transport technologies of the Industrial Revolution, described in Chapter 8 of this volume, dramatically reduced transport costs. Geopolitically, new industrial military technologies increased the relative power of Europe and its most important overseas offshoot, the United States. The half-century following Waterloo saw major European imperial advances in India, North Africa, and elsewhere, as well as the infamous Opium Wars, which forcibly opened Chinese markets to trade. Meanwhile, the United States expanded overland across North America, while Russia continued to expand in Asia. European states forced more or less free trade on their imperial possessions or on nominally independent countries such as China, Japan, and Siam.

The period also saw a gradual move towards trade liberalization in Europe. Early liberalizers were typically smaller countries, such as the Netherlands and Denmark. The latter country had abolished import prohibitions and adopted low tariffs as early as 1797, while the Dutch moved to a relatively liberal trade policy in 1819, having seen the Dutch East India Company being destroyed during the war. The first major economy to liberalize was Britain, where power was shifting to export-oriented urban interests. Liberal reforms in the 1820s and 1830s were followed by Robert Peel's historic decision to abolish the Corn Laws in 1846, and move the United Kingdom to a unilateral policy of agricultural and industrial free trade, against the objections of landlords and much of his own Tory Party. There followed further moves towards liberalization in countries such as Austria-Hungary, Spain, the Netherlands, Belgium, Sweden, Norway, and Denmark (Bairoch, 1989, pp. 20–36). For example, in 1849 Spain abolished its navigation laws and suppressed prohibitive tariffs, and the Spanish went on to liberalize imports of inputs into railway construction in the mid-1850s. Average tariffs were falling throughout the 1850s in the major European powers (Accominotti and Flandreau, 2008).

Trade liberalization was not universal. Russia and Austria-Hungary remained extremely protectionist throughout almost all the period, only liberalizing slightly in the late 1860s. The Ottoman Empire actually became more protectionist during the period, not less, although this is explained by the fact that it had previously been limited to a maximum 3 percent tariff as a result of various treaties signed with west European powers. In 1838, the Turks obtained the right to raise their tariffs to 5 percent, but at the cost of abolishing all monopolies and prohibitions. Overall, however, the period between Waterloo and 1870 was one in which both trade policy and technology were integrating international commodity markets. The switch from mercantilism to modernity was now complete.

Quantitative trends, 1700–1870

Trade volumes

Using the shipping data in Figure 4.1, Jan de Vries (2003) estimates that the tonnage returned from Asia to Europe grew at 1.01 percent per annum during the sixteenth century, 1.24 percent during the seventeenth, 1.16 percent during the eighteenth, and at 1.1 percent over the three centuries as a whole. O'Rourke and Williamson (2002a), using a more eclectic mix of data, calculate average growth rates per annum of European trade with both Asia and the Americas of 1.26 percent during the sixteenth century, 0.66 percent during the seventeenth,

1.26 percent during the eighteenth, and 1.06 percent per annum overall. An average growth rate of roughly 1 percent per annum over a period of three centuries was an impressive achievement relative to what had gone before, and led to Europe, or at least the maritime powers of western Europe, becoming more open, albeit from very low levels. According to Maddison (2003a), west European GDP grew at roughly 0.4 percent per annum between 1500 and 1820, implying rising ratios of intercontinental trade to GDP.[1] As a result, trade with Asia, Africa, and America was a very important share of European trade in 1790 (Table 4.1).

The wars of 1792–1815 and the Industrial Revolution were a turning point for European trade, dramatically increasing the relative importance of the United Kingdom (contrast Tables 4.1 and 4.2 with Table 4.3), and reducing European trade-to-GDP ratios. Both phenomena are partly explained by the fact that pre-1800 trade-to-GDP ratios were inflated by entrepôt trade (Table 4.4), which declined following the end of the "first" French and Iberian colonial empires and the collapse of the Dutch East India Company. Trade started growing again during the 1830s. Between 1820 and 1870, the volume of trade grew ninefold (Table 4.3) and the European trade-to-GDP ratio more than doubled (Table 4.5).

Commodity price convergence

Perhaps surprisingly, the increase in early modern trade volumes between Europe and the rest of the world was not accompanied by commodity price convergence, at least according to the data that have been analyzed up to now (O'Rourke and Williamson, 2002b). Figure 4.2 shows that the ratio of the Amsterdam to the Asian prices for pepper and cloves did not fall before the nineteenth century, and there was substantial price divergence for cloves in the 1650s, coinciding with the establishment of Dutch control over clove supplies around that time. Mercantilist policies could have directly prevented price convergence during this period, as the figures for cloves suggest, but mercantilism also created an international political environment in which wars were frequent, and this was perhaps the key factor preventing long-run price convergence. Peaks in the clove price gaps during the first and second Anglo-Dutch wars, the Seven Years War, and the wars of 1792–1815, lend credence to this view. More systematic price evidence is available for the latter conflict, and shows clearly that warfare led to a dramatic, worldwide

---

[1] The Maddison figures probably represent an upper bound, given the lower growth figures (around 0.1% per annum) calculated by van Zanden (2005a) and Álvarez-Nogal and Prados de la Escosura (2007).

Table 4.1 European trade *c.*1790

	Imports		Exports		Reexports		Total	Share rest of world
	From Europe	From ROW	Toward Europe	Toward ROW	Toward Europe	Toward ROW		
			£ million					
Britain (1784–86) (including trade with Ireland)	11.3	11.5	6.3	7.3	2.8	0.8	**40.0**	49%
France (1787)	12.8	11.7	9.7	5.3	6.0	0.4	**45.9**	38%
Netherlands (using 1770 trade composition)	9.3	3.6	8.3 (including reexports)	0.7 (including reexports)	3.8 (colonial goods) 2.4 (European goods)		**21.9**	20%
Spain (1788–92) (ROW: Americas)	7.2	2.8	3.5	1.9	1.4	2.2	**19.0**	36%
Portugal (1796–1806) (ROW: Brazil)	4.6	2.7	1.4	1.3	3.9	1.4	**15.3**	35%

Sources: See Table 4.5, and Pedreira, 1993; Cuenca-Esteban, 1989; and Marshall, 1833.

Table 4.2 European merchant fleet, *c*.1790

	Tons	Percentage
United Kingdom	881,963	26.2%
France	729,340	21.6%
Netherlands	397,709	11.8%
Denmark and Norway	386,020	11.4%
Italy, Trieste, and Ragusa	352,713	10.5%
Hamburg, Bremen, Lubeck, Rostock, Dantzig, and Prussia	181,308	5.4%
Sweden	169,279	5.0%
Spain	149,460	4.4%
Portugal	84,843	2.5%
Russia	39,394	1.2%
Total	3,372,029	100%

Source: Romano, 1962.

Table 4.3 European real trade, 1820–1870

	1820	Growth 1820–1870
	$million 1990	
Austria	47	+894%
Belgium	92	+1,245%
France	487	+621%
Italy	339	+427%
Spain	137	+550%
Switzerland	147	+653%
United Kingdom	1125	+988%
Weighted average		+793%
United States	251	+12,010%

Source: Maddison, 2001.

disintegration of commodity markets (O'Rourke, 2006). For example, the price of wheat rose by over 40 percent during 1807–14 relative to textiles in Britain, which imported wheat and exported textiles, but it fell in France, which was a wheat exporter and cotton textile importer. Similarly, the price of raw cotton rose relative to textiles in Europe, but fell substantially in the United States.

Figure 4.2 shows dramatic price convergence between Southeast Asia and the Netherlands once the wars had ended, and a vast array of evidence documents international price convergence more generally during the nineteenth century. Figure 4.3 shows that while the Anglo-American wheat price gap fluctuated widely before 1840 or so, around a roughly constant trend, it started to drop dramatically after that date, coinciding with the commencement of large-scale shipments of wheat between the United States and Britain. Jacks (2005, p. 399)

Table 4.4 Entrepôt and special trade

	Retained imports (1) = total imports – Reexports	Domestic exports (2)	Reexports (3)	Special trade (4) = (1)+(2)	Special trade as a share of total trade = 100*(4)/ [(4)+(3)+(3)]
	£ million				
Britain (1784–86)	19.2	13.6	3.6	32.8	82%
France (1787)	18.1	15.0	6.4	33.1	72%
Netherlands (using 1770 trade composition)	6.7	9.0	6.2	15.7	43%
Spain (1788–92)	6.4	5.4	3.6	11.8	62%
Portugal (1796–1806)	2.0	2.7	5.3	4.7	31%

Note: Retained imports are computed assuming that the value of a good is recorded identically when it is imported and when it is reexported. Special trade excludes both reexports and non-retained imports.
Source: Tables 4.1, 4.5.

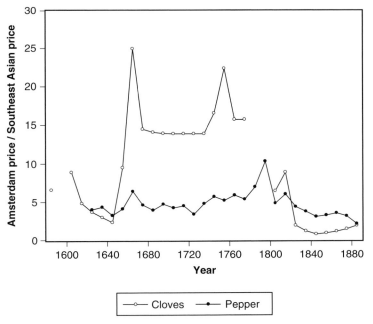

Figure 4.2 Spice markups, 1580–1890 (Bulbeck et al., 1998)

concludes that there is evidence of a "truly international market for wheat from around 1835." This evidence (cf. Federico and Persson, 2007) is important, since it shows that international price convergence characterized the nineteenth century as a whole, not just the years after 1870.

Table 4.5 Exports plus imports as share of GDP

	c. 1655	c. 1720	c. 1755	c. 1790	1820	1830	1840	1850	1860	1870
Austria						11.4%	14.2%	13.2%	18.7%	29.0%
Belgium							19.0%	26.7%	31.3%	35.6%
Denmark					7.5%	17.5%	27.5%	36.5%	29.7%	35.7%
Finland									20.7%	31.7%
France		5.5%	14%	20%	9.8%	8.2%	10.7%	13.0%	20.2%	23.6%
Germany								19.2%	23.2%	36.8%
Greece									42.7%	45.6%
Hungary										19.4%
Italy									16.1%	18.3%
Netherlands	85%	82%	84%	110%	33.0%	25.8%	53.4%	64.0%	96.4%	115.4%
Norway										33.9%
Portugal								42.4%	33.9%	33.7%
Spain			16%			6.0%		8.5%	10.6%	12.1%
Sweden						5.7%	6.8%	13.8%	20.0%	29.4%
United Kingdom		19%	20%	24%	21.4%	18.8%	25.2%	27.8%	41.8%	43.6%
Best guess at total European trade-to-GDP ratio					13.5%	11.5%	15.4%	18.1%	24.8%	29.9%
Ibid., net of intra-European trade						3.8%		6.4%	8.9%	9.2%

Note: Ottoman Empire, Albania, Bulgaria, Romania, and Serbia are not included in total Europe. "United Kingdom" pre-1800 is just England and Wales.
Sources: Pre-1800: Deane and Cole, 1962, 1969; Davis, 1969, 1979; Officer, 2001; Crafts, 1985a; Maddison, 2001; de Vries and van der Woude, 1997; McCusker, 1978; Arnould, 1791; Daudin, 2005; Marczewski, 1961; Prados de la Escosura, 1993. Post-1800: Bairoch, 1976; and data underlying Prados de la Escosura, 2000.

Another important change after 1800 concerns the types of commodities which could be transported profitably between continents. As Table 4.6 shows, European imports from the rest of the world before then were mostly high value-to-weight ratio commodities, which could bear the cost of transport because they were not produced in Europe at all, or only with some difficulty. There was a gradual evolution, to be sure. During the sixteenth century, silver and spices were the dominant imports from the Americas and Asia respectively. Around the middle of the seventeenth century, Indian textiles became the leading European import from Asia, but the European textile industry was still uncompetitive relative to Indian weavers. Around the same time, "colonial goods" such as sugar and tobacco were becoming important New World exports, but these were warm-climate commodities

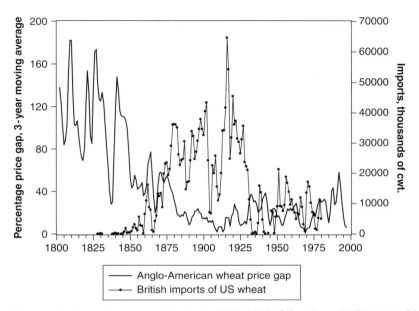

Figure 4.3 Anglo-American wheat trade, 1800–2000 (O'Rourke and Williamson, 2005, p. 10)

that could not be easily grown in western Europe. There was thus an evolution in the nature of intercontinental trade during the early modern period, towards bulkier commodities, but the period before 1800 did not, for the most part, involve large-scale intercontinental trade in basic, heavy commodities such as wheat, which could be easily grown both inside and outside Europe.

The new transport technologies of the nineteenth century meant that such basic, "competing" commodities could indeed be shipped across the oceans of the world. European prices for temperate-climate agricultural commodities now started to reflect American, Australian and Russian factor endowments rather than demand and supply in western Europe alone, implying that, in line with Heckscher–Ohlin logic, cheap overseas food started to place European land rents under pressure (O'Rourke and Williamson, 2005). This would only become important in the years after 1870, when these Heckscher–Ohlin forces would have important political repercussions. However, the seeds of that retreat from globalization were sown in the half century following Waterloo.

Trade, empire, and growth

Recent aggregate evidence suggests that trade was positively associated with growth in Europe during the seventeenth and eighteenth centuries. Both the urbanization rate and GDP grew more rapidly in the "Atlantic" European

Table 4.6 Composition of European overseas imports, 1513–1780

A Imports from Asia to Lisbon, 1513–1610 (% by weight)

	1513–19	1523–31	1547–8	1587–8	1600–3	1608–10
Pepper	80.0	84.0	89.0	68.0	65	69.0
Other spices	18.4	15.6	9.6	11.6	16.2	10.9
Indigo	0.0	0.0	0.0	8.4	4.4	7.7
Textiles	0.2	0.0	0.0	10.5	12.2	7.8
Misc.	1.4	0.4	1.4	1.5	2.2	4.6
Total	100.0	100.0	100.0	100.0	100.0	100

B Imports of Dutch East India Company into Europe, 1619–1780 (% by invoice value)

	1619–21	1648–50	1668–70	1698–1700	1738–40	1778–80
Pepper	56.5	50.4	30.5	11.2	8.1	9.0
Other spices	17.6	17.9	12.1	11.7	6.1	3.1
Textiles	16.1	14.2	36.5	54.7	41.1	49.5
Tea and coffee				4.2	32.2	27.2
Drugs, perfumes, and dye-stuffs	9.8	8.5	5.8	8.3	2.8	1.8
Sugar		6.4	4.2	0.2	3.7	0.6
Saltpetre		2.1	5.1	3.9	2.6	4.4
Metals	0.1	0.5	5.7	5.3	1.1	2.7
Misc.		0.2	0.1	0.4	2.3	1.7
Total	100.0	100.0	100.0	100.0	100.0	100

C Imports of English East India Company into Europe, 1668–1760 (% of invoice value)

	1668–70	1698–1700	1738–40	1758–60
Pepper	25.25	7.02	3.37	4.37
Textiles	56.61	73.98	69.58	53.51
Raw silk	0.6	7.09	10.89	12.27
Tea	0.03	1.13	10.22	25.23
Coffee	0.44	1.93	2.65	
Indigo	4.25	2.82		
Saltpetre	7.67	1.51	1.85	2.97
Misc.	5.15	4.52	1.44	1.65
Total	100	100	100	100

economies (England , France, the Netherlands, Portugal and Spain) than in the rest of western Europe or Asia between 1500 and 1800 (Acemoglu et al., 2005; Maddison, 2003a). Allen (2003) also finds a strong positive relationship between trade and growth in Europe during this period, concluding that "the intercontinental trade boom was a key development that propelled north-western Europe forwards" (p. 432).

Table 4.6 (cont.)

D Estimated annual sales of colonial imports, England and Netherlands, 1751–4

	Total sales (1000 pesos)	Percentage of sales	
		From Asia	Of total
Textiles	6750	41.7	21.1
Pepper	1100	6.8	3.4
Tea	2800	17.3	8.7
Coffee	1000	6.2	3.1
Spices	1850	11.4	5.8
Misc.	2700	16.7	8.4
Total from Asia	16200	100.0	50.5
		From Americas	Of total
Sugar	8050	50.8	25.1
Tobacco	3700	23.3	11.5
Misc.	4100	25.9	12.8
Total from Americas	15850	100.0	49.5
Total overseas imports	32050		100.0

Source: Findlay and O'Rourke, 2007, pp. 308–09.

The conclusion that trade and growth were positively related during the period is an important one. However, it is less clear what the mechanisms linking trade with economic growth were. Different authors, discussing the impact of trade on various European countries, tend to assume different mechanisms, while to make matters even more complicated the literature very often (if understandably, given the realities of mercantilism) conflates two conceptually distinct issues, namely the impact of trade in general and the effects of countries' colonial policies. In what follows we therefore look at the mechanisms through which, it has been suggested, trade might have influenced growth. We then consider the link between imperialism per se and economic welfare, using the Iberian loss of its Latin American colonies as a "natural experiment." Finally, we take a more detailed look at the various links between trade and the central economic event of this period, the British Industrial Revolution.

Mechanisms

How might trade have affected growth during this period? One crucial issue is whether or not all resources in the economy were fully employed. With full employment, allocating resources to exports had an opportunity cost, as they could alternatively have been used in production for the domestic market. While a "comparative advantage" perspective leads to the conclusion that trade was beneficial for economies, it also tends to imply that the gains involved were small (since the Harberger triangles measuring the gains of moving to free trade from some protectionist equilibrium are small relative to the size of the overall economy). Thus Thomas and McCloskey (1981) among others conclude that if the British economy had been shut off from trade at the time of the Industrial Revolution, it would have produced a lot less cotton, but a lot more of other commodities, and sustained only a small welfare loss.

An alternative Smithian "vent for surplus" perspective assumes that resources in many eighteenth-century economies were unemployed, or at least underemployed, and that trade could bring these resources into productive (or more productive) employment at little or no opportunity cost. In this case, trade would have a bigger effect on economic growth, as O'Brien and Engerman (1991) argue for the British case.

Faced with these two alternatives, some researchers have adopted the eclectic solution of providing upper (unemployment) and lower (full employment) bounds for the impact of trade or empire on particular economies. Nevertheless, both approaches tend to produce small numbers, with the estimated contribution of empire or trade to growth remaining modest compared with the expansion of the domestic market. This is not surprising, since both approaches are essentially static, whereas economic growth is a dynamic process, involving both capital accumulation and technological change.

While any rigorous assessment of the impact of trade on economic growth requires specifying a theoretical model, be it static or dynamic, many traditional economic historians have preferred to give qualitative accounts emphasising the impact of trade on particular regions or sectors. In the case of eighteenth-century France, for example, Butel and Crouzet (1998) have depicted imperial expansion in (and thus trade with) America and Asia as a non-negligible contribution to growth that was, however, concentrated both by region – in the Atlantic ports (Bordeaux, Nantes, Le Havre) and their immediate hinterlands – and by sector. Colonies represented a significant market for French industry, since they accounted for 45 percent of the total increase in manufactured exports during the eighteenth century. While such figures should be tempered by the fact that on the eve of the French Revolution exports represented only 7 percent of industrial output, and colonial exports even less (only 2.5 percent), the impact of these exports was concentrated in a few sectors (linen especially), implying proportionately greater effects there. Similarly, around 15 percent of Portuguese linen output was exported to Brazil in the early nineteenth century (Pedreira, 1993). Butel and Crouzet also stress the feedbacks from colonial trade to non-exporting industries, including sugar refining, shipbuilding and its ancillary activities, and the shipping industry, since transportation was on French ships.

In the case of Spain, trade with America increased between 1714 and 1796, especially during the late eighteenth century, promoting monetization and market orientation at a time of growing population pressure and rising land rents. Trade stimulated industry and services, in particular shipbuilding and its associated activities (iron, timber, and cordage industries). Exports to the colonies benefited some industries and regions, but the small share of industrial goods and commercial services supplied to Latin America by Iberian firms and merchants before the breakup of their empires stands in contrast to the linkages forged between the British economy and Britain's overseas territories and markets. Monetization, the commercialization of agriculture, and the stimulus of particular industries, such as the iron industry, are also seen as major benefits of foreign trade in Russia during this period (Kahan, 1985).

Recent research has downplayed Spanish gains from colonial trade (Prados de la Escosura, 1993). The composition of trade suggests that the possibility of increasing production by reallocating resources was small, and that most gains possibly resulted from changing consumption patterns. By 1792, over 60 percent of retained imports consisted of cocoa and sugar. Furthermore, these colonial products could have been acquired on international markets. Consequently, gains from colonial trade would only occur if, given colonial rule, Spain acquired the same commodities at lower prices. Furthermore, Spain's dependence on the colonies for raw materials was very small (raw cotton and dyestuffs only represented 4 percent of retained imports in 1792). This is, of course, a measure of the weakness of domestic manufacturing. In the Catalan cotton textile industry (one of the most dynamic industries at the end of the eighteenth century), European cotton yarn imports were more important than colonial raw cotton imports, suggesting how weak the Catalan spinning industry was at the time.

Industrial exports, concentrated in a few sectors (textiles: 36.6 percent in 1792; iron and steel: 3.2 percent; paper: 4.4 percent; and food: 22.3 percent) stimulated industrial expansion and were associated with some external economies in their regions of origin. Colonial protectionist legislation made Spanish manufactures artificially competitive on the Spanish American market. An upper bound computation suggests that exports of domestic manufactures to the colonies made a 5 percent contribution to industrial value added before the Napoleonic wars (ibid.).

One way of gauging the importance of overseas trade to the economies of western Europe is to see what happened when the trade between continental Europe and the Americas was suppressed by British blockades after 1807.

Crouzet (1964, p. 571) presents a vivid picture of a deindustrializing west European seaboard during this period: "Harbors were deserted, grass was growing in the streets, and in large towns like Amsterdam, Bordeaux, and Marseille, population did actually decrease." Industries which particularly suffered included shipbuilding and those processing colonial raw materials such as sugar and tobacco. A variety of food-processing industries were also badly affected, as well as cotton printing, but the most important victim was the linen industry in regions such as western France, Flanders, Holland, and Germany. According to Crouzet (p. 573), the damage done to the outward-oriented Atlantic economy of continental western Europe was permanent. On the other hand, trade disruption also led to the development of import substituting industries protected from British competition by wartime blockades, notably the cotton textile industry. To repeat, in a world with scarce resources which can be transferred from one activity to another, there is a limit to how great can be the static welfare losses associated with trade disruption, unless one assumes asymmetries across sectors (for example, associated with externalities: Engerman, 1998).

Daudin (2006) abandons this essentially static perspective in favor of a more dynamic one, focused on profits and capital accumulation. The question he addresses is the extent to which colonial profits contributed to capital formation in France before the Revolution. Net reinvested profits linked to the overseas sector represented up to 6 percent of French savings, and were responsible for approximately 7 percent of French GDP per capita growth between 1715 and 1790. This implies that by 1790 GDP would have been only 3 percent smaller in their absence. However, a further conjectural exercise (Daudin, 2004), assuming that high overseas profits encouraged investment throughout the economy, suggests that they might have been responsible for as much as one-third of French growth.

A very different mechanism linking trade and growth was proposed by Voltaire more than two centuries ago. He argued that Britain's success in trade and the freedom of its constitution mutually reinforced each other in a virtuous circle: "trade, which has made richer the citizens of England, has helped to make them free, and this freedom has, in turn, enlarged trade" (cited in Findlay and O'Rourke, 2007, p. 347). Similarly, Acemoglu et al. (2005) claim that Atlantic trade strengthened the political power of merchants, who obtained a strengthening of property rights in consequence. According to these authors, such beneficial political consequences of trade did not occur in states which had initially been more absolutist than, say, Britain, and there is certainly a case to be made that imperialism strengthened rather than weakened absolutist monarchs in Iberia at this time. In early modern Europe state power was constrained by the crown's need to raise taxes. The more kings depended on taxes, the less sovereign and autonomous they became. Colonial revenues allowed the rise of a strong political center which concentrated power without being drawn into extensive bargaining with its more prominent subjects and institutions. In Portugal, the tax on gold accounted for some 10 percent of public revenue in 1716, while by the 1760s, just before the gold and diamond mines started to decline, it provided a fifth of state receipts. Brazil supplied around 40 percent of government tax returns at the time of the Marquis of Pombal. In Spain, prior to the Napoleonic wars, crown revenues of colonial origin (including the surplus from colonial chests and those derived from customs duties) represented one-fourth of the total. In Spain, as in Portugal, bullion not only underpinned regal power but augmented the incomes of the aristocracy and thereby reduced their need to increase taxation and rents from the population. Thus the colonial empire helped to consolidate and stabilize traditional institutions and structures of power, status, and property rights within Iberia, implying comparatively few representative institutions there.

The emancipation of the American colonies at the start of the nineteenth century marked the end of the Iberian *ancien régime*, and opened the way to liberal revolutions in Spain and Portugal with implications for the economic development and international position of Iberia that have remained largely unexplored. Accounts of economic backwardness in nineteenth-century Iberia have often placed the blame on the loss of empire, but this may in fact have contributed significantly to the economic and social modernization of the peninsula.

In summary, the existing literature on the relationship between trade and growth is unsatisfactory in several respects. While the cross-country evidence indicates that there was a clear positive relationship between trade and growth, individual country studies have for the most part not identified mechanisms that can account for this. The political economy analysis of Acemoglu et al. (2005) seems promising, but this is clearly an area where more research is required.

Empires and welfare

The question of why European countries chose to build empires has long been controversial. Several hypotheses have been proposed, ranging from the purely economic to the purely political, with several intermediate cases as well. Among the more economic explanations is the Vinerian view which we have already encountered, that in the absence of integrated international markets, caused largely by insecurity in an age of widespread piracy and warfare, overseas expansion permitted the creation of reserved markets, thus intertwining conquest and trade. If Spanish merchants, say, were to be able to trade in a given area, the Spanish government would have to make this possible by excluding other merchants and governments from that area, since otherwise the Spanish would themselves be excluded. This is not to deny that a generally free trading situation would have been preferable to one in which each country pursued a mercantilist strategy which might have been individually rational, from a military or even economic viewpoint, but which produced a collectively suboptimal outcome. From a historical point of view, however, one can ask: is this a realistic counterfactual, in a world without a collective security regime? Findlay and O'Rourke (2007, p. 229) argue that for the individual European state, pondering what such a unilateral conversion to peaceful free trade might bring, "in the absence of … a clearly defined hegemonic power, military defeat and exclusion from foreign markets" seems a plausible answer.

Other less economic explanations for empire have also been proposed. For example, in response to the question of why, once the technological constraints that impeded long-distance oceanic voyages had been removed, only some European countries established colonies overseas, Elliott (1990) proposed an explanation based on previous histories of expansion. Iberian plunder, settlement, and colonization in the Americas, in this view, represented a follow-up to the reconquest ("reconquista") of territories previously under Muslim control, while England's overseas expansion in the seventeenth century followed the conquest of Ireland in the previous century. Why did other countries in Europe eventually join them? Here Elliott points to competition between European nation-states, which triggered an emulation process leading to the seizure and occupation of New World lands. In this scenario, the fact that all of Europe ultimately became involved in overseas expansion was at least in part unintended.

Another view points to the interconnections between empire and nation-state building, with countries in Europe struggling not to be left behind. This interpretation regards as economistic and anachronistic the view that states and merchants needed reserved markets and supply sources in an uncertain world, and regards colonies not as an investment, but rather as costs paid for non-economic ends (Engerman, 1998). The costs of empire are undeniable, since colonies needed to be acquired, settled, and defended. Wars, loss of life, and ships represented – from a purely economic perspective – a diversion of resources from alternative uses. War costs had to be financed through taxes, inflation, or public debt. Besides, the colonial system involved navigation laws that imposed an implicit tax on consumers, as they usually had to pay a price above that of the most efficient producer.

A recurring theme in the Iberian literature is whether Portugal and Spain did not develop because, when building their empires, the metropolitan economy was disregarded. Did empires represent a significant opportunity cost, absorbing resources that could have been allocated to productive investment (Fontana, 1991), or were such costs a prerequisite for economic development?

In order to realize the potential inherent in the discovery of the resource-abundant but labor-scarce Americas, the Iberian powers required continuous investment in social overhead capital (ports, roads, housing, internal transportation, and oceanic shipping) and the establishment of new political and commercial organizations. This task, while benefiting the rest of Europe, was mainly undertaken by Iberians for at least 150 years after Columbus (O'Brien and Prados de la Escosura, 1998). In the case of Portugal, it might be argued that emigration deprived the country of manpower, skills, and entrepreneurship, since emigrants were young males, and more literate and ambitious than average. On the other hand, emigration made possible the colonization of new territories, opening new markets and providing luxuries and tropical groceries at lower cost. Furthermore, emigration eased economic conditions in the more densely populated areas, especially in the northwest.

Ironically, in the light of this literature, it may be the flow of resources *from* the Americas *to* Iberia that did the most damage to the Spanish and Portuguese economies in the long run. First, as we have already seen, bullion flows strengthened absolutist monarchies and central governments, with damaging political and economic consequences. Second, the inflow of specie, gold in Portugal and silver in Spain, may have provoked a "Dutch disease" of sorts, damaging the competitiveness of local manufacturing industries (Forsyth and Nicholas, 1983; Drelichman, 2005).

One way of assessing the importance of empire to the Iberian economies is to explore what happened after the loss of those empires. By 1827, once Brazil had severed its links to Portugal and declared full independence, real Portuguese domestic exports represented just two-thirds of their average level in 1796–1806. However, this conceals a switch from industrial to agricultural exports, with Portugal reorienting its economy towards Britain by selling its primary produce in exchange for manufactures, in the context of improving terms of trade. Trade in services also suffered, with reexports contracting by one-fifth in real terms between the same dates. For example, Portugal could no longer be an entrepôt for the produce of Brazil. Pedreira (1993) suggests that the loss of Brazil implied an upper bound loss of 8 percent of GDP. A widespread consensus views Portugal as being now confined to the role of supplier of foodstuffs and raw materials, with no opportunities to specialize within the more dynamic industrial sector. However, since the old colonial system did not bring Portugal to the verge of modern industrialization, its breakdown can hardly be blamed for the country's failure subsequently to industrialize.

In contrast to Great Britain and the thirteen North American colonies, where commercial links were immediately and vigorously renewed after their independence (Shepherd and Walton, 1976), Spain and the new Latin American republics practically cut ties (except for the trade using Cuba as an entrepôt). From the beginning of the war with Britain in October 1796, Spain maintained almost no link with the colonies for more than two decades. The subsequent decline in domestic exports (roughly 25 percent between 1784–96 and 1815–20) can be attributed almost exclusively to the fall in colonial commerce (which shrank by 40 percent). The consequence was the end of the long-standing equilibrium distribution of domestic exports between the colonies and Europe (roughly one-third and two-thirds, respectively), and the establishment of a new distribution that continued throughout the nineteenth century (with foreign markets absorbing four-fifths). Retained imports of colonial goods for domestic consumption (which had represented one-third of total retained imports) were halved, but this was offset by imports from Europe. The collapse of trade with the empire was particularly significant for services (financial, insurance, transportation), as is revealed by the contraction of real reexports by three fifths between 1784–96 and 1815–20. The Spanish balance of trade also felt the effects of colonial independence. Before the loss of empire, Spain had a deficit on current account with foreign countries that was balanced by a corresponding surplus in colonial trade. With colonial emancipation this balancing mechanism disappeared, with deflationary consequences for the domestic economy. Fortunately, a favorable terms of trade – resulting from an improvement vis-à-vis Europe, more than matching a deterioration with respect to the colonies – increased the purchasing power per unit of exports by 20 percent between 1784–96 and 1815–20, allowing Spain to avoid further deterioration in the current-account balance.

Prados de la Escosura (1993) has attempted a rough estimate of the real cost to Spain of the loss of its colonies, making assumptions favorable to the generally accepted view that the loss was significant. The first assumption is that the productive resources embodied in exportables did not have alternative uses in the domestic economy. A similar assumption is made regarding the services (shipping, insurance, mercantile) provided by Spanish subjects in the colonial trade. In contrast to the non-colonial trade, almost totally carried on non-Spanish ships, Spanish colonial legislation ensured that the Indies trade used only national shipping. Therefore, with the decline of Spanish American trade, a decline in Spanish maritime services closely followed. The loss in revenues due to the cessation of precious metal shipments, and the reduction of customs duties resulting from colonial independence, were also taken into account, the assumption being that public revenues from the colonies were productively used in the domestic economy. The upper bound estimate of Spanish losses implied by these assumptions was not more than 8 percent of national income. And while it could be argued that the profits from colonial trade represented a high proportion of the funds used to finance investment in Spain, an upper bound estimate of their contribution to total capital formation is below 18 percent by 1784–96.

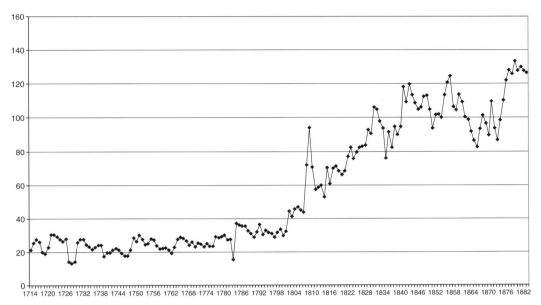

Figure 4.4 Spanish terms of trade vis-à-vis Britain, 1714–1882 (Prados de la Escosura, 1994)

The long-term consequences of the loss of the colonies depended on the flexibility and dynamic nature of the industry concerned. The decline in manufactured exports from many sectors illustrates the lack of competitiveness of Spanish industries: Spain could not offer the Latin American consumer either the prices or the quality of its west European competitors, specifically Great Britain. For example, the Basque iron and steel industry (which sold at least a third of its output to colonial markets at the end of the eighteenth century) became uncompetitive from the 1770s onward. A similar situation characterized the Valencia silk industry. Between the 1790s and the 1820s net exports of raw silk rose while net imports of silk textiles increased. Catalan shipping was yet another industry which had grown under colonial protection and suffered afterwards. However, Catalan cotton textiles developed further once the colonial market had been lost. The more competitive and flexible sectors of the economy eventually adapted to new circumstances, particularly commercial agriculture, which turned towards growing markets in western Europe. As mentioned earlier, the nineteenth century was a good time to do this, in that the terms of trade moved favorably for agricultural producers, with technological progress lowering the prices of industrial goods and growing demand raising relative agricultural prices (Figure 4.4). The loss of the colonies had a less profound and widespread impact upon the Spanish economy than the historical literature has suggested.

Trade and the Industrial Revolution

Chapter 1 of this volume provided a broad overview of Europe's transition to modern economic growth. We now focus on one particular aspect of this transition and ask: what was the impact of trade (and therefore empire, since the two were so closely related during this period) on the British Industrial Revolution? As we have seen, the cross-country econometric evidence indicates that there was a positive relationship between trade and growth during this period, but uncertainty remains about what was driving this correlation. What can we say about the relationship between trade and growth in this canonical case?

The literature on this issue has largely been shaped by the dominant economic theories of the day. One particularly influential strand of thought has been inspired by the assumption of classical economists, from Smith to Marx, that growth depends on investment, which depends on savings, which depends on profits (since workers were assumed to be too poor to save, and landlords too frivolous). In a famous book, Eric Williams (1966) argued that Atlantic slave trade profits financed the Industrial Revolution. His largely anecdotal evidence consisted of enumerating cases in which those associated with slavery made investments in domestic British industry. The classic quantitative responses to Williams were made by Engerman (1972) and O'Brien (1982), both of whom measured the profits associated with the slave trade (or, in the case of O'Brien, with Britain's transoceanic activities more generally), and found these to have been too small to have possibly mattered. For example, O'Brien found that the total profits accruing to those engaged in trade and commerce with the 'periphery' in 1784–86 amounted to £5.66 million. If 30 percent of these profits were saved and reinvested, then that would have financed roughly 15 percent of British gross investment during that period. Since 15 percent was, for O'Brien, a small figure, the Williams thesis 'foundered on the numbers' (p. 16).

There is a more fundamental problem with the Williams thesis, which is that technological change rather than capital accumulation was the ultimate driving force behind the Industrial Revolution. By focusing on profits as the possible link between overseas trade, empire, and slavery on the one hand, and European growth on the other, Williams and others have been barking up the wrong channel. If Marxist economic theory is ill-suited to explain the Industrial Revolution, so too is Keynesian theory, by definition, since Keynes was concerned with the short-run determination of output and employment, not with long-run economic growth. This has not prevented various historians from attempting to argue that overseas demand exogenously boosted British industrial output during the transition to modern growth. As almost 60 percent

Price

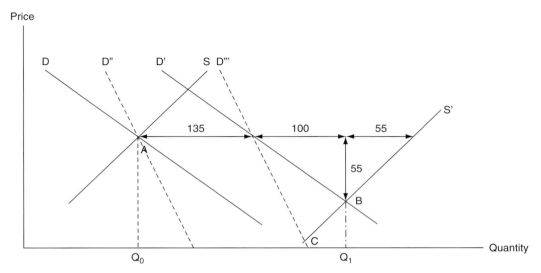

Figure 4.5 Demand versus supply during the Industrial Revolution (Findlay and O'Rourke, 2007, p. 306)

of British cotton textile exports went to non-European countries during 1784–6 (Davis, 1979), such a claim is understandable. However, growth is ultimately a supply-side phenomenon, and, indeed, if growth had been due to rising over-seas demand, then Britain's terms of trade should have increased during the Industrial Revolution, whereas in fact they fell, reflecting the cost-reducing nature of the innovations concerned (McCloskey, 1981; Mokyr, 1977). Figure 4.5 makes the point in a simple manner. According to Crafts and Harley (1992), industrial output rose by roughly 235 percent between 1780 and 1831, while GDP rose by roughly 135 percent. If the income-elasticity of demand was unity, and foreign incomes rose at the same rate as British ones, then the demand for British manufactures at constant prices rose by roughly 135 percent. This can be illustrated by the outward shift of demand from D to D' (ignore D" and D'" for now). If the industrial supply curve were vertical, it would have shifted out by 235 percent, intersecting D' at the new equilibrium, denoted by point B. The available data on the British terms of trade suggest that at this point, relative manufactured goods prices were (very roughly speaking) 55 percent lower than in the initial equilibrium A. If the elasticity of supply were unity, on the other hand, the supply curve would have shifted out (at constant prices) by 290 percent (=135+100+55), far more than the 135 percent outward shift in demand.

Findlay (1990) provides a simple general equilibrium model of the late-eighteenth-century Atlantic economy which, although it is static, can still help in thinking about how trade really mattered during the Industrial

Revolution. That revolution was initially heavily concentrated in cotton textiles, and British imports of raw cotton came exclusively from outside Europe, particularly from the Americas.[2] The American supply was highly elastic, as a result of the then seemingly limitless endowment of New World land, and the highly elastic supply of slave labor. The Industrial Revolution meant a large increase in the demand for raw cotton, and hence a rise in its price at home and abroad, implying a deterioration in Britain's terms of trade. High American supply elasticities minimized this terms of trade loss – in the absence of slaves and New World land, relative raw cotton prices would have increased by more than they actually did, potentially choking off growth in this crucial sector. The existence of overseas markets also implied a higher demand for cotton textiles, and a more elastic demand as well. As can be seen from Figure 4.5, a given supply shift due to industrial innovation would have had a smaller output effect, and reduced cotton textiles prices by even more than was actually the case, with inelastic demand (compare the shift from D to D' with the shift from D" to D'").

Not only did trade ensure that a given supply side impulse travelled further; it also probably ensured more innovation, which was both motivated by profits and expensive (Allen, 2006). Large fixed research and development costs implied that innovators had to make profits just to break even, and larger markets helped innovators recoup those fixed costs. Furthermore, under certain circumstances larger markets imply more elastic demand curves for individual monopolistically competitive firms (Desmet and Parente, 2006). Thus a given price-reducing innovation will imply larger sales and revenue increases in larger markets, meaning that as markets expand, innovation becomes more likely. While this mechanism has yet to be quantified, presumably a closed Britain (even a closed Britain miraculously enabled to grow cotton) would not have experienced as much innovation as was in fact observed. Unlike China or the Mughal Empire, it was too small to rely on its domestic markets. As it was, increases in exports were equivalent to 21 percent of the total increase in GDP between 1780 and 1801 (Crafts, 1985a, p. 131), over 50 percent of additional industrial output during the same period (Cuenca Esteban, 1997), and over 60 percent of additional textiles output between 1815 and 1841 (Harley, 1999, p. 187).

Furthermore, between 1780 and 1801 the Americas accounted for roughly 60 percent of additional British exports (O'Brien and Engerman, 1991, p. 186). British innovators were largely dependent on overseas markets as their industries expanded. The implication, in a mercantilist world in which nations

---

[2] Pomeranz (2000) emphasizes the benefits to Europe of access to the raw materials of the New World, an advantage denied to the Chinese economy of the time.

systematically excluded their enemies from protected markets, is that British military success over the French and other European rivals was one ingredient in explaining its subsequent rise to economic prominence. It was certainly not on its own a sufficient condition – since domestic conditions had to be right in order to spur innovation in the first place – but possibly a necessary one.

CHAPTER

5

Business cycles

Lee Craig and Concepción García-Iglesias

Contents

In Western civilization, the periodic deviations from long-run trends in real economic activity, which we have come to know as business cycles, can be identified at least as far back as the sixteenth century.[1] The causes and consequences of these cycles have changed over time, and cycles before 1700 may have differed in effect, frequency, and possibly magnitude from those after 1870; however, the most salient difference was in their causes. The literature on the early cycles tends to associate them with **technological change**, **demographic shocks**, **specie flows**, **disruptions in trade**, **agricultural crises** (typically associated with climatic shocks), and/or **war**. In contrast, by the last decades of the nineteenth century the disruptions in **financial markets** and the **manufacturing sector** are usually the suspects in swings in economic activity, though modern business cycle theory still links technological change with cyclical activity.

Scholarly study of the business cycle dates at least from Adam Smith, who discussed the causes of cycles by contrasting the fluctuations in the textile and corn markets, as well as the potential role of monetary shocks via specie flows (1966[1776], pp. 66–75, and pp. 35–55, respectively). By the late nineteenth and early twentieth centuries it had become common in scholarly circles to emphasize the length and supposed regularity of various economic cycles. Thus Joseph Schumpeter (1939, pp. 162–65) could organize cyclical behavior into five broad categories. Seasonal cycles, driven as they were by the rhythms of the agricultural sector, typically ran their course in a calendar year. Kitchin cycles, lasting three to five years, were reflected, supposedly, in the behavior of financial indicators (for example, bank clearings and interest rates) and wholesale prices. Juglar cycles, of ten years or so, marked more fundamental changes in financial markets, as well as demographic indicators. Kuznets cycles, of roughly twenty years, followed structural changes in key technologies, leading industries, and, especially, long swings in construction activity. Finally there were Kondratieff cycles, which were as long as fifty or sixty years, which represented historic shifts in the economy, such as the Industrial Revolution.

Although Schumpeter's approach can be found in European macroeconomic histories as recently as the 1980s (see, e.g., Trebilcock, 1981), subsequent studies, particularly those found in the economics literature, downplay or reject outright the systematic nature of those earlier categories, focusing instead on the statistical properties of key macroeconomic time series – including real GDP and its components, price indices, trade data, and interest rates – or the causes and consequences of specific cyclical episodes.[2] The primary objection

---

[1] In major trading centers, such as Venice, cycles went back centuries (Lane and Mueller, 1985), and they were not limited to the West (Chaudhuri, 1985).

[2] Tellingly, recent summaries of business-cycle research neither mention nor cite Schumpeter's taxonomy (see Basu and Taylor, 1999; DeLong, 1999; Long and Plosser, 1983; Mankiw, 1989; Plosser, 1989; Romer, 1999; and Zarnowitz, 1999, to cite just a few).

to the earlier approach is its low predictive power. Indeed, the recent literature rejects the notion that there exists *a* business cycle outside the historical context in which the cyclical activity occurs. In analyzing cross-country cycles covering roughly 130 years, Basu and Taylor observe that "The interpretation of these results is not straightforward, since over such a long time span the structure of the economy has probably changed" (1999, pp. 50–51). Similarly, Romer notes that "Only by establishing how economic fluctuations have changed can we know the phenomena to be explained" (1999, p. 24). Following these admonitions, we focus on the changes in both economic structure and the causes of economic fluctuations between c. 1700 and c. 1870.

Today, macroeconomic data are universally organized along the lines of nation-states. Key business cycle indicators – for example gross domestic product, price indices, and unemployment rates – track national economic activity. Thus the rise of the business cycle as a notion of intellectual interest coincided with the rise of the nation-state. Not coincidentally did Smith inquire about cyclical activity in *Wealth of Nations*. Although, as we argue below, aggregate cyclical activity is tied to geographically specific markets – a decidedly microeconomic notion – by the late-eighteenth century the integration of the European economy was extensive enough that large cyclical shocks in specific markets, in specific regions, had ramifications for economic activity in other regions, often without regard to national boundaries. Thus there emerged something like a pan-European cycle, even before the national income and product data were well defined. In what follows, we document how this came about.

Cycles before 1816[3]

Modern business-cycle theorists emphasize the role of **technological change** as a key causal factor in so-called "real business cycles" (McCallum, 1989; Plosser, 1989). In these models the cumulative (and thus aggregate) impact of a number of 'micro' technological changes increases labor productivity and, via the labor–leisure trade-off, leads to an increase in hours worked and in output, and thus to an upturn in real economic activity. In this respect Jan de Vries's (1994) notion of an "industrious revolution" before the Industrial Revolution, as well as Joel Mokyr's (1990, 1993) characterization of technological creativity as the foundation of the Industrial Revolution itself, are not inconsistent with

---

[3] The dating here, which marks the end of the Napoleonic wars and England's subsequent adoption of the gold standard, is admittedly somewhat arbitrary. Some scholars put the break much earlier, around 1770 (Hoppit, 1986); whereas the work of others suggests a later break (Williamson, 1987b).

specific institutional or technological changes in specific geographical areas that could generate an upturn in the local business cycle through, for example, productivity shocks. Through other factors, such as migration (see below), these shocks impacted other regions and countries.

Conversely, in some versions of modern business-cycle theory, downturns occur as firms that experience technological change and positive productivity shocks do not increase output proportionally and thus reduce hours and employment (Francis and Ramey, 2005).[4] A similar process appears to have been at work as Europe's agricultural sector modernized and increased productivity as employment declined. Of course, with sweeping changes characterized by expressions like "'Industrial Revolution' or 'Agricultural Revolution'," one must be careful "to distinguish between growth and cycles" (Craig and Fisher, 2000, p. 114). Indeed, broad institutional and technological changes are more likely to impact long-run trends in growth than short-run cycles. Although recent macroeconomic histories do not find substantial discontinuities in the long-run trend rate of growth until well into the nineteenth century, Mokyr himself notes that "There is typically a long lag between the occurrence of changes in technology, even those of fundamental importance, and the time they start affecting aggregate statistics" (1993, p. 10). Thus, if nothing else, the Industrial Revolution probably made modern business cycles possible.

Early business cycle theorists often interpreted **demographic change** as a major indicator of cyclical activity (for example, Juglar, 1889[1860]). Births, deaths, and net migration could all reflect, as well as influence, aggregate economic activity. While an increase in the birth rate relative to the death rate could impact aggregate demand and aggregate supply in both the short run and the long run, quantitatively these impacts were small relative to the potential impact of a mortality crisis. Thus in standard portrayals of the demographic transition, although premodern birth rates fluctuated, these fluctuations were typically small compared with fluctuations in death rates, which resulted largely from infectious disease.

[S]hort-run movements of fertility in early modern Europe were primarily responses to disturbances of the demographic equilibrium brought about by the mortality crises; their function was the speedy restoration of "normality." With mortality, on the other hand, short-run instability was endemic and at the mercy of exogenous forces. (Flinn, 1985, p. 47)

Among these exogenous factors, plague proved to be the most effective and persistent killer. It also created an early modern pan-European cycle: "Bubonic plague epidemics moved around Europe throughout most of the

---

[4] Smets and Wouters (2007) obtain essentially the same result employing a different model with different assumptions.

period ... there were few years when the disease was not attacking somewhere" (Flinn, 1985, p. 51). Plague tended to affect the economy in two ways. One way was through disruption of the labor market. The lost production of the sick and the dead impacted real output, and the spectre of famine could follow plague, even in the absence of a harvest failure. The second way was through the disruption of trade. Plague typically entered through port cities, and the subsequent damage to trade – through lost labor, ostracism, and quarantine – could be quite sharp. After the crisis of the fourteenth century, however, plague outbreaks tended to be more geographically localized affairs, often moving from port to port. Still, these episodes could be particularly troublesome when they hit several ports in the same country at the same time. Also, epidemics could affect aggregate economic activity when they coincided with harvest failures (see below). As for specific episodes of mortality-induced cycles, outbreaks in southern Italy (1743) and Spain (1799–1800) appear to have been limited largely to urban areas. However, the combination of plague and agricultural problems further inland led to major economic downturns in Sweden and the Baltic region of the Continent more generally (1709–10) and France (1720–22). Both of these episodes were associated with economic downturns elsewhere in Europe – though cause and effect are difficult to disentangle.

As for migration, on the whole, even prior to the great transatlantic migrations, European migration during the period was on quite a large scale. This internal migration tended to be seasonal, revolving as it did around a long-run, rural-to-urban trend. However, as Brinley Thomas (1973) observed, this migration both responded to and was caused by real cyclical activity. Although Thomas's empirical work focused on the nineteenth century, his theoretical arguments apply for earlier periods. Institutional or technological change, broadly defined, that increased economic activity and labor productivity in a specific region would lower production costs, increase output and wages along with the demand for labor, and lead to in-migration. Conversely, regions not experiencing this change would lose capital and labor and experience a downturn in the cycle. Thus, via migration, (countercyclical) shocks are spread to other regions, and these shocks could be exacerbated by war and harvest failures (see below). Foreman-Peck notes in a review of Thomas that this "central theme translates well as a real business cycle" (2006, p. 2).

Up to the eighteenth century, much of the traditional narrative of early modern European growth emphasizes the economic effects of New World **specie flows**, which caused the general inflation known as the 'price revolution' (Hamilton, 1934). One must be careful to disentangle the impact of specie flows on price levels from their effects on real economic activity. In its simplest form, disentangling these influences involves differentiating between anticipated and unanticipated flows. To the extent that the flows were anticipated, both sides of the market could have adjusted their price expectations to offset the effects of any resulting economic shock – the most conspicuous of which would have been inflation. Based on the logic of the quantity theory of money, one should be skeptical of placing too much weight on the association of specie flows and the resulting inflation with either economic growth or even real activity of a cyclical nature (Craig and Fisher, 2000).

That said, to the extent that the magnitude of or fluctuations in these flows were not fully anticipated, they represented an early modern version of a monetary shock. The specie was after all money, and discoveries of precious metals represented an increase in the purchasing power of the discoverer and provided one of the primary motives for the establishment of European-based, worldwide trading empires. It is hard to imagine that all the effort expended on seeking gold and silver from the four corners of the earth was merely to test the neutrality of money. Those who traded in precious metal, and the crown which derived seignorage from its coinage, received an initial windfall, which only subsequently manifested itself as a European-wide inflation. That initial windfall, however, would result in some deviation from the long-run trend in real economic activity, or as Cipolla put it, the specie flows "acted as a stimulus to even greater [cyclical] activity during the long periods of development" (1972, p. 45).

The propagation of these monetary shocks and the magnitude of their real impact remain a subject of dispute, but the presence of *some* real impact is generally accepted (see the survey in Fisher, 1989). It is likely that this impact was not unlike unanticipated money in a modern monetarist framework – that is, the specie flows, while arguably neutral in the long run, had a real impact in the short run. Indeed, the expansion of trade resulting from the quest for specie may well have contributed both to economic growth – that is, to an increase in the long-run trend rate of growth – and to deviations from that trend – that is, to business cycles. If nothing else, the specie flows served as a metric of expanding trade, and this expansion was itself associated with real economic growth and increasing international integration, which in turn provided a vehicle for cross-country influences on growth rates, business cycles, and, in the end, inflation: in short, a pan-European cycle.

The creation and expansion of New World (as well as African and East Indies) **trade** networks offers another mechanism by which early cycles could begin and be propagated. The trading companies were largely private, though publicly sanctioned, enterprises that continued for roughly four centuries. In this way, international trade can reasonably be said to have increased the long-run trend in growth rates of European countries. Associated with this positive trend, however, were occasional temporary deviations in the rate at which trade expanded. The disruption in trade was often a function of other factors that also caused cycles. Military action or plague, for example, caused short-term deviations from long-run trends, and the quest for specie proved a persistent driver of trade. In addition to its links to other causal agents, the expansion of trade could generate cycles in another, more modern, way – specifically, through financial markets.

Reviews of specific episodes of financial crises during this period often emphasize events surrounding the so-called "South Sea Bubble." The British South Sea Company was chartered in 1711 and, in what was essentially a debt-for-equity swap, assumed some of the national debt in return for monopoly rights in the overseas trade (Neal, 1990). Subsequently, in France, John Law, the Scottish adventurer-cum-financier, founded the Banque Generale (later the Banque Royale) and the Compagnie d'Occident (later the Compagnie des Indes), and took over the mint and the collection of taxes. According to Velde (2003, p. 1),

The operation resulted in the conversion of the existing French public debt into a sort of government equity. Strictly speaking, a publicly traded company took over the collection of all taxes in France, ran the mints, monopolized all overseas trade and ran part of France's colonies. This company offered to government creditors the possibility of swapping their bonds for its equity, making itself the government's creditor … Thus, bondholders became holders of a claim to the stochastic stream of fiscal revenues [from trade].

The ambitious fiscal, monetary, and financial plans surrounding these companies were ultimately based on their profitability as trading enterprises. The debt-for-equity swaps made sense only as long as the companies generated returns from their real overseas activities and their affiliated financial institutions could credibly manage their liabilities. The latter depended on the former, and when either failed, the system as a whole would fail. As Neal notes, "the South Sea scheme came to an end" when the Bank of England pressured the South Sea Company's correspondent bank to redeem its notes in specie or Bank of England notes (1990, p. 106). Similarly, in France, "It was a crucial aspect of Law's scheme that the [trading company] share price remain high" (Velde, 2003, p. 28). Aside from Law's short-run manipulations, the only way to assure that was the flow of profits from the company's trading activities. When those failed to materialize, the scheme collapsed in summer 1720. The damage, which spread to Amsterdam through credit markets, was by contemporary accounts real enough, and the downturn was felt throughout the economies of France and Britain; thus the connection between trade and finance, albeit public finance, resulted in swings in (pan-European) real economic activity.

While institutional and technological change, mortality shocks, migration, unanticipated specie flows, and disruptions in international trade all impacted the early modern economy, prior to the nineteenth century **agricultural shocks** were the most frequent, and arguably the largest, sources of cyclical downturns.

In order to understand the importance of agricultural events in the early modern cycle, it is important to note that, in terms of national income accounting, the agricultural sector tended to dominate other sectors of the economy. Using Britain, a relatively early economic developer, as a benchmark, something like 50 percent of the British labor force was still directly employed in agriculture in 1700, and the typical British agricultural laborer, one of Europe's more productive, produced enough food to feed himself and only two other people.[5] So the overall economy was quite sensitive to agricultural shocks, the most prominent of which were significant short-run deviations from climatic norms.

The most obvious climatic problems included late and early frosts and unusually dry or wet periods around or between sowing and harvest. These climatic shocks could cover much of Europe or be highly localized. In either case, depending on the length and severity of the crisis, given the relatively high transportation costs at the time, the resulting crop failures would yield lower nutritional consumption, if not outright famine. This in turn would have made the human population more susceptible to disease, which reduced labor inputs and further reduced agricultural output, thus further exposing humans to the ravages of disease. Generally speaking, "[t]here was a close and exact correlation between food prices and mortality" (Flinn, 1985, p. 51).

Beyond the local economy, the transmission of a weather-related agricultural shock could be quite complex. Poor yields associated with a crisis in one region would increase the demand for grain from other regions, which might well result in a cyclical upturn in those other regions. Thus the impact of a crop failure on the business cycle of a national economy depended crucially on the geographical extent of the crisis. If it were quite local, then the net result might be merely a redistribution of income from one agricultural area to another or from town to countryside; however, if much of a country's agricultural sector were hit, then food would be imported under worsening terms of trade, *ceteris paribus* of course, and aggregate output would be negatively affected.

Furthermore, prior to the mastery and widespread use of steam power in manufacturing and transportation, the same weather problems that affected agriculture could impact manufacturing and trade, and understanding the impact of weather-related shocks is further complicated by their impact on the urban sector.

[S]ome industries were directly affected by changes in the weather. The frost that killed the sprouting corn, or the heavy rain that beat down the straw, might simultaneously put a stop to the water-wheels or interfere with the delivery of

---

[5] This is only an estimate based on figures in Allen (2004) and Wrigley (2004a).

materials ... a fall in the output of copper in Cornwall and of broad cloth in the West Riding resulted from a great frost ... In most years of dearth there was a sharp rise in the price of coal, not at the pit-head but in London and other urban centres. But, it was the severe weather preceding the harvest that was responsible. (Ashton, 1959, pp. 34–35)

As Europe industrialized and the share of economic activity taking place in urban areas expanded, urban populations became vulnerable to crop failures. This had always been the case, but as agricultural productivity grew, each farmer supported a larger number of non-farm, and increasingly urban, households; thus the shock of each agricultural failure had the potential to be felt more broadly in non-farm sectors. Supply shocks resulting in high prices and small quantities of foodstuffs were a constant threat to urban dwellers, and to the political leaders who faced their wrath. As one contemporary put it, "Who could forget the terrible years of soaring prices ... that so harshly oppressed almost the whole of Europe" (cited in Craig and Fisher, 2000, p. 119). Of course, unusually low prices resulting from abundant harvests had their own risks. "If the price of corn became too low, the tenant farmer tended to leave his fields untilled ... A crisis arose and soon spread to the towns simply because corn was sold too cheaply" (Abel, 1980, pp. 11–12). Craig and Fisher summarize the narrative accounts of agricultural crises thus: "In other words, if prices were too high that was bad for the economy, but if prices were low that was bad, too" (2000, p. 120).

The confusion reflected in commentaries on early cycles is the result, at least partly, of reliance on prices as the main indicator of economic activity. This reliance derives from the relatively plentiful data on prices and the general absence of output figures. Of course, the timing and distribution of the impact varied depending on the nature of the shock, and observations about the nature of early cycles often reflect the distributional effects of short-run agricultural shocks. Given the inelastic demand for basic foodstuffs, a harvest failure resulted in higher incomes for those farmers who generated a disproportionate share of the marketable surplus, which in most cases included those who owned or managed larger farms and those in regions not affected by the poor weather. The redistribution was from urban consumers to the large or non-affected producer. Small farmers in the affected areas also suffered. Conversely, an abundant harvest, which is just another type of shock, would reduce farm incomes and confer a windfall on urban dwellers in the form of lower prices and greater quantities. Farmers who experienced a shortfall due to extreme local conditions in a year of general abundance would suffer the most in this scenario, as they would see lower prices and smaller yields. With respect to a shock's impact on aggregate economic activity, however, of the two scenarios the loss of agricultural output in the wake of bad weather, if geographically widespread enough, was the one most likely to produce a substantial aggregate business cycle decline.

As for specific episodes of these shocks, there are few macroeconomic time series for European countries before 1750; however, narrative accounts combined with price data, especially those that reflect urban food prices, and real wage data can be employed to identify various cycles, particularly after 1750. In short, large decreases in real wages accompanied by increases in prices suggest economic stress in these economies. In Britain there were crop failures of varying degrees in 1708–09, 1724, 1727–29, 1740, 1756–57, 1771–74, and 1792. Each of these coincided with a downturn in the broader economy. In France the years 1769, 1771–72, and 1789–90 appear to be particularly poor ones in the agricultural sector (Craig and Fisher, 2000, pp. 171, 217–18), and each of these downturns in France coincided, within a year, with an aggregate downturn in the Low Countries (Table 5.2).

Although financial crises revolving around fractional reserve banking systems were largely a feature of the later European economy (see below), because of the importance of short-term credit in agricultural economies there were crises in credit markets in the eighteenth century. These typically reflected real crises in either trade or agriculture or, as was the case in England and France in 1720 and France in the 1780s, in public finance (Hoppit, 1986). A review of the historiography of Ashton (1955) identifies the following as years of crisis: 1701, 1710, 1715, 1720, 1726–28, 1745, 1761, 1763, 1772, 1778, 1788, 1793, and 1797. All but two of these episodes (1772 and 1788) involved the public sector in one way or another (Hoppit, 1986, p. 45), and four of them (1710, the late 1720s, 1770s, and 1793) were associated with harvest failures. Although the exact timing of change remains a subject of dispute, scholars of the era recognize that as the century progressed, the causes of cycles changed fundamentally. "What distinguishes [later] financial crises … from those before is that they were in large part caused by economic growth" (Hoppit, 1986, p. 51). This growth lay disproportionately in the manufacturing sector, and was supported by the evolution of the financial sector (see below).

The early crises in public finance noted above were not entirely caused by trade problems. Indeed, in one way or another they were often associated with **war**. War could also lead to agricultural shocks, through either direct destruction or via the labor market as a result of conscription of the farm labor force. Of course, there was another side to this: destruction in one region could increase the demand for the products of another, unaffected region, leading to a windfall there. More generally, the economic impact of wars is often misunderstood. Although in modern times it is not uncommon for standard measures of economic output, such as gross domestic product, to increase during wartime, it does not follow that such increases necessarily result in increased economic well-being for the citizens of the warring states; rather it is due to the greatly increased government consumption of scarce resources. Furthermore, almost inevitably, wars produce a negative effect on investment spending through "crowding out" – though the extent to which crowding out was an important component of cyclical behavior associated with wartime public expenditures has been much debated in the literature (Crafts, 1987; Mokyr, 1987; Williamson, 1987a).

The geographical area in which the war is fought may face economic disruption and the destruction of local infrastructure, circumstances that typically lead to a reduction in economic output, at least in the short run. A war that disrupted agricultural production over a region of some size for a notable period of time would have had a potentially devastating effect on the economy; indeed, a short war would produce a shock and a long war a significant, and possibly enduring, deviation from the long-run trend growth rate. In practice, disruptions took several forms. The confiscation of output by military authorities reduced current civilian consumption and, if an army or armies remained in the vicinity, reduced the incentive for future production. Fields, fences, and structures were damaged by campaigns. Diseases were introduced and/or spread as a result of mixing different populations. Finally, farm labor was often conscripted, both at home and in conquered territories. Taken together, these negative effects on food production, coupled with exposure to new disease pools, could lead to famine and/or a reduced capacity for work, both of which lowered output as well. Finally, it is not necessarily the case that the economic growth that sometimes follows war is "caused" in any meaningful economic sense by the war.

As for specific wars that most likely had some negative aggregate impact, they include the Great Northern War (1700–21), the War of the Spanish Succession (1701–14), the Wars of the Austrian Succession (1740–48), the Seven Years War (1756–63), and the wars of the French Revolution from 1792.

What, then, can we make of this summary of the various causes and specific cyclical episodes before 1816? Craig and Fisher (2000) argue that in agricultural economies downturns in wages coinciding with a general increase in the price level, particularly increases in grain prices, suggest economic stress. By combining that logic with narrative accounts and secondary data sources, we have identified downturns in the business cycles of seven countries or regions of Europe, dating from 1700 for Great Britain, and from 1750 for other areas, including France, the Low Countries, the German states, the Italian states, Austria-Hungary, and Spain.[6] The pre-1750 years of downturn in the British

---

[6] For countries and years for which there exist output or financial market data, we have followed Craig and Fisher (1997, 2000) in identifying downturns. For countries and years for which we have only price and wage data, we have identified

Table 5.1 Economic
downturns in Great
Britain, 1700–1750

Great Britain
1702
1705–1706
1709–1710
1714
1718
1720–1721
1724
1728–1729
1734
1737
1740–1742
1745

economy, arguably the most advanced at the time, are shown in Table 5.1, and
the post-1750 downturns are shown in Table 5.2.

Downturns occurred roughly every three to four years, more frequently than
one finds in Europe today. Of course, this might simply be the noise and biases
of the indicators employed to identify downturns and, tellingly, the list reflects
the specific episodes of trade, war, and agricultural problems that show up in
various narrative accounts. Also, every downturn in the British economy is
accompanied within a year by a downturn in two or more other countries or
regions. One could interpret this as evidence of an early pan-European cycle, or
it might simply reflect the overall volatility of these largely agricultural economies. Together, the Italian states, Austria-Hungary, and Spain show a downturn roughly every three years.

If one is willing to define a continent-wide recession as one in which several
countries or regions faced economic stress simultaneously, then it appears that
there was one such episode, lasting two to three years, roughly every decade
(Table 5.3). While the agricultural sector and war must be suspects in most of
these cases, there are considerably more downturns than there were major
agricultural "crises." Given agriculture's share of total output during the eighteenth century, one would be justified in concluding that the tables include a few
"false positives." That said, the agricultural sector was quite volatile, and that

downturns as years in which prices went up and wages went down. Increasing food prices suggest an agricultural supply
shock in these economies, and, if accompanied by a decrease in wages, rising food prices suggest stress beyond the
agricultural sector. For example, in Austria-Hungary in 1752–53 wages declined by nearly 15 percent; while wheat, barley,
and oat prices all increased; thus we have identified those years as downturns.

Table 5.2 Economic downturns in seven European countries, 1750–1816

Great Britain/ United Kingdom	France	Low Countries	German states	Italian states	Austria-Hungary	Spain: agriculture	Spain: manufacturing
1754		1752	1753	1750	1752–53	1750–51	1750–51
1756		1757		1755		1753	1754
				1757–59	1756–58	1757–58	1758
1762	1763	1761–62	1761		1761	1760, 1762	1761, 1763
1765		1766	1765 & 67	1763–66	1766–1767	1764–65	1765–1766
1768		1769				1767	1768
			1770	1770–72	1770–71	1769	1771
		1771–72				1772–73	
1773–74	1772–74		1775	1774			1778
1778–79		1780		1777–78	1777–79	1779–80	1780
			1781–82	1781–83			1783
1785				1786–87		1784–85	
	1789–90	1788	1789	1790	1787–89	1787, 1789	1787–88
1793–1794	1793	1793		1792–93		1792–93	1792–93
			1794–95		1794–95	1796–98	1796
1797				1795–98	1797		
		1799–1801		1799–1800	1799–1800	1800–01	1801
1801			1803 & 05		1804–05	1803–04	1806
1808	1806–07		1808		1807		1808–10
1812		1811–12	1812	1810–11		1810–12	
	1815	1814		1814–16			1815

Sources: Allen, 1992; Craig and Fisher, 1997, 2000; Grytten, 2007; Hoffman et al., 2002; Jacks, 2004; Komlos, 1983; and Roses et al., 2007.

Table 5.3 Candidates for continent-wide recessions, 1750–1816

Continent-wide recession years
1761–62
1765–66
1770–72
1778–80
1789–90
1792–93
1811–12

volatility would be reflected in overall economic activity. In any case, agriculture's relative decline would mirror the increasing importance of the financial and manufacturing sectors, and in turn these would play a more important role in subsequent cycles.

Cycles from 1816 to 1870

As agriculture's role in the business cycle diminished in the closing decades of the eighteenth century, a decreasing correlation between harvest failures and cyclical activity would prove to be a good indicator of a country's overall economic development. Although eighteenth-century downturns often had a financial component, largely through public finance or the financial sector's connections to agriculture, these crises typically reflected, rather than caused, real problems in agriculture, trade, or manufacturing. The growing importance of commercial banks in providing financial intermediation, and the growth of manufacturing's share of aggregate output, suggest that increasingly the business cycle was driven by developments in the banking and industrial sectors.

With respect to the evolution of the **financial sector**, using Britain as an early benchmark, as late as 1750 there were probably no more than a dozen or so banks outside London (Neal, 1994, p. 168). By 1775, there were still only 150 banks in England and Wales, with a total capital of £3.5 million (Cameron, 1967, p. 33). By 1800, however, there were more than 400 banks with a combined capitalization of £5.5 million. While scholars might quibble with these figures, the point is that the growth of the banking sector was dramatic by almost any reasonable standard, and, as both the breadth and depth of bank activities expanded, so too did the customer base. In addition, bank assets grew faster than the overall economy, and financial markets evolved from a system dominated by commercial credit and delegated lending, transactions that were conducted by a variety of financial intermediaries, to a system increasingly marked by external bank credit. This dramatic expansion meant that what happened in the banking sector was increasingly felt throughout the economy.

Although the evolution of banking followed a varied path throughout Europe, it was often the case that banking at the metropolitan core (in, for example, Amsterdam, Paris, Berlin, and Vienna) differed from practice in the hinterlands. At the time the key to a successful bank was information, specifically information about the quality of the loans in the local economy – that is, literally in the geographical area in which the bank issued loans. Although there might have been more opportunity for diversification in the secondary or re-discount market, the reputation of the issuer (i.e. the seller) of the loan still mattered. The tendency of the largest and most important metropolitan banks only to discount "blue-chip" loans has been a source of criticism in the literature (Craig and Fisher, 1997). However, more generally, reputation, on the part of both borrowers and lenders, was the key component of the system.

Although the structure of the English banking system differed from those found elsewhere in Europe, the evolution of the system is instructive in evaluating the increasing role of banks in the business cycle. The Bank of

England served as the government's bank, and the other London banks concentrated on underwriting government debt, issuing and trading in foreign bills of exchange, and maintaining a correspondent business with the non-London, or so-called country, banks (Neal, 1994; Quinn, 2004). In addition to issuing banknotes, the country banks served as the intermediaries between London and the hinterlands and "between the savers (for example agricultural landlords) and investors (for example artisanal manufacturers)" (Neal, 1994, p. 168). These banks were not large, but they were at the center of the agriculture–trade–manufacturing nexus, and as they increased in number, size, and importance so too did their role in the business cycle.

Despite the declining relative importance of agriculture, even as Britain and the Continent industrialized, problems in financial markets were not divorced from those in the agricultural sector. With improvements in transportation and the general integration of the European economy, the impact of local crop failures was ameliorated by trade. Furthermore, as a result of the increases in agricultural productivity, fluctuations occurred around a higher mean level of output. Unless the entire continent was subject to the crisis – an unlikely event – food could be imported, at a higher price to be sure, but starvation and bread riots were increasingly a thing of the past. Still, country banks relied on agricultural surpluses to provide liquidity on the liability side of their balance sheets. The combination of a (locally) poor crop year unaccompanied by dramatically higher prices could dry up the flow of deposits. The result could be a general downturn. As Quinn observes, "banks failed in waves of runs between 1810 and 1813 caused by bad harvests and the downturn in foreign trade" (2004, p. 163). Depending on the strength of bank balance sheets (i.e. bank capital), the simultaneous liquidation of deposits and a decline in the value, and liquidity, of loans could transfer an agricultural problem into the financial sector, and from there the crisis could find its way into other sectors, trade being the most likely, as a general tightening of credit accompanied by higher interest rates could result.

As for specific episodes of stress in the post-Napoleonic agricultural sector, there were several in both England and France, and, with the notable exception of the Low Countries, elsewhere in Europe agriculture still dominated aggregate output. There were poor harvests in England in 1816, 1829, 1831, 1837–38, and 1848. In France indices of agricultural production suggest that 1818, 1820, 1822, 1825, 1833, 1836, 1842, 1845–46, 1848–49, 1851, 1853, 1855, 1859, 1861, 1865, 1867, and 1870–71 were unusually bad years. And Spain's agricultural sector lurched from one bad year to the next.

Narrative evidence yields specific years for other countries, but exactly how one interprets this information in terms of its implications for European business cycles should be mitigated by three factors. First, the agricultural sector was of declining importance during this period. So, in terms of the impact of a shock on aggregate output, it would be smaller in 1842 than 1742, *ceteris paribus*. Second, both the narrative and the quantitative evidence indicating a shock are subject to interpretation. Any historian familiar with the primary or secondary sources recognizes that hard times are not difficult to find, if that is what one is looking for. Third, as discussed in the previous section, it is possible that what much of the narrative history considers to be a negative shock was in fact a windfall for at least a good portion of the agricultural sector. A decrease in the supply of foodstuffs can increase farm incomes. In short, before one leaps from harvest failures to downturns in the business cycle after 1815 or so, one should first investigate what was going on in the banking and manufacturing sectors.

With respect to the rise of banking, in some ways the experiences of the British South Sea Company and Law's assorted French institutions foreshadowed subsequent financial crises, in that with fractional reserve banks, the pressures on both sides of their balance sheets defined their role in the crisis. In the absence of a true lender of last resort, the rise of the small note-issuing bank in the late-eighteenth and early nineteenth centuries set the stage for any number of crises. Bad, or often simply illiquid, loans in an undiversified portfolio combined with the liquidation of deposits proved to be the bane of small fractional reserve banks well into the twentieth century. On occasion these local crises could become large general crises. This was particularly true once the domestic and international banking systems were linked through the specie-flow mechanism of the gold standard. As García-Iglesias and Kilponen note, although the gold standard "may have contributed to economic growth," it also "affected the business cycle and variations of the economies joining" the system (2004, p. 4). If perceived as credible, the commitment to gold could improve the terms under which a country's borrowers received credit; however, such a commitment also tied the hands of the monetary authorities (Craig et al., 1995).

The wars that followed the French Revolution had a strong impact on the long-run trend in the English banking sector (Neal, 1994; Quinn, 2004). First, the suspension of convertibility and Parliament's authorization of the issuance of small-denomination banknotes – important during a period in which specie was quite scarce – led to even further growth in the number of country banks. There were nearly 800 by the end of the era. At the same time the London banks, and especially the Bank of England, severely rationed their discounting of bills emanating from the country banks. One might see in this an early effort to regulate the money supply, in that the Bank's actions discouraged an over-expansion of notes during a wartime suspension of convertibility. With the continued growth of the industrial sector, itself at least partly related to wartime expansion (see below), the demand for credit in the industrial regions remained relatively high. Thus there emerged a booming market in the brokering of bills between the banks that were lending to manufacturers and those that were accepting deposits, which, as a result of the wartime disruption of imports and, later, of the Corn Laws, were disproportionately in agricultural regions. The brokerage business arguably improved the efficiency of British credit markets and facilitated the expansion of the country banks, as they grew in size and number. At the same time, "[t]he spread of commercial banking across Britain also brought banking panics" (Quinn, 2004, p. 163).

Although every bank panic has its own story to tell, some scholars have attempted to identify common themes that run through them (Kindleberger, 1989; Minsky, 1982). In this view the seeds of the panic are sown through a "speculative boom" in some asset, for example, stock in a specific company, such as the South Sea Company; or a sector, such as canals or country banks; or in government debt. Investors (speculators, to use a pejorative), seeking to capitalize on the further expected increase in asset prices, turn to credit markets.

The boom is fed by an expansion of bank credit that enlarges the total money supply … as the speculative boom continues, interest rates, velocity of circulation, and prices all continue to mount. At some stage, a few insiders decide to take their profits and sell out … There may then ensue a period of "financial distress" … It is time to withdraw … The specific signal that precipitates the crisis may be the failure of a bank. (Kindleberger, 1989, pp. 18–21)

Loans, and thus loan portfolios and banks themselves, were not homogeneous products. Some lenders may have had better information and made more accurate forecasts than others. However, once one institution began to fail, depositors at other institutions could put pressure on the fractional reserve system by liquidating deposits at otherwise perfectly sound institutions. Also, banks that were caught holding loans to firms that were facing a *temporary* downturn in their fortunes could be pulled down as well. The pressure from depositors to liquidate loans could unnecessarily worsen a bad, but otherwise not critical, situation. The development of modern central banking would do much to alleviate these problems.

As for specific episodes of financial crises, the British country banks had first felt distress on a large scale in 1793. At the time, the combination of a collapse in the market for canal debt and a decline in trade resulting from the onset of war between Britain and revolutionary France disrupted the bill market. A similar collapse in 1799–1800, centered on the free city of Hamburg, resulted from the ebb and flow of the British blockade of the Continent. The next major crisis in Britain resulted from the aforementioned combination of agricultural and trade problems in 1810–13, and the end of the Napoleonic wars brought "rapid deflation" while the Bank of England kept nominal rates high. The resulting increase in real rates led to a decline in trade in 1816 (Kindleberger, 1989, Appendix B; Quinn, 2004, p. 162). In Britain a major panic ensued in 1825, when, after a rapid expansion of credit to the recently independent Latin American countries, the market collapsed following the onset of war between Argentina and Brazil over Uruguay. Banks holding Latin debt failed, taking the deposits of their correspondent banks with them. At the same time, Kindleberger (1989) argues that, across the Channel, Restoration France witnessed considerable speculation in lands, the titles to which had been placed in dispute as a result of the Revolution and the Napoleonic era. This market crashed in 1828, causing considerable distress to lenders.

The most widespread international crisis of the era spanned from 1836 through 1839 and reached across the Atlantic to the United States. Since Britain returned to the gold standard following the end of its wars with France, the Bank of England was charged with maintaining convertibility. As a result it closely monitored the nation's monetary gold reserves. With London serving as the financial center of an expanding world trade network, other financial markets became sensitive to the Bank of England's discount policies. An increase in rates, to protect reserves, accompanied by a collapse in the market for US canal debt, reverberated throughout the banking systems of the West. The crisis of 1836–39 was rivalled by that of 1847–48, which in terms of breadth, depth, and political ramifications was the worst of the era. There was also an international downturn in 1857, which stretched across the Atlantic as well as the continent.

Today, the speed at which shocks are transmitted from the financial sector to real economic activity can be quite rapid (see, e.g., Hansen, 2003), but central banks stand ready to pump liquidity into the banking system. The crises of 1836–39, 1847–48, and 1857 spread at varying speeds, but each demonstrated the potential role of a lender of last resort with public responsibilities above and beyond its own balance sheet. The financiers and politicians learned. Table 5.4 illustrates that by mid-century there were at least ten institutions that could or would subsequently fulfill the obligations of a modern central bank. However, even as late as the crisis of 1866, these institutions were still struggling with how and when to exert their control over the money supply and serve as a lender of last resort. Their struggles with these functions were related to the fact that most were private institutions, charged with maintaining the convertibility of their liabilities. Since the directors had private stockholders to whom they answered during a panic, these institutions would protect their own portfolios and deposits rather than run the risks associated with aiding the banking system more generally. As a result, their discount policies became very conservative at exactly the time when the economy called for liquidity. Similarly, their goal of maintaining convertibility often meant raising discount rates during a crisis, exactly the opposite of what subsequent monetary theory would suggest was efficacious.

Table 5.4 Summary of European central banking before 1914

Country	Bank	First founded or taken over by the state	Note issue monopoly	First decade as lender of last resort	First year on gold standard
UK	Bank of England	1694	1844	1850s	1816 (1819)
France	Bank of France	1800	1848	1880s	1878
Germany	Reichsbank	1875	1875	1870s	1871
Belgium	National Bank	1850	1850	1850s	1878
Netherlands	Bank of the Netherlands	1814	No	Unknown	1877
Denmark	National Bank of Denmark	1818	1818	1900s	1873
Finland	Bank of Finland	1811	1886	1890s	1878–79
Norway	Bank of Norway	1816	1816	1900s	1875
Sweden	Riksbank	1668	1897	1900s	1873
Italy	Bank of Italy	1893	No	1900s	1884–93, 1902
Austria-Hungary	Austro-Hungarian Bank	1816	1816	No	1900
Portugal	Bank of Portugal	1822	No	No	1854–90
Spain	Bank of Spain	1829	1874	No	No
United States	None	–	–	–	1879

Note: For details of the dating of the various actions, see Craig and Fisher, 1997, p. 117; Muhleman, 1896; and Tarkka, 1993.

Finally, then, we turn to the most common and persistent source of modern business cycles, fluctuations in the non-agricultural, non-banking **industrial sector**. The relative decline of agriculture and the maturation of banking systems across the continent were accompanied by the spread of industrialization and, just as the spread of banking made bank panics more common and their consequences for the economy more severe, increasingly what happened in the industrial sector influenced aggregate economic activity. As the research on modern real business-cycle theory suggests, exactly why modern economies remain subject to downturns in real economic activity, even after all of the above-mentioned causes have been ameliorated, remains something of a mystery. Modern business-cycle theorists have focused on "technology," which in this context is a rather amorphous term that might stand in for something as specific as an energy price shock related to, say, political unrest in a major petroleum producing area, or it might simply stand in for "all else." Of course, these downturns in aggregate activity are just the net impact of firm-level decisions and, here, nineteenth-century downturns looked a lot like their late-twentieth-century counterparts, in that they often coincided with layoffs, which in turn tended to follow the accumulation of inventories.

Because this accumulation of inventories was often financed by short-term credit, the manufacturing sector was tied to the financial sector, just as trade had been for centuries. Until the late nineteenth century, these loans tended to be short-term and used to finance operations rather than long-term investments in physical plant. Although they could be rolled over and thus used to finance some plant and equipment, they were more often used for working capital and wages, covering short-term deficits, as "when the inflow of credits (accounts receivable) proved too slow to cover payments due (accounts payable) a demand for external borrowing was created" (Quinn, 2004, p. 158). When the short-run cash flow was negative, manufacturers had to go into the bill market to cover expenses, and thus became subject to the vagaries of interest rates. As the bill market matured, manufacturers could go into the market and raise funds for expansion, even when accounts payable and receivable were roughly in balance. Conversely, when discount rates soared, manufactures would have to borrow at unfavorable terms or face layoffs and a reduction in output.

This story is not so far from current real business cycle theory. Assuming that the initial prosperity was at least partly associated with an increase in productivity, which itself might be related to a technological change in key – that is, large and growing sectors – then the borrowing that led to the expansion of inventories was nothing more than a reflection of an upturn in the (real) business cycle. The downturn came when some exogenous factor – an agricultural crisis, for example, or war, which disrupted the trade with suppliers or customers – caused actual conditions to diverge from forecast conditions. There was nothing irrational about the behavior of either borrowers or lenders; however, they occasionally made forecast errors. There was no simple or low-cost way to hedge against that possibility. Although the result was swings in aggregate real output that might look systematic in retrospect, there was nothing systematic about them. The forecast errors of 1816 were made by different men, in different industries, from those of 1848 or 1868.

As for specific episodes, in Great Britain there were major declines, as measured by the Crafts–Harley (1992) index, in 1816, 1819, 1826, 1829, 1837, 1840, 1842, and 1847, and, using gross national product (GNP) figures from Mitchell (1978, 1992), we would add 1866. For France, Toutain's (1987) index of industrial production shows downturns in 1819, 1828, 1830–31, 1839, 1847–48, and using GDP figures from Mitchell (1978, 1992) we would add 1851, 1853, 1855, 1859, 1861, 1865, 1867, 1870–71. For Belgium, Craig and Fisher (2000) create what is essentially a consumption index and infer downturns in 1818, 1822, 1828, 1831, and 1837–38. Also, more generally, the years 1842–50 appear to be bad ones. Similarly, using production and interest rate data for "Germany," they identify downturns in 1816–17, 1836, 1838, 1845, and 1848–50, and using industrial production figures from Mitchell (1978, 1992), we would add 1853. As for the European "periphery," narrative accounts and price and

Table 5.5 Economic downturns in eight European countries, 1816–1870

United Kingdom	France	Low Countries	German states	Italian states/Italy	Austria-Hungary	Spain: agriculture	Spain: manufacturing	Scandinavia
1816		1817–18	1816–1818	1814–16		1817	1817	
1819	1820		1821	1820–21	1821	1820	1819, 1821	1820–21
	1822	1822			1823		1823	
1826	1825	1828	1826	1825	1828	1825	1825–26	1824–25
				1827–28		1828	1828	
1832	1832	1831	1831–32			1831–32	1831–32	1833
					1833–34	1834		
1837		1837–38		1835–37		1836–38		1838
	1839			1839	1839		1839	
1840–42	1842	1842			1841	1841–44	1841–43	1841
	1845–46	1845	1845	1846–47				1846
1848	1848	1848–49	1848–49		1847–48			1848
	1851						1850–51	
	1853		1853	1853–54	1853	1853	1853–54	
	1855				1855	1855	1856	
1857	1859				1858–59	1859		1857–59
	1861				1862–1864	1861	1862–64	1861–62
	1865					1865	1866	
1866	1867			1867–68		1867		1867–68
	1870–71					1870		

Sources: See Table 5.2.

Table 5.6 Candidates for continent-wide recessions, 1816–1870

Continent-wide recession years
1816–19
1820–21
1825–26
1831–32
1837–38
1840–42
1848–49
1853–54
1857–59
1861–62
1866–68

wage data suggest that the volatility of the agricultural sector continued to drive the business cycle well into the nineteenth century.

Combining the narrative accounts of harvest failures, financial panics, and industrial downturns with the empirical evidence constructed by economic historians and offered in the secondary literature yields Table 5.5, which shows the years in which eight European countries or regions (the United Kingdom, France, the Low Countries, the German states, the Italian states, Austria-Hungary, Spain, and Scandinavia) experienced declines, and what might arguably be considered a recession in the current meaning of the term. Downturns involving multiple countries occur roughly every four to five years. Like the eighteenth-century data in Tables 5.1 to 5.3, these figures show more frequent recessions than one finds in post-World War II Europe. Of course, as Basu and Taylor (1999) and Romer (1999) note, one should be wary of comparisons such as this over long periods of time, because of the changes in the underlying structure of the economy. Table 5.5 shows that even by 1816 there was an identifiable European business cycle, with downturns in one country frequently coinciding with those in other countries, and Table 5.6 contains the years that would appear to be good candidates for continent-wide recessions.

These observations suggest that there was something like a European-wide recession roughly twice every decade. This accounting yields more frequent downturns than Europe subsequently experienced, and it certainly reveals more frequent downturns than in recent decades, which include the so-called Great Moderation (of the business cycle). We conclude by noting that, while the frequency of downturns might be a function of how the data and events were recorded, an important part of the "lessons of history for pan-European development" is the amelioration of key factors – the role of agriculture, metallic monetary standards, and the absence of a consistently credible lender of last resort – through economic modernization, as well as learning and institutional change, particularly in the banking sector and on the part of public policymakers.

PART

II Sectoral analysis

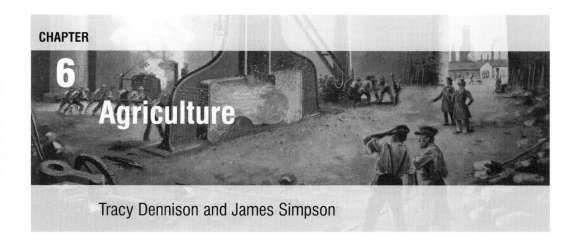

Agriculture

Tracy Dennison and James Simpson

Contents

Agriculture and long-run growth

In 1700, all economies were based very largely on agricultural production. The agricultural sector employed most of the workforce, consumed most of the capital inputs and provided most of the outputs in the economy. In some ways this is obvious. People in 1700 were much poorer than they are today but required similar levels of food intake, so food must have constituted a higher percentage of economic activity – whether measured from the production, consumption, or expenditure side of the national income identity. Hence at the onset of the Industrial Revolution in England , around 1770, food accounted for approximately 60 percent of the household budget, compared with just 10 percent in 2001 (Feinstein, 1998). But it is important to realise that agriculture additionally provided most of the raw materials for industrial production: fibres for cloth, animal skins for leather, and wood for building houses and ships and making the charcoal used in metal smelting. There was scarcely an economic activity that was not ultimately dependent on agricultural production – even down to the quill pens and ink used by clerks in the service industries.

The very large share of agriculture in economic activity has several important economic implications. First, the growth rates of agricultural output and productivity within each country were the primary determinants of overall growth rates in each country. Similarly, agricultural productivity differentials across countries were the primary determinants of overall productivity differentials across countries. Second, Crafts (1985a) has emphasized that substantial food imports were unavailable to any country in the eighteenth century because no country was producing a sufficient agricultural surplus to be able to supply the food demanded by another. Therefore any transfer of labor resources from agriculture to industry required high output per worker in domestic agriculture, because each agricultural worker had to produce enough to feed both himself and some fraction of an industrial worker. This is crucial, because the transfer of labor resources out of agriculture and into industry has come to be seen as the defining feature of early industrialization. Alternative paradigms of industrial revolution – such as significant increases in the rate of productivity growth, or a marked superiority of industrial productivity over that of agriculture – have not been supported by the empirical evidence.

Measuring the importance of the agricultural sector in each economy in 1700 and tracing its evolution over time with any degree of precision are impossible. The standard modern approach would be to calculate for each year the share of agriculture in GDP in each country. By contrast, the best that we can do is to estimate the percentage of the workforce employed in agriculture for a selection of countries at benchmark dates. Nonetheless, this proves to be quite a useful statistic if we follow the Crafts definition of industrialization. Brunt and Fidalgo

Table 6.1 The percentage of the European workforce employed in agriculture

	1705	1775	1845	1870
Austria	n.a.	75	72	64
Belgium	n.a.		26	17
Denmark	n.a.	n.a.	n.a.	45
England	35	29	20	14
France	70	65	59	59
Ionia	n.a.	n.a.	68	60
Ireland	48	48	75	49
Malta	n.a.	n.a.	50	50
Netherlands	n.a.	38	34	35
Norway	n.a.	n.a.	33	33
Poland	n.a.	n.a.	89	58
Prussia	80	70	60	49
Russia	n.a.	n.a.	81	81
Scotland	n.a.	50	23	17
Spain	71	66	61	61
Sweden	n.a.	n.a.	n.a.	80
Wales	n.a.	n.a.	n.a.	53

Source: Brunt and Fidalgo, 2008.

(2008) recently reexamined the available data on the European agricultural workforce and we report their findings in Table 6.1.

We can see that the relative importance of agriculture declined fastest in England, Scotland, and Belgium, with the Netherlands being some way behind. Norway was also low, but this is almost certainly due to the extraordinary importance of fishing in GDP, rather than a sign of early industrialization. Most other European economies remained predominantly agricultural through to 1870.

Measuring agricultural productivity in this period is very difficult owing to the severe data constraints. The data on labor and land inputs are poor; but the data on capital inputs are non-existent, which precludes any attempt to estimate total factor productivity. The data on arable agriculture are considerably better than the data on pastoral agriculture. This is partly because arable agriculture is immobile and tends to be taxed, whereas pastoral agriculture can be highly mobile and is therefore seldom or ineffectually taxed. But, also, there is a clear distinction in arable agriculture between inputs (such as seed and fertilizer) and outputs (such as grain and straw). By contrast, in pastoral agriculture an animal can be either an input (such as a breeding cow that gives milk and calves) or an output (such as a cow that is sent to the slaughter house for meat and leather); tax and census data on animals almost never distinguish between these different possibilities.

Table 6.2 European agricultural labor productivity (England = 100 in 1800)

	1600	1700	1750	1800
England	53.1	80.4	107.7	100.0
Belgium	88.1	83.9	85.3	77.6
Netherlands	74.1	86.7	103.5	100.7
France	50.3	51.7	55.9	58.0
Italy	58.0	56.6	49.0	39.9
Spain	53.1	60.8	55.9	49.0
Germany	39.9	37.8	39.2	46.9
Austria	39.9	51.7	69.9	51.5
Poland	54.5	65.7	65.0	74.8

Source: Derived from Allen, 2000, p. 20.

An alternative procedure is to derive agricultural output from the demand side. The crudest procedure is to assume constant consumption per head. However, economists have long established that the demand for food varies with income and relative prices. Using abundant historical data on wages and prices, together with standard assumptions concerning the price and income elasticities of demand, Allen (2000) derives the demand for food for a number of European economies for the period 1300–1800. Making allowances for known imports and exports of food then provides estimates of agricultural output. Dividing agricultural output by the agricultural labor force yields the results reported in Table 6.2.

We can see that England, Belgium, and the Netherlands were far more productive than other countries. This fits broadly with the emerging literature that stresses the divergence between northwestern Europe and the rest of the continent during the early modern period. This pattern of comparative productivity can also be seen in the later nineteenth century, when better quality data become available, based on direct observation of outputs. The data for 1890 in Table 6.3 show a very similar pattern of comparative productivity within Europe, with output per worker substantially higher in the northwest than in the rest of the continent.

There are a number of well-known and important difficulties in using labor productivity as an indicator. One problem is that we are measuring annual labor productivity as total output divided by all workers, rather than productivity per hour worked, and there could be systematic differences across countries in workforce utilization. For example, agricultural labor in traditional societies often had several sources of employment and these could include alternative sectors such as services (especially transport), construction, mining, or industry. Also, workers could be seasonally unemployed; their earnings

Table 6.3 European agricultural labor productivity in 1890 (United Kingdom = 100)

	1890
United Kingdom	100
Netherlands	82
Denmark	44
France	52
Italy	28
Spain	33
Germany	63

Source: O'Brien and Prados de la Escosura, 1992, p. 531.

might be enough to keep them living in the countryside year-round but there was not enough work to keep them occupied in the slack periods. This distinction was perhaps less important in a country such as England, where in 1700 the agricultural workforce consisted of family labor supplemented by young adults hired on annual contracts (Allen, 1994, p. 106). But it was important on the large Italian and Spanish *latifundios*, where the highly seasonal demand for labor led to temporary contracts and farm employment for the landless that was perhaps half that of those in northern Europe. The problem for much of southern and eastern Europe was the lack of year-round employment opportunities in agriculture.

However, if we take the above estimates as broadly representative then we need to consider just why labor productivity and rural living standards differed so markedly across Europe. This requires us to explain both why productivity and farmers' living standards failed to rise over much of eastern and southern Europe, and why labor productivity surged ahead in some areas of northwest Europe. Successive sections below look at technological change and population growth, urban markets and specialization, and institutional factors. We conclude with some general comments on the contribution of the agricultural sector to industrialization.

Technological change and the growth of productivity and population

The significant increase in Europe's population over the period 1700 to 1870, described in Chapter 2 of this volume, required an increase in food output if living standards were not to decline. Much of the European continent had long been settled, hence changes in the size of the population equate largely to changes in the density of population, rather than expansion at the geographical frontier as in North America or Australia. Much, though not all, of the increase in output between 1700 and 1870 is attributable to an increase in the intensity of rotations and the switch to new crops. In exceptional cases this could involve the planting and production of a high-value crop, such as grapes in the Médoc, but usually it involved much humbler ones such as the potato, which was high in calories and low in cost.

The Malthusian model of population notes that rising population makes land increasingly (relatively) scarce. We would expect this to prompt the adoption of land-saving techniques and result in a reduction in output per worker, since each worker has less land to cultivate. At first glance, the European evidence is consistent with this interpretation. For example, land was in limited supply in the Netherlands. Therefore, as the economy and population boomed in the seventeenth century as a result of the Dutch monopoly of the spice trade to Asia, it made sense to respond by both creating new land and intensifying production on existing land to meet the urban demand for food. This prompted both the reclamation of land from the sea using dykes, and the application of much more fertilizer to each unit of land. A comparable change in England in the eighteenth century was the replacement of fallow land by crops such as turnips and clover, thus making more intensive use of land resources and effectively increasing the area of cultivated land per worker. This technique reached its apogee in England in the mid-nineteenth century with the widespread adoption of the "Norfolk four-course" crop rotation, in which wheat cultivation in one year was followed by turnips in the next year, barley in the next, and clover in the next. This system was adopted in the nineteenth century in modified form in other northern European countries. In the English system the turnips and clover were fed to animals, which raised meat output for the voracious English market. In France and parts of central Europe the turnips were substituted with sugar beet; this made sense because the farmers faced a lower demand for meat (since incomes were lower and meat is an income-elastic good) and sugar was more expensive (since countries such as Germany did not have tropical colonies which could produce cheap cane sugar). Attempts were made around the Mediterranean to introduce the new rotations of northern Europe, but they usually failed because of the very different farming and market conditions found there.

Yet southern farmers were not necessarily disadvantaged in the same way as their northern counterparts when it came to rising population pressure. One of the problems of southern Europe was the periodic unemployment that occurred through the year, and intensification of production could help to solve this problem. First, in some areas the land, which had once provided only poor-quality natural grazing, was plowed up and cereals sown instead. Second, cereal rotations, which had provided just a single harvest every three or more years, were shortened so that crops were taken more frequently. Finally, the area under crops such as vines and olives increased. While a hectare of cereals in southern Spain in the 1880s provided only about 20 days' employment per year (less if fallow is taken into consideration), the vine required 80 days and the olive 30 days (Simpson, 1995). Contemporaries in Spain at this time considered that their natural resource endowment was favorable, and cereal producers in the 1850s and winegrowers in the 1870s looked to become major exporters. Their hopes were ruined only as the integration of global food markets led to New World countries capturing these export markets and then threatening Spain's domestic markets themselves. The situation was similar elsewhere in the Mediterranean. Tariffs were significantly increased on cereals in Spain in 1891, just as they were in France (1885–94), Italy (1887–94), and Portugal (1889–99). Spanish contemporaries came to reflect bitterly on what were then perceived as their country's poor natural resource endowments. In effect, the integration of the North Atlantic grain and livestock economy had shifted the comparative advantage of large areas of the Mediterranean from land-intensive agriculture to capital-intensive agriculture. The difficulties for farmers to adapt to this change were considerable, and the final stage in the process of crop intensification only came with modern irrigation, which required both the construction of large-scale reservoirs to store the water (as opposed to simply using free-flowing rivers and streams) and the development of biotechnologies to create new specialist crops to sell in national and international markets. Certainly there were some signs of change in the Mediterranean as early as 1870, but the process only acquired any real importance from the mid-twentieth century.

In eastern Europe, too, especially in the areas still dominated by serfdom, the introduction of new agricultural technologies occurred more slowly and unevenly than in the northwest. There were some entrepreneurial landlords who introduced new rotations and crops on their demesne lands. For example, in the mid-eighteenth century the Kleist family initiated a move from the traditional three-field grain system to a system of fallow-free convertible farming, which resulted in a substantial increase in output (Hagen, 2002, pp. 314–15). Further east, demand grew among more enterprising Russian landlords for English books on agricultural improvements.[1] There were even instances of Russian peasants themselves introducing modifications such as new fertilizers and non-grain crops on their own allotments (Moon, 1999, pp. 130–31). On the whole, however, the three-field system of grain cultivation (mainly wheat, rye,

---

[1] Konstantin Levin, the enthusiastic reformer in Tolstoy's *Anna Karenina*, was modelled on such a landlord. It is worth noting that in the end Levin abandons his reforms, having decided that English innovations were impossible in a Russian context.

and oats) remained in place throughout eastern Europe until well into the nineteenth century (in much of Russia it remained in place even after the abolition of serfdom in 1861). This was to some extent due to the different ecological conditions in this region (shorter growing seasons, different soils) and, in the case of the Russian empire, to an abundance of land, which reduced the pressure to intensify production. But even more important in central and eastern Europe were the institutional constraints imposed by serfdom and strong rural communities, about which more will be said later.

One example of crop intensification which achieved widespread success was the introduction of the potato. Although it had been known since the sixteenth century, when it had been brought by the Spanish from its native habitat in the Peruvian and Bolivian Andes, the potato was rarely grown in Europe before the late eighteenth century. Then a combination of growing population pressure, grain shortages, and famine, together with the development of new seed varieties, encouraged its spread – in the early 1770s to parts of Switzerland, Germany, and Austria, in the 1790s to France, and in the 1810s to Hungary and Poland (Blum, 1978, pp. 271–76). While France had about 20,000 hectares planted on the eve of the Revolution, the figure had risen to 3 million by the first decade of the nineteenth century. The potato provided many more calories per hectare than wheat or rye (but not necessarily in terms of hours worked), and allowed many small farmers to subsist, freeing them to use the rest of their land and labor to grow cash crops. Yet there were limits on an agricultural system excessively dependent on the potato, as it was both difficult to store and transport, which made it difficult for growers to accumulate savings as an insurance against crop failure (Mokyr, 1985).

Technological change could provide a way for the population to grow while simultaneously improving labor productivity and living standards. According to Boserup (1965), technological change occurs as a direct result of population pressure, as it is the increasing difficulty in meeting the current standard of living that spurs people to innovate. One could argue that the development of European agriculture fits this characterization, especially the increasing population pressure in the northwest and the response of increasing capitalization and the introduction of new crops to use land resources more intensively. But there are two caveats to this straightforward and attractive line of reasoning.

First, it is usual to draw a distinction between "technological change" and the "choice of technique." The former is a dynamic concept: new technology is created in response to high or rising input prices. The latter is a static concept: farmers are already aware of a range of possible production techniques and they choose the least-cost method of production given the prices that they face. Many of the fertilization techniques (such as liming and marling) that came into fashion in the eighteenth century in England and the Netherlands had been known for many years (even in Roman times), and farmers had merely chosen to reintroduce them because relative prices had shifted in such a way as to make it profitable once again. The same may also be true of some aspects of crop rotation, such as the increasing use of clover in England. In that sense, the changes that we see were simply a change in the choice of technique rather than technological change.

Second, England had one of the highest land–labor ratios in the world and should really have been inventing labor-saving technologies if it were responding to resource constraints in the way that Boserup suggested. But the evidence on this is very mixed. For example, attempts to introduce steam threshers in the 1820s sparked the Swing Riots, and the machines vanished in southern Britain until the 1850s (Hobsbawn and Rudé, 1968). Also, it seems likely that innovation in English plow technology was driven by local knowledge spillovers rather than local resource shortages (as signalled in the market place by the local relative prices of labor and capital) (Brunt, 2003). However, England did manage to introduce some labor-saving machinery at a relatively early date. Notably, by 1871 an estimated 25 percent of wheat in England and Wales was harvested by mechanical reapers, considerably more than in Germany (3.6 percent in 1882) or France (6.9 percent in 1882) (Collins, 1969). Some Mediterranean farmers also tested the new labor-saving equipment but rejected it in preference for the cheaper, traditional methods (Simpson, 1995; Federico, 2003).

It may be that a deeper understanding of technological change requires a more holistic view of agricultural production. Labor productivity in agriculture was greatly influenced by the ratio of draft animals to human labor. O'Brien and Keyder (1978, pp. 115–19) have suggested that English farmers had perhaps two-thirds more animal power than their French counterparts in 1800, helping to explain the differences in labor productivity.[2] The role of horsepower was crucial to increasing output both on and off the farm, and this was one of the areas where the Mediterranean region, for example, appears to have been at a major disadvantage compared with northern Europe. While the technological barrier to increasing the number of farm animals in northern Europe was the lack of winter fodder, a problem overcome with the planting of crops such as turnips, in southern Europe the seasonal shortages of feed occurred during the summer months. South of Poitou in France the possibilities of growing spring cereals were limited, cereal yields were perhaps only as much as a third of those in the north, and the long dry summers produced poor-quality grass. Irrigation was an expensive solution, and this energy

---

[2] Wrigley (1991, p. 329) calculates that French farm workers had about 2.1 "man-hours" of horse labor to assist him for each hour worked, compared with a figure of 3.5 hours for the English workers.

restriction remained in the Mediterranean region until the massive introduction of tractors in the second half of the twentieth century.

Urbanization, markets, and farm specialization

Adam Smith (1966, Book 3, Chapter IV) wrote that "through the greater part of Europe the commerce and manufactures of cities, instead of being the effect, have been the cause and occasion of the improvement and cultivation of the country." The concentration in cities of consumers with high incomes gave farmers a major incentive to specialize in commodities whose income elasticities of demand were higher than that of cereals. Economic historians such as Jack Fisher or Tony Wrigley in particular emphasized the role played by London. Outside England and the Netherlands (with its urbanization rate of 30 percent) the pull of the urban market was much weaker for most farmers. In 1850, on the eve of the railway age, levels of urbanization were 15 percent in France, 11 percent in Germany, 17 percent in Spain, 20 percent in Italy, and just 8 percent in Austria–Bohemia and 9 percent in Poland (de Vries, 1984, table 3.8).

A high degree of urbanization might encourage farmers to specialize, but it was the efficiency with which food could be brought from the countryside to the city which would play a major factor in determining the size of the city in the first place. Therefore if Smith could write in the 1770s that the prices of bread and butchers' meat were generally the same, or very roughly the same, throughout the greater part of Britain, this was hardly the case in some parts of Europe even a century later.

Two types of obstacle to domestic trade can be identified. First, there was the physical cost of transportation. Second, there were institutional impediments such as taxes or the need for official transport permits, or the outright prohibition of the movements of goods and (in the case of eastern Europe) people. These two features were not entirely separate. In England communications were good because of the abundance of settlements located close to navigable water, the relatively small distances, and the good flow of market information. The risk of famine was also low. On the one hand, government policy encouraged farmers to continue planting even at times of abundance, since there were effectively guaranteed minimum prices to farmers because bounties were paid on exports in times of low domestic prices. On the other hand, in times of unexpectedly small harvests (due, for example, to several consecutive seasons of bad weather), the workers' relatively high incomes attracted imports to make up the shortfall.

The English case can be contrasted with the situation in much of continental Europe. Grain marketing there was very heavily controlled, especially in the eighteenth century, with only certain places being permitted to hold grain markets and farmers being obliged to market any surplus grain through those markets; selling outside the market was illegal and subject to very harsh legal sanctions (Persson, 1999). Transport was costly and information on the size of harvests and stocks was limited or non-existent for consumers. Rumors of shortages could set off panic buying in towns and this encouraged merchants to move grain from the countryside, where consumers had limited savings, for resale in urban markets. Yet *ancien régime* governments used a whole battery of measures to protect further urban consumers: maximum prices, restrictions on grain movements, government granaries, and so on. The urban policy bias could discourage grain planting, especially after poor harvests when price ceilings effectively expropriated the profits of farmers. Farmers might try to increase their profits by switching to other crops such as the vine, but often found that they were prohibited from doing so. Another obstacle for much of continental Europe was that goods transported and introduced into urban areas were taxed, a feature that continued well into the twentieth century in some countries.

Famine was a significant problem in early modern Europe, as can be seen by the "massive famines of the 1690s in France, Sweden and Finland, 1708–09 in France, and 1740–41 in Ireland" (Ó Gráda, 2007, p. 31). The Irish famine of 1846–52 led to an excess mortality of perhaps a million people. But by 1870, serious famine was history in most of western Europe, with a few exceptional cases such as the Netherlands or Greece in 1944–45. By contrast, wars and Stalinism led to at least three major famines in the east during the first half of the twentieth century. Research on developing economies shows that famines are not necessarily caused by an overall lack of food in an economy; instead they are caused by a maldistribution of food, either because some social classes cannot afford the food they need or because the food cannot be transported to the place where it is most needed (Sen, 1981). The same was largely true of Europe in the period from 1700 to 1870: the structure of local food markets profoundly affected how well the agricultural sector met the demands placed upon it by the wider economy.

Despite the physical and legal constraints they faced, grain merchants did their best to trade with one another when price differences were sufficient to overcome the institutional and transport costs. But how big were these inter-city prices differences and how did they change over time in response to increasing political stability and improved communication networks? These price differences provide one metric of the degree of market integration. A second metric is that of the speed of adjustment. How long does it take merchants in London to respond to a price spike in Paris by arbitraging the two market prices back down to the level of the transport cost between the two cities? Consumers and producers will both be better off, on average, if the speed of adjustment is faster.

Jacks (2005) examined grain price series for 100 cities in Europe and North America between 1800 and 1913. He found that markets in northwestern Europe – such as England and Belgium – were generally already well integrated by 1800, both within countries and between them. Price differences were low and adjustment speeds were high. Moving further south and east in Europe was associated with generally lower levels of market integration on both measures, with Austria-Hungary and Spain performing particularly badly. Jacks found considerable evidence of falling price differentials up to 1870 for all countries, but no improvement in adjustment speeds. Regression analysis of both price differentials and adjustment speeds revealed the type of economic behavior that we would expect to find: better transport links (canals, railways, ports, and river connections) resulted in smaller price differentials and higher adjustment speeds. However, it is interesting to note that Jacks (2006) shows that improvements in market integration over time were not due to improvements in transport networks; instead, they were due to improved political stability. Whilst Jacks's results are certainly interesting, Coleman (1999) argues that tests of market integration based on prices alone may be misleading, because it is difficult to distinguish between increased synchronicity of shocks and increased speed of adjustment. Brunt and Cannon (2007) address this problem by breaking down price differentials into four components: the average price differential, the variance of the price shocks, the correlation between the shocks and the two price series, and the speed of adjustment of one series to the other. They find that for England between 1770 and 1820 virtually all the deviation from the "law of one price" was due to the average price differential, rather than the adjustment speed; like Jacks, they find that the marked improvement in roads and canals over the period had very little effect.

For some regions, export markets were of particular importance. By the late eighteenth century the major trade flows in basic foodstuffs, such as grain, were from the Baltic (especially East Prussia and Poland) towards northwest Europe (especially the Netherlands, which was both a consuming center and a distribution hub). From the early nineteenth century onwards, England became the major European importer and began to draw grain additionally from Russia through the Black Sea. The total quantities shipped were nonetheless quite small compared with overall consumption; even in England in the 1850s, after the move to free trade, wheat imports amounted to only around 25 percent of total consumption. There was very little impact from trade with the New World before 1870 (O'Rourke, 1997; O'Rourke and Williamson, 1999).

Wine had been an important commodity in international trade in earlier periods, but between the mid-seventeenth and the late eighteenth centuries the production of specialized fine wines underwent major transformations that changed the patterns of trade and consumption. Port was a drink developed by British merchants in Portugal for consumption in Britain. The development of fine wines in the Bordeaux region can be dated to the period between about 1650 and 1740, involving the draining of the Médoc and the introduction of cylindrical bottles and corks that allowed the best wines to be matured in bottles. Producers in Champagne learnt to overcome the difficulties of a second fermentation in the bottle and began to market their wine as a luxury product worldwide (Guy, 2003). The poor keeping-quality of most wines, high transaction costs, and high levels of taxation everywhere limited the possibility for European farmers to utilize labor more intensively and obtain productivity gains through market specialization in wine. Nevertheless, wines were very important export items, accounting for about half of all Portugal's exports in 1850, a quarter of Spain's, and a tenth of France's.

Institutions

The empirical findings described in the previous sections indicate significant variation in labor productivity, technological progress, and market integration across Europe in this period. Still, a broad pattern can be discerned: southern and eastern Europe lagged behind the northwestern regions – especially England and the Netherlands – in all these areas until well into the nineteenth century. How can we account for these differences? While climate, geography, and differences between cultures may well have had some effect on outcomes, the role of institutions – in particular the procedures established to uphold property rights and enforce contracts – must not be overlooked.

An institutional approach seeks to explain differences in productivity as resulting from differences in the economic, social, or legal frameworks that characterize a particular society. For instance, without secure property rights farmers – regardless of cultural beliefs or length of growing season – were unlikely to invest in agricultural innovations, since they could not be sure that the returns to such investments would accrue to them. Without a reliable system of contract enforcement, peasant farmers could not obtain credit, and thus could not undertake expensive innovations. Property rights and contract enforcement varied substantially across Europe (and within any given country) in this period. How these processes worked in any given place was largely determined by the local institutional framework – in particular, by the strength of local corporate entities, such as landlords, churches, and communities.

In England these groups were relatively weak. Instead, there was a remarkably centralized legal framework and system of courts, which developed at a very early date. Even in the medieval period, when the Church and landlords were quite powerful and had much control over their peasant tenants (serfs), an integrated system of courts was used, even by serfs, for the resolution of property and credit disputes.[3] Not only were there manorial courts, where disputes regarding transactions among serfs were heard, there were also royal courts, to which cases could even be brought against landlords who violated customary agreements by raising rents or demanding additional labor. This legal framework was not nearly as sophisticated as that which exists today, but it nonetheless sufficiently reduced the risk involved in transactions to enable the existence of lively rural markets in land and credit, as well as grain and livestock. (English agricultural productivity was aided by later developments, such as the enclosure of open fields, which resulted in even more clearly defined property rights.)

In much of southern Europe, rights to property were less clearly defined, and improvements in agriculture were hindered by disputes between powerful local groups over control of resources. Due to uncertainty in property rights in parts of *Ancien Régime* France, landlords and villagers could often claim rights to the same lands (Rosenthal, 1992; Hoffman, 1996). While France did have a system of courts to decide such questions, this system did not function particularly well. The litigation process was slow and costly, and decisions that were granted could be appealed repeatedly. This did little to reduce uncertainty, and innovation remained a risky undertaking. The situation only improved, with greater investment in technological innovation, when a uniform system of clearly assigned property rights was introduced by the Revolution.

Agriculture in Spain, too, was affected by uncertainty in property rights. "Ownership" in Spain often had several layers, with those who had rights to the rents from land being distinguished from those who had the right to cultivate it (*dominium directum* and *dominium utile*) (Simpson, 1995). Agricultural innovations were further hindered by powerful local groups, who held special privileges from the crown. One such institution was the Mesta, a powerful association of shepherds and sheep owners on which the crown, in exchange for payment, had bestowed rights to pasture on all traditionally unsown land. While there has been some debate in recent years over the broader economic effects of Mesta privileges (Nugent and Sanchez, 1989), many historians maintain (as did contemporary observers) that the powers of the Mesta made it difficult to enclose property and delayed bringing pasture under cultivation, and thus limited the possibilities for improving agricultural production.

Landlords' powers had similarly negative effects on agricultural productivity. In some parts of Italy (such as Tuscany) landlords were able to control the way

---

[3] Even in a place as centralized as England there was institutional variation. Recent research on rural debt litigation in the thirteenth and fourteenth centuries suggests that manorial court procedures – and the way courts were perceived to function by local inhabitants – had a significant effect on the size and shape of local credit markets. See Briggs (2006).

in which tenants' lands were allocated and used. Many retained the right to terminate leases at will. Insecurity of tenure and the regular confiscation of surpluses made it unlikely that tenant farmers in these regions would invest in improving yields. In central and eastern Europe, landlords had even greater powers. Much of Europe east of the river Elbe was in this period still under the "second serfdom,"[4] a tenurial system in which landlords had significant control over the allocation of their tenants' labor. Serfs are often said to have been "tied to the land" because, in most serf societies, they were not free to leave their landlords' holdings. They cultivated land which they rented from their lords and for which they usually paid an annual fee in cash or kind. In addition, many serfs were obliged to spend several days a week cultivating their landlord's own land (demesne). Serfs were thus unable to allocate their full supply of labor to their own plots, and any attempt to increase productivity was undermined. And they had no incentive to use their labor efficiently on the demesne, as the benefits of their exertion accrued mainly to the landlord.

Landlords under the second serfdom engaged in various forms of rent seeking. Some held monopolies on brewing and insisted their tenants buy local beer at inflated prices. Some held monopolies on milling and insisted their tenants bring grain to the manorial mill. Most landlords extracted fees from their tenants for permission to marry or to travel beyond the estate boundaries.[5] It might be argued that serfs were often able to evade estate policies, thus minimizing their effects on productivity. However, getting round rules and regulations was also costly. Serfs often had to pay bribes to estate officials and risked fines for violating estate rules. The end result was a steady confiscation of surpluses which made it very difficult for peasant farmers to accumulate the wealth necessary to invest in improving their yields. Such rent seeking simultaneously provided a disincentive for such investments, since the returns were anyway likely to be siphoned off by landlords.

Incentives for innovation were further undermined by strong local communities. In much of central Europe, communities controlled access to land through their power to regulate transfers. For instance, in the Württemberg Black Forest, peasant farmers could not sell or bequeath holdings without the permission of the community. Village communities in this region regulated access to common resources, and were responsible for deciding how arable land would be used. Those who wished to plant new crops or adopt new technologies had to have the permission of village officials.[6] Strong local communities also existed under the second serfdom. Like the communities in Württemberg, they,

---

[4] "Second" because it came after medieval serfdom or "feudalism," though it is worth noting that not all places which experienced a "second" serfdom had experienced a "first."

[5] Examples of such practices can be found in Ogilvie (2001); Hagen (2002), Dennison (2006); Dennison and Ogilvie (2007).

[6] See discussion in Ogilvie (1997), esp. ch. 3; Warde (2006).

together with landlords, had the power to regulate transfers and take decisions about the use of commons and arable. In many places, serf communities had the power to take land away from households they viewed as not economically viable. On estates in Bohemia and in Prussia, for instance, widows could be forced by the community to remarry in order to retain their holdings (Ogilvie and Edwards, 2000; Hagen, 2002). In Russian serf society, where most arable was held in communal tenure, communal officials allocated land in accordance with the number of laborers and consumers in each household. When a household changed in composition, these officials had the power to reallocate some portion of its land to another, larger household.

Restrictions on mobility, enforced by both landlords and communities, affected the pace of urbanization and market integration in central and eastern Europe. In serf societies, those who paid rents in cash or kind could often get permission to engage in migrant labor in nearby towns or cities, though they were not generally permitted to migrate permanently. They were still required to fulfill certain annual obligations on the estate – or at least hire someone to fulfill them in their absence. Serfs who owed regular labor on the landlord's demesne were less likely to obtain permission to leave, even temporarily. Communities in serf societies, as well as in areas without serfdom, often had a say in whether their members were allowed to travel, as well as in whether new householders could settle in the village. Many landlords required that a serf obtain the permission of the community before he or she would agree to issue travel documents. Not surprisingly, then, this region urbanized much more slowly. Even at the beginning of the nineteenth century, there were no cities as big as London or Paris in central or eastern Europe.

Conclusion

It is no coincidence that those places where agricultural productivity improved first were also the first to industrialize. For industrialization to occur, it had to be possible to produce more food with fewer people. England was able to do this because markets tended to be more efficient, and incentives for farmers to increase output were strong. As labor flowed to the cities, agricultural output and imports of food and raw materials increased. By 1840, labor productivity in agriculture was as high as that of the rest of the economy (Crafts, 1985a).

Why did other countries, especially those in eastern and southern Europe, take longer to increase farm output and productivity? Natural resource endowments were clearly different from those of northwest Europe, which perhaps made it harder to develop and introduce new farming techniques and commercial crops. However, a greater obstacle would appear to have been the fact that there were fewer incentives for farmers to change production systems, either because they faced major difficulties in reaching potential consumers, or because institutional arrangements failed to overcome problems of market failure.

When new techniques, crop rotations, or the reorganization of land owner-ship were rejected, it was not necessarily because economic agents were averse to change, but because the traditional systems were considered more profitable by those with vested interests. Agricultural productivity in southern and east-ern Europe may have been low, but the large landowners were often exceed-ingly rich, and were successful in maintaining policies which favored the current production systems. In Britain, the abolition of the Corn Laws and the collapse in domestic cereal prices, especially after 1873, not only seriously challenged the economic and political base of the country's aristocracy and landowning classes, but also increased urban real wages, thereby providing new opportunities for other forms of farming, such as labor-intensive market gardening. Outside northwest Europe, changes did take place between 1700 and 1870, but tended to be more localized. Only in the twentieth century did parts of southern and eastern Europe begin to achieve productivity levels found in the northwest in the late nineteenth century.

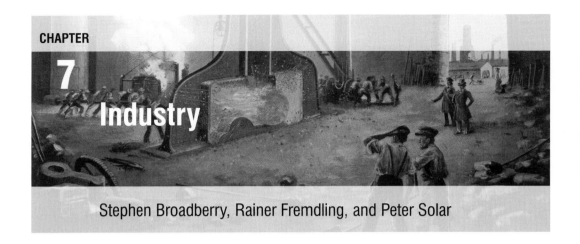

Industry

Stephen Broadberry, Rainer Fremdling, and Peter Solar

Contents

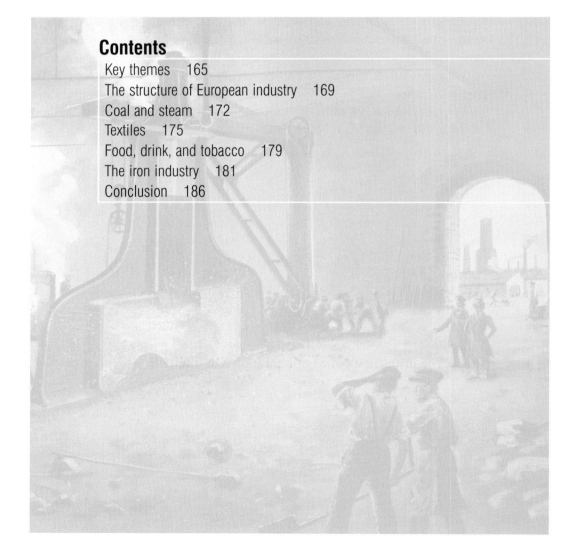

The transition to modern economic growth occurred in Europe between the mid-eighteenth and mid-nineteenth centuries. The decisive breakthrough was made in Britain, and centered on the adoption of new technologies and methods of organization in industry. Although economic historians now see these changes as quite drawn out, building on already high shares of economic activity in industry, and involving only a modest increase in the growth rate before 1830, the term "Industrial Revolution" has continued to be widely used (Crafts, 1985a; Shaw-Taylor and Wrigley, 2008). As de Vries (2001) argues, the changes associated with industrialization were revolutionary in the sense that they proved to be irreversible and became an "ideal type," like the French Revolution. Although the rest of Europe did not merely copy the British example – there were "different paths to the twentieth century" – the idea of "catching up" remains a useful starting point for thinking about continental industrial developments between the late eighteenth and the late nineteenth centuries (O'Brien and Keyder, 1978; Gerschenkron, 1962; Fremdling, 2000). Working at the pan-European level helps to make clear the fundamental significance of the Industrial Revolution for the history of mankind, something which can be lost when focusing on national developments.

Key themes

Technological progress

It is common in the literature on technological progress to make distinctions between invention, innovation, diffusion, and imitation (Mokyr, 1994, pp. 13–16). An invention is defined as a new discovery, while an innovation is the commercial application of an invention. Although the distinction is blurred in practice, there are some obvious examples, such as Leonardo da Vinci's technical sketches for a helicopter, which remained dormant for centuries. The distinction between innovation and diffusion is between the first commercial application of an invention and its widespread use. This distinction may also be blurred in practice, because an innovation often requires some modification before it can become widely diffused. Similarly, the distinction between innovation and imitation can become blurred if a company or a society that sets out to imitate ends up innovating. Twentieth century Japan is a well-known example of this, but there is also an element of it in Britain during the Industrial Revolution.

Economists have recently used the idea of a General Purpose Technology (GPT) to shed light on periods of accelerating economic growth. Lipsey,

Carlaw and Bekar (2005, p. 98) define a GPT as "a single generic technology recognisable as such over its whole lifetime, that initially has much scope for improvement and eventually comes to be widely used, to have many uses, and to have many spillover effects." The concept was born to explain the acceleration of economic growth with the recent widespread adoption of information and communications technology (ICT), but has obvious historical parallels in earlier periods of accelerating growth such as the Industrial Revolution. We shall examine the extent to which steam power can be seen as the first GPT, and assess its contribution to economic growth during the Industrial Revolution.

Wages and technology

Factor prices may be expected to affect the choice of technology. However, although this idea has received a lot of attention in explaining technological differences between Europe and the United States in the nineteenth century, it has received rather less attention in the context of the differences between Europe and Asia during the early stages of the Industrial Revolution. Writing about transatlantic differences in the nineteenth century, Habakkuk (1962) argued that high wages in the United States induced a substitution of capital for labor (more machines) and a labor-saving bias in the direction of technological progress (better machines). Broadberry and Gupta (2006) have recently pointed out that the scale of the wage gap between northwest Europe and Asia was substantially larger on the eve of the Industrial Revolution than the wage gap between Britain and the United States during the nineteenth century. This is important, because the breakthrough to modern factory industry occurred in the British cotton textile industry, which displaced the Indian industry as the major producer and exporter of cotton textiles. Faced with money wages that were five or six times as high in Britain as in India, British firms could not hope to compete using labor-intensive Indian production methods.

Factor prices are also important in explaining the sometimes long delay in the adoption of modern British technology in much of continental Europe. Whilst writers such as Landes (1969) have seen this as the result of entrepreneurial failure, this view does not do justice to the conditions actually faced by entrepreneurs who had to take account of the differences in factor prices between Britain and the rest of Europe. This often meant that the new technology, which had been developed to suit British factor prices, could not be used profitably on the Continent without further technological improvement or adaptation to local circumstances (Fremdling, 2004; Broadberry, 1997).

Energy

Another important factor price was that of energy. With a growing shortage of wood, there was an increasing incentive to substitute coal for wood as the major source of energy. This can be seen as leading to the innovation of coke smelting (Hyde, 1977). Allen (2006) argues that the combination of high wages and cheap coal was important in explaining both the development of the key technologies of the Industrial Revolution in Britain, and the delay in their adoption in other European countries.

Wrigley (2004b) sees this substitution of coal for wood as a crucial development, enabling Europe to escape from the constraints of the "organic economy" by tapping into the stored-up energy of millions of years embodied in coal seams. Coal replaced wood as a source of heat energy in a growing range of industries during the eighteenth century. This occurred initially in processes such as boiling salt and sugar refining, where the source of heat and the object to be heated could be separated by a physical barrier to prevent chemical contamination. Over time, it extended to industries such as bricks, pottery, glass, and brewing, as a result of technical developments which prevented pollution from ruining the product. The culmination of this process was the use of coke for smelting iron. Coal, via the steam engine, also provided the solution to the constraints on mechanical energy provided by reliance on animals, wind, and water power. Steam power played an important role in many sectors of the economy, spreading from its initial role in pumping water out of mines to providing motive power in manufacturing, driving steamships and trains, and powering agricultural machinery such as threshers (Crafts, 2004).

Knowledge and human capital

Economists today generally place a great deal of emphasis on the contribution of knowledge and human capital to growth. Until recently, however, economic historians and historians of science have tended to be rather skeptical about their contribution to the Industrial Revolution. On the role of knowledge, although there was an attempt by Musson and Robinson (1969) to argue for a strong link between science and innovation during the Industrial Revolution, most economic historians remained skeptical. As von Tunzelmann (1981, pp. 148–51) noted, science had not been brought into a consistent framework and much of it was simply wrong. Furthermore, the crucial innovations of the Industrial Revolution were a long way from the major areas of scientific enquiry, and anyway science was in better health in continental Europe than in Britain where the decisive breakthroughs were made. More recently, however, Mokyr (2002) has argued for a more general interrelationship between "propositional knowledge" (science) and "prescriptive knowledge" (engineering). Interactions between these two types of knowledge are seen as important in preventing the cluster of innovations during the Industrial Revolution from petering out and running into diminishing returns, as had happened after previous bursts of innovation.

Economic historians have often been quite dismissive of the role of the patent system during the Industrial Revolution, pointing more to its shortcomings than its advantages (Landes, 1969; MacLeod, 1988). However, a number of authors have recently suggested a more positive role for the patent system, drawing on the importance attached to intellectual property rights in the recent literature on technological change, and pointing to the large sums that inventors were prepared to pay for patent protection (Sullivan, 1989; Broadberry and Gupta, 2008). Of course, much crucial knowledge was also embodied in skilled workers and passed on by doing rather than by being written down. Both types of knowledge can be shown to have played a role in the industries discussed below.

Although human capital has been seen as crucial to economic growth in recent times, it has rarely featured as a major factor in accounts of the Industrial Revolution. One problem is that the machinery of the Industrial Revolution is usually characterized as de-skilling, substituting relatively unskilled labor for skilled artisans, and leading to a decline in apprenticeship (Mitch, 2004, p. 347). A second problem is that the widespread use of child labor raised the opportunity cost of schooling (Mitch, 1993, p. 276).

The organization of industry

Before the Industrial Revolution, much of industry was conducted on a small-scale and part-time basis in the countryside. Of course, there were exceptions, such as mining, metal smelting, and grain milling, which required large fixed investments, and even in industries without such large capital requirements there were always craftsmen working full-time in towns and cities (Clarkson, 1985, pp. 9–10).

Mendels (1972) used the term "proto-industry" to describe this type of rural production, which he identified as the "first stage of industrialization." The stage approach was further developed by Kriedte et al. (1981), who tried to identify a more detailed progression. In the first stage, or *Kaufsystem*, artisanal producers retained control over production in rural workshops. In a second stage, or *Verlagsystem*, merchants took control by putting out work to rural producers working in their homes. The third stage is seen as the development of "centralized manufactories and mechanized factories" (Ogilvie and Cerman, 1996, p. 4). Although the specific theory of proto-industrialization, and the dynamics of the progression between stages, have received much criticism, most economic historians have continued to see the emergence of the factory system as an important part of the Industrial Revolution.

One aspect of economic development highlighted in the proto-industrialization framework is the importance of the region, sometimes cutting across national borders, as a unit of analysis (Pollard, 1981, pp. 63–78). However, notice that this framework, by focusing on industrial employment in the countryside as a sign of economic dynamism, sits uneasily with work emphasizing the links between urbanization and economic development (de Vries, 1984). It is only with the emergence of factory employment in towns that we see the emergence of genuine "Marshallian industrial districts," characterized by external economies of scale. As cotton mills clustered together in Lancashire towns, although each individual firm faced constant returns to scale, the industry as a whole faced increasing returns to scale. The external economies arose through learning (knowledge spillovers between firms), matching (thick markets making it easier to match employers and employees), and sharing (giving firms access to customers and suppliers in the presence of significant transport costs) (Duranton and Puga, 2004).

The structure of European industry

Tables 7.1 and 7.2 present a rough quantitative picture of European industry around 1870. Table 7.1, which shows the overall distribution of industry, reveals that the process of industrialization had gone much further in some parts of the continent than in others. The share of industry in GDP was over 30 percent in only four countries: the United Kingdom, France, Belgium, and Switzerland, a contiguous area that could be seen as the industrial heartland of Europe at this time. Similarly, these were the only countries for which their share of European industrial production was greater than their share of European GDP. Germany, on the eve of its great burst of industrial development, was the only country with between 25 and 30 percent of its GDP coming from industry, and its share of European industry was similar to its share of GDP. In all other countries the share of European industry was a good deal less than the share of European GDP. A number of countries had an industrial share of between 20 and 25 percent: greater Austria, which at this time included much of what is now the Czech Republic and Slovenia, Italy, Spain, the Netherlands, Denmark, and Sweden. With Germany these countries formed a contiguous ring around the heartland. Finally, there were a number of

Table 7.1 Industry in Europe, c.1870: overall distribution

	Industry share in country GDP	Country share in European industry	Country share in European GDP
	%		
Northwestern Europe			
Belgium	30	3.9	3.4
Denmark	20	0.6	0.8
Finland	17	0.3	0.6
Netherlands	24	1.8	2.1
Norway	12		
Sweden	21	1.0	1.3
United Kingdom	34	30.3	25.5
Southern Europe			
France	34	18.9	15.8
Italy	24	10.0	11.6
Spain	22	3.6	4.7
Portugal	17	0.7	1.1
Central and eastern Europe			
Austria-Hungary	19	9.0	13.1
Austria	*23*	*7.2*	*8.8*
Hungary	*12*	*1.8*	*4.4*
Germany	28	19.8	20.0
Switzerland	36		

Sources: GDP in 1870 boundaries: Broadberry and Klein, 2008; Belgium: personal communication from Antoon Soete; Denmark: Hansen, 1970, pp. 11, 18, 71–73; Finland: Hjerppe, 1989, pp. 78, 218; Netherlands: Smits et al., 2000, pp. 130–41; Norway: personal communication from Ola Grytten; Sweden: Schön, 1988, pp. 208–17; United Kingdom: Feinstein, 1972, table 51; Broadberry, 1997; France: Lévy-Leboyer and Bourguignon, 1990, pp. 272, 314; Lévy-Leboyer, 1968, p. 806; Italy: Fenoaltea, 2003, p. 1084; Spain: Prados de la Escosura, 2003, pp. 259–74; Portugal: Lains, 2003, p. 138, 2006, p. 152; Austria-Hungary: Schulze, 2000, pp. 316, 339–40; Germany: Hoffmann, 1965, pp. 390–91, 451; Switzerland: personal communication from Thomas David.

countries on the periphery of Europe – Portugal, Norway, Finland, and greater Hungary (including Slovakia and parts of Poland and Romania) – that had industrial sectors accounting for less than 20 percent of GDP. These countries are representative of the even less industrialized countries – Russia, Turkey, and much of southeastern Europe – for which reliable statistical information is wanting.

Table 7.2 shows, in the first instance, the broad composition of Europe's industrial production in 1870. More than half, accounting for about 17 percent of European GDP, catered to what were still the basics of life – food, clothing, and shelter. The other notable manufacturing activity was metals and metal working, which took in primarily the production of iron and steel and their transformation into rails and locomotives, ships, steam engines, and other machines. Mining supplied raw materials and energy for some industrial

Table 7.2 Industry in Europe, c.1870: major branches and countries

	Share of European GDP	Share of European production			
		UK	France	Germany	Big three
		%			
Food, drink, tobacco	5.7	21	16	19	57
Textiles, clothing	7.6	29	24	22	75
Metals	3.4	45	5	24	74
Other manufacturing	4.5	16	23	25	64
Construction	3.7	17	32	13	62
Mining	3.0	70	5	12	87
Utilities	0.3	43	20	11	74
Total industry	28.0	30	19	20	69
GDP		26	16	21	63

Sources: As Table 7.1.

activity, but much of its output was coal for domestic heating. Around 1870, before the advent of electricity, the small utilities sector was mainly occupied with the production of gas for lighting.

Table 7.2 also shows the shares of Europe's three biggest economies – the United Kingdom, France, and Germany – in production by sector. Together they accounted for over two-thirds of industrial output, as against about 60 percent of European GDP. Their shares in construction and food processing, both activities in which there was little or no trade, were similar to their shares in GDP. The big three stand out in textiles and clothing, and metal and metalworking. Here they accounted for about three-quarters of European output, with the United Kingdom being particularly important in metals and metalworking. The most remarkable feature of this table is that the United Kingdom alone was responsible for over two-thirds of all mining activity in Europe.

How had European industry changed since 1700? Table 7.3, based on the work of Bairoch (1982), provides a rough quantitative picture of the scale and geographical unevenness of the expansion of European industry between the mid-eighteenth and mid-nineteenth centuries. The way in which Bairoch assembled the data is not transparent, but with one important exception, the results fit well with the large secondary literature on the subject, and can at least be seen as providing a broad guide to the orders of magnitude. The exception is the case of the United Kingdom, where a major revision of the Hoffmann (1955) industrial production index used by Bairoch (1982) has been undertaken by Crafts and Harley (1992) and incorporated here. This results in a substantially slower rate of growth of UK industrial output between 1750 and

Table 7.3 Per capita levels of industrialization, 1750–1860 (UK in 1860 = 100)

	1750	1800	1830	1860
Northwestern Europe				
Belgium	14	16	22	44
Denmark	–	13	13	16
Finland	–	13	13	17
Netherlands	–	14	14	17
Norway	–	14	14	17
Sweden	11	13	14	23
United Kingdom	28	30	39	100
Southern Europe				
France	14	14	19	31
Greece	–	8	8	9
Italy	13	13	13	16
Portugal	–	11	11	13
Spain	11	11	13	17
Central and eastern Europe				
Austria-Hungary	11	11	13	17
Bulgaria	–	8	8	8
Germany	13	13	14	23
Romania	–	8	8	9
Russia	9	9	11	13
Serbia	–	8	8	9
Switzerland	11	16	25	41
Europe	13	13	17	27
World	11	9	11	11

Sources: Derived from Bairoch, 1982; UK data before 1830 amended using the industrial production index from Crafts and Harley 1992.

1830, and hence a much higher level of industrialization in 1750 and 1800 than was suggested by Bairoch.

Table 7.3 shows us that on a per capita basis the United Kingdom was already by far the most industrialized country in Europe in 1750, before the classic Industrial Revolution period, as emphasized by Crafts (1985a). Elsewhere in Europe the differences in levels of industrialization in the mid-eighteenth century were modest.

Coal and steam

From the sixteenth century onwards, Britain led the way in the use and exploitation of coal, as wood could no longer meet the increasing demand for energy, particularly for heating London, by 1700 the largest city in Europe. A shift of relative prices in favor of coal, with which Britain was relatively well endowed, led to a process of substitution. Since the possibilities of substituting

Table 7.4 Output of coal in 1860

	000 tonnes	% of Europe
Austria	3,189	2.7
Belgium	9,611	8.0
France	8,304	6.9
Germany	16,731	13.9
Great Britain	81,327	67.6
Hungary	475	0.4
Italy (1861)	34	0.0
Russia	300	0.2
Spain	340	0.3
Sweden	26	0.0

Note: Hard coal and brown coal (lignite) are lumped together.
Source: Mitchell, 2003.

coal for wood were less than perfect, this process also brought about large-scale technological change (Buenstorf, 2001). Coal was increasingly used in industrial processes requiring heat, culminating in the use of coke for smelting iron, and was also used to create mechanical energy through the steam engine. The high costs of transportation meant that industrialization in Europe during the early nineteenth century became strongly linked to location on or near a coalfield (Pollard, 1981, pp. xiv–xv). Eventually, coal played an important role in reducing transport costs by means of the railways and steamships, thus freeing industry from the need to locate on or near a coalfield.

In the early exploitation of coal for various purposes and in the sheer size of this industry, the British Isles tremendously outstripped any other European country far into the nineteenth century. Table 7.4 shows the dominance of the British coal industry around 1860, when Britain alone produced more than twice the coal of all other European countries taken together. British coal mines not only supplied domestic customers but during the nineteenth century increasingly also foreign markets, including the rapidly expanding international fleet of steamships (Fremdling, 1989, 1996). In the middle of the nineteenth century, imports of coal from Britain helped continental countries and regions poorly endowed with coal to apply British-style coal-consuming technologies and thus catch up with the British model of industrialization.

To a large extent the success of early industrializing Belgium was based on the coal deposits in the Sambre-Meuse region (Pollard, 1981, pp. 87–90). After France, Germany was the second largest importer of British coal during the nineteenth century. Nevertheless, Germany also became the second largest exporter of coal after Britain. This peculiar development reveals important features of coal production and coal markets. For hard coal, the two most important German mining districts, namely the Ruhr and Upper Silesia, were both located far away from the coast and closer to the western or southeastern borders than to northern, central and southern parts of Germany. All coal mining districts became major centers of industry. Above all, the Ruhr with its heavy industry was to become the most important industrial region of continental Europe (Holtfrerich, 1973).

In the long run, coal mining could cope with the growing demand only by exploring coal deposits deep beneath the surface. The major problem was pumping out water, and the solution was the steam engine. The steam engine is conventionally associated with James Watt, who obtained his first patent on this innovation in 1769. As with many inventions, Watt's achievement has to be placed in a long process of trial and error, stretching back to Newcomen's atmospheric engine of 1712 (Mokyr, 1990, pp. 84–90). The diffusion of the Newcomen engine, which relied on harnessing the atmosphere as a source of power by creating a vacuum, was limited because of the machine's enormous appetite for fuel. During the eighteenth century, the steam engine was almost exclusively applied to the drainage of mines, where coal was available at cheap prices. The Watt engine, with its separate condenser, raised fuel efficiency by nearly five times compared with Newcomen's design. Watt also designed a transmission mechanism which converted the up-and-down-motion of the beam engine into a rotary motion. This way, the steam engine became the prime mover for machines in the textile industry and various other applications, such as the steamship and the steam locomotive.

Some writers have tended to play down the role of the steam engine, since it was not widely used during the early phase of the Industrial Revolution. Kanefsky (1979) shows that waterwheels generated as much power as steam engines as late as 1830. Thus the finding of von Tunzelmann (1978) that the social saving of the stationary steam engine in Britain was only 0.2 percent of GDP in 1801 is not too surprising. However, this may understate the importance of the steam engine if what matters is the avoidance of the onset of diminishing returns and if the steam engine helped to sustain productivity improvements across a wide range of activities. Calculations of the social savings of railways later in the nineteenth century suggest a much larger impact of just this one aspect of steam technology. For 1865, Hawke (1970) estimates the social savings of the railways of England and Wales at 6.4 to 11.4 percent of GDP, depending on the treatment of passenger comfort. Leunig (2006), with a more sophisticated treatment of the saving of time, arrives at a similar figure. Crafts (2004) assesses the role of steam power as a general-purpose technology, using the accounting framework of Oliner and Sichel (2000), which includes the effects of capital deepening as well as total factor productivity (TFP) growth. The results are shown in Table 7.5, with separate calculations for stationary steam engines, railways, and steamships. Although the steam engine made very

Table 7.5 British labor productivity growth and the contribution of steam technology

| | Economy-wide labor productivity growth | Contribution of steam technology | | | |
		Stationary steam engines	Railways	Steamships	Total
		% per annum			
1760–1800	0.2	0.01			0.01
1800–30	0.5	0.02			0.02
1830–50	1.1	0.04	0.16		0.20
1850–70	1.2	0.12	0.26	0.03	0.41
1870–1910	0.9	0.14	0.07	0.10	0.31

Source: Derived from Crafts, 2004.

little contribution to economy-wide labor productivity growth in the early phase of the Industrial Revolution, its contribution increased after 1830, and accounted for around a third of economy-wide labor productivity growth after 1850. Furthermore, Crafts (2004, p. 348) accepts that this ignores important TFP spillovers from steam in the second half of the nineteenth century, when transport improvements permitted increased agglomeration and specialization along lines of comparative advantage (Rosenberg and Trajtenberg, 2004).

Textiles

After agriculture and food processing, the production of textiles and clothing was the largest economic activity in Europe during the eighteenth and nineteenth centuries. Around 1870 it accounted in most countries for 4–6 percent of GDP and 15–30 percent of manufacturing output. Around 1700 its share in a much smaller manufacturing sector was probably higher, perhaps 40–50 percent. Until the second half of the nineteenth century most clothing was produced in the home or by local seamstresses and tailors. Other than the increasing importance of fashion among the middle and lower strata of the income distribution (Roche, 2000, ch. 8), there was little in the way of technological or organizational change in clothing production before sewing machines became available from the 1850s. The rise of the ready-made clothing industry is largely a development of the period after 1870.

If the clothing industry remained for the most part unchanged over this period, the same was not true of the textile industry that supplied its raw materials. The locus of production for yarn and cloth shifted from the home to the factory, and increasingly from the countryside to the towns. The processes of preparing, spinning, weaving, and finishing were mechanized, making possible large increases in productivity and steeply falling prices to consumers. The mix of textile fabrics changed, as cotton cloth, which in the early eighteenth century had been an exotic luxury good, became the stuff of which most underclothing, shirts, dresses, sheets, and towels were made.

This transformation of the textile industry is mainly about what happened in the British Isles and secondarily about how the rest of Europe reacted to it. By the mid-nineteenth century the United Kingdom dominated the textile industries not just of Europe, but of the world. It is astonishing that in the cotton industry over half of the mechanical spindles and power looms in the world were in British factories (Farnie, 2003, pp. 724, 727). UK linen and jute producers, mainly located in Ireland and Scotland, operated over 40 percent of the world's mechanical spindles and over 60 percent of the power looms (Solar, 2003, pp. 818–19). The English woolen and worsted industry used over a quarter of the world's new wool, supplemented by large supplies of recycled wool (Sauerbeck, 1878). Only in the silk industry was the United Kingdom surpassed by other countries, notably by France and Japan (Federico, 1997, p. 64).

These figures for equipment and raw material use understate British dominance during much of the early nineteenth century, since one reaction by other countries was to maintain their own industries by erecting tariff walls. In the mid-1850s the United Kingdom was a large net exporter of all textiles, except silk goods (Davis, 1979). During the early nineteenth century British goods had flooded markets in the Americas, Africa, and Asia, as well as those in Europe which had remained open. Only in the mid-century did some European producers start to become competitive in these markets (Jenkins and Ponting, 1982, pp. 146–48).

The United Kingdom had not always been so dominant in textile trade and production. As late as the 1780s, whilst it was a large net exporter of woolens, it was still a small net exporter of cotton, linen, and silk goods (Davis, 1979). Earlier in the eighteenth century, under pressure from woolen and silk producers, the British Parliament had felt it necessary to prohibit imports of Indian cotton goods. It had also raised tariffs on imports of German linen cloth in order to protect Scottish and Irish producers. O'Brien et al. (1991, p. 418) argue that these and other "pragmatic" measures helped to "construct a benign legislative framework for the long-term development of a cotton industry."

In the early eighteenth century the textile industry was spread across the countryside of Europe (Clarkson, 2003; Jenkins, 2003; Solar, 2003; van der Wee, 2003). Much output was for local consumption, but there were rural areas where spinners and weavers were more densely settled and where goods were produced for more distant markets, either for urban centers of consumption, such as London, Paris, or Amsterdam, or for colonial markets in the Americas.

The traditional centers of commercial textile production in Europe were in northern and central Italy, the region around Ghent and Courtrai in the southern Netherlands (what is now Belgium), and Lille and Amiens in France. Parts of southern England were also major producers of woolens. But by the eighteenth century these areas were being challenged. In woolen textiles they faced competition from producers located in the neighborhoods of Leeds and Bradford in Britain, Montpellier in France, Chemnitz and Aachen in Germany, and Verviers in the southern Netherlands. In linens the more dynamic areas were around Belfast in Ireland, Dundee in Scotland, Landeshut in Germany (now in Poland), and Trautenau in Austria (now in the Czech Republic).

The cotton industry was quite small in the eighteenth century. In Britain as late as 1770 it accounted for less than 6 percent of value-added in textile production (Crafts, 1985a, p. 22). Some pure cotton fabrics were produced, but most output took the form of fustians – mixed fabrics made of cotton and linen. Centres of European fustian production were near Manchester in England, and in the border area taking in parts of eastern France, southern Germany, and northern Switzerland. The most dynamic sector of the cotton industry was printing, often in imitation of Indian calicoes. Printing works were large establishments which required the mobilization of significant amounts of capital and labor (Chassagne, 2003).

It is interesting to note that the technological breakthrough in the mechanization of textile production in Britain occurred in cotton, a sector where there was no local supply of the raw material. However, as Broadberry and Gupta (2008) note, wages were five to six times higher than in India, the largest producer and exporter of cotton textiles during the early modern period. If British producers were to succeed in displacing India in world markets, it would clearly not be using the labor-intensive Indian production methods. The canonical textile inventions – the spinning jenny and the water frame in the 1760s, the mule in the late 1770s, and the power loom in the early 1780s – can thus be seen as a response to the particular factor price environment faced by British producers. Allen (2007) shows that the spinning jenny was highly profitable at British factor prices, but not at French or Indian factor prices. The fact that England had a patent system which offered protection to innovations embodied in machinery also helped to realize the potential for import and reexport substitution offered by the success of Indian cottons in English and overseas markets (Sullivan, 1989; Broadberry and Gupta, 2008).

By 1830 cottons accounted for almost half of British textile output, and their share in the textile industries of other European countries had also risen. Several factors account for the cotton industry's rapid and sustained growth. The most obvious is the mechanization of spinning and weaving noted above.

Perhaps equally important was the elasticity with which raw cotton was supplied. The invention of the cotton gin in 1793 made it possible to extend the cultivation of short-staple cotton across the American south. The availability of land on the frontier and of slaves to cultivate it led during the following half-century to an enormous increase in supplies of raw cotton at the same time as its real price was falling. Cotton prices were also falling relative to the price of flax, which, along with the much slower pace of mechanization in the linen industry, helped cotton replace linen in a wide variety of uses. Finally, it should be noted that for consumers cottons were attractive fabrics. They were light and easy to maintain. They could also be colorful since they lent themselves well to dyeing and printing.

The early inventions were not universally applicable. Initially they worked only with cotton, often only with certain sorts of raw cotton. The new spinning technologies were quite rapidly taken up in the cotton industry in the 1770s and 1780s, but were not widely used in the UK woolen and coarse linen industries until the 1790s, in the worsted industry until the 1800s and in the fine linen industry until the late 1820s. The power loom, even though invented in the 1780s, did not start to be widely used in the UK cotton industry before the 1810s, in coarse linen and worsted industries before the 1820s, in the woolen industry before the 1840s, and in the fine linen and silk industries before the 1850s. Some finer cotton fabrics were still being woven by hand until the 1850s. These long delays in mechanization owed much to the differing elasticities of the various textile fibres. Where the fibres broke easily, too much hand labor was needed to piece together the yarn during spinning and weaving. Better ways to prepare fibres and to run the machines more smoothly had to be found before mechanization became economically viable.

There were also long delays in the adoption of the new spinning and weaving technologies by countries other than the United Kingdom. In 1800 there were 3.4 million mechanical spindles working cotton in the United Kingdom, but only about 100,000 elsewhere in the world (Farnie, 2003, p. 724). This was not for want of trying to copy the British example. French governments, both royalist and republican, provided ample subsidies to would-be cotton spinners in the 1780s and 1790s (Chassagne, 1991, ch. 3). To take another example, the wet spinning of flax, which made possible the production of fine linen yarns, was taken up rapidly in England and Ireland in the late 1820s, but did not start to be adopted in France, Belgium, and Germany until the late 1830s and early 1840s (Solar, 2003). The difficulties experienced by other continental countries in successfully applying the new British textile technologies can readily be explained by the fact that wages were lower than in Britain. Hence the labor savings offered by the new technologies did not initially justify the higher capital costs (Allen, 2001, 2006).

Within Britain the various textile industries became increasingly localized during the early nineteenth century. The cotton industry became concentrated in south Lancashire and adjoining parts of Yorkshire, Derbyshire, and Cheshire. Within west Yorkshire the woolen and worsted industries were increasingly segregated, around Leeds and Bradford respectively, and both of these areas gained relative to other UK producing areas. The coarse linen industry became clustered around Dundee and the fine linen industry around Belfast.

The localization of the UK textile industries suggests that there were advantages to firms in being located near the center of the industry. It is difficult to get a firm quantitative grip on the value of these external economies, as Marshall called them, but they may have arisen from several sources. One would be technological. The sort of incremental technical change involved in getting machines to run faster and more efficiently was not likely to be written down. Such knowledge was embodied in the skilled workers who maintained and repaired the machines. These workers were often the vehicle through which new inventions spread to other countries, either because they left to try their hand elsewhere, like Samuel Slater, the pioneer of the US cotton industry, or because they were enticed away by foreign entrepreneurs or governments (Jeremy, 1981; Chassagne, 1991). However, once they left, they cut themselves off from the font of new technical knowledge.

Another potential source of external economies was the concentration of mercantile activity. Reliable and timely information about the state of demand and about the sorts of fabric that were wanted was crucial in an industry where a prime cause of bankruptcy was unsold merchandise. A notable feature of the early nineteenth century was the shift in the locus of mercantile activity away from London toward the regional centers of production (Edwards, 1967, p. 180; Solar, 1990). During this same period the value of the United Kingdom's stock of mercantile expertise and connections probably gained from the relative isolation of continental merchants from non-European markets during the wars from 1792 to 1815. From the 1820s foreign cotton merchants setting up in Manchester reinforced its commercial status (Farnie, 2004, p. 33).

Food, drink, and tobacco

The food, drink, and tobacco industries grew significantly during the eighteenth and nineteenth centuries. Population growth from the mid-eighteenth century was one driving force. So, too, was urbanization. As a greater share of the population lived in towns and cities, fewer people could bake their own bread or brew their own beer. This was also a period when the consumption of exotic goods such as sugar, tea, coffee, and tobacco penetrated further down the social scale and became items of mass consumption.

Much of the growth in this sector was based on traditional techniques. There were few major breakthroughs: the most notable was continuous distilling, patented by Aeneas Coffey in 1830 (Weir, 1977). Much change was incremental and benefited from developments in other sectors. Better metals and metal-working techniques made machinery more reliable and permitted increases in the size of machines. Steam power was applied in some industries, notably in milling and brewing, though wind, water, and animal power remained important right up to 1870. However, even water-powered mills became larger and more sophisticated in their exploitation of water resources and in the organization of production. As industrial structures, the three- and four-storey mills built from the mid-eighteenth century onward were precursors of the early cotton spinning mills.

Perhaps the most important force for change in this sector was more rapid and reliable transportation, first by steamship from the 1820s, then by rail from the 1830s. Whilst better transport merely facilitated the distribution of the high-value, low-volume exotic goods, it significantly widened markets for more perishable low-value, high-volume food products such as flour and beer. For example, Guinness, which had initially relied on the Dublin market, was, by the 1860s, shipping its dark stout throughout Ireland and to many cities in England. Its Dublin brewery had become one of the largest in the world (Bielenberg, 1998).

Whilst the impact of transport changes was already apparent by 1870, it was still incomplete in the perishable goods industries (Mingay, 1989). Country mills, driven by water or wind power, still produced most of the flour used in small towns and rural areas. The beer consumed in these places was home-brewed or made by publican-brewers or small breweries. Other perishable goods industries generally remained on a very small scale and were spread fairly evenly across space. Even in towns, bakers, cheese-makers, and meat processors rarely employed more than a handful of workers unless they were working for the military or other large institutional customers.

There was more concentration in the production of non-perishable goods, though here the organization of production was also heavily influenced by state policy. Tobacco, sugar, tea, coffee, and cocoa and chocolate were all imported commodities, so processing, where necessary, often took place in the major ports. Sugar refineries, which were very capital- and fuel-intensive, were major features of the urban landscape in Amsterdam, London, and other cities, not only for their size but for their smell and smoke (de Vries and van de Woude, 1997, pp. 326–29). Because some of these exotic goods were also heavily taxed, governments tried to prevent smuggling and tax evasion by restricting the number of producers. In the extreme, some countries, including France,

Austria, and Spain, created state-owned tobacco monopolies. These monopolies were some of the largest industrial enterprises of the eighteenth and early nineteenth centuries, though they remained highly labor-intensive (Goodman, 1993, ch. 9). The production of spirits, another important source of tax revenue, was also highly regulated. In addition, the introduction of the patent still led to a highly concentrated industry. In 1860 just eight distilleries produced all the spirits made in England (Weir, 1977, p. 138).

The iron industry

Deposits of iron ore were scattered across most of Europe and were thus widely available and in abundant supply, whereas in the most populated and thriving regions, wood had become a scarce resource. In the long run, to overcome this *Holzbremse* or "wood brake," which was binding in the seventeenth and eighteenth centuries, societies had to proceed to a new technology independent of wood (Sombart, 1928, p. 1137). In the meantime, there were transitory strategies which either economized on wood consumption or drew on the resources of remote regions with still-abundant supplies of wood. This is precisely what Britain did during the eighteenth century, with Sweden and later Russia delivering iron produced with charcoal technology for the increasing British iron consumption. Table 7.6 provides some crude estimates of annual

Table 7.6 National shares of iron production in Europe, 1725–50 and 1860–61

	Wrought iron 1725–50	Pig iron 1860–61
	%	
United Kingdom	8.1	59.5
France	27.0	13.7
Sweden	25.4	2.6
Germany	8.7	8.1
Spain	8.0	0.6
Austria/Hungary	8.7	4.8
Italy	2.5	0.4
Russia	6.2	4.9
Belgium	?	4.9
Rest of Europe	5.3	0.5
Europe (000 tonnes)	165–214	6,539

Sources: 1725–50: King, 2005, p. 23; Wertime, 1962, p. 101; Paulinyi, 2005, p. 97; Hildebrand, 1992, p. 22; 1860–61: Fremdling, 1986, pp. 260, 262, 285–86, 324–25, 385; Mitchell, 1988.

Stage of production	Process		Product
	traditional	modern	
First Stage	Smelting in the blast furnace		Pig iron
	with charcoal	with coke	
Second Stage	Refining		Wrought iron (steel)
	in a hearth with charcoal	in a puddling furnace with coal	
	Shaping		Bar iron (rails)
	by the hammer	by a rolling mill	

Figure 7.1 Primary wrought-iron industry

production of wrought iron in the main iron-producing countries of Europe around 1725–50, drawn mainly from assessments of contemporary travellers.

Figure 7.1 provides a brief overview of the production stages and processes in the iron industry, emphasizing the distinction between traditional and modern methods. In the first stage of production, iron ore was smelted in the blast furnace. In the traditional method, the fuel was charcoal, derived from wood, while the modern process used coke, derived from coal. The output, "pig iron," contained a lot of impurities and a high content of carbon, which made it brittle and unsuitable for shaping. It could, however, be turned into final products by casting while in a molten state. Otherwise, the pig iron had to be further refined at the forge to produce malleable or wrought iron, which was suitable for shaping by hammering or, later, by rolling. This refining largely involved reduction of the carbon content and required re-heating, again either using charcoal in the traditional process or coal in the modern puddling process. Distinguishing between the two stages of production is essential, because smelting on the one hand and refining/shaping on the other were not necessarily integrated in one production unit or even at the same location.

Sweden and Russia: the charcoal-based iron industry

Iron-making in Sweden during the seventeenth and eighteenth centuries was closely connected with traditional agriculture (Hildebrand, 1992). Cheap peasant labor was available for burning charcoal and mining the iron ore and smelting it in blast furnaces. Water wheels provided mechanical power for the bellows of the blast furnace and the hammers of the forge. Bar iron, manufactured by specialist forge-men, was the major product, much of which was exported. Iron-making was heavily regulated by state authorities. From the middle of the eighteenth century, production and thus exports were deliberately limited in order to protect the forests against over-felling. High prices on the international market, as a result of growing demand from Britain and supply restrictions in Sweden, created a favorable environment for a new competitor, namely bar iron from Russia (Agren, 1998, p. 6). Russian iron production also depended on wood as fuel and on the intensive use of peasant labor (Florén, 1998).

Britain: the first coal-based iron industry

At the beginning of the eighteenth century the British iron industry was small and unable to meet domestic demand, with imports exceeding domestic production (Hyde, 1977). British costs of production were high, largely because of the high cost of charcoal. The transition from charcoal to mineral fuel techniques, which made possible a process of import substitution, was a long drawn-out affair, lasting the whole of the eighteenth century, as can be seen from Figure 7.2. As late as 1755, only 20 percent of pig iron produced in England and Wales was being smelted using coke, and the proportion did not reach 90 percent until 1790.

Abraham Darby is usually credited with being the first successfully to operate blast furnaces using coke, from 1709 onwards. The diffusion of coke smelting gained momentum in the 1750s and 1760s, mainly due to the increasing use of the coke pig iron for castings. New casting techniques could use coke pig iron made molten again in reverberatory or cupola furnaces fired by coal (Beck, 1897, pp. 380–85, 753–56).

In 1784, Henry Cort obtained a patent for his famous puddling and rolling process. Very quickly this method of refining pig iron came to prevail in the production of wrought or bar iron (Figure 7.1). The large increases in production turned Britain from one of the foremost importers of iron products in the eighteenth century into a net exporter by the early nineteenth century (Fremdling, 2004, pp. 151–52). Within a century, the British iron industry had transformed itself from a small high-cost producer into the leading supplier of iron products for the world market. Using the new technology, its disadvantage (the "wood brake") had been turned into a competitive advantage in a long drawn-out process of innovation, diffusion, and improvement.

The Continent: partial adoption of the new techniques

Despite Landes's (1969, p. 126) statement that the process innovations of the coke-using blast furnace, the puddling furnace, and the rolling mill were vastly superior to the traditional procedures both technically and economically, traditional or partly modernized processes could survive very well within their native districts and in their traditional markets. Moreover, as they were diffused across continental Europe, the new techniques did not follow the British model strictly. Rather, there was a coexistence of techniques adapted to local circumstances, particularly different factor prices (Fremdling, 2004; Broadberry, 1997).

Wallonia, the southern part of Belgium, was the first and almost the only continental region to follow the British model in its entirety. In the middle of the 1820s, numerous works comprising coke blast furnaces as well as puddling and rolling mills were built in the coal mining areas around Liège and Charleroi (Reuss et al., 1960). As in Britain, iron ore and coal were situated close together. Transportation costs and moderate protective duties screened Wallonia from British competition, while an ambitious government program for industrial development was framed on the British model (Fremdling and Gales, 1994). In a favorable economic environment, with proximity to customers and a relatively high-cost traditional industry, the technology transplanted from Britain could prosper. Whilst by the 1840s the old-fashioned way of smelting iron ore with charcoal still dominated in Germany and France, it served only niche markets in Wallonia (Figure 7.2).

In France, as well, imports from Britain had shown that there was a demand for coal-smelted iron. With customs policy fending off British competition from 1822 onwards, a guaranteed high price level and large profits seemed to be in prospect for establishing British-type ironworks. Large establishments were actually set up in the coal districts of the Loire valley and the Massif Central, but they had no economic success until well into the 1830s. This was largely because of the high costs of shipping ores to production sites and the final products to centers of consumption, where they had to compete with the products of the traditional or partly-modernized iron industry. Thus for a long time traditional iron production based on charcoal technology remained viable (Vial, 1967). Before railway demand created a new situation, a similar story could be told for Germany (Fremdling, 1986, pp. 117–75; Banken, 2005).

The Continent: adaptations in the traditional sector

Some German and French regions managed to compete with the British iron industry for a transitional period covering several decades. Total factor productivity in smelting iron ore with charcoal increased considerably in the Siegerland, Württemberg, and Sweden between 1820 and 1855, largely as a result of remarkable economies in charcoal use (Fremdling, 1986, pp. 155–60). Furthermore, elements of the new coal-based technology were integrated into traditional iron production. Small forges could, for instance, substitute the new

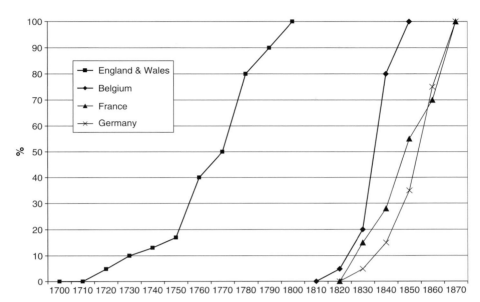

Figure 7.2 Share of coke pig iron (King, 2005, pp. 3, 7; 2006, p. 264; Fremdling, 1986, p. 342; 2005, pp. 49, 51–52; Banken, 2005, p. 56)

puddling furnace for the old refining furnace without changing the rest of the operations. As puddling furnaces were fuelled with coal, the effects of rising charcoal prices were mitigated. These partial modernizations were widespread in the most important regions of the traditional iron industry in Germany and France, namely the Siegerland and the Champagne region. Nevertheless, during the 1860s German and French charcoal-using ironworks retreated into niches and in the end sank into insignificance beside the large-scale technology coming from Britain (Figure 7.2).

In Sweden, however, charcoal iron production did remain viable, but not without adaptation (Rydén, 2005). Around 1830, a Swede came across in Lancashire a refining technique very similar to that of puddling, but using charcoal. This highly productive British charcoal technique became the dominant process of Swedish iron making in the 1840s. Austria also persisted in the use of charcoal technology (Paulinyi, 2005). Only with the coming, from the 1860s, of the new liquid steel Bessemer and Thomas/Gilchrist processes and the open-hearth (Siemens-Martin) method, did technological convergence occur across Europe's iron and steel industries.

Table 7.6 shows output of pig iron and steel in the major producing countries around 1860. Britain was heavily dominant, with the next largest country, France, producing less than a quarter of the British output. The other large producers were Belgium and Germany in western Europe, and Austria-Hungary and Russia in central and eastern Europe.

Conclusion

Industry was a relatively small part of the European economy at the beginning of the eighteenth century, with economic activity dominated by agriculture and services. By 1870, much of Europe had undergone an industrial revolution, with the development of modern technology leading to an acceleration in the growth rate of industrial output and productivity, accompanied by a dramatic structural shift of economic activity towards industry. Unlike earlier, pre-industrial episodes of economic expansion, this burst of economic growth did not peter out, but ushered in a new era of continuously rising living standards, which has continued to the present.

The process began in Britain and spread to the rest of Europe. However, the process of technology transfer from Britain to the Continent should not be seen as a process of slavish copying. Rather, it was a long-drawn-out affair, involving the adaptation of technology to local circumstances. This process has been illustrated here with examples drawn from the classic industries of the Industrial Revolution, including iron making and textiles. We have also pointed to the importance of steam power as the first general-purpose technology in sustaining the process of growth.

The services sector

Regina Grafe, Larry Neal, and Richard W. Unger

Contents

The commercial revolution that arose from the opportunities of long-distance trade created in the two centuries before 1700 penetrated local markets throughout continental Europe over the next 170 years. In the process, the dominant form of employment in the services sector switched from local and household services required by largely self-sufficient households and villages, engaged primarily in agriculture and handicraft manufacturing, to specialized commercial, financial, and transportation services organized between specialized centers of production and commerce. Increased specialization led to continued advances in productivity, in services as well as in agriculture and industry. Services may, in fact, have been the most dynamic sector in the European economy throughout this period. While the Industrial Revolution occurred in Great Britain, industrialization did not dominate the economies in the rest of Europe until after 1870. In contrast, the earlier British innovations in providing services in finance, shipping, and wholesale distribution were more readily adopted in the rest of Europe and their diffusion led to continued dynamic growth of the services sector throughout Europe.

The importance of productivity advances in services for growth in the general economy was not recognized as clearly in the eighteenth century as it is now. Only in recent decades, after stunning improvements in information and communications technology, have economists begun to identify the importance of advances in finance for overall economic growth, as well as for continued trade in goods and services among diverse regions. While trade was recognized as the engine of economic growth by many economists of the eighteenth century, the importance of financial innovations for facilitating trade was typically not. Economic well-being, however, measured as the satisfaction derived from current consumption by everyone in an economic unit (indicated by the prices they are willing to pay), depends upon the "right" goods and services being delivered at the "right" place at the "right" time for the ultimate consumer. Getting everything "right" in an economy is the function of the services sector as a whole, and each component has a useful and complementary role to play, from finance to shipping to distribution at the wholesale and retail levels. Consequently, the major components of the services sector – finance, transportation, communication, and distribution – comprise the largest and still-growing part of the domestic product, capital stock, and labor force in modern economies.

The rise in the share of services within European economies in the period 1700–1870, however, was overshadowed by the more dramatic rise of manufacturing and the decline of agriculture. In 1700, the services sector in its modern form appeared primarily in Europe's cities, which were just beginning their rise (Chapter 10 of this volume). By 1870, however, services had emerged as the leading sector in the first industrial country, Britain, as well as in the Netherlands, the first commercial country. In the rest of Europe, services rose in importance as commercialization and industrialization spread throughout Europe in the wake of railway expansion.

Overall, the volume of goods transported within and beyond Europe rose dramatically and at an increasing pace from the end of the seventeenth century to 1870. Existing services expanded in the face of rising output, while new services were added to accommodate changes in the geography and range of production. New goods found markets and new lands were brought into production because of falling costs of moving goods. Improvements in many of the technologies of transportation, combined with capital investment in infrastructure, and shippers taking advantage of economies of scale all combined to bring greater efficiency to transportation. Governments supported and subsidized transportation facilities and promoted trade. Increased international competition, a by-product of the creation of nation-states, stimulated further growth in trade. The development of wholesale distribution networks in Europe, however, was neither a steady nor a uniform process. Between 1700 and 1870 deep interregional differences persisted and probably deepened across Europe.

We take up first the developments in financial technology that had spread through mercantile Europe by 1700 and gradually spread thereafter until 1815, when the pace of financial innovation kept quickening and its scale kept increasing. Then we examine the rise of transportation, where improvements in technology and organization led to sustained productivity increases even before the epoch-defining shift from sail and draft animals to steam power after 1815. Finally, we explore the resulting expansion of commercial ties and the growth of distribution networks for the benefit of European consumers. In the face of an unprecedented increase in private capital demanded to expand transport and distribution services throughout Europe over the entire period 1700–1870, the remarkable fact is that the cost of capital remained low. Absent direct measures of productivity in the services sector overall, this finding alone indicates that the productivity of both capital and labor in the services sector must have risen substantially.

This chapter will focus on the major private services of finance, shipping, and distribution, while government is discussed in Chapter 3 of this volume. Within a national accounting framework, the other parts of the services sector are housing, which is simply an imputed rent, and domestic service, which we know accounted for around 15 percent of services-sector output in the most advanced parts of Europe in the mid-nineteenth century (Deane and Cole, 1962; Hoffmann, 1965).

Finance

By 1700, European leadership in financial innovation, especially with respect to war finance, was passing from the Dutch Republic to England. The essentials of the financial revolution in England were to implement the most efficient aspects of Dutch mercantile and public finance within a much more centralized tax and payments system centered on London, while taking full advantage of the superior payments system already developed in Amsterdam. The initiative came from the duress of war finance that Britain's new Dutch king, William III, placed on the resources available to the English monarchy when he seized power in 1688. With the help of numerous Dutch advisors who had assisted him as *Stadhouder* of the Dutch Republic in his wars with France, he forced a series of financial innovations that developed into a "financial revolution" (Dickson, 1967).

Founding the Bank of England in 1694 proved unexpectedly important and useful (Clapham, 1994a). While the Exchange Bank of Amsterdam (1609) provided efficient payment services for the wholesale trade of Amsterdam and then of much of western Europe from the Mediterranean to the Baltic (Gillard, 2004), the Bank of England added new features. As well as providing payment services by transfer of balances from one account to another, the Bank of England could also expand the money supply of the kingdom because it needed only a fraction of its silver or gold on hand to redeem its notes. Because of their convenience the notes stayed in general circulation. The Bank could also discount bills presented to it before they were due for final payment by providing the payee bank notes rather than coins of the realm. For the remainder of the eighteenth century, the bank's discount facility helped to finance wholesale trade and capital market transactions during peacetime and then to provide subsidies to Britain's European allies during wartime (Dickson, 1967; Roseveare, 1991; Quinn, 2004).

From 1700 through 1793, then, European merchants could combine the payments systems of the Bank of England and the Amsterdam Exchange Bank to finance trade throughout Europe. The outbreak of war between revolutionary France and the monarchies of Europe disrupted the basis of trade credit in foreign bills of exchange until peace was finally restored in 1815. Until then, the significance of the increased negotiability of foreign bills of exchange drawn on either Amsterdam or London was that it allowed multilateral settlement of trade balances to occur in place of the previous system of bilateral settlements. This meant that persistent payments deficits by one part of Europe against another, for example the persistent deficit of England with the Baltic, could be settled by surpluses earned in another part of Europe, for example the English reexport to continental Europe of sugar and tobacco produced in its American colonies.

Multilateral settlement of differences in merchant accounts had long been recognized as a more efficient way of organizing payments systems. In previous centuries, however, access to these giro services in Barcelona, Florence, Venice,

Genoa, or Lyon was limited to local citizens and selected foreign merchants. Initiatives to encourage trade through Antwerp and then Amsterdam broadened access to the exchange banks there to include anyone willing to make a deposit in silver or gold, coin or bullion. Every increase in use of these services by merchants from any part of Europe increased the potential for trade as well. The result was to provide the basis for continual improvements in the extent of the market within Europe for all goods produced anywhere in the world. By 1720, manuals produced for the benefit of European merchants instructed them on the methods of drawing and paying bills of exchange throughout Europe (Justice, 1707; see Figure 8.1).

Network (in degrees)

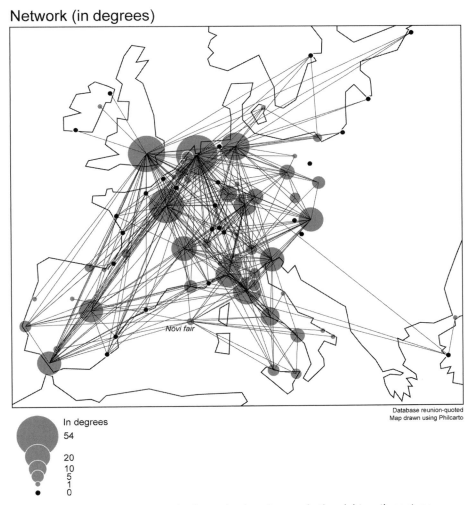

Figure 8.1 The European network of merchant exchanges in the eighteenth century (contemporary merchant manuals described means of payment between each pair of cities connected on the map) (Flandreau et al., 2009)

Sugar and tobacco especially were bulk goods in heavy demand throughout Europe, adding to the already rising demand for pepper and other spices in addition to the continued demand for salt. The distribution channels created by the competing East Indies companies of the Dutch, English, French, Danes, and Austrians continued to expand into the rest of Europe over the rest of the eighteenth century, albeit with disruptions and dislocations during the various wars. Despite the increasing demands of war finance, however, commercial credit continued to be available at low interest rates. The self-regulating beneficence of the resulting system of international payments by bills of exchange within Europe and between Europe and the various mercantile out-posts established by Europeans overseas was described and extolled by Isaac Gervaise in 1720 and elaborated by Abbé Condillac and Adam Smith, both in 1776.

The work of Flandreau et al. (2008) demonstrates that commercial credit was available to merchants with contacts in Amsterdam at rates between 3 and 4 percent annually throughout the period 1688–1789, despite the increasing presence of state finance throughout Europe. There were occasional spikes created by the uncertainties of war, especially at moments when the outcome of a lengthy war was uncertain. But because the increased debt issued by Britain (3 percent Consols) and Holland (bearer obligations) consisted of negotiable instruments easily transferred between merchants, war finance simply increased the possible means for settling their accounts with each other, regardless of nationality. Throughout the eighteenth century, London merchants enjoyed interest rates only slightly higher than in Amsterdam, while Paris merchants had to endure higher rates, but which were still below those paid by merchants in Italy and Spain.

The main effect of the wars on the financial systems of Europe was to demonstrate the surprising usefulness of the capital market for British government debt in peacetime as well as in war. As a result, Britain's national debt continued to expand with each war from 1700 through 1815. Isaac de Pinto (1771) attributed Britain's success precisely to the useful role that Amsterdam's stockjobbers played in providing a liquid market for the new issues of British government debt that each war required. Increasing tensions between the Dutch and the British, however, cut off that symbiosis by the end of the American War, which culminated in the Fourth Anglo-Dutch War of 1780–84. Thereafter, financial innovations in Britain relied more on importing financial talent and capital from the Continent, a process that was greatly facilitated by the French Revolution and its spread to the rest of Europe after 1793.

French troops carried with them the ideals of the French Revolution – liberty, equality, and fraternity – but when imposed on conquered territories these translated into high taxes and the removal of previous privileges and exemptions, not just for religious organizations and feudal lords, but also for merchant and trade guilds. In France itself, however, the accumulated strains upon French public finances following the conclusion of the American War of Independence caused the entire monetary and financial structure of that country to collapse as the French Revolution of 1789 unfolded. In sequence over the next four years from 1789 to 1794, (i) free banking was allowed to emerge as the previous system of privileges and tax exemptions was abolished; (ii) price controls and restrictions on banking practices were then imposed as the revolutionary governments attempted to legitimize their regime in place of the deposed monarchy; and (iii) the issuance of *assignats* ran well beyond either the value of the Church and *emigré* lands put up for sale as backing for them or the value of the stock of circulating specie in France that they had displaced. The hyperinflation that followed destroyed once again the private credit structure of France, just as had the inflation during the John Law episode in 1720 (Hoffman et al., 2000). It also destroyed the credit of the state, since there was no legitimate government in sight to reestablish political credibility à la Louis XV in 1723. Consequently, the Directory tried to implant in France the financial and monetary practices that had proved successful in England and the Netherlands (Bordo and White, 1991; Hoffman et al, 2000; Sargent and Velde, 1995; and White, 1995).

First, two-thirds of the debt was defaulted on while creditors were assured that interest would be paid on at least the remaining one-third. Then a major currency reform was undertaken, replacing the discredited *livre tournois* with a new unit of account, the *franc germinal*, defined like the Dutch guilder in terms of both gold and silver with a fixed mint ratio. Finally, a public bank was established in 1801, the Banque de France. While it was required to maintain the value of the *franc germinal*, the Banque was also expected to help the government avoid fresh deficits by improving the efficiency of its payments system. In the event, French public finances maintained their solidity by virtue of Napoleon's military victories. The satellite kingdoms, subjected to the new tax regime of the French revolutionaries and required to accept the *franc germinal* at fixed prices for military supplies, were able to support the continued war effort of France in a throwback to Roman-style war finance (Bordo and White, 1991). Chief among the satellite kingdoms from a financial perspective was that of Holland.

To avoid seizure by the French occupation troops the specie reserves of the Exchange Bank of Amsterdam had been completely withdrawn by the time the French troops entered Amsterdam. Repeated payments to support the French forces forced the Batavian Republic and then the Kingdom of Holland to issue more annuities, now issued by the national government. In 1814, the Kingdom of the Netherlands consolidated these into 2½ percent perpetual annuities, modelled on the successful British example. Amounting to over four times the national income of the kingdom, however, only a small part of the annuities, the activated portion, were actually paid by the government in any year (t'Hart, Jonker, and van Zanden, 1997).

The British reorganized their war finance in stages as the pressure mounted in view of French successes. As French monetary reforms threatened to encourage a speculative return of funds to France at the end of 1796, the Bank of England was allowed to suspend convertibility of its banknotes into specie. The resulting "paper pound" lasted from February 1797 to May 1821, when the gold standard was formally resumed. Then the government of William Pitt moved to competitive bidding among underwriting syndicates for placement of new issues of Three Percent Consols, with interest payments guaranteed against the increased revenues of the income tax. The income tax allowed the government to tap into the profits of European merchants who now directed all their affairs from London rather than dividing them among London, Paris, Amsterdam, and Hamburg. The existing liquid market for British debt allowed huge sums to be raised on the capital markets (Neal, 1990, 1991).

As most of the money raised for war finance was used after 1803 for paying and supplying British forces directly, rather than laying out subsidies to continental allies or hiring mercenary armies from Germany, domestic expenditures rose greatly. Entrepreneurs from all over Europe flocked to Britain to take advantage, either with direct or portfolio investment, of the profit opportunities that emerged in textiles, iron and steel, dockyards, waterworks, gas works, and agriculture (Neal, 1990, 1991). The capital flight to safety by the mercantile classes of French-occupied Europe, certain to be taxed heavily and dispossessed of privilege by Napoleon's forces, alit in large part in Great Britain. The result was to make London the new financial capital of Europe, displacing Amsterdam permanently.

The dramatic success of British finance by the end of the Napoleonic wars led other European states to imitate, as best they could within their diverse political structures, the key elements as seen by foreign observers. Public banks of issue like the Bank of England or the Banque de France were the first to emerge. It took longer to create national debt in the form of perpetual annuities, as these required a perpetual source of tax revenue to service them, and that required a permanent legislative authority, a parliament. Gradually, however, imitations appeared – *rentes* in France, funded by the taxes voted by the Parlement, *renten* in the Kingdom of the Netherlands, and even perpetual annuities maintained as book entries in the Kingdom of Naples but marketed in Paris and Vienna by the Rothschild brothers. The House of Rothschild, a multinational family investment bank, proved to be the organization chiefly responsible for diffusing the basic elements of British finance to the rest of Europe (Ferguson, 1998).

The success of British finance, however, was not so obvious to the British authorities in 1815. The income tax was repealed in 1816, and in 1819 Parliament required the Bank of England to resume convertibility of its bank notes in gold at the pre-war rate by 1821. The East India Company had to accept the end of its monopoly on trade with the East Indies by 1833 after increasing encroachment by competitors and the return of Dutch East India Company properties in Asia. Moreover, country bank notes, which had risen to inflationary levels during the war, could no longer be redeemed in Bank of England notes. These were being withdrawn by the Bank to increase its gold reserves before resuming convertibility of its notes. The financial panic that eventually resulted in 1825 was quickly resolved, but with major changes in legislation that laid the basis for future developments in British finance. These were (i) the beginnings of joint-stock banking, (ii) the establishment of Bank of England branches, (iii) the displacement of private banks by joint-stock dis-count houses for the business of re-discounting inland bills of exchange, and (iv) the assumption of some central banking functions by the Bank of England. The combination of these four factors allowed the rise of the most distinctive feature of the British financial system in the later nineteenth century, the inland bill of exchange market. (See W. T. C. King's classic account, 1936.)

The rise of the inland bill of exchange market in London meant that the previous means of financing foreign trade, a four-party bill of exchange, could also now be modernized. Instead of paying immediately in local currency for a foreign bill of exchange to pay a foreign supplier in his currency, an importer could now ask his bank to arrange accommodation finance with the bank of the exporter. Under acceptance house practices in the nineteenth century the Amsterdam exporter could get immediate payment from his bank upon show-ing the order from the importer in London. The bank in Amsterdam then ordered the importer's discount house in London to pay it the sum it had promised the exporter. The London house, in turn, would charge the London importer the amount, plus its service fee, but in British currency kept on account (Chapman, 1984).

Governments also tried to innovate along the lines of British finance. The attempts of continental countries to follow the example of Britain in creating a stable market for their long-term government debt were valiant, but under-mined by recurring political uncertainties – repeated regime changes in France, the breakup of the Kingdom of the Netherlands with the creation of Belgium in 1830, and the continued expansion of Prussia after the revolutions of 1848. Not until the universal adoption of the gold standard by the European followers after 1870 could any of the European continental countries claim to have

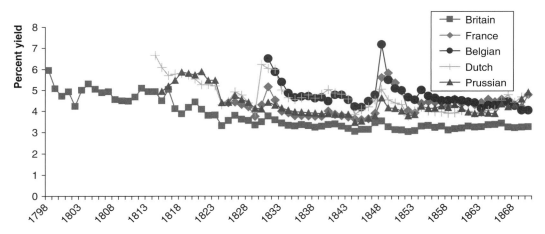

Figure 8.2 Government bond interest rates, 1789–1870 (Homer and Sylla, 1991)

emulated the British lead in finance, whatever may have been their accomplishments in agriculture or industry (Figure 8.2). By 1870, then, the innovations and productivity advances in the services sector of northwestern Europe had contributed to large and growing differences in levels of per capita income among the territories of continental Europe. The growth of the shipping industry demonstrates this well.

Shipping

Significant improvements in transportation efficiency on both land and sea in the years after 1700 preceded the transformation in shipping generated by the slow adoption of steam propulsion in the first seventy years of the nineteenth century. Moving goods over land was always more expensive than moving goods over water. Simply put, there was less friction between the liquid and the solid vehicle. In the years up to 1815 investment in better roads did not overcome the physical problem, but did make land transport more efficient and redirected trade. The extension of the road network and improvements in roads made possible faster and more consistent shipping services, including the transport of people and mail in regularly scheduled coaches, the latter being an emerging feature of eighteenth-century western Europe.

Short-distance transport from farms to markets was the most resistant to improvements. The products of agriculture started their journeys carried by animals, including people, or in wheelbarrows or carts. Some farm products transported themselves. Massive cattle drives from Denmark to the Low Countries and from Hungary to western Europe might have declined from pre-1700 heights but the growing cities required increasing supplies of animals, which made their way along the roadways, spreading out to grazing lands around as they passed (Gijsbers, 1999, 485–99).

Roads and bridges, long neglected, got new attention from governments and private investors in the first half of the eighteenth century. In 1716 the kingdom of France established a department of civil engineering responsible for roads and bridges. That led in 1747 to the creation of the École des Ponts et Chaussées in Paris to train new engineers who would improve the quality of French land transportation. In England it was private entrepreneurs who were the source of most major road improvements. The turnpike trusts anticipated returns on their investments from tolls. Charging for the use of roadways and footpaths was not new, but the scale of road construction and the contribution to overall transport efficiency were unprecedented. Over long hauls – distances of about 300 km – improved roads could lead to at least a doubling of productivity in land transport by the 1760s and a tripling by the 1830s. There were significant gains from a shift to using wagons in place of pack animals, something made possible by better roads. There were also gains from bigger and better animals to pull the wagons and better organization as firm size among shippers grew (Gerhold, 1996, 494–511). Pavement was created or improved, increasing speed, especially in poor weather. In the Austrian Netherlands, for example, new brick or stone roads replaced mud tracks, the Habsburg monarchs increasing the road network from 200 km in 1700 to nearly 2,850 km by 1793 (Serruys, 2008).

Governments promoted investment in inland transport by water. The Dutch Republic in the sixteenth and seventeenth centuries created a system of canals that could carry bulk cargoes as well as passengers on regularly scheduled routes, all while controlling the flow of water to prevent flooding (de Vries, 1981). In the seventeenth and even more in the eighteenth century other European states imitated the Dutch pattern, using canals to supplement or supplant existing river transportation. People still exploited rivers, some of them in rather modest ways – for floating goods downstream or for carrying goods on sailing barges. The difficulties of going upstream always presented problems in the narrow confines of rivers. Using poles and oars for propulsion meant large crews and undermined the advantages of moving goods by water. Canals solved the problem with vessels pulled by draught animals walking along towpaths alongside the waterways.

More powerful absolutist governments sought and exercised the power to do away with property rights so that canals could be built. Louis XIV's France embarked on an ambitious program of canal construction, including a canal through the Midi, completed in 1681, to connect the Atlantic to the Mediterranean. While French canals, often built with a political purpose in mind, might have engineering and financial problems, the products of the English canal construction boom in the second half of the eighteenth century avoided many of those pitfalls. As with somewhat earlier building in the Austrian Netherlands, the result was a network of interconnected waterways. Financing in England came from private investors, the sums required being sizeable, given the scale of the work (Deane and Cole, 1969, 237–38). Distances might be only scores of kilometers, but any hills or uplands meant building a number of locks. The shorter canals in areas with few gradients proved the most successful, while more ambitious projects that tried to emulate that success often fell short. Even Peter the Great in Russia, a ruler with coercive powers and seemingly limitless drive, could not complete the projected canal to link the Volga and Don rivers in the first years of the eighteenth century. The impact of canals increased as kilometers increased and connections among waterway systems became more common. Those connections tended to be internal to states and so served to integrate markets within them.

The expansion of ocean shipping services drew government attention in the eighteenth century. States throughout Europe introduced policies to promote shipping, conscious of the potential and anxious that potential benefits be accrued – from greater trade, from earnings from the sector itself, and from possible streams of income from easily taxed streams of commerce. The total tonnage of the European merchant marine grew rapidly (Table 8.1), more than doubling through the eighteenth century, with the most rapid growth in north-western Europe but with impressive expansion throughout the continent (Unger, 1992, 258–61; van Zanden, 2001, 81–82).

The supply of shipping services grew even more rapidly as vessels spent more time each year at sea carrying goods. Various factors made it possible for ships and crews to work more effectively. Investment in port facilities including docks and cranes continued, as did improvements in the organization of work in port. Guilds of cargo handlers were the norm, and having their labor available when needed sped up the handling of cargo. The flow of information also improved. The establishment of regular and predictable exchanges of certain goods through certain ports where cargoes were marshalled made it easier for shippers to fill a larger proportion of their holds. Reliable trades made possible and promoted the development of back cargoes, so that vessels made return trips not empty but carrying paying goods. The improvements in ports and in information served to decrease turnaround time for ships and so made possible the more intensive use of the capital sunk in ships.

Better ships also contributed to the increase in the supply of shipping services. In the eighteenth century shipbuilders elaborated and better exploited earlier breakthroughs. The sailing packet of about 500 tons with a standard three-masted rig of square sails on the fore- and mainmasts and a fore-and-aft

Table 8.1 Tonnage of merchant marines in Europe, 1675–1870

Year	Britain	Netherlands	Germany	France	Spain and Portugal	Italy	Denmark-Norway and Sweden	Norway	Total (van Zanden)	Total (Unger)	Total world (Maddison)
1670	500,000								1,050,000	1,500,000	1,650,000
1676		900,000		100,000							
1686	340,000										
1700		500,000									
1702	320,000										
1750		500,000									
1761	460,000										
1775	700,000										
1786	751,626										
1786 (Lucassen and Unger)	881,963	397,709	155,349	729,340	224,303	311,964	555,299		3,372,000	3,000,000	4,160,000
1788	1,055,299										
1788	1,200,000										
1790	1,290,000										
1800	1,856,000										
1824		130,792									5,880,000
1830	2,202,000							131,445			
1850	3,565,000							303,080			
1851			516,410								
1860	4,659,000	479,000						567,431			
1865								747,489			
1870											24,900,000

Sources: Lucassen and Unger, 2000, pp. 4–5; Maddison, 2003b, p. 59; van Zanden, 2001, pp. 81–2; Unger, 1992, pp. 260–1; Brautaset and Grafe, 2004.

sail on the sternmost mast or mizzenmast was the workhorse of international and especially intercontinental trades. A highly divided sail plan and greater use of staysails kept crew size down. On a number of routes, shippers increasingly used two-masted ships. Those brigs and snows and other vessels with less rig grew in tonnage without an increase in crew size.

The decline in piracy and the greater provision of enforced convoy protection during the many wars of the eighteenth century changed the character of navies and, critically, relieved shippers of the need to put guns and extra crew on their ships. Governments took ever more seriously the task of protecting ocean shipping and increased the number of warships deployed to protect merchant vessels beyond as well as within Europe (Unger, 2006b, 50–53; Glete, 1993). Charts became readily available and more European waters were charted as governments promoted the creation of reliable maps of their own waters (Lang, 1968, 50–66). The sextant, along with abundant tables filling greater numbers of books on navigation in various languages, gave sailors an easier way to estimate their latitude. John Harrison's reliable chronometers of the 1750s which could keep time at sea finally solved the problem of establishing longitude. For much shipping carried on over shorter distances and where landfalls were frequent, the improved navigational aids served as a supplement to traditional knowledge and practices.

Not all routes at all times were able to generate gains in efficiency and there is some doubt about the scale of gains as a whole (Menard, 1991). However, the many changes in technology and organization apparently led to a general improvement in the productivity of shipboard labor. Gains that were already being made in the sixteenth century spread widely in the eighteenth, as more parts of Europe found ways to increase shipping services more quickly than the number of men was increased to supply those services.

While best practice would generate a ratio of about 10 tons per man in the late seventeenth century, by the 1760s that figure was rising, reaching 15 tons per man by the 1780s and 20 tons per man at the end of the century. Those regions of Europe best able to exploit the new efficiencies saw their merchant marines grow and saw a shifting of trade routes in their favor with rapid expansion of their ports. Centers of trade and especially long-distance intercontinental trade continued to shift from the Mediterranean and southern Europe to the northwest and especially to Britain, which by the 1780s emerged with the largest merchant marine tonnage of any European state.

The wars that plagued Europe for many of the years between 1793 and 1815 disrupted transportation on land as well on rivers, canals, and the seas. The ever larger armies involved in those wars could only take the field and carry on extensive campaigns, in some cases travelling hundreds of kilometers, because of the long-term improvements in transportation. The better logistics that allowed Napoleon to sustain almost annual French imperial military

Table 8.2 Manning ratios in Europe: tons served per man

Year	Venice	France	England	Germany	Netherlands	Denmark–Norway	Norway
1425	3.22						
1450			4				
1525				10			
1550	2.9				7		
1582			4.53				
1585			4.96	11			
1605					7.27		
1635					8.7		
1670		2					
1676				10.4			
1678					18		
1686			7				
1725					10.1		
1755			7.14				
1773			11				
1775			10				
1780					8.82		
1786						14.7	
1790		13.3					
1800			17.67			20	
1825					5.5		
1830			16.48				13.57
1850			18.45	17.36			20.24
1860			27.15		34.37		23.98

Sources: Lucassen and Unger, 2000, pp. 129–30; Brautaset and Grafe, 2004.

adventures grew out of the improved roads and canals. The ability of Britain to undermine enemy efforts to dominate Europe depended on improvements in shipping which supplied troops overseas and brought in much-needed tax revenue to sustain the military and naval effort.

Despite the actions of governments and despite the wars, many of the trends in transportation common to the years up to 1793 continued, not just in western but also in central and eastern Europe. After a lull in the 1770s there was a wave of new canal building in England in the 1790s followed by major projects on the Continent. The trends in the construction of roads and the rising productivity of land transport continued during the Napoleonic wars and after they ended. Using animal and wind power Europeans proved capable of generating significant gains in transportation efficiency into the 1830s. At that point, however, a new technology appeared which, by 1870, had transformed each sector of shipping services, one after the other, beyond recognition.

The steam engine developed and improved by James Watt through the 1760s and 1770s had the potential to supply motive energy, and it was transportation over land which was first to feel the effect of steam power. As early as 1801 an English engineer took a steam carriage from his home in Cornwall to London. Unreliability and the weight of the steam-powered vehicle were problems solved by improvements in the machining of parts and in metallurgy. Heavier rails made it possible to use steam engines to haul coal out of mines, and further technical improvements, allowing more of the energy to be transferred to the driving wheels, made it possible for such engines to venture further from their principal source of fuel. In 1825 in northern England a railroad more than 38 km long went into operation. By 1829 engines capable of speeds of almost 60 kilometers an hour could serve as effective people carriers, in addition to their typical original function as vehicles for moving coal. In England in 1830 about 100 km of railways were open to traffic; by 1846 the distance was over 1,500 km. The following year construction soared, and by 1860 there were more than 15,000 km of tracks.

The building of point-to-point lines led to the emergence of a railroad network. Obtaining rights of way and the construction of rails and building rolling stock, including engines, all represented considerable capital investment. English railroad builders insisted on minimal gradients, so that costs of construction were high and represented a much more sizeable sunk cost than had canals (Deane and Cole, 1969, 230–3). The advantages of rail transport and the sizeable capital investment led governments on the Continent to subsidize construction. The first French rail line opened in 1828. From 1835 there was a regular rail service in Belgium. Lines in various German states followed. Russia got its first public railway in 1836. In western and central Europe, and more slowly in eastern Europe, the connection of various lines created networks with standard track and interchangeable rolling stock. A whole range of new goods invaded unfamiliar markets as the railroads reached more parts of Europe (Figures 8.3a, 8.3b, and 8.3c).

As early as 1790 innovators had shown that the new improved steam engine could power a boat. The first commercially viable use of steam power on water came in ports and on rivers and canals. Steam-powered tugboats made it

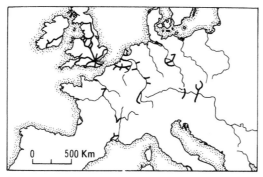

Figure 8.3a Railways in Europe, 1840 (Pounds, 1990, pp. 433–34)

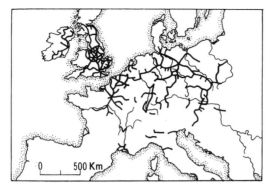

Figure 8.3b Railways in Europe, 1850 (Pounds, 1990, pp. 433–34)

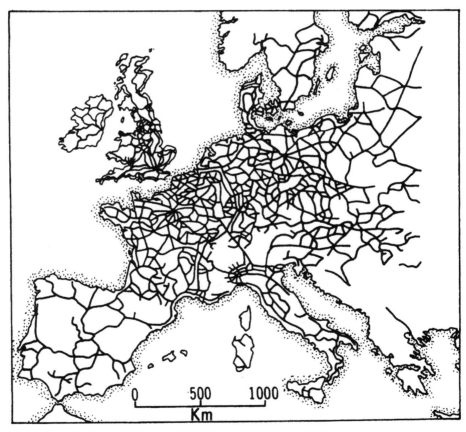

Figure 8.3c Railways in Europe, 1880 (Pounds, 1990, pp. 433–34)

possible for sailing ships to enter and leave port without having to wait for favorable winds and tides. That offered potentially sharp reductions in turn-around time, making seagoing ships even more productive.

Steamboats were especially valuable as ferries, for short hauls on protected waters, and on rivers, where they could consistently go upstream against the current. More frequent trips within a year and smaller and lighter engines made it possible for river boats to reach the highest rates of productivity increase in any part of the shipping sector in the nineteenth century (Mak and Walton, 1972, pp. 623–29).

The biggest problem for all steam-powered vehicles was their voracious appetite for fuel. The introduction of the tube boiler after 1835 and improvements in the pressure of steam engines, reaching twenty-five times their early-nineteenth-century levels by 1870, sharply reduced fuel needs. So, too, did the development of the compound engine, which reused steam in a second cylinder. That was first tried in 1825; by 1870, triple and even quadruple compound engines were in operation on seagoing ships. Greater efficiency meant that steam displaced sail on short hauls, though not until the 1850s and 1860s. Only after 1870 did sailing ships lose out in long-distance ocean trade (Harley, 1971, p. 216). The slow success of steam at sea was in part the result of continued and simultaneous improvements in the efficiency of sailing ships (Harley, 1988, 861; Rosenberg, 1972, 26–8). The increasing efficiency of sailing vessels meant that their numbers and tonnage grew and as late as 1860, for example, they made up more than 90 percent of UK merchant marine tonnage. The shift to steam began in earnest after 1870, so that by 1883 the share of steamships was over 50 percent. The future was clear.

Steam as a motive force transformed European transportation in the years from 1815 to 1870. Not only did its use on land and on water lower transport costs, but it also opened many places in Europe and beyond to trade and exchange. Steamboats and steam locomotives contributed to the reorientation of trading patterns within and beyond Europe. However, steam appeared in the context of an already growing, improving, and expanding shipping sector, subject to greater efficiencies generated by economies of scale, technological improvements, and better organization, advances already well under way in the sector in the years from 1700 through 1815.

Distribution

The significant efficiency gains made in deeper and wider capital markets and transport services fed into improvements in the overall wholesale distribution of goods, benefiting European consumers substantially. But gains from the transformation of the services sector penetrated local, regional, and interregional markets in different ways. Innovations in transport and finance developed and diffused unevenly, as did market regulation through corporations such as guilds and/or emerging nation-states. The net outcome of these factors was substantial changes to the geographical concentration of European markets between 1700 and 1870.

Productivity gains in wholesale distribution can only be traced indirectly. Economic historians use at least three methods. The most traditional way to analyze market efficiency from an economic point of view is to measure deviations from the law of one price – that is, the assumption that tradable goods should cost a consumer the same in geographically diverse markets if these markets are fully integrated (Persson, 1999, pp. 91 ff.). If prices of staple foodstuffs, such as grain, diverge over longer periods of time, then the differences can be interpreted as the cost of transacting between these markets. Transaction costs include the amount of time and money needed to procure information about the market, the cost of shipment, the legal fees involved, and the cost of accounting for diverse currencies and measures, as well as other costs, such as the protection of cargo from theft and pilferage, and of traders from extortion by corrupt officials.

The second way to approach the efficiency of markets is to analyze the organizational changes that occurred in wholesale distribution. The expansion of overseas and colonial trades was often subject to strong state-sanctioned monopolies. Within Europe the picture was more varied. Corporate, town, and state control of internal markets was increasingly on the defensive in the later eighteenth century. It all but disappeared by the mid-nineteenth century, but the process showed wide diversity across Europe, and the survival of corporate regulation could at times be both the source of poor market integration and a consequence of it.

Finally, the introduction of new goods into the European markets tells the story of the impact across Europe of early globalization, which made consumers familiar with, and regular purchasers of, a greater variety of goods. These ranged from colonial stimulants such as cacao and tobacco to non-European goods adapted into European agricultural production, such as maize and potatoes, and supplies such as Atlantic salt cod that substituted for animal products that had become rare in Europe due to their over-exploitation. Supply created its own demand and notably more sophisticated consumer behavior became apparent over this period.

Throughout European history the development of efficient distribution systems went hand in hand with urbanization, and the fast growth of Europe's ports over the course of the eighteenth century is indicative of the way in which Europe's increasing integration with the rest of the world fed into the transformation of the European hinterland (Acemoglu, Johnson, and

Robinson, 2005). Smaller coastal towns, from Glasgow to Cadiz, often grew fastest, but many medium-sized ports such as Bordeaux or Barcelona also doubled their population, and even at the top end, in cities such as London and Naples, rapid growth continued (Chapter 10; de Vries, 1984). However, Amsterdam, Europe's prime commercial hub of the seventeenth century, stagnated throughout the eighteenth century, illustrating another characteristic feature of European development: the successive leadership of different regions throughout time.

In 1700 many regions, especially in southern and central Europe, were only just emerging from a phase of disintegrating markets (Jacks, 2004) caused by wars and economic dislocation during the late sixteenth and much of the seventeenth centuries. Local harvest failures could still have devastating effects and bore witness to the consequences of thin and narrow markets. Shortages led to price hikes and the high transport-cost-to-value ratio of goods such as grains and slow information flows meant that it took a long time for supplies from elsewhere to fill the gap. Local famines were the consequence. Persson (1999) has estimated that in the early eighteenth century a local grain supply shock in Paris might only have affected northern Italian markets after a delay of two to three years. As a result price volatility was high, too.

There were only few exceptions: from the late fifteenth century large-scale shipments between the Baltic city of Gdansk and Amsterdam made up grain deficiencies in the Netherlands (van Tielhof, 2002). English domestic grain markets were probably fairly well integrated by the first half of the eighteenth century (Granger and Elliot, 1967). In the 1770s Adam Smith claimed in his *Wealth of Nations* that "the prices of bread and butchers' meat are generally the same, or very nearly the same throughout the greater part of the United Kingdom." Elsewhere, market efficiency increased only slowly: over the course of the eighteenth century adjustment times between markets probably halved overall (Persson, 1999, p. 100). Political boundaries slowed the process and even within domestic markets change took place at very different speeds across Europe. Nevertheless, in the later eighteenth century price movements were largely synchronized within the internal markets of France and Spain, even if true price convergence between markets remained elusive in most of continental Europe (Llopis Agelán and Jerez Méndez, 2001).

Wholesale distribution of any good suffered severely from the continent-wide military turmoil of the Napoleonic campaigns. Military activity and occupations, naval blockades, general insecurity, the dislocation of local economies caused by the absence of able-bodied laborers who had been drafted into service, and the presence of large armies that had to be fed all conspired to destroy existing marketing networks. Extremely volatile prices for staple foodstuffs and other goods alike were the consequence (O'Rourke, 2006).

After 1815, trends towards more integrated wholesale markets resumed, but again the European experience remained varied. Using grain price data, Jacks argues that three patterns could be observed across European countries (Jacks, 2005). The first one is epitomized by Great Britain, where, after the dust of war had settled, both domestic and international integration improved markedly. The second could be represented by the Austro-Hungarian Empire, which experienced over the period 1815–70 a process of improved internal distribution networks reflected in grain price behavior. At the same time, the empire was apparently less well connected to the remaining European economies. Finally, Spain exemplified a European economy that did not become particularly integrated either internally or externally.

The evidence from grain price studies is controversial, however, and points to the complex forces at work in market integration. Because grain and bread were of prime importance to European consumers, they were also subject to regulation in many parts of Europe well into the eighteenth century. Bread riots were feared by towns and rulers alike. Political and corporate regulations – aimed at providing a regular, affordable supply – had been ubiquitous since the Middle Ages, and the price of grain relative to wages was a concern to urban, regional, and national commentators as much as their volatility. The regulations employed could include fixed prices for grain and/or bread, urban storage, tight controls over grain trade in the urban hinterland, forced sale of grains, and all kinds of ad hoc measures against "speculators." Town or regional authorities sometimes engaged in government-sponsored missions to buy grain abroad, while the international grain trade was prohibited or subject to very high tariff rates in many places.

Throughout the early and mid-eighteenth century voices against such regulation grew stronger. The charge was that they restricted the development of marketing networks. Proponents of flexible prices in grain and other goods argued that instead of guaranteeing plentiful supplies at low and stable prices, regulated trade and prices lowered supply and thus raised both price levels and volatility. The history of the Netherlands, which had relied on open grain markets for centuries and enjoyed some of the most stable prices, seemed to contemporaries an instructive example. Also, in vastly larger urban centers administering any kind of market regulation became increasingly difficult (Ringrose, 1996, ch. 10).

The 1760s saw large projects designed to abolish regional restrictions in the grain markets in several places, notably France (Persson, 1999) and Spain (Llopis Agelán and Jerez Méndez, 2001). The effects of this liberalization, however, were disappointing, at least in the short run. As it turned out, "free trade" was no panacea for poorly integrated markets. With thin markets and high transaction costs, large producers could ration supplies. Prices and volatility rose, and since the experiments coincided with bad harvests the effects were magnified. The popular response was as expected. Unrest and rioting cost the Spanish minister his job and led to the withdrawal of such reforms in France.

These episodes illustrate a central problem of the development of markets and distribution networks. Strong corporate or state control over markets tended to slow down the process of market expansion and deepening, one of the main sources of service-sector growth. At the same time, thin markets could not function efficiently without regulation that enforced competition by check-ing the power of a few large operators. Early modern town aldermen in parts of Europe where markets were poorly integrated were not acting irrationally when they worried that freeing their trades from regulation might actually increase volatility and prices, at least in the short run. It stands to reason that one important impact of the improvements in transport and finance discussed above was that they served to accelerate the process of market integration enough to help overcome the tension between regulation and competition.

Throughout the eighteenth century the fast-growing intercontinental and colonial trades were in many parts of Europe subject to state-sanctioned trading privileges in the form of regulated merchant "companies," such as the English, Dutch, Danish, and Swedish East India Companies or the Spanish Casa de Contratación that regulated trade with Spanish America (Tracy, 1990). Here, too, the early nineteenth century constituted an important break. The existing supply lines previously established by regulated and joint-stock commercial companies were largely interrupted. The independence of North, Central and South American colonies transformed colonial trades into open supply chains. The Dutch East India Company had been liquidated in 1798 and its English counterpart lost most commercial privileges by 1813.

Within Europe craft guilds continued to self-regulate the production and marketing of a large variety of products in the eighteenth century, in particular those involving specialist skills. By contrast, traditional merchant guilds were fast disappearing in intra-European trade. In some cases guilds transformed themselves relatively successfully into company-like structures. The Compañia General y de Comercio de los Cinco Gremios Mayores de Madrid was by the 1760s acting as a deposit and credit bank, running royal factories, and perform-ing as a tax administrator, while engaging in trade on an international and national level (Capella Martínez and Matilla Tascon, 1957). In large parts of continental Europe, the Napoleonic invasions put an end to long domestic controversies over corporate control of marketing.

Napoleonic rule over continental Europe helped trade in the long run by fostering the unification of weights and measures and legal systems, though it is hard to assess the size of the impact. The same is true for the outcome of widespread taxation reforms within European states as a response to the French assault, which had demonstrated that the jurisdictionally fragmented systems prevailing in much of late-eighteenth-century Europe were unfit for raising war finance (Dincecco, 2009). Some states, such as Prussia and Austria-Hungary, responded early in the nineteenth century with reforms, while elsewhere conflicts over regional customs and tax privileges continued to disrupt internal marketing networks. In Spain, these internal disputes led to civil war as late as 1872.

After the 1820s trade barriers were – in different degrees of magnitude – reduced, through the creation of customs unions, monetary unions, and unified systems of taxation. The notable exception to this trend, surprisingly, was Britain, which introduced high tariffs on the grain trade in the aftermath of war. The traditional emphasis on the German Zollverein and the Austro-Hungarian customs union as being instrumental in creating internal markets has been challenged by more recent research, which claims that improved transport technology, namely railways, rather than political integration drove the improved efficiency of European commodity markets in the nineteenth century (Komlos, 1983; Shiue, 2005).

Given the complex interactions between the regulation of markets on the one hand and improvements in transport, finance, and distribution on the other, the fast and successful inclusion of new consumer goods in the diets and households of European consumers is probably one of the better indicators of the increasing overall efficiency of marketing within the continent. Historians of consumption have stressed the importance of the lure of addictive beverages, such as cacao, coffee, and tea, but also sugar for increasing economic incentives and altering diets and social behavior (de Vries 2008). In 1725, barely one in five lower-class households in Paris had special pots and utensils for the preparation of tea or coffee. By 1785 almost half had one such item and were presumably consuming these beverages regularly (Fairchilds, 1993). Chinese porcelain and Indian textiles mutated from exquisite goods available only to the upper classes to everyday items for increasingly fashion-conscious middle- and lower-income groups.

The first important step in the creation of these entirely new patterns of consumption was that an increasing variety of goods had to be marketed across ever-larger sections of European society. Even if colonial goods were often imported by monopoly companies, their distribution networks within European territories were rarely subject to any corporate control. In the most integrated internal markets of Europe – the Netherlands and England – supply networks for rapidly changing fashion goods probably developed first. Many new products were quickly successful all over Europe and penetrated rural as well as urban markets and all social classes. This shows that measuring the efficiency of wholesale distribution is more complex than finding price convergence or synchronization. When consumer demands changed, distribution channels had to provide a changing mix of goods with a new set of complementary services.

The dislocation caused by international warfare in the late eighteenth and early nineteenth centuries was felt particularly by trade in "new" goods, with their dependence on uninterrupted intercontinental trades. Consumer-driven market development was seriously curtailed by the hardships endured by large parts of the European population. Even in unoccupied England, real earnings were subject to strong fluctuations during this period and presumably limited the market for non-essentials (Feinstein, 1998). An at least partial setback in their distribution networks was the consequence.

Still, by the early nineteenth century many aspects of the organizational structure of marketing networks had been radically transformed. Where once regional fairs and local markets had linked wholesale and retail trades, beginning in England the travelling salesman became the agent of integration in the eighteenth century. Specialist factors represented increasingly large firms across the country, which were creating their own distribution systems. As early as the 1770s, even smaller English manufacturers from Birmingham or Sheffield cut out intermediaries by sending elaborate patterns and price lists directly to retailers. The creation of the large industrial firm changed not only production but also the way in which marketing was organized (Daunton, 1995, p. 231). Producers as well as consumers adapted to thicker markets, where close relations with customers, rapid distribution of novelties and fashion, and advertising of products became increasingly important. Larger commercial centers in turn created dynamic agglomeration benefits. There, know-how travelled fast, young merchants could learn their trade from experienced peers, consumer preferences were revealed more clearly, and market news from all over Europe and beyond arrived regularly and was publicly accessible in the form of price lists and other tools.

Before the 1800s the improvements in transport services and finance discussed above clearly contributed to the slowly increasing efficiency of marketing in Europe. The picture that emerges from grain market studies is one of moderately integrated markets in 1700, slow improvements over the eighteenth century and much faster advances after the first half of the nineteenth century. But at a European level it is also one of substantial divergence across countries in the eighteenth century, and only partial convergence after the Napoleonic wars up to 1870; the efficiency of markets in Europe differed more across regions in 1870 than it had in 1700.

The determinants of such different paths were complex. Technological improvements such as canals and railways impacted differently in the various

European economies. Notably, in parts of southern Europe canals never played a role and railways arrived late. Paradoxically, where political obstacles to trade were removed, as in the Germanies, economic historians have found that improved technology mattered more, while in southern Europe railways seem to have produced only modest social savings, presumably because other obstacles, such as political instability, persisted (Herranz-Loncan, 2007). The slow but steady freeing of markets from political and corporate control contributed in the long run, but often not in the short. Increased purchasing power of larger numbers of European consumers, changing tastes, and an increasing desire for more sophisticated and varied consumer goods began characterizing rural areas as they had towns earlier. The interactions between political and economic market integration as well as changing demand patterns were multi-dimensional and complementary. The dynamism of market development and wholesale distribution was rooted in the fact that improvements in one area increased the benefits from advances in another.

Conclusion

As Table 8.3 shows, in 1870 the growth in services as a share of the labor force was positively associated with the degree of industrialization across the nation-states of Europe. Moreover, the advances that took place in the services sector of the leading maritime countries of Europe stimulated economic development throughout Europe. Structural change within each country typically reduced the share of agriculture in both the labor force and GDP, but also changed the internal structure of the services sector. From there having been mainly female labor in relatively self-sufficient households, shops, and farms, the services sector drew in increasing numbers of male laborers, who had to be both numerate and literate to fulfill their functions in the growing economies of Europe.

Throughout the period 1700–1870, investment in physical and human capital devoted to services were never subject to diminishing returns during peacetime. In wartime, the increasing scale of conflicts both on land and sea led to economies of scale in important parts of the services sector, especially shipping and distribution.

The disruptions of war and the changes in national boundaries and policies that resulted from the treaties that ended the wars did alter the incentives for merchants and their financiers for innovating within each country. Countries open to competition from overseas responded by adapting the new organizations and infrastructure that had proved their value for the winning side. Countries less open to competition, such as Spain and Turkey, maintained

Table 8.3 Comparison of services sector and industrialization, c.1870

	Services, percentage of working population, c. 1870	Per capita levels of industrialization in 1880, UK in 1900 = 100
Northwestern Europe	*33.3*	
Belgium	17.8	43
Denmark	30.3	12
Finland	14.4	15
Netherlands	38.2	14
Norway	27.5	16
Sweden	15.2	24
United Kingdom	35.4	87
Southern Europe	*18.2*	
France	22.2	28
Greece		7
Italy	15.7	12
Portugal	10.1	10
Spain	15.5	14
Central and eastern Europe	*17.6*	
Austria-Hungary	17.5	15
Bulgaria		6
Germany	21.4	25
Romania		7
Russia		10
Serbia		7
Switzerland	15.9	39
Average, Europe	*21.4*	*23*

Source: Volume II of this book, Chapter 3.

traditional markets with state regulation. Unlike previous wars in Europe, however, the wars of the eighteenth and nineteenth centuries did not deter continued investment in services by permanent destruction or dislocation of population or infrastructure. Indeed, the logistical demands of Europe's wars, which were fought over wider areas than ever before, required the mobilization of greater resources to the point of conflict. The increased ability of states to finance the enlarged demands of modern warfare helped sustain progress in the technology and institutions of the services sector, while altering permanently its structure and significance for economic growth throughout Europe.

Figure 8.1 above shows that the density of payments networks in eighteenth-century Europe was greatest along the trade routes of medieval Europe, while Figures 8.3a–c show that the density of transportation networks expanded along the pattern already existing in the 1700 payments network. It is not surprising, then, that the process of agricultural improvement and later industrial advance throughout Europe was destined to follow a similar pattern. Behind these historical forces lay the differential productivity growth of the services sector across Europe. By 1870 the resulting differences in per capita income and growth potential between the advanced economies of western and northern Europe and the laggard economies of eastern and southern Europe were so much larger than in 1700 that all governments had to respond somehow in the succeeding decades.

Overall, productivity in the services sector, especially in the Atlantic port cities of western Europe, must have increased substantially throughout the period 1700–1870. Despite the increased scale of shipping and distribution services, first at sea and on inland waterways, and then on land with the creation of the railroad network of continental Europe, interest rates remained at the low levels already obtaining in the Netherlands by 1700. This fact alone demonstrates that productivity in the services sector increased steadily and permanently. Each advance in finance, shipping, or distribution led to spin-offs of improved productivity in the rest of the sector. Increased marketability of various products available to European consumers from around the world surely stimulated advances in the productivity of European agriculture and then European manufacturing. Enlarged markets, in turn, created incentives for further improvements in finance, shipping, and distribution. The responses to the incentives, however, depended on the institutional framework within which firms operated.

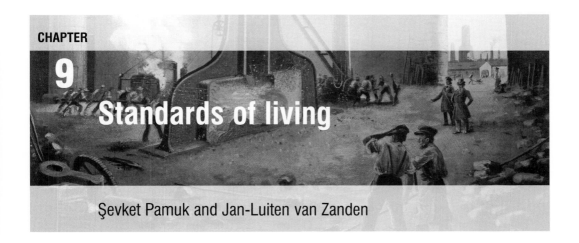

Standards of living

Şevket Pamuk and Jan-Luiten van Zanden

Contents

In 1844, Friedrich Engels, the son of a German textile merchant who had lived in Manchester during the early 1840s, published *The Condition of the Working Class in England in 1844* (originally in German), in which he presented a very pessimistic analysis of the "standard of living" of English laborers at the time. Because the book was initially written for a German audience, he often made comparisons with the – in his view – more favorable position of the German population. "But far more demoralizing than his poverty in its influence upon the English working-man is the insecurity of his position, the necessity of living upon wages from hand to mouth, that in short which makes a proletarian of him. The smaller peasants in Germany are usually poor, and often suffer want, but they are less at the mercy of accident, they have at least something secure. The proletarian, who has nothing but his two hands, who consumes today what he earned yesterday, who is subject to every possible chance, and has not the slightest guarantee for being able to earn the barest necessities of life, whom every crisis, every whim of his employer may deprive of bread, this proletarian is placed in the most revolting, inhuman position conceivable for a human being."[1]

To this stark assessment was added a wealth of information about the crime rate (which was rising rapidly), health care (death rates in the big industrial cities were much higher than elsewhere), the poor state of the education of the proletariat, and the harmful effects of child and female labor – all leading up to the conclusion that the workers in England were worse off than they had been in the past, or than their counterparts in Germany. For this, "the invention of the steam-engine and of machinery for working cotton" was to be blamed: "These inventions gave rise, as is well known, to an industrial revolution, a revolution which altered the whole civil society."

Since 1844, when Engels's book was published, the debate on the long-term consequences of the Industrial Revolution for the living standards of the working class has remained center stage in social and economic history. With hindsight it is clear that in the long run this led to a strong acceleration of economic growth in Europe and to a vast increase in the standard of living of Europeans, continuing until today (a fact which was also acknowledged by Engels in the 1892 preface to the English translation of the book: "Accordingly, the most crying abuses described in this book have either disappeared or have been made less conspicuous"). For contemporaries this was not always clear, however. Industrialization often led to the increased concentration of the poor in urban conglomerations dominated by "dark satanic mills," to increased exploitation of women and children, to declining incomes for craftsmen who

---

[1] We cite the translation of 1969, available on line at www.marxists.org/archive/marx/works/1845/condition-working-class/.

had to compete with the new steam-driven technology, and to increased inequality in income and wealth, fuelling the social movements rising in the wake of industrialization that tried to resist or modify these changes. Recent research has added that, indeed, there was an "early growth paradox," that economic growth (in terms of an increase in per capita GDP) only after some decades resulted in increases in real wages earned by industrial and agricultural laborers, and that the "biological standard of living" as read from the evidence on heights sometimes tended to lag behind even more. All this points to the fact that industrialization went hand in hand with a major redistribution of income – a few profited quickly, many had to wait a lifetime before returns came in. But to this it must be added that no industrialization – or economic stagnation – was of course no alternative, and also that patterns of rising inequality inside Britain and across Europe began to be reversed after 1870.

We shall focus on two related questions: what were the consequences of industrialization for the standard of living, and how did it affect (income and wealth) inequality in different parts of Europe and across Europe as a whole? The direction of change in standards of living in the first industrializing country during this period has been the focus of extensive debate between the so-called optimists and the pessimists. The inconclusive nature of the evidence has encouraged the search for new measures of the standard of living and evidence, supplementing the information on the development of real wages and of GDP per capita. A quarter of a century later, it is clear that improvements in standards of living were limited until 1870, especially in comparison with later decades. This chapter will present and analyze evidence related to the standard of living – including data on heights, literacy, and life expectancy. We will also study what happened in those countries and regions which did not industrialize – or began to industrialize only after 1830 or 1850 – for which less evidence has been available until recently.

A closely related debate focuses on what happened to income and wealth inequality during the 1700–1870 period. This discussion goes back to Simon Kuznets's (1955) seminal contribution on the relationship between income distribution and economic growth, in which he argued that during the first stages of growth inequality tended to increase, due to processes of structural change and widening income gaps within sectors of the economy. In the later stages of "modern economic growth," he found a decline in income inequality. This Kuznets curve has been the subject of much research, which will be briefly reviewed in this chapter. Again, the discussion of Britain will be the starting point, but we shall also pay attention to what is known about levels and trends in income and wealth inequality in the rest of the continent. In the conclusion we hope to be able to offer an answer to the question of how the benefits from industrialization and economic growth in Europe were distributed before 1870.

Economic growth

Before examining the various measures of standards of living, we shall briefly review the existing evidence regarding income per capita across Europe. Economic historians agree that increases in per capita GDP remained limited across Europe during the eighteenth century and even during the early decades of the nineteenth century. In the period before 1820, the highest rates of economic growth were experienced in Great Britain. Recent estimates suggest that per capita GDP increased at an annual rate of 0.3 percent per annum in England or by a total of 45 percent during the period 1700–1820 (Table 9.1). In other countries and regions of Europe, increases in per capita GDP were much more limited – at or below 0.1 percent per annum or less than 20 percent for 1700–1820 as a whole. As a result, at some time in the second half of the eighteenth century per capita incomes in England (but not the United Kingdom) began to exceed those in the Netherlands, the country with the highest per capita incomes until that date. The gap between the Netherlands and Great Britain on the one hand, and the rest of the continent on the other, was already significant around 1820. Italian, Spanish, Polish, Turkish, or southeastern European levels of income per capita were less than half of those occurring around the North Sea (Table 9.1). In view of the higher rates of growth in Great Britain before 1820, it is clear that these inter-country or regional differences inside Europe were smaller during the eighteenth century (van Zanden, 2001). With the acceleration of industrialization and economic growth, however, these west–east differences would increase considerably until World War I.

From the 1830s and especially the 1840s onwards, the pace of economic growth accelerated significantly. Whereas in the eighteenth century England, with a growth rate of 0.3 percent per annum, had been the most dynamic, from the 1830s onwards all European countries realized growth rates that were unheard of during the preceding century. Between 1830 and 1870 the growth of GDP per capita in the United Kingdom accelerated to more than 1.5 percent per year; the Belgian economy was even more successful, with 1.7 percent per year, but countries on the periphery, such as Poland, Turkey, and Russia, also registered annual rates of growth of 0.5 percent or more (Table 9.1). Parts of the continent then tended to catch up, with rates of growth exceeding 1 percent per annum after 1870. Catch-up or convergence applied especially to France, Germany, Austria, and the Scandinavian countries. Southern European countries such as Italy and Spain experienced rates of growth only marginally higher than those of Great Britain after 1870. As a result, their catch-up was weak, but the gap between them and the higher-income parts of the continent did not continue to expand in the years before World War I. In contrast, even though eastern and southeastern Europe began to experience increases in per capita

Table 9.1 Estimates of GDP per capita in European countries, 1700–1913
(United Kingdom, 1820 = 100)

	c. 1700	c. 1750	1820	1870	1913
England/UK	73	87	100	187	288
Netherlands	109	109	107	162	237
Belgium	69	76	77	158	247
France	n.a.	n.a.	72	110	205
Italy	71	76	65	88	150
Spain	61	58	62	71	132
Sweden	66	67	70	97	181
Poland	38–42	34–37	41	55	102
Russia	n.a.	n.a.	40	55	84
Turkey	35?	38?	40	52	71

Sources: van Zanden, 2001; Maddison, 2001; Pamuk, 2006; Álvarez-Nogal and Prados de la Escosura, 2007.

incomes after 1820, rates of increase in GDP per capita in most countries of these two regions remained below those of the rest of the continent in the years before World War I. It would thus be more appropriate to use the term "growth without convergence" for the experience of these two regions during both sub-periods of the nineteenth century (Maddison, 2003a).

To sum up, the gap in per capita incomes between northwestern Europe and the rest of the continent was wider in 1870 than it had been in 1820. The disparities between the early industrializers and the rest of the continent tended to decline for parts of Europe after 1870. Other countries of western Europe and the Scandinavian countries, and to some extent Italy, tended to catch up until 1914, but the income per capita gap between other parts of the continent and the northwest widened even further. On the eve of World War I, the gap, measured in percentage terms, between western and northern Europe, on the one hand, and southern, eastern and southeastern Europe, on the other, was wider than it had been in 1820. At the same time, however, average income per head had increased enormously, compared with the eighteenth century – already in 1870 all Europeans enjoyed an average income that was 50 to 200 percent higher than in the eighteenth century (Maddison, 2003a). What this average tells us about the living standards of the mass of the population is the focus of the rest of this chapter.

Real wages

One of the big debates among economic and social historians in the 1960s and 1970s was whether and to what extent the growth that occurred during the

Industrial Revolution resulted in an increase or a decline in the standard of living of the working population – in particular in Great Britain, but also in Belgium, the Netherlands and elsewhere on the Continent. The development of real wages was one of the key variables on which the debate focused. One of the limitations of this debate was that it tended to deal with individual countries in isolation, because an international comparative framework for analyzing real wage trends was missing. In recent years, however, indices of the real wages of construction workers have been developed for many parts of the continent for the period since the fourteenth century. Even if these wage series offer narrow coverage and exclude manufacturing, they have the very attractive advantage of providing a common measure for virtually the entire continent. For these reasons, the wage series are probably the best place to begin to compare standards of living in different regions of the continent during and after the Industrial Revolution. In fact, for the period before the Industrial Revolution, real wage evidence arguably provides more insights into income levels and the standards of living in different parts of Europe than any other measure.

The British Industrial Revolution standard of living debate between optimists and pessimists has greatly expanded the coverage and improved the quality of wage and cost of living indices. Thanks to this effort, the wage series for Great Britain now include farm laborers, artisans engaged in various trades, and white collar employees, as well as manufacturing and construction workers. In the early 1980s Lindert and Williamson constructed new indices with broader coverage to argue that standards of living improved sharply in Britain, by as much as 50 percent or more from 1780 to 1830, and about 100 percent for the period 1780 to 1850 as a whole (Lindert and Williamson, 1983). The optimists' position was later challenged, however, by Feinstein, whose critical contribution to the debate was a new cost of living index including many new goods, which indicated that prices fell less in the decades after the Napoleonic wars than was earlier thought (Feinstein, 1998). In contrast, there was little disagreement about the nominal wage series. The Feinstein indices showed much smaller increases for real wages, about 20 percent for the period 1820–50 and less than 40 percent for the entire period 1780–1850. They indicated another increase of 9 percent for the period 1850–1870. When adjustments were made for unemployment, the gains were even lower for the period before 1850 and higher for the later period.

Another development that has important implications for this debate is the recalculation of the growth rates in Great Britain for the early decades of industrialization. GDP series constructed by Crafts and Harley indicate that industrial and overall growth in Britain until the 1830s was much slower than estimated earlier. These estimates made it very difficult to sustain the optimists' case for the period before 1830, because they argued for wage increases

Table 9.2 Estimates of economic growth and real wages in Great Britain, 1780–1870

	GDP per capita	Real wages		
	Crafts–Harley, Maddison	Lindert and Williamson	Feinstein	Allen	Clark
	Total increase for each sub-period, %				
1780–1830	25	50	14	12	35
1830–1850	33	30	20	4	13
1850–1870	37	n.a.	9	20	24

Sources: Estimates for GDP per capita increases are from Crafts and Harley (1992) for 1780–1830 and from Maddison (2003a) for 1830–1870.

significantly higher than the rates of increase in GDP per capita before 1850 suggested by Crafts and Harley. The downward revision in economic growth rates indicates that standards of living improved slowly in the early decades of industrialization, not only because of the uneven distribution of the benefits of growth as assumed earlier, but also because these benefits were limited. Even with the lower rates of economic growth, however, the pessimists' case remains: Feinstein's indices continue to indicate that real wage increases lagged well behind GDP per capita increases until 1870 (Table 9.2; Harley, 1982; Crafts, 1985b, 1997a; Crafts and Harley, 1992).

More recently, two additional indices of real wages have been constructed for Great Britain during and after the Industrial Revolution. These long-term indices are limited to skilled and unskilled construction workers, but are still useful for the light they shed on the standard of living debate. The series by Allen, which will be discussed in greater detail below, are limited to London and Oxford, and indicate that real wage increases until 1850 were small, comparable with or even less than those suggested by Feinstein. On the other hand, the long-term series constructed by Clark for England point to real wage increases somewhere between the original optimist and pessimist positions for the period 1780–1870. (Table 9.1) (Allen, 2001; Clark, 2005). These more recent indices for the wages of construction workers also suggest that wage increases lagged behind increases in per capita GDP, not only in the earlier decades of industrialization, until 1830, but also in the mid-century decades, until 1870.

Evidence for real wages in the rest of the continent has not been studied to the same extent. In an important recent study, however, Allen (2001) examined the real wages of skilled and unskilled construction workers in the leading cities in Europe from the second half of the fifteenth century until World War I. He utilized a large body of data, most of which had been compiled during the early part of the last century by studies commissioned by the International Scientific Committee on Price History (Cole and Crandall, 1964). In order to facilitate

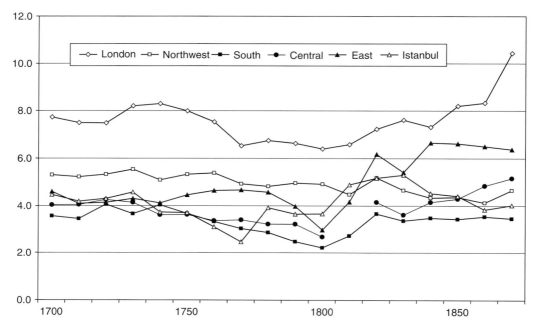

Figure 9.1 Real wages of European unskilled construction workers, 1700–1870 (Allen, 2001; Ozmucur and Pamuk, 2002)

cross-sectional and inter-temporal comparisons, he converted all price and wage series into grams of silver, and deflated nominal wages in grams of silver by a common consumer price index which allowed for north–south differences in the consumer basket to arrive at new real wage series. While his series cover only one sector, they have the important advantage of facilitating intertemporal and interregional comparisons.

Allen's series indicate that while there were short- and medium-term movements, urban real wages did not show upward or downward trends during the eighteenth century in any region of Europe. Moreover, levels of urban wages were close to each other in most parts of Europe, with one significant exception. Real wage levels in Great Britain and the Low Countries were distinctly higher than the rest of the continent during the eighteenth century, even as real wage levels in the Low Countries were declining (Figure 9.1).

Since increases in real wages in Great Britain were limited before the middle of the nineteenth century, one should not perhaps expect large real wage movements in the rest of the continent until the 1850s or even 1870. In most parts of western and northern Europe real wages declined modestly, by 10 to 20 percent during the last decades of the eighteenth century and the Napoleonic wars, and then recovered in varying degrees after 1820. The impact of the Industrial Revolution on real wages was limited outside Great Britain until the middle of the nineteenth century and even until 1870, except for the recovery after the Napoleonic wars. Allen's real wage series also indicate that there was a slight widening of the gap in urban real wages between Great Britain and northwestern Europe, on the one hand, and the rest of the continent, on the other, during the decades before 1870. One exception to this pattern was Poland, where urban wages rose faster than they did in Great Britain during the first half of the nineteenth century. Similarly, indices recently constructed for Istanbul by Ozmucur and Pamuk (2002) and for St. Petersburg by Boris Mironov (2004) indicate that real wages in these cities rose sharply between 1800 and 1870. Real wages in Leipzig also went up more than in other parts of Germany. There may be a common pattern here for eastern and southeastern Europe. One possible cause of these wage increases may be the rise in the prices of cereals and other agricultural commodities which were being exported by these regions during this period.

Workers in all parts of western Europe seem to have benefited only marginally from the large advances in productivity taking place during the Industrial Revolution. Nonetheless, it is also clear that wages did not decline in the face of rapid population growth during this period. In previous periods – in particular during the sixteenth century (and the thirteenth century) – rapid population growth had resulted in a strong decline in real wages, arguably as a result of Malthusian forces (Wrigley and Schofield 1989; Clark 2007b). That this did not happen before 1870 can also be seen as proof of the emerging economic resilience of the new economy.

The rest of the chapter will discuss the extent to which one may observe a similar pattern in other measures of the standard of living and measures of inequality.

The pessimistic case revisited

Incomes or wages as a measure of economic welfare or well-being have been greatly criticized in recent decades. Focusing on incomes tends to ignore the various disamenities of urban life and economic growth, for example. Real wages generally concern the earnings of men, who developed into the "male breadwinner," but trends in the standard of living of children and women may have been different. More generally, while incomes are an "input," welfare or well-being is an "output" or an outcome measure. For this reason, other, broader measures of welfare or human development have been gaining in popularity. Similarly, recent attempts to use body measurements, and height in particular, to establish trends in living standards have generated much enthusiasm. The search for evidence about the standard of living of children and women has also led to the use of indicators related to health, mortality, and life expectancy.

John Komlos has recently reviewed the evidence on height from different parts of Europe and what it might mean for the possible links between urbanization, economic growth, and the biological standard of living in the early stages of industrialization (Komlos, 1998). A large body of evidence indicates that average heights of males born in different parts of western and northern Europe began to decline, beginning with those born after 1760 for a period lasting until 1800. After a recovery, average heights resumed their decline for males born after 1830, the decline lasting this time until about 1860. The total reduction in average heights of English soldiers, for example, reached 2 cm during this period. Similar declines were found elsewhere: in the Netherlands, for example, where the economy did rather well from the 1820s onwards, the average height of recruits tended to decline from the mid-1830s to the mid-1850s. In particular, in the case of England, it is clear that the decline in the average height of males born after 1830 occurred at a time when real wages were rising, albeit gradually, as we have seen.

This pattern has brought into question the conventional wisdom that increases in per capita income should bring about an unambiguous improvement in human welfare. It has also led some to question whether height and socioeconomic variables were causally related during this period. Komlos emphasizes that the causal linkage between socioeconomic and structural changes and heights should be retained for this period as well. He argues that a number of developments may have adversely influenced average height during the early decades of industrialization. Amongst them, he cites rapid population growth and rising relative prices of nutrition that may have led to the substitution of more carbohydrates for proteins, rapid urbanization, which may have put town dwellers at a disadvantage as regards nutrition, growing inequalities in income, and intensification of labor. These structural changes may have created a divergence between average incomes and wages, on the one hand, and biological well-being on the other. Komlos concludes that the limited gains in incomes during these early decades of industrialization may have been too low to offset the decline in health in the newly created social environment. Baten, on the other hand, found that in most cases real wages and height appear to move more or less in the same direction, suggesting that the "early growth paradox" is limited to England (and the United States) (Baten, 2000).

Another important piece of evidence that has become available in recent years is life expectancy at birth, which takes into account infant as well as adult mortality. Life expectancy at birth for selected countries, as summarized in Table 9.3, points to a similar pattern: in the period 1820–70, the greatest improvement in life expectancy at birth occurred not in Great Britain but in other western and northwest European countries, such as France, Germany, the Netherlands, and especially Sweden. The demographic record of industrializing

Table 9.3 Life expectancy at birth across Europe, 1820–1870

	UK	France	Germany	Netherlands	Sweden	Italy	Spain	Poland	Turkey	Russia
1820	40	37	32	32	37	30	30	29	27	25
1870	41	42	36	37	45	33	34	32	31	30

Source: Baten and Pamuk, 2007; and Riley, 2005.

Europe is indeed mixed: population growth accelerated, but life expectancy rose very slowly until the 1870s – and in some regions not at all. Some of the best evidence pointing towards "pessimistic" interpretations of changes in the standard of living relate to infant mortality, which increased in large parts of western Europe until the middle decades of the nineteenth century. The record is better only in Scandinavia, where infant mortality declined continuously from about 1810 onwards. Even in industrializing northern England this measure of the standard of living only began to register progress after the middle of the nineteenth century – before the 1850s, infant mortality still went up (Huck, 1995). Similarly, rather pessimistic stories of increasing infant mortality are found in Germany and Austria (where it continued to be extremely high: three out of ten babies died before age 1 in Germany in the 1860s), the Netherlands, Belgium, and Spain (Lee and Marschalck, 2002; Chesnais, 1992, pp. 58–59, 580–81).

Urban disamenities are clearly part of this story. Simon Szreter (1997) has demonstrated that in "laissez-faire" England investment in social overheads by cities lagged behind urban growth, causing four "D"s to occur: "disruption, deprivation, disease, and death." Cities on the Continent generally did not fare much better – in the case of Hamburg, for example, the wake-up call came only during the cholera epidemic of 1892, which disclosed the extent to which investment in social overheads had lagged behind the strong economic expansion of the city (Evans, 2005). Spatial patterns in this measure of hygiene and health care show no clear correlation with income per capita; Scandinavia led the way in the mortality decline (except for Finland), but the dismal record of Germany in particular is striking. One of the explanations for this poor demographic record is the decline in breast feeding: as more and more women participated in the labor market, breast feeding gave way to less hygienic ways of feeding infants.

The evidence thus points strongly to slow improvements in the standard of living in industrializing western Europe before the 1870s. Changes in relative prices are another important part of any explanation of this pattern. For the Netherlands, for example, it has been established that the agricultural sector profited a lot from the industrialization that occurred in the United Kingdom, leading to growing exports of livestock products across the North Sea. This drove up food prices (and especially the prices of high-quality products such as butter, cheese, and meat), and led to a worsening diet, helping to explain the stagnation in average height until the mid-1850s (van Zanden and van Riel, 2004). More generally, until the "agricultural invasion," beginning in the 1860s and 1870s, food prices in Europe showed a rising trend, which tended to undermine some of the gains in terms of purchasing power resulting from the increase in nominal wages. In this respect, the real breakthrough in standards of living only occurred after *circa* 1865 (or even 1870), when growing imports of cheap cereals and livestock products from the other side of the Atlantic radically changed price trends and led to a sudden and very strong increase in real wages during the "agricultural depression" of the 1873–96 period.

The other side of the same price movement applied to the more agricultural areas of Europe. The sharp decline in the prices of cotton textiles and the rise in agricultural prices in eastern and southeastern Europe from the 1820s onwards encouraged the importation of factory-made cotton textiles and led, in varying degrees, to the decline in existing manufacturing activity and increased specialization in agriculture. While these price movements benefited consumers and rural producers in the short and medium term, they may have also delayed the onset of industrialization and more rapid economic growth in these poorer regions of the continent (Williamson, 2006).

More generally, while improvements in average life expectancy at birth occurred only slowly in industrializing western Europe, less detailed evidence, as summarized in Table 9.3, indicates that increases in average life expectancy at birth were even more limited in the rest of the continent until 1870. As a result, along with average incomes and real wages, the gap in average life expectancy at birth between western Europe, on the one hand, and southern (Italy and Spain) and eastern Europe (Russia and Turkey, as well as others), on the other, widened during the period 1820–70.

A third element in the pessimistic interpretation is related to the negative effects of the rise of the factory system. This meant that laborers had to be disciplined (because the capital-intensive mode of production of the factory system demanded constant labor input to keep the machines going), that working hours were extended, and that on top of this the labor of women and children was also increasingly "exploited." It is this transformation (as analyzed already by Engels in 1844; see also Thompson, 1967) that may have held back real improvements in the standard of living of the urban or industrial population. That working hours went up until the middle decades of the nineteenth century is now well documented, in particular for England (Voth 2001a), but similar tendencies are apparent in other industrializing countries as well. Social reformers from the 1840s onwards saw this as one of the main drawbacks of the factory system, and began to argue in favor of new social policies to limit the harm that was being done.

The story is probably more complex, however. According to Jan de Vries's hypothesis of an "industrious revolution," the increased working hours and more intensive use of women's and children's labor were a response by households to growing market opportunities or incentives arising from a developing market economy offering new goods (tea, sugar, coffee, etc.) in return for the extra income that was generated in this way (de Vries 1994). There is a substantial literature arguing that already, in the eighteenth century, western Europe underwent a "consumer revolution," of which the increased consumption of these colonial goods was perhaps just the tip of the iceberg, since, for example, consumers also owned increasing numbers of "luxury" consumer goods, such as high-quality textiles, clocks, stoves, and porcelain. The jury is still out on this issue, but it is clear that the arrival of new consumer goods to Europe – from potatoes and polenta to coffee, tobacco, and tea – meant that consumers had more options for satisfying their needs – an advance in living standards that standard measures of real wages and purchasing power omit to take into account.

The increased labor input of women and children had its negative effects as well, however. What is remarkable about England's development in the eighteenth and nineteenth centuries is that it probably made much more intensive use of female and child labor than did industrialization on the Continent (Horrell and Humphries 1995). A side effect of this specific pattern of labor-intensive industrialization that was arguably characteristic of the English Industrial Revolution (in which textiles and other industries making heavy use of cheap female and child labor were quite important) was that in a period of strong economic expansion human capital formation stagnated.

Another important indicator of the standard of living is literacy. The level of literacy remained more or less constant during the eighteenth century, and increased rather slowly during the first half of the nineteenth century. As Table 9.4 indicates, and as Crafts (1985a, p. 64) has demonstrated in greater detail, levels of human capital formation during the British Industrial

Table 9.4 Literacy* across Europe, 1820–1870

	UK	France	Germany	Netherlands	Sweden	Italy	Spain	Turkey	Russia
1820	53	38	65	67	75?	22	20	6?	8
1870	76	69	80	81	80?	32	30	9?	15

*Ability to sign a document (%).
Source: Crafts, 1997b, 2002; Baten and Pamuk, 2007.

Revolution were much lower than those of similar continental countries during their industrialization. Sweden, Norway, Denmark, Scotland, the Netherlands, and Prussia simply outperformed England in this respect; only Belgium seems to have followed the same path of labor-intensive industrialization based on low, perhaps even declining, levels of human capital formation (Vandenbroeke, 1985). The catching-up of the south in terms of literacy – of Spain, Italy, and also Austria – did not begin until the second half of the nineteenth century. Until 1850 or even 1870, the gap between the north and the south as well as the east continued to widen (Boonstra, 1993, pp. 20–28).

On top of this, under the guidance of liberal economics, states developed policies that hardly favored the working population. Following the new insights of political economists, commons – traditional sources of subsistence for large parts of the rural population – were distributed among their owners, often leaving the poor dispossessed (de Moor et al., 2002). Guilds, in many cities an important part of the urban networks supplying social security, were similarly abolished in the wake of the French Revolution. Poor laws were "reformed" in order to limit the number of people dependent on them and thus lower their costs; most famous is the 1834 reform of the English poor law, but similar reforms were carried out elsewhere (the Netherlands carried out a similar reform in 1854). The economic rationale behind this program was perhaps sound, and some measures may even have enhanced the living standard of the working population (such as the abolition of the Corn Laws and other forms of protectionism), but in the most developed parts of Europe it was often the poor who in particular bore the burden of the liberal reforms.

Liberal economic policies were not always bad news for the mass of the population, however. Jerome Blum has shown in his seminal study, *The End of the Old Order in Rural Europe* (1978), how traditional forms of bondage and serfdom were abolished in large parts of Europe, a reform movement that began as a result of the initiatives of enlightened rulers in Savoy, Denmark, and Austria in the 1760s and 1770s, accelerated under the impact of the French Revolution, and culminated in the abolition of serfdom in central Europe and Russia in the 1840–60 period. It is unclear to what extent these reforms had an impact on the standard of living, however – often peasants had to pay for their liberation quite heavily, and sometimes, as in the Russian case, they continued to be bound to the village and to the debts incurred during emancipation.

The Human Development Index

Growing dissatisfaction with GDP per capita or real wages as a measure of living standards, and the conviction that more attention needs to be paid both

Table 9.5 Human Development Index, 1820–1870

	UK	France	Germany	Netherlands	Sweden	Italy	Spain	Turkey	Russia
1820	0.383	0.303	0.344	0.380	0.403	0.221	0.210	0.134	0.129
1870	0.489	0.456	0.448	0.473	0.481	0.284	0.284	0.182	0.196

Source: Calculations based on Crafts, 2002, and Baten and Pamuk, 2007.

to aspects of well-being that are not determined by purchasing power, and to the quality of life, has led in recent years to the development of alternative measures. One more comprehensive measure of socioeconomic welfare that has gained popularity recently is the Human Development Index (HDI) which has been devised and is regularly used by the United Nations in its annual Human Development Reports. In this approach human development is seen as a process of expanding people's choices. The HDI is then defined as an index with three basic components, longevity, knowledge, and income. Longevity is measured by life expectancy at birth in years, knowledge by a weighted average of adult literacy and school enrollment percentages, and income by purchasing power parity adjusted GDP per capita in 1990 US dollars. These three components are combined into a single index by measuring each in terms of the percentage of the distance travelled between an assumed minimum and maximum. The HDI thus takes values between 0 and 1. While the United Nations has focused on gathering information and calculating annual values for HDI for individual countries for the recent period, economic historians have been pushing the estimates of HDI backwards in time towards the nineteenth century (Crafts, 1997b, 2002). With the information on the three components already presented above, we can calculate the HDI for selected countries and obtain another view of the changes in standards of living in different parts of Europe between 1820 and 1870. Table 9.5 summarizes these calculations.

The HDI values presented in Table 9.5 are consistent with our earlier conclusions. They show that rapid increases in GDP per capita in the United Kingdom after 1820 were not matched by similar improvements in human development. In fact, despite the more rapid rise in GDP per capita in the United Kingdom, improvements in human development were more significant in other west European countries until 1870. On the other hand, improvements in both income and social-economic welfare were even slower in the rest of the continent, in southern and eastern Europe where industrialization was slow, or did not begin at all during the same period. In other words, while differences in human development tended to decline inside western Europe, they tended to increase in comparison with the rest of the continent, including southern Europe, until 1870.

A Kuznets curve?

Summing up the evidence so far, we have seen that GDP per capita started to grow quite rapidly after about 1820, whereas real wages and other measures of the (biological) standard of living tended to lag behind. It has been argued that social inequality exploded, in particular in those parts of Europe that profited most from the new industrial age (Williamson 1985). This increase in inequality came on top of an already rising inequality in distribution of income and wealth, the result of economic expansion and urbanization in the centuries before 1700. In the most dynamic parts of the continent– in England, Holland, and France – levels of inequality in the eighteenth century were already very high – due to the concentration of land ownership and of mercantile wealth (van Zanden, 1995). Proto-industrialization often added to the growing inequality, creating a class of wage laborers, on the one hand, and a group of wealthy merchants, on the other. In other parts of western Europe – in southern Italy for example – income inequality was probably much lower than in the northwest (Malanima, 2006a).

Different explanations have been offered for the growing inequality of income. Kuznets's original insight was that changes in sectoral composition and increases in the urbanization ratio may in themselves have led to growing inequality; in a simple "unlimited supply of labor" model, in which real wages in the urban sector are determined by low productivity in agriculture, "modern economic growth" will initially result in an increase in income inequality, until about 50 percent of the wage earners are in the urban sector or until real wages begin to increase substantially because of the drying up of the labor surplus in agriculture. The real-wage evidence reviewed here suggests that such a turning point occurred in the post-1850 (or even 1870) period, when real-wage growth accelerated. A different interpretation of the Kuznets curve has been supplied by Williamson (1985) in his study of British capitalism; he saw as the driving force the "race between technology and education" (already analyzed by Tinbergen, 1975). During the first stages of the industrialization process, the increased demand for skilled labor led to an increase in the skill premium, driving up income inequality. Williamson argued that education expansion seriously lagged behind the demand for skills during this early period, and that only after a few generations was the supply of skills sufficiently large to result in a decline in skill premia. The evidential basis for this analysis has been questioned, however, by Feinstein (1998). Finally, there is probably a political economy story here as well: the rise of parliamentary democracy during the (second half of) the nineteenth century, and in particular the extension of the franchise to middle and lower social classes, had important consequences for government policies. It led, for example, to a growing supply of education, resulting in a further acceleration of growth (Lindert, 2004), and to social programs aimed at transferring income to the lower classes (Acemoglu and Robinson, 2005; for a case study of the Netherlands, see van Zanden and van Riel, 2004). Again, the third quarter of the nineteenth century was probably the turning point: the "social question" that emerged in the consciousness of European politicians after 1848 – the long-term question of how to integrate the "proletariat" into the political system – led in many countries to the gradual reforms that helped to stem the tide of rising inequality. Not all states responded in this way, however; where the checks and balances of parliamentary democracy were absent or weak, as was the case outside western Europe, the road to reform was not equally available. The evidence we have presented also indicates, however, that economic growth and the increases in the already existing inequalities did not occur to the same extent outside western Europe.

Conclusion

This assessment demonstrates that Friedrich Engels was addressing real concerns about the growing inequality and the continued poverty of the mass of the British working population, but that he was not entirely correct on all counts. It is clear that economic growth accelerated during the 1700–1870 period – in northwestern Europe earlier and more strongly than in the rest of the continent; that real wages tended to lag behind (and again, were higher in the northwest than elsewhere); and that real improvements in other indicators of the standard of living – height, infant mortality, literacy – were often (and in particular for the British case) even more delayed. The fruits of the Industrial Revolution were spread very unevenly over the continent – both in spatial terms (but that is perhaps not altogether surprising, since the Industrial Revolution emerged in one corner of Europe), and in socio-economic terms. Spatial inequality increased, and social inequality exploded, in particular in those parts of Europe that profited most from the new industrial age (Williamson, 1985). This increase in inequality came on top of an already rising inequality in the distribution of income and wealth, the result of economic expansion and urbanization in the centuries before 1700. It should also be added, however, that many of the basic patterns of rising intra- and inter-country inequality that we have examined in this chapter began to be reversed between 1870 and 1914, but that is a story for another chapter.

Industrialization in western Europe did therefore occur in an environment of high income inequality, and tended to sharpen it. Theorists who have sought to understand the links between inequality and growth can therefore not refer to western Europe as an example of growth occurring in an environment of low income or low wealth inequality. This statement has to be qualified, however; in terms of political rights, and the protection of their property rights, citizens of western Europe may have been better off than the inhabitants of other parts of the world. In the wake of the "Atlantic Revolution" and of course in particular of the French Revolution, new concepts of citizenship developed which – in theory at least – gave the citizens of western Europe increased political rights, a change that was not really undone by the conservative movement that dominated national and international politics in the decades after 1815. The price paid was that traditional ways of organizing a "voice" – through guilds, cities, and other corporations – were suppressed. Again, the rather difficult transformation of political systems occurring in the 1776–1848 period laid the basis for the real progress that was made during the second half of the nineteenth century.

Paolo Malanima*

Contents

* I thank Oliver Volckart for his cooperation on the first draft of this chapter.

The nineteenth century marks the passage of Europe from a civilization based on agriculture and the countryside to a civilization based on industry, services, and cities. Urbanization was one of the main changes taking place during the modernization of the last two centuries.

In the past, a dualistic economy and society prevailed, and the urban and rural worlds were two deeply different spheres from both a social and an economic viewpoint. In the countryside family ties and integration in village and community formed the basis of human relationships. In the cities, by contrast, relations prevailed among individuals cooperating within a wider system of social and economic contacts and exchanges.[1] Innovation and technical change characterized cities, while stability and tradition were the hallmarks of the countryside.

From Max Weber onwards Western urban centers have frequently been defined as "producer cities," distinguishing them from ancient and non-Western cities which have often been labelled as "consumer cities."[2] This distinction, however, does not correspond to reality – production and consumption are intertwined features of any city.[3] In pre-modern European capital cities, centered on the court and the associated bureaucracy, there was a need for services, which are also productive activities.[4] Early modern European cities offered a wider range of employment opportunities and thereby attracted people from the countryside.[5]

As a result of economic modernization the urban–rural divide began to fade and ultimately disappeared. Structural change, characterized by the diminishing share of agriculture in employment and output and the rising share of industry and services, implied the relative decline of agriculture and the countryside within both the economy and society.

The phase of urbanization we shall describe in this chapter marks the passage from the traditional world, where cities were islands in the sea of the traditional agrarian system, to the modern world, where cities have a pervasive influence on any feature of social and economic life. After an examination of European urban geography, we shall trace the passage from the old to modern urbanization, and examine the relationship between these changes in urban systems, on one hand, and the beginning of modern growth, on the other.

---

[1] See the still useful Wirth (1938).

[2] Weber (1921) is still a landmark on the topic of medieval and early modern cities.

[3] Several suggestions on the topic can be drawn from Feldbauer, Mitterauer, and Schwentker (2002).

[4] On this see the remarkable article by Brunner (1968).

[5] Migration to the cities was further encouraged by the existence of "disguised unemployment" in premodern agriculture, similar to that in any mainly agricultural economy; see Harris and Todaro (1970) on modern cities in developing countries.

The geography of urbanization

Cities

Various definitions of the city have been proposed by scholars. The differences between these definitions reflect the social, political, religious, and economic characteristics of the urban world. From an economic viewpoint, a city can be defined as *a stable settlement of population mainly devoted to industrial and service activities*. This definition would also cover "consumer cities" – that is, cities where services prevail. If the criterion for defining a city is the percentage of employees in industry and services, it is hard to specify the urban character of a particular center in past societies because of the lack of information on the employment structure of the population. In some parts of northern Europe, centers with as few as 2,000 inhabitants showed an urban professional structure. Conversely, in the south there were centers of more than 10,000 people in which peasant families were in the majority.

Sizes of 5,000 and 10,000 inhabitants have often been adopted by scholars when examining past urbanization. They are a necessary simplification when we try to extend our inquiry beyond regional borders and to compare different urban structures and levels.[6]

A global view

In past agricultural societies only a tiny minority of the population lived in cities. In modern societies, by contrast, the majority is concentrated in urban centers. In Europe, in the early modern age, fewer than 10 percent of the population lived in urban centers with more than 10,000 inhabitants. At the end of the twentieth century, this had increased to about 70 percent.[7]

In 1800 the population of the world was 900 million, of which about 50 million (5.5 percent) lived in urban centers of more than 10,000 inhabitants: the number of such centers was between 1,500 and 1,700, and the number of cities with more than 5,000 inhabitants was more than 4,000.[8] At this time Europe was one of the most urbanized areas in the world (Table 10.1), with about one third of the world's cities being located in Europe. The urbanization rate in

---

[6] When not otherwise specified, in the following pages I shall refer to centers with over 10,000 inhabitants.

[7] See the brief, but useful presentation of these changes in Bairoch (1992).

[8] The figures here proposed for the number of cities in the world in 1800 exceed those presented by de Vries (1984), p. 349. They seem more plausible on the basis of the figures referring to Europe in our tables in the appendix, which are higher than those of de Vries.

Table 10.1 Urbanization rate in 1800 (cities with 10,000 inhabitants and over)

		%
1	China	3–4
2	Japan	12
3	Russia	3
4	Europe	8–9
6	Middle East	12
7	India	6
8	Rest of Eastern hemisphere	1.5
9	North America	3
10	South America	7
11	Central America–Caribbean	3.5
	World	5

Sources: De Vries, 1984, p. 349; appendix to this chapter; Maddison, 2007, p. 39.

western Europe was greater than 15 percent, even higher than in Japan and the Middle East.[9]

European urbanization in 1700 and 1800

In 1800 the urbanization rate for Europe (8–9 percent) exceeded the average for the world (5 percent). There were, however, major regional variations (Figure 10.1). Although in some eastern regions of the continent urbanization rates were only about 3 percent, in other countries the level was higher than 20 percent and in Holland it was almost 30 percent.

If we divide the continent into four more or less homogeneous areas in terms of urbanization,[10] we find that in 1700 the highest rates were in the north – from Flanders to Holland and England – and in Mediterranean countries. In both areas the urban percentage was around 12–13 percent in 1700 and more than 15 percent in 1800. In the central countries, such as France and Germany, it was below 10 percent,[11] and in the east[12] less than 5 percent.

---

[9] Including Egypt, Syria, Iraq, and Turkey. In Table 10.1 the differences in the level of urbanization depend on the choice of the extent of the areas covered. The high level of Middle Eastern urbanization is the result of the existence of seven big cities (with 1 million inhabitants on the whole) (de Vries, 1984, p. 350). If we exclude some regions of eastern Europe, European urbanization figures would increase appreciably and exceed those for both Japan and the Middle East.

[10] See Figure 10.3 on the countries included in the four European areas.

[11] For Germany the *Statistik des Deutschen Reichs* (1877) has also been used.

[12] With the exception of the Balkans, on which see the remarks below.

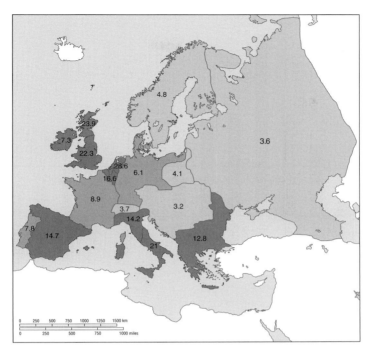

Figure 10.1 European urbanization in 1800

The core of European urbanization

At the country level, the highest urbanization rates in the mid-eighteenth century were along an imaginary line running from southern England, through the Low Countries and northern France, to Italy (Figure 10.2). West of this line, urbanization rates, although high in Spain, were less than 10 percent overall.

On the whole, European urban patterns were not very different from those of the late Middle Ages (i.e. between the tenth and the fourteenth centuries). The only difference was the rise of urbanization north of Flanders, especially in the Netherlands and England.[13]

In contrast, urbanization in Italy and Spain had declined in both relative and absolute terms. However, in both cases figures on urbanization are misleading, given the wide presence of peasant families in the cities in the southern regions of these two countries. In 1800, the urbanization rate in Spain was around 14 percent, using centers with over 10,000 inhabitants, and 24 percent using those with over 5,000. If peasant families are excluded, these figures fall to 11

---

[13] DeLong and Shleifer (1993) attempt the hard task of connecting this change with the features of the different institutions in the North and South.

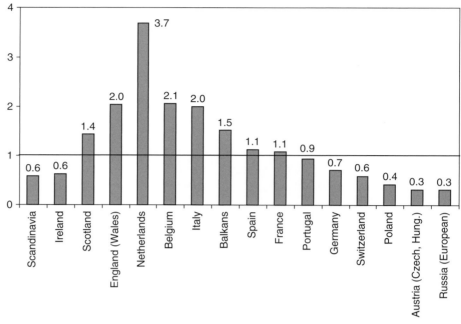

Figure 10.2 Urbanization in 1750 (European average = 1)

and 14 percent respectively.[14] In southern Italy, the presence of agro-towns had been a feature since ancient times (Malanima, 1998, 2002, 2005). Taking cities with over 5,000 inhabitants, Sicily in 1800 would boast an urbanization rate of 66 percent, perhaps the highest in the world. If urbanization was an indicator of wealth and progress, Sicily would have been the most advanced region in the world: more advanced than England, whose urbanization rate, in the same year, was a mere 30 percent. Data on cities need to be used carefully in order to avoid simplifications and mistakes.

The peripheries of urban Europe

The regions around western Europe were much less urbanized. In Scandinavia big centers were rare,[15] and urban inhabitants accounted for only about 5 percent of the total population. The percentages were even lower in eastern Europe, from Austria through Bohemia, Slovakia, Hungary,[16] Poland, and

---

[14] These figures, however, provided by Llopis Agelán and Gonzáles Mariscal (2006), are higher than those presented in the appendix. Also higher are the figures proposed by Álvarez-Nogal and Prados de la Escosura (2007), who derive their series from Bairoch, Batou, and Chèvre (1988). A good basis for Spanish urbanization is Carreras and Tafunell (2005). I followed their data on urban population in 1800 Spain.

[15] Data on Scandinavian cities have been revised using Galletti (1822).

[16] To single out eastern cities under the sovereignty of Austria we utilized Sommer (1839).

Russia.[17] The Balkans, by contrast, had relatively high urbanization rates. In the eighteenth century, with a total population of 8.5–12 million inhabitants, urbanization rates exceeded 12 percent.[18]

However, more than half of the urban population of this area lived in Constantinople, which in 1700 was the biggest European center, with more than 685,000 inhabitants.[19] Constantinople was the capital of a large Asian empire, and if it is excluded the urbanization rate for the Balkans falls to a mere 6 percent. London, the second city in Europe, then numbered 575,000 inhabitants, overtaking Constantinople only around 1750. It was the biggest city in 1800 (with 865,000 inhabitants), when Paris was the second, with 581,000, and Constantinople the third with 560,000. The next largest cities were Naples (320,000), Moscow (300,000), Vienna (231,000), St. Petersburg and Amsterdam (both around 220,000), and Madrid, Lisbon, Dublin, and Berlin (between 150,000 and 200,000).

Urban geographic structure

What was the distribution of cities within Europe? Geographers and demographers have shown that today, in some regions, the urban distribution follows the rank–size rule,[20] which can be summarized by the equation:

$$S_r = \frac{S_1}{r}$$

where S_r is the size (that is population) of a particular city, S_1 the size of the largest city in the region; and r the rank (represented by the series of natural numbers from *1* – the main city – to *n*). According to this rule, the city ranked 2 would have half the population of the first, the third city one third, and so on. If, in past agrarian societies, the spatial distribution of cities in a given region followed the same pattern, an estimate of the urban population could be easily obtained by knowing only the size of the first city. We would simply use the previous formula and increase the rank until the result for S_r is 10,000 or 5,000 (according, that is, to the threshold chosen). Then we could sum up the population of all cities in order to obtain the number of urban inhabitants.

[17] See, on Russia especially, Kappeler (2002).

[18] Data on cities and population in the Balkans are from Carter (1977), McGowan (1981), Palairet (1997), and Todorov (1983). I thank S. Pamuk for the many suggestions both on population and urbanization in the Balkans.

[19] This was the population of the European part, which was, in any case, much bigger than the Asian one. Some 15–20 percent of the total urban population lived in the Asian part of Istanbul (*Meyers Konversations-Lexikon*, 1885–90).

[20] The rank–size rule has been the subject of many debates. Scholars do not agree on the presence of this pattern of distribution in the modern world. The topic is discussed from a historical perspective by de Vries (1984, pp. 49 ff.).

The rank–size rule has been verified for some modern urban regions (though with many exceptions).[21] However, in any region, the first five to ten cities do not follow closely the rank–size pattern in their distribution. Cities below 2,000 inhabitants do not follow any statistical rule either. It has been verified, by contrast, that the intermediary cities – between, that is, about the fifth main city and centers of 2,000 inhabitants – are distributed according to a particular pattern easily represented in a double-scale logarithmic graph by an interpolating straight line.[22] The higher the slope of the interpolating curve, the more the cities' distribution is hierarchical – that is with some big cities, surrounded by smaller centers. The slope is lower wherever the urban hierarchy is less evident and the urban system is more polycentric. In any case, defining in a non-arbitrary way the extent of the region for which the rule is tested is difficult where premodern Europe is concerned. The result is influenced by the width of the region we are dealing with: ordinarily the smaller the region, the higher the slope.

Dispersion and hierarchy depend on the functions any city develops together with geography and the transport costs facing the individuals exploiting these urban functions. While agglomeration forces push towards hierarchical structures, transport costs imply the dispersion of the functions among many different towns. The nineteenth-century transport revolution played an important role in pushing European urban systems towards more hierarchical structures.[23]

Two case studies

The pre-modern European urban landscape is made up of hierarchical structures, on the one hand, and clusters of big cities, on the other. Italy and England in 1800 are clear examples of two extremes (Figure 10.3). Since the late Middle Ages, England has been characterized by a few modestly sized cities and a large capital, or primate city, London.[24] In 1700, although England and Italy shared the same urbanization rate – about 13 percent – in England the second-largest city was Norwich, with 29,000 inhabitants (one twentieth the size of London), and there were only eleven towns with over 10,000 inhabitants. In Italy there were 66 cities with more than 10,000 inhabitants – many big cities, but not a single truly dominant one.[25]

---

[21] The literature on the rank–size distribution has increased rapidly in the last few years. Among the many contributions, Nitsch (2005) has a useful summary of recent research. See also Soo (2003) and Gabaix and Ioannides (2004).

[22] On the rank–size distribution and its use in the chapter, see the appendix.

[23] See, however, the remarks below about the first phase of European modern urbanization.

[24] On the relationship between London and the English economy as a whole, see Wrigley (1967).

[25] The English population was, however, less than half the Italian population (see appendix).

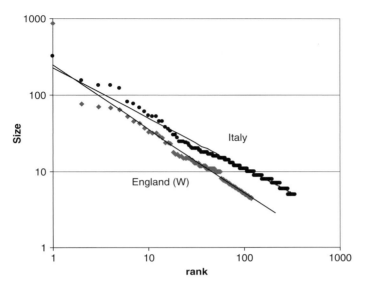

Figure 10.3 Rank–size distribution England (Wales) and Italy 1800 (cities with 5,000 inhabitants or more)

This distribution did not change much in the following centuries. The slope of the interpolating curve in 1800 England is high – 0.84.[26] For Italy, the slope of its urban system in 1800 is among the lowest in Europe – 0.66. Germany is nearer to Italy (0.67); France and Spain occupy a intermediary position (0.77 and 0.79), while Austria-Hungary (0.81), the Balkans (0.86), Poland (0.86), the Netherlands (0.87), and Russia (0.88) are closer to England.

The chronology of urbanization

A long view

We know that urbanization in Europe progressed during the high Middle Ages. The percentage of the European population living in centers with more than 5,000 inhabitants rose from 6–8 percent in the ninth century to about 10 percent in 1300 (Bairoch, 1988, pp. 118, 137).[27] Urban populations were more severely affected by the Black Death in 1348–50 than the countryside (especially in Mediterranean regions) and urbanization declined as a consequence. A recovery took place from 1400 until 1600. The following two centuries were characterized

---

[26] This applies whenever London is included in the regression, as in Figure 10.2. If London is excluded the slope falls to 0.65. The coefficient is always negative (see appendix).

[27] On the late Middle Ages see the still useful Russell (1972).

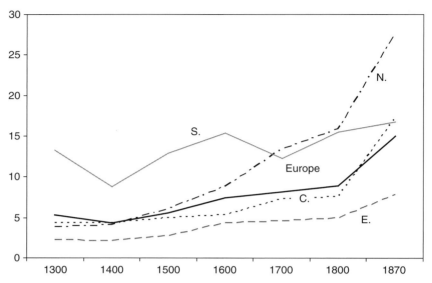

Figure 10.4 European urbanization, 1300–1870
Note: the thick curve refers to the whole of Europe. *North (N.)*: Scandinavia, England and Wales, Scotland, Ireland, Netherlands, Belgium; *Centre (C.)*: Germany, France, Switzerland; *South (S.)*: Italy, Spain, Portugal; *East (E.)*: Austria, Bohemia, Hungary, Poland, Balkans, Russia.

by a slow rise. In the nineteenth century the pace of urbanization increased. From 1800 until 1870, the proportion of the population living in urban areas almost doubled when we refer to centers with over 10,000 inhabitants, and rose by about 60 percent when we take centers with over 5,000 (Figure 10.4).[28]

The long-term trend of European urbanization could therefore be divided into three distinct phases: growth in the high Middle Ages, 900–1300; relative stability, 1300–1800; modern growth, from 1800.

The growth rates attained at the end of the twentieth century are unlikely to be exceeded in the future, although some increase is possible – the level for 2030 is forecast to be only a little higher compared with the 2000 rate of 70 percent. Once a certain level has been reached, the pace of urbanization must inevitably slow down and finally stop.

The period 1700–1870 can be divided into two phases (Table 10.2): the last epoch of *pre-modern stability*, between 1700 and 1800;[29] and the start of the *modern urban transition*, from 1800 until 1870.

---

[28] The sources of this figure and the following tables are given in the appendix. In Table 10.2 and in the appendix I present some series excluding England, in order to isolate the role of English urbanization from European urbanization as a whole.

[29] See the remarks by Wrigley (2004b).

Table 10.2 European urbanization, 1700–1870 (cities with >10,000 and >5,000 inhabitants and indices)

	Europe (>10,000)	Index (>10,000)	Europe without England (>10,000)	Index without England (>10,000)	Europe (>5,000)	Index (>5,000)
1700	8.2	1.00	7.9	1.00	11.4	1.00
1750	8.0	0.97	7.6	0.96	11.7	1.03
1800	9.0	1.10	8.3	1.05	12.4	1.09
1870	15.2	1.85	13.0	1.64	19.7	1.73

Two epochs

During the first of these two phases (1700–1800), urban growth would be even slower if we were to subtract the rise in agricultural population living in the big centers of southern Spain and southern Italy. On the other hand, we know that in both the eighteenth and nineteenth centuries proto-industrial activities developed in the countryside,[30] and the slow pace of urbanization between 1700 and 1800 reflected the spread of industry outside the city walls.[31]

The lack of growth in urbanization during the eighteenth century (or, in any case, its modest growth) is not a solely European phenomenon. On the world level urbanization diminished during this century by about 10 percent. China and India were more urbanized in 1700 than in 1800. Only in North America was there a 7–8 percent increase.

Things changed during the second phase, between 1800 and 1870. In the nineteenth century urban populations rose in Europe by 27 million (Bairoch, 1988, p. 291) (by 22.5 million in 1800–70) and the number of cities with over 5,000 inhabitants grew from 1,600 in 1800 to 3,419 in 1870. On the whole, in today's developed regions, urbanization rates tripled in the nineteenth century, from 10 to 30 percent (Bairoch, 1988, p. 495). This was an urban growth unknown in the history of mankind (Figure 10.5).

Even though urbanization rates rose very little in the eighteenth century, it is important to notice the increasing role that cities played in Europe during this century and to a greater extent later on. On the European continent the number of cities rose rapidly even where the urbanization rate fell or remained stable (Table 10.3).

With regard to centers with over 5,000 inhabitants, their number was 86 percent higher in 1800 than in 1700, and this figure increased fourfold by 1870.

---

[30] See the general overview by Cerman and Ogilvie (1994).   [31] See also de Vries (1994).

Table 10.3 Number of European cities and their population, 1700–1870 (cities with >10,000 and indices)

	Number	Index	Inhabitants	Index
1700	287	1.00	9,375	1.00
1750	361	1.26	11,492	1.23
1800	585	2.04	16,936	1.81
1870	1,299	4.53	47,259	5.04

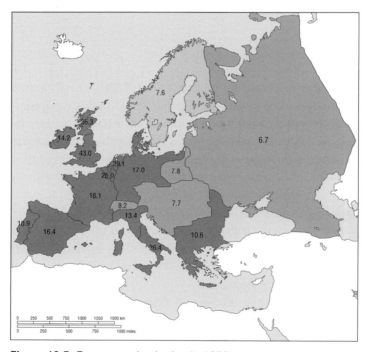

Figure 10.5 European urbanization in 1870

Between 1700 and 1800 centers with more than 10,000 inhabitants doubled. If we look, then, at the ratio between urban population and space rather than at the urbanization rate we see growth. The change in the number of urban inhabitants is a good approximation of the process of human capital formation. It is always in urban centers that human interaction is strongest and the exchange of useful knowledge most intense.[32] Within the borders of present-day Europe the urban population was three times more extensive in 1800 than in 1300, and nine times more in 1870. Urban culture was much closer to any European inhabitant in 1800 than in 1700 and much more so in 1870.

---

[32] On the possibility of a quantification of human capital formation through urban growth, see the interesting remarks by Lucas (1988).

Urban population and urban centers

In order to analyze eighteenth-century urban stability and subsequent nineteenth-century growth, it is helpful to divide the process of urban development into two components: the rise in urban population within already existing cities, and the rise in the number of cities. In some periods cities grow considerably, whereas their number remains almost the same, whilst in other periods the population of the existing cities remains stable whilst their number increases. In Table 10.4 both changes are reported for the period we are dealing with, on the basis of a threshold of 10,000 inhabitants, for the whole of Europe.

We could summarize the results of the table by saying that, between 1700 and 1800, the decline in urbanization rates was more than counterbalanced by the growth in the number of urban centers, and that from 1800 until 1870 both the urbanization rate and the number of cities increased. However, the overall rise of the urban percentage depended on variations in the number of cities rather than on the growth of existing centers. There were 862 cities with over 5,000 inhabitants in 1700, 1,170 in 1750, 1,600 in 1800 and 3,419 in 1870. While urban population rose only slightly more rapidly than the whole population, many more centers became cities.

Four areas

A division of the continent into four areas provides a clearer view of these two periods in the chronology of European urbanization (Table 10.5).

In relative terms, nineteenth-century growth (1800–70) was higher in the Centre (129 percent), characterized by a lower starting point, and the North (75 percent). Growth was lower in the East (56 percent) and even lower in the South (a mere 8 percent). The nineteenth century was the last phase of the redistribution of European urbanization, which had started in the late Middle Ages. The South accounted for 51 percent of Europe's urban inhabitants in 1300, 41 percent in 1400 and 42 percent in 1500 and 1600. It was only 30–31 percent in 1700–50, 29 percent in 1800 and 17.2 percent in 1870. From the urban viewpoint, the Euro-Mediterranean continent was becoming less and less Mediterranean (Table 10.6).

Deviations from the average

On a regional scale we can identify several remarkable deviations from the European average. These deviations concern specific regions which were

Table 10.4 Number of European centers with 10,000 inhabitants or more and urban percentage of a sample of 147 cities, all exceeding the threshold of 10,000 inhabitants in the period between 1700 and 1870

	Number	Urban percentage (147 cities)
1700	287	6.2
1800	585	4.6
1870	1,299	5.8

Note: The rate of urbanization is based on the number of cities with 10,000 inhabitants or more.

Table 10.5 European urbanization rate in 1700–1870, per area (cities with 10,000 inhabitants and more)

	1700	1750	1800	1870
North	13.3	13.2	15.8	29.7
Centre	7.3	7.3	7.5	17.2
South	12.3	12.8	15.5	16.8
East	4.6	4.4	5.0	7.8
Europe	8.2	8.0	9.0	15.2

Note: See Figure 10.4 for the countries comprising the North, South, Centre, and East.

Table 10.6 Percentage of the European urban population by area in 1700–1870 (cities with 10,000 inhabitants and more)

	1700	1750	1800	1870
North	21.8	21.2	24.6	31.7
Centre	28.6	27.7	24.5	29.8
South	30.1	30.5	28.8	17.2
East	19.5	20.5	22.1	21.3

Note: See Figure 10.4 for the countries comprising the North, South, Centre, and East.

important economic centers in the past but which, in the period we are interested in, were declining. With the exception of the south of the peninsula, the rise of whose urbanization depended on the growth of many agro-towns, Italian urbanization was stationary at around 13–14 percent between 1700 and 1870. It was declining if we refer back to the late Middle Ages, when urbanization was 18 percent.[33] The Netherlands also declined between 1700 and 1750, but then remained relatively stable until 1870. Spain also decreased in comparison with the sixteenth century, but recovered between 1750 and 1870,

---

[33] I refer here only to northern and central Italy (excluding the south in order to avoid the effect on urbanization of the increasing number of southern agro-towns).

while Portuguese urbanization was lower in the eighteenth century than in 1600, when it was 11.4 percent, and increased only slightly in the nineteenth century.[34] In the Balkans urbanization declined between 1700 and 1870. The Austrian empire's extensive urbanization started from the very low level of 4 percent, but progressed at a faster rate than England , even though, in 1870, its urban percentage was still half the average European level. The Scandinavian population increased, while urbanization hardly rose, between 1800 and 1870.

The rise in England, Scotland, Ireland, Belgium, Germany, and France is much higher than the average. The geography of urban growth is the same as that of the first European wave of industrialization. England, Scotland, and Ireland account for 26 percent of all European urban growth between 1800 and 1870.

Urban hierarchies

It is often assumed that the urban transition resulted in a more hierarchical rank–size distribution in every state or area. The new techniques of transportation allowed a higher mobility of population and consequently the concentration of functions in bigger cities, often the capitals. The forces of agglomeration were stronger than the forces of urban dispersion. This trend has often been confirmed by research into specific regions during the nineteenth century. The situation was different in the first phase of modernization with which we are dealing. The slope of urban distribution was declining in several European regions between 1700 and 1870, which meant a tendency towards dispersion rather than towards centralization. We are not surprised by the discovery of a decline in these 170 years in regions which were stationary from an urban viewpoint, such as Italy (0.71, 0.67), Spain (0.81, 0.74), the Balkans (1.12, 0.80), Russia (1.08, 0.79), or even Belgium (0.92, 0.82).[35] However, the decline also affected England (1.42, 1.03).[36] Only the Netherlands (0.84, 0.91), France (0.73, 0.88), Germany (0.66, 0.75) and Poland (0.67, 0.96) reveal a clear trend towards a stronger hierarchy in urban distribution in the European area. The main reason is that, as we have seen in Table 10.4, in this first phase of modern urbanization many small cities were exceeding the threshold of 5,000 to 10,000 inhabitants. The consequence was the widening of the base of urban pyramids in most European regions.

---

[34] Data on Portuguese cities are from Valerio (2001).

[35] The first figure in parentheses refers to 1700 and the second to 1870. All figures are computed using regressions according to the equation presented in the appendix.

[36] London is included in the coefficients of the regressions, while it is excluded from data presented in the appendix. The inclusion or exclusion of London implies big changes in the coefficients.

The urban transition

Structural change and the urban transition

The urban transition is an important element in the major change often referred to as *modern growth* and in the structural change which accompanied the strong increase in productive capacity of modern economies.[37] Even in past agrarian economies we find examples of urban transition and migration to the cities (e.g. during the medieval period), but in the nineteenth and twentieth centuries this phenomenon acquired an intensity unknown in the past. The urban population, which had formerly represented a tiny minority of the total European population, rose rapidly from less than 10 percent in 1800 to 25–30 percent in 1900 (de Vries, 1984, pp. 45–48) and 60–80 percent in 2000. The developing countries outside Europe caught up at the end of the nineteenth century and reached similar rates in the second half of the twentieth century. On the world scale, urbanization was about 5 percent in 1800, 15–20 percent in 1900, and 40 percent in 2000 (Bairoch, 1988, p. 405; see also, more synthetically, Bairoch, 1992).

Urbanization is a particular case of internal migration. Over the period which we have considered, mortality was higher in the cities than in the countryside due to poor hygiene conditions. The increase in the urban population, in absolute and relative terms, is thus attributable to population flow from rural areas. Migration from the countryside has, in past societies, been the immediate cause of urbanization. In the nineteenth and twentieth centuries, growth of the migration and urbanization rates followed the trends represented in Figure 10.6. Migration followed a parabola or inverted U-curve, whilst urbanization rates described a logistic curve, from the low level of the pre-modern world to the substantial increases during the first phase of modern growth and stability during the last decades of the twentieth century (de Vries, 1990, p. 54).

Only at the end of the nineteenth century did hygiene improve sufficiently to allow the natural increase in the urban population to outstrip that in the countryside. As a consequence, the flow of immigration was now adding population to the internal demographic rise.

A dualistic system

As regards the determinants of migration from the countryside, they can be represented through the two-sector models often used in economics to explain

---

[37] Hohenberg and Lees (1985, chs. 6–8) provide a good reconstruction of the European urban transition.

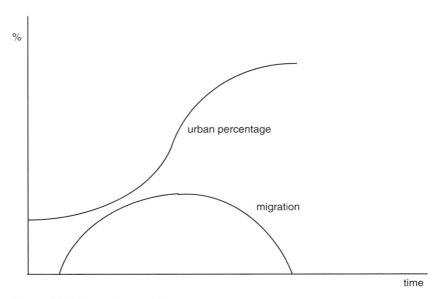

%

urban percentage

migration

time

Figure 10.6 The urban transition

migratory flows. Our departure point is a *dualistic economy*, such as the premodern one, where:

1. The countryside is characterized by the production of food and raw materials and the city by industries and services. Of course, we know that reality is more complex: industrial production and services are not exclusive to cities, while agricultural workers often live in urban centers. However, this dualism is a useful approximation when we look at past societies.
2. Primary goods produced in the countryside are characterized by low-income elasticity, while secondary goods and services have high-income elasticity. Therefore a lasting rise in per capita income results in ever lower relative demand for primary goods, and in an economy-wide shift towards the production of secondary goods and services.

The determinants of urban growth

Let us therefore now presume that a flow of innovations initially permits an increase in the level of productivity in industry and subsequently in agriculture. This is exactly what happened at the start of the nineteenth century with the Industrial Revolution. In this case the curve of marginal productivity in industry rises and so do wages. A higher percentage of workers is now attracted by urban activities than before, and it is likely that the process will continue and employment in the primary sector diminish further. The capacity to produce, however, must also increase in agriculture, but since primary goods are inelastic to income growth, the increase in agricultural productivity also results in a diminishing relative demand for primary goods, followed by diminishing employment in the countryside. Migratory flows originate in the countryside and move towards the cities. Thus the center of gravity of the economy gradually shifts from the agricultural to the industrial sector.

Wages reflect the rise in urban labor productivity, and the differential between urban and rural wages widens. The demand for labor in the most innovative sectors and the migratory flow towards these are followed by further migration towards dependent activities. Through the employment multiplier, growth in one or several urban sectors spreads and involves new urban activities (building, services, administration, etc.). The attraction of rural workers from outside the city is the consequence of the inner, new dynamism of the urban economy and the consequent demand for labor. The effect of the exogenous shock to the city's economy on the whole can be represented as:

$$\Delta T = \frac{T}{B} \cdot \Delta B$$

where ΔT is the change in total employment; ΔB is the change of employment in the innovating sector and T/B is the employment multiplier.[38] Nineteenth-century urbanization implied deep transformations in the urban environment: the building of houses to accommodate the rapidly rising population, new urban infrastructure, the widening of sewers and water supply, and so forth. The interrelationship betwen several different factors in urban growth has been referred to as the "law of proportional effect": the bigger the city the more it is able to attract immigrants, given the multiplying effects of its new activities (Hohenberg and Lees, 1985, ch. 7).

Agriculture, industry and urban transition

If agricultural productivity does not follow the rising path of industry then the process cannot continue, unless there is a sufficient importation of food. Agricultural prices increase as soon as agricultural workers are not able to support the rising urban demand. The value of agricultural marginal labor productivity rises as a consequence of rising food prices, and rural wages rise as well. Migratory flows towards the cities stop and sometimes people abandon the cities.

There are many examples, in past societies, of de-urbanization caused by the inelasticity of agricultural production following an increase in productivity in the

[38] See the useful analysis by O'Sullivan (2003, pp. 119 ff.).

more advanced and innovative urban centers. We have seen how, during the first modernization of the European economy, some European regions did not immediately follow the rising path of northern European economies. This was partly a consequence of the stationary conditions of the primary sector. The novel feature of the growth which has taken place from the first decades of the nineteenth century is the rise in productivity in the primary sector together with those in industry and services. In contrast, in past agrarian economies innovations were frequent in the cities, whilst agriculture remained stationary for long epochs, thus hindering structural change and the development of the economy as a whole.[39] Things changed rapidly from the nineteenth century onward, and urbanization was one of the main effects of this overall economic expansion.

Nineteenth-century England and Wales witnessed a period of rapid industrialization, during which wages rose together with productivity in industry;[40] however, agriculture also progressed contemporaneously. Laborers' wages in building increased compared with those in agriculture. In real terms the difference in wages between the town and the countryside has been estimated as approximately 30 percent. Rural migration towards industries rose dramatically from 1820 onwards: between 0.9 and 1.6 percent per year (while in the 1960–80 Third World they never exceeded 1.2 percent per year) (Williamson, 1987c, p. 50; 1991, ch. 2; see also Clark, 2005, 2007b, for series on industrial and agricultural wages). Italy represents, in contrast, the example of a declining economy, where the ratio of urban to rural wages diminished relative to the end of the sixteenth century (Malanima, 2005).[41] The declining trend was correlated with the diminishing importance of cities in the economy as a whole up to the 1880s (Malanima, 2005; Federico and Malanima, 2004).

Urbanization and structural change

Urbanization is therefore a dynamic process correlated with growth. Since growth results in a diminishing relative importance of agricultural production, structural change follows. However, on the other hand, we could also modify the direction of this relationship and consider growth as the result of the development of useful knowledge based on the human interactions which are possible only within cities. Yet the possibility of assessing the relationship between growth and urbanization is far from easy. In fact, until the end of the nineteenth century, data on structural change are lacking or unreliable[42] and even output estimates

[39] The problem was particularly stressed by Bairoch (1992).
[40] Useful for data on urban inhabitants in England is Great Britain, Census Office (1968).
[41] I exclude here southern Italy for the reason already noted.
[42] See, in any case, the attempts made in this direction by van Zanden (2005b).

for the decades 1800–70 can only suggest trends and some of the more important differences among groups of countries. Additionally, the data on urbanization are far from perfect, despite probably being of a better quality.

Over the period with which we are dealing it is difficult to discern any meaningful relationship between population growth and those variables which explain urbanization.[43] However, some long-term correlation between population density and urbanization is likely to exist, although not during the first phase of modern growth. We have seen that, while population was rising during the eighteenth and nineteenth centuries in every European region, the trend of urbanization differed both in intensity and direction.[44]

Attempts at checking the determinants of past urbanization have already revealed that several variables such as cereal imports, progress in transportation, industrialization, and exports contribute to the explanation of urban growth, while the main determinant is labor productivity (Bairoch and Goertz, 1986; Bairoch, 1990). Since per capita output is a summary index for the process of growth, checking its correlation with urbanization is quite reasonable. The result of doing this is that a correlation exists in the period 1800–70, with the correlation being stronger whenever we include the level of urbanization in 1800 among the determinants. While we discover a positive relationship between urbanization and growth, the relationship with the level of urbanization at the beginning of the century is negative: the higher the level of urbanization in 1800, the lower the rate of annual increase, indicating convergence.[45]

Inequalities in urbanization

Whereas during the last epoch of the traditional European agrarian economy urbanization was stationary, modern growth engendered a fast change in urbanization, first in Europe and later in the rest of the world. As with many other economic variables, inequalities in urbanization also increased worldwide (Table 10.7).

In 1800 the level of urbanization in Europe was only slightly higher than the world average, whereas in 1900 it was twice that level. Europe and the Americas were at the same level, whilst in Asia and Africa the level was three to six times

---

[43] For instance by Boserup (1965).

[44] Population change is not significant when included in the regression reported below.

[45] I ran the following regression: $\ln u = \alpha + \beta_1 \ln y + \beta_2 \ln U_{t1} + \varepsilon$ where u, y, U_{t1} are the annual rates of growth of urbanization (u between 1800 and 1870) and of per capita product (y), and the level of urbanization (U_{t1}) at the beginning of the period in which we are interested (in our case 1800). For Italy I used the per capita GDP estimate in Malanima (2006b), while the data for the other countries are from Maddison (and refer to the decades 1820–70). The result of the regression is: $\ln u = 1.28 + 0.84 \ln y - 0.81 \ln Ut_1$ with an R^2 of 0.8. The coefficients on $\ln y$ and $\ln U_{t1}$, have associated p-values of 0.000028 and 0.027 respectively.

Table 10.7 Levels of urbanization in the continents and the world
in 1800–1980 (cities with more than 5,000 inhabitants)

	1800	1900	1950	1980
Europe	12	30	43	64
America	12	29	48	64
Africa	4	5	12	25
Asia	9	9	15	26
World	9	16	26	38

Source: Bairoch, 1988, p. 495 (with some changes).

Table 10.8 Inequality in urbanization in Europe, 1300–1870
(cities with more than 5,000 inhabitants)

	17 regions	4 areas
1300	0.95	0.77
1400	0.90	0.56
1500	0.86	0.66
1600	0.80	0.57
1700	0.71	0.42
1750	0.68	0.45
1800	0.69	0.53
1870	0.67	0.48

Note: See the appendix for the method used to calculate inequality in
urbanization.

less. As can be noted, inequality subsequently diminished (at least in terms of
urbanization per continent).

We know that, during the first phase of economic modernization, personal
and regional inequalities increased. With urbanization, by contrast, things
developed differently. When considering the seventeen regions and four areas
(North, South, Centre and East) into which the continent has been divided in
this chapter, it may be noted that inequality diminished from the late Middle
Ages onwards (Table 10.8).

In the late Middle Ages, the southern part of the Euro-Mediterranean world
was considerably more advanced. This was the legacy of late antiquity, when
civilization and cities characterized the South, whilst the North was backward
and scarcely urbanized. In 1300 this was still the case. Beyond the Alps and
north of the Pyrenees cities were few and modest. The inequality within the
continent was notable, with the inequality in urban distribution suggesting
inequality in economic levels. In the early modern age some convergence began
to take place and previous sharp contrasts faded gradually. The period we have
dealt with in this chapter was the last phase of the old agrarian world and the

beginning of the new economy. Already around 1700 urbanization in the South had been overtaken by that in the North. During the nineteenth century, urbanization progressed more in the North and the Centre. As a result, the differential in urbanization was lower than it had been five centuries before.

Conclusions

From stability to growth and from inequality towards convergence: thus we could succinctly summarize the main changes in eighteenth- and nineteenth-century European urbanization. In 1800 the geography and the levels of European urbanization were still similar to those of the late Middle Ages, the main changes being the rise of England and Scotland and the spread from Flanders towards the Netherlands in the early modern age. Inequality between North and South had diminished for this very reason.

In 1870, by contrast, both the level and geography of urbanization were significantly different. An evident dominance of the northern European countries over the Mediterranean regions and a fast rise in urbanization rates were the main differences with the past. The rise in urbanization occurred within the context of the great transformations of the European economy during the first epoch of modern growth. Since modern growth took place primarily in the cities, and was based on the application to the economy of that useful knowledge which had developed in urban centers since the distant past, we can speculate whether structural change and urban development were the consequences of the ongoing economic changes, or if urban culture has to be seen as the main determinant of modern growth. The determination of the direction of the causal link, in this case as in many others, is not straightforward.

Appendix

The series presented in this appendix are new. They are based on a revision both of data on urban inhabitants and of the population of Europe per country. The series refer to the whole of Europe (within the present borders of the continent). The starting bases for the urban populations have been the revision and merging of the urban databases by Bairoch, Batou, and Chèvre (1988) and de Vries (1984). The new database has then been checked with the more recent literature on the subject (quoted in the footnotes and in this appendix). The necessity of a new urban database for the period 1700–1870 comes from the fact that the existing ones do not cover the whole continent and do not include the nineteenth century (see below).

1 European population

European population per country or area and their extent in sq km

		Sq km	1700	1750	1800	1870
			000			
1	Scandinavia	1,198	2,900	3,600	5,250	9,540
2	England (Wales)	151	5,450	6,300	9,250	23,000
3	Scotland	79	1,200	1,260	1,630	3,420
4	Ireland	84	1,900	3,120	5,200	5,800
5	Netherlands	33	1,950	1,950	2,100	3,650
6	Belgium	30	1,900	2,300	2,900	4,900
7	France	544	21,500	24,600	29,000	38,000
8	Italy	301	13,500	15,500	18,100	28,000
9	Spain	505	7,400	9,300	10,500	16,200
10	Portugal	92	2,000	2,600	2,900	4,300
11	Switzerland	41	1,200	1,300	1,700	2,700
12	Austria (Hungary)	626	15,500	18,300	24,300	35,700
13	Germany	543	14,100	17,500	24,500	41,000
14	Poland	240	2,800	3,700	4,300	7,400
15	Balkans	516	8,550	9,900	12,000	23,700
16	Russia (European)	5,400	20,000	22,000	35,000	63,000
	Europe	10,383	121,850	143,230	188,630	310,316
	Europe (without Russia)	4,983	101,850	121,230	153,630	247,316

Note: Data in the table refer to the European population within the 1870 political borders. The extent of every country or area is recorded in the first column. Poland is in fifteenth-century borders. Scandinavia includes Finland, Sweden, Norway, and Denmark. Austria includes Hungary, Bohemia, Croatia, Slavonia, Transylvania. The Balkans include Greece, Serbia, Montenegro, Bosnia-Herzegovina, Romania, Bulgaria, Crete, and the European part of Turkey. Iceland, Malta, and some minor islands are excluded.

Sources: Among the following works, only Urlanis provides data on a country basis for all our period and for every country: Reinhard, Armengaud and Dupâquier (1968) (several countries); Urlanis (1941), p. 414; Wilson and Parker (1977) (some countries, early modern); de Vries (1984), pp. 36–37 (western Europe); Wrigley and Schofield (1989) (England, 1700–1870); Beloch (1937–61) (Italy, 1700–1800); Bardet and Dupâquier (1997) (several countries); Maddison (2001, 2003a) (several countries); de Vries and van der Woude (1997)(Netherlands); Valerio (2001) (Portugal); McEvedy and Jones (1978)(several countries); Glass and Grebenik (1965) (several countries); Woods (1989) (early modern United Kingdom); Carreras and Tafunell (2005) (Spain); Palairet (1997) (Balkans).

2 Different estimates of European urbanization (1700–1870)

As can be seen (Figure 10.7), the differences between the three series are relatively modest from an aggregate viewpoint (at least for the period we are dealing with in the present chapter, but not for the late Middle Ages). Much stronger are the differences for regional data on population and urbanization.

Three estimates of urbanization in Europe from 1700 to 1850–70 (cities with more than 5,000 inhabitants and cities with more than 10,000 inhabitants).

	Bairoch >5,000	Index	Bairoch >10,000	Index
1700	11.4	1.00	7.8	1.00
1750	12.0	1.05	8.1	1.04
1800	11.9	1.04	8.1	1.04
1850	18.9	1.66		
	De Vries >5,000	Index	De Vries >10,000	Index
1700	11.9	1.00	9.2	1.00
1750	12.4	1.04	9.5	1.03
1800	13.0	1.04	10.0	1.09
1850			16.7	1.81
	New >5,000	Index	New >10,000	Index
1700	11.4	1.00	8.2	1.00
1750	11.7	1.03	8.0	0.97
1800	12.4	1.09	9.0	1.10
1870	19.7	1.7	15.2	1.85

Sources: Bairoch, Batou, and Chèvre, 1988; Bairoch, 1988, p. 216 (for >5,000 in 1850); de Vries (1984); present appendix.

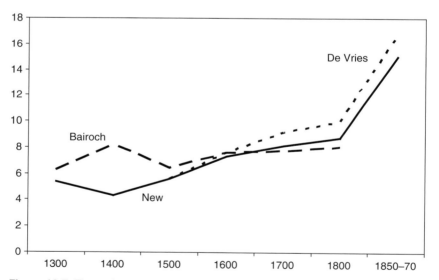

Figure 10.7 Three views on urbanization 1300–1870 (> 10,000 inhabitants)

The coverage of the three series is also different. While in the new series the whole continent is covered, Bairoch dealt with Europe as a whole, but without European Turkey, and did not elaborate data for nineteenth-century Europe in Bairoch, Batou, and Chèvre (1988). Data on European nineteenth-century urbanization were, however, provided by Bairoch (1988). De Vries (1984) provides a database concerning western Europe (with Poland) from 1500 until 1800. Data on urban inhabitants after 1800 are not presented in the database, although concise series are provided in the book.

3 Number of cities, urban inhabitants, and urbanization (10,000 inhabitants and above)

For the preparation of the database on which the following tables are based, for the year 1870 I exploited the geographic dictionary by Predari (1871), with information drawn from contemporary statistical sources. The following dictionaries have been used to check and improve the series: Marmocchi (1854–62); Metzger (1888); Muzzi (1854); Vivien de Saint-Martin (1879–95).

Number of cities (10,000 inhabitants and above)

		1700	1750	1800	1870
1	Scandinavia	3	3	7	21
2	England (Wales)	11	22	57	147
3	Scotland	3	7	14	23
4	Ireland	3	3	8	15
5	Netherlands	20	18	19	29
6	Belgium	13	14	20	45
7	France	62	63	88	161
8a	Italy CN	34	40	51	66
8b	Italy SI	32	49	75	136
9	Spain	25	30	60	107
10	Portugal	2	4	3	14
11	Switzerland	3	4	4	11
12	Austria (Hungary)	10	18	31	98
13	Germany	34	38	64	222
14	Poland	4	5	5	18
15	Balkans	20	24	43	65
16	Russia (European)	8	19	36	121
	Europe	287	361	585	1,299

Urban inhabitants (10,000 inhabitants and above)

		1700	1750	1800	1870
		000			
1	Scandinavia	125	167	251	727
2	England (Wales)	718	1,031	2,065	9,891
3	Scotland	64	145	390	1,242
4	Ireland	96	159	382	822
5	Netherlands	634	577	600	1,061
6	Belgium	404	363	482	1,225
7	France	1,877	2,136	2,592	6,881

8a	Italy CN	1,043	1,264	1,447	2,131
8b	Italy SI	873	1,203	1,658	2,893
9	Spain	714	846	1,542	2,649
10	Portugal	190	196	225	470
11	Switzerland	39	60	63	222
12	Austria (Hungary)	263	473	770	2,753
13	Germany	767	992	1,489	6,965
14	Poland	106	124	176	580
15	Balkans	1,195	1,214	1,536	2,519
16	Russia (European)	267	542	1,268	4,228
	Europe	9,375	11,492	16,936	47,259

Urbanization rates (10,000 inhabitants and above)

		1700	1750	1800	1870
		%			
1	Scandinavia	4.3	4.6	4.8	9.1
2	England (Wales)	13.2	16.4	22.3	43.0
3	Scotland	5.3	11.5	23.9	36.3
4	Ireland	5.1	5.1	7.3	14.2
5	Netherlands	32.5	29.6	28.6	29.1
6	Belgium	20.3	15.8	16.6	25.0
7	France	8.7	8.7	8.9	18.1
8a	Italy CN	13.0	13.6	14.2	13.4
8b	Italy SI	16.1	19.4	21.0	26.4
9	Spain	9.6	9.1	14.7	16.4
10	Portugal	9.5	7.5	7.8	10.9
11	Switzerland	3.3	4.6	3.7	8.2
12	Austria (Hungary)	1.7	2.6	3.2	7.7
13	Germany	5.4	5.7	6.1	17.0
14	Poland	3.8	3.4	4.1	7.8
15	Balkans	14.0	12.3	12.8	10.6
16	Russia (European)	2.1	2.5	3.6	6.7
	Europe	8.2	8.0	9.0	15.2
	Europe (without England)	7.9	7.6	8.3	13.0

4 Number of cities, urban inhabitants and urbanization (5,000 inhabitants and above)

In order to calculate urbanization rates for cities with over 5,000 inhabitants (in the following table) on the basis of direct data for European cities with over 10,000 inhabitants, we start with the following equation (see above):

$$S_r = \frac{S_1}{r}$$

This equation is estimated by altering it in the following way:

$$S_r = \frac{S_1}{r^u} \text{ or } S_r = S_1 r^{-u}$$

where u is the slope of the curve. Both the constant term S_1 and the coefficient u can be computed through the following regression:

$$\log S_r = \log S_1 - u \log r$$

This regression has been used to calculate the population of cities with more than 5,000 inhabitants. In order to work out data for 1700, 1750, 1800, and 1870, I used direct data for S_1 and calculated u for any country on the basis of direct data on cities with over 10,000 inhabitants. Then, using the results of the regressions, it was possible to complete the series with the calculated population of cities between 10,000 and 5,000 inhabitants. For all regressions the R^2 was higher than 0.90, and the regressions were all significant at the 1 percent level. When calculating the regressions for England, London was considered to be a special case and therefore excluded. If we include the data for the city the coefficient (the slope) of the regression is too high, and, as a consequence, the number of cities between 5,000 and 10,000 too low. Only for Portugal did I use direct data on cities between 5,000 and 10,000 inhabitants because of the few cities in the country and the unreliable results of the regression.

Number of cities (5,000 inhabitants and above)

		1700	1750	1800	1870
1	Scandinavia	7	8	12	44
2	England (Wales)	26	84	174	374
3	Scotland	5	15	45	43
4	Ireland	7	8	17	28
5	Netherlands	57	48	49	74
6	Belgium	35	49	55	103
7	France	185	205	251	371
8a	Italy CN	84	93	102	138
8b	Italy SI	130	184	238	378
9	Spain	74	99	140	287
10	Portugal	5	22	28	35
11	Switzerland	21	19	11	41
12	Austria (Hungary)	17	37	63	270
13	Germany	123	173	205	637
14	Poland	29	29	25	39
15	Balkans	40	51	96	195
16	Russia (European)	17	46	89	362
	Europe	862	1,170	1,600	3,419

Urban inhabitants (5,000 inhabitants and above)

		1700	1750	1800	1870
		000			
1	Scandinavia	150	204	266	872
2	England (Wales)	793	1,407	2,767	11,407
3	Scotland	76	193	597	1,370
4	Ireland	121	212	444	904
5	Netherlands	884	771	791	1,357
6	Belgium	551	596	702	1,576
7	France	2,653	3,067	3,613	8,190
8a	Italy CN	1,363	1,576	1,788	2,590
8b	Italy SI	1,520	2,138	2,756	4,489
9	Spain	1,034	1,302	2,025	3,995
10	Portugal	221	324	416	620
11	Switzerland	147	152	105	413
12	Austria (Hungary)	303	586	950	3,803
13	Germany	1,333	1,894	2,369	9,596
14	Poland	288	292	330	711
15	Balkans	1,324	1,388	1,834	3,366
16	Russia (European)	325	712	1,607	5,799
	Europe	13,087	16,813	23,362	61,058

Urbanization rates (%) (5,000 inhabitants and above)

		1700	1750	1800	1870
		%			
1	Scandinavia	5.2	5.7	5.1	9.1
2	England (Wales)	14.6	22.3	29.9	49.6
3	Scotland	6.3	15.3	36.6	40.1
4	Ireland	6.4	6.8	8.5	15.6
5	Netherlands	45.3	39.5	37.7	37.2
6	Belgium	29.0	25.9	24.2	32.2
7	France	12.3	12.5	12.5	21.6
8a	Italy CN	13.0	13.6	14.2	13.4
8b	Italy SI	16.1	19.4	21.0	26.4
9	Spain	14.0	14.0	19.3	24.7
10	Portugal	11.1	12.5	14.3	14.4
11	Switzerland	12.3	11.7	6.2	15.3
12	Austria (Hungary)	2.0	3.2	3.9	10.7
13	Germany	9.5	10.8	9.7	23.4
14	Poland	10.3	7.9	7.7	9.6
15	Balkans	15.5	14.0	15.3	14.2
16	Russia (European)	2.5	3.2	4.6	9.2
	Europe	11.4	11.7	12.4	19.7
	Europe (without England)	11.2	11.3	11.5	17.3

5 Urban Inequality

Differentials in urbanization have been calculated according to the following equation:

$$D = \sqrt{\sum_{i=1}^{n} \left(\frac{U_i}{U_a} - 1\right)^2 \cdot \frac{p_i}{p_w}}$$

where:

D differential in urbanization;
U_i urbanization in a specific region or area;
U_a average European urbanization;
p_i population of the region or area;
p_w total European population.

11

Europe in an Asian mirror: the Great Divergence

Bishnupriya Gupta and Debin Ma*

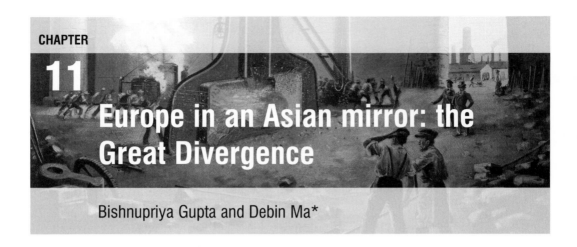

Contents

* We want to thank the editors, Stephen Broadberry and Kevin O'Rourke, Joachim Voth
and Tirthankar Roy for comments and suggestions. We are solely responsible for the errors.

Europe is a peninsula to Asia.

Fernand Braudel

Why did sustained industrialization and modern economic growth first take off in western Europe and not elsewhere? Attempts to address this historical conundrum have spawned a large literature related to the theme of "European exceptionalism." It champions the view that Europe, in particular northwest Europe, had superior, and in some cases exceptional, economic conditions and social institutions long before its economic take-off in the modern era. This widely prevalent and often contentious view has recently been contested by a new wave of historians and specialists on Asia such as Ken Pomeranz, Bin Wong, and Prasannan Parthasarathi. They marshalled evidence to show that living standards in the advanced parts of China and India were on a par with those of northwest Europe in the eighteenth century. The revisionists have also put forward various hypotheses to reinterpret the traditional story of the "rise of the West and the fall of the Rest" in terms of factor and resource endowments, the impact of Western colonization and, most importantly, historical path dependencies.

This chapter provides a broad but selective survey of the major hypotheses and evidence regarding historical comparisons of the economic performances of India and China versus western Europe. We begin with a review of the latest research on the comparison of real wages across Eurasia, which reveals that living standards in the advanced parts of China, Japan, and India as measured by real wages seem to have been closer to the lagging parts of Europe – namely, southern and central Europe – than to northwest Europe, as was claimed by the revisionists. We follow the review with a comparative survey of other complementary evidence such as anthropometric indicators, literacy rates, consumption patterns, and urbanization rates.

To shed light on the divergence in living standards and levels of development across pre-Industrial Revolution Eurasia, this chapter offers a preliminary survey of the early modern economic, political, and social institutions and organizations that underpinned the operation of goods and factor markets. It reviews the emerging research on comparative degrees of efficiency in grain market integration, as well as the different patterns of commercial organization and trading networks in Europe and Asia. Our chapter ends with a brief comparison of the differential impacts of Western imperialism on India and China, and their contrast with modern Japan, which made a successful transition to modern economic growth in the shadow of Western dominance.

We do not deny that a comparative study on this scale and size is likely to be over-ambitious, and our generalizations too broad. As noted by Braudel, the sheer size of India and China often meant that differences within or between these two countries could be just as large as they were between themselves and Europe. Therefore our survey below is highly selective and at times contentious or even speculative.

Living standards across Eurasia

Silver wages and grain wages

A recent systematic comparison of living standards based on wage information is summarized in Broadberry and Gupta (2006), who put together silver wages for different regions of India using a variety of sources. These are earnings of artisans, employees in the Mughal court, as well as employees of the European companies at a number of points between 1595 and 1874, in units that facilitate a comparison with Europe. The data are also subdivided into regional categories. Table 11.1 presents data on the daily wages of unskilled and skilled laborers in terms of both their silver content and the amount of grain that they could purchase. Part A provides data for northern and western India, based on the cities of Agra and Surat. Wages in rupees are converted to grams of silver using information from Habib (1982) and Chaudhuri (1978). Part B shows the trend in southern India using wages from different parts of this region. The broad trend is for the silver wage to rise, with the skilled wage about double the unskilled wage.

Table 11.2 compares the Indian wage with the wage in England. It shows that the Indian silver wage for unskilled laborers was little more than one-fifth of its English counterpart at the end of the sixteenth century, and fell to just over one-seventh of the English level during the eighteenth century.[1] Table 11.3 presents Chinese wage data, which show the same basic patterns in comparison with England as the Indian wage data. The silver wage was already much lower in China than in Britain by the Late Ming period.

As a first step we use the price of grain to convert the money wages into grain wages. We have been careful to use an average price rather than a price below or above the average. Grain prices varied greatly from area to area and year to year. Using a price that reflected a famine situation would make the grain wage very low, while using a low price would lead to the opposite bias. Tables 11.2 and

---

[1] Table 11.1B shows that the skilled wage used by Parthasarathi (1998, 2001) for 1750 was well above the average wage of the region. There was great differentiation among weavers. Many worked as assistants and earned below the average; weavers with one loom made close to the average earnings. There were skilled weavers with more than one loom who employed men to work as assistants. The earnings of skilled weavers were higher and some were likely to have enjoyed a high skill premium. This was clearly not the average wage of the region, as implied by Parthasarathi. We have thus excluded Parthasarathi's estimates from Table 11.2. If these estimates were included, Indian silver wages would be up to about 40 percent of the British level in the first half of the eighteenth century.

Table 11.1 Indian silver and grain wages, 1595–1874

A Northern and western India

	Silver wage		Wheat grain wage		Rice grain wage	
	Unskilled	Skilled	Unskilled	Skilled	Unskilled	Skilled
	grams per day		kg per day		kg per day	
1595	0.67	1.62	5.2	12.6	3.1	7.5
1616	0.86		3.0		2.4	
1623	1.08		3.8		2.9	
1637	1.08	2.37	3.8	8.3	2.9	6.5
1640	1.29		4.5		3.5	
1690	1.40		4.3			
1874	1.79	5.27	2.5	7.5		

B Southern India

	Silver wage		Rice grain wage	
	Unskilled	Skilled	Unskilled	Skilled
	grams per day		kg per day	
1610–13	1.15		5.7	
1600–50	1.15		3.2	
1680	1.44	2.44	3.9	6.9
1741–50	1.49		2.1	
1750	(3.02)	(7.56)	(4.2)	(10.5)
1779	0.86		1.1	
1790	1.44		1.8	

Source: Broadberry and Gupta, 2006.

11.3 show that, in contrast to the rising trend in silver wages, grain wages trended downwards in northern and western India as money wages failed to keep up with rising grain prices, particularly during the early seventeenth century. Brennig (1986) argues that subsistence consumption for a household of six was 3.1 kg of rice per day. Taking the wheat/rice ratio of calories per lb from Parthasarathi (1998) yields a subsistence consumption of 4.7 kg of wheat per day for a family of six. On this basis, grain wages were always above subsistence for skilled workers, but fell below the subsistence level for unskilled workers during the early seventeenth century.

Table 11.2 makes possible a direct comparison between Indian and English grain wages for unskilled workers. The Indian grain wage for unskilled laborers remained relatively high, at above 80 percent of the English level, until the

Table 11.2 A comparison of the daily wages of English and Indian unskilled laborers, 1550–1849

A Silver wages

Date	Southern England	India	Indian wage
	grams of silver per day		as % of English wage
1550–99	3.4	0.7	21
1600–49	4.1	1.1	27
1650–99	5.6	1.4	25
1700–49	7.0	1.5	21
1750–99	8.3	1.2	14
1800–49	14.6	1.8	12

B Grain wages

Date	England	India		Indian wage as % of English wage
	Wheat, kg of grain per day	Wheat, kg of grain per day	Rice, on wheat equivalent basis	
1550–99	6.3	5.2		83
1600–49	4.0	3.8		95
1650–99	5.4	4.3		80
1700–49	8.0		3.2	40
1750–99	7.0		2.3	33
1800–49	8.6	2.5		29

Source: Broadberry and Gupta, 2006.

seventeenth century, but fell to only about a third of the English level by the late eighteenth century. Although less detailed, Table 11.3 reveals a similar trend for the Chinese, with the grain wage falling decisively behind after the mid-Qing period.

The silver wage data suggest unambiguously, then, that the Great Divergence was already well established in the sixteenth century. Broadberry and Gupta (2006) show that as in today's industrialized countries, high money wages reflect a higher level of economic development. Although Asian grain wages remained close to the English level until the end of the seventeenth century, the data indicate a sharp divergence during the eighteenth century. This divergence occurred partly as a result of a rise in the English grain wage, but also partly as a result of a decline in the Indian grain wage. The finding in terms of silver and grain wages is that India and China look much more like the backward parts of

Table 11.3 A comparison of the daily wages of English and Chinese unskilled laborers, 1550–1849

A Silver wages

Date	Southern England	Yangtze delta	Chinese wage
	grams of silver per day		as % of English wage
1550–1649	3.8	1.5	39
1750–1849	11.5	1.7	15

B Grain wages

Date	England	Yangtze delta		Chinese wage
	Wheat	rice, kg of grain per day	Rice, on wheat equivalent basis	As % of English wage
1550–1649	5.2	3.0	4.5	87
1750–1849	7.8	2.0	3.0	38

Source: Broadberry and Gupta, 2006.

Europe than like the most developed parts of Europe from the sixteenth century, with high grain wages reflecting an abundance of grain and low silver wages reflecting low levels of overall development.

Grain wages and agricultural productivity

One explanation for the relatively high grain wage is the low grain price. Parthasarathi (2001, pp. 43–53) claims that the high productivity of southern Indian agriculture was the result not of geographical factors and high yields in rice, but of high levels of investment during the seventeenth and eighteenth centuries. Parthasarathi's explanation of how the investment in southern Indian agriculture came about, and how it led both to high levels of economic development and to low silver wages, raises a number of logical difficulties, however. The investment in agriculture was the result of rulers competing to attract and fix mobile labor. The puzzle is why competition for labor did not lead to higher silver wages. Investment in land in this account led to an abundance of grain and low food prices, rather than to the movement of labor out of agriculture. Although Desai (1972) argues that labor productivity in agriculture was twice as high in 1595 compared with 1961, Moosvi (1973) scales this down to about 29 percent for food grains and 45 percent in all agriculture. Habib (1969), in his seminal work on the potential for capitalist development in Mughal India, argued that although agricultural *land* productivity might have been comparable with other countries including those of western Europe, the scale of the surplus was small given the high level of taxation. Furthermore, technology was described by foreign travellers as rudimentary. The implications for labor productivity in the economy are well captured by Pelsaert's statement that "a job that one man would do in Holland passes through four men's hands before it is finished." Therefore Indian agriculture had low wages and high labor intensity, but relatively higher land productivity (Habib, 1969, p. 60).

We find the argument that there was high labor productivity in Indian agriculture not only counterintuitive in light of the theoretical framework for modern economic growth and structural change, but also contrary to other historical evidence. In the developing parts of northwest Europe, investment in agriculture did indeed lead to high agricultural labor productivity. However, this higher agricultural labor productivity did not lead to an abundance of grain and low food prices, because labor moved out of agriculture into industry and services. Rising living standards came from increasing consumption of cheaper industrial goods, together with a relatively constant consumption of food. A similar logic applies to Chinese and east Asian agriculture, where wet-rice cultivation had achieved possibly one of the world's highest land productivity levels using traditional technology. However, despite this high land productivity, labor productivity was relatively low compared with highly commercialized English and Dutch agriculture.

Real wages of unskilled workers

The use of grain wages is a highly simplified exercise that suffers from various biases in the absence of a more comprehensive consumption basket. Contemporary accounts suggest that the diet of the common Indian man was rice, millet, and pulses, and fish in the coastal regions. Wheat was less common. Housing was considered to be of poor quality. Contemporary writers also commented on the rudimentary state of clothing (Moreland, 1923, pp. 270–78). There are also shifts in relative prices to be considered when comparing living standards over time. Moosvi (1973) argues that while the purchasing power of cereals was the same in 1595 as in 1874 and products like milk, butter (ghi), and meat were cheaper in Mughal India, sugar was more expensive. Desai (1972) found that industrial goods were more expensive in 1595 compared with 1874, and the average consumption of cloth and metal goods was low. Of course, there are also the large questions of how to deal with differences in climatic factors and cultural preferences when making cross-country comparisons.

A series of recent studies (Bassino and Ma, 2005; Allen et al., 2010) has attempted a relatively rigorous comparison of the purchasing power of real wages of unskilled laborers in Asia and Europe, based on more systematic price data and consumption baskets. As opposed to grain wages, these comparisons are based on fairly comprehensive consumption baskets of representative goods and services that extend beyond staple grains to include items such as meat, vegetables, clothing, and fuel. They also focus exclusively on unskilled workers in major urban centers. Allen et al. (2010) contains detailed discussions of the wage and price data, as well as of methodological problems.

Table 11.4 presents a sample of the kind of basket constructed for a China–Europe comparison. The next step is to compile nominal wages of unskilled laborers in major urban centers across Eurasia. Allen et al. (2010) focuses on three major cities in eighteenth- to twentieth-century China: Beijing,

Table 11.4 Comparison of consumption basket costs, c.1750

	Bare bones basket		Respectable basket		London prices	Beijing prices
	Europe	North China	Europe	North China		
					grams of silver	
Oats/Sorghum	155 kg	179 kg			0.76	0.48
Bread			182 kg	182 kg	1.28	0.95
Beans			40 kg	40 kg	0.5	0.84
Meat/Fish	5 kg	3 kg	26 kg	31 kg	3.19	2.04
Cheese			5.2 kg		2.07	
Eggs			52 pc	52 pc	0.37	0.074
Butter	3 kg		5.2 kg		6.45	
Oil/Cooking		3 kg		5.2 kg		4
Beer/Rice Wine			182 l	49 l	0.39	1.98
Soap	1.3 kg	1.3 kg	2.6 kg	2.6 kg	6.36	1.65
Linen/Cotton	3 m	3 m	5 m	5 m	4.87	6.14
Candles	1.3 kg	1.3 kg	2.6 kg	2.6 kg	5.4	3.3
Lamp Oil	1.3 kg	1.3 kg	2.6 kg	2.6 kg	2.8	3.3
Fuel (M BTU)	3	3	5	5	5.59	11.2
Total Basket Cost (Grams of Silver)	213	182.6	558.6	499.3		
Europe/Beijing ratio					Geometric average	
	Bare bones basket		Respectable basket			
	1.17		1.12		1.14	

Source: Allen et al., 2010.

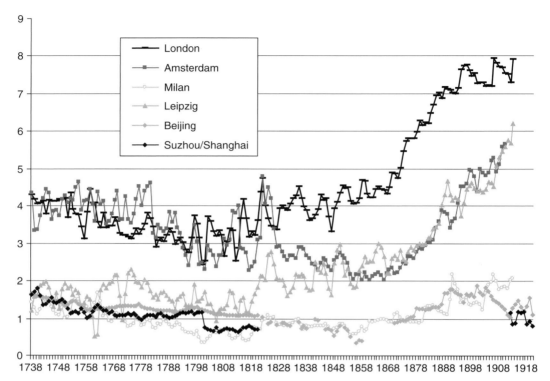

Figure 11.1 Real wages in Europe and China (Allen et al., 2010)

Suzhou/Shanghai (in the lower Yangzi Delta), and Canton, comparing these with major European cities. They survey an extensive sample of nominal wages and choose an average wage level that is likely to have been at the upper end for unskilled workers in major Chinese cities. Deflating nominal wages by the costs of the consumption baskets yields the data plotted in Figures 11.1 and 11.2.

The data broadly confirm the outcome of the grain wage comparisons. We can summarize as follows. First, the Yangzi Delta is reputed to have enjoyed the most advanced economy of any Chinese province, but the real wage there was not noticeably higher than the real wage in Beijing or Canton. Overall, Chinese cities tied for last place with Italian cities, which had the lowest standard of living in Europe. Chinese real wages were far behind those in London or Amsterdam – only about 30–40 percent of earning levels there in terms of purchasing power. Second, unskilled laborers in the major cities of China and Japan – poor as they were – had roughly the same standard of living as their counterparts in central and southern Europe for the larger part of the eighteenth century.

Figure 11.2 suggests that living standards in Japan and India in the eighteenth century were quite similar to those in major Chinese urban centers, and that eighteenth-century living standards were close to subsistence for unskilled

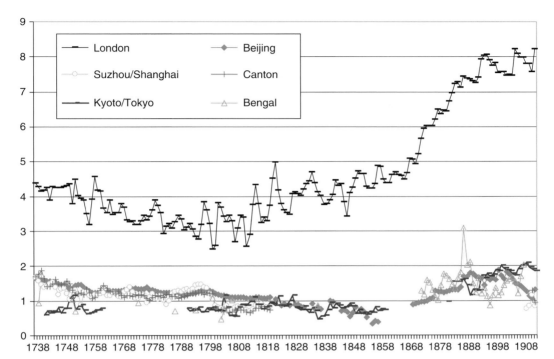

Figure 11.2 Real wages in Europe and Asia (Allen *et al.*, 2010)

workers in much of the non-industrializing world. This calls into question the validity of the extensive "rise of the West" literature that sees western Europe as a whole surpassing the rest of the world in the early modern era.

Finally, these real wage studies confirm a second "greater" divergence that occurred with the onset of the Industrial Revolution. The gap in living standards between unskilled workers in northwest European cities and Chinese cities widened after the middle of the nineteenth century. Industrialization swept through previously laggard European countries such as Germany, so that by World War I their workers' standards of living had greatly increased relative to their counterparts in Beijing or Shanghai. The standard of living in China and India remained low and on a par with the regions of Europe untouched by the Industrial Revolution.

It remains for future research to identify the timing of the first divergence in living standards. It is likely that, for India, living standards may have started to fall from the sixteenth and seventeenth centuries.[2] Future research should also construct much longer time series for real wages for both China and India.

---

[2] Moosvi's revised estimates show that per capita food grain consumption in 1595 was 1.05–1.32 times the level of 1961. There is a consensus that if we compare wages between 1595 and the late nineteenth century for different categories of workers, living standards did fall. Moosvi estimates that in 1595 the average unskilled worker had 10 percent of income left over after paying for necessities, but that in the 1870s there was deficit of 16 percent. For skilled workers the difference is smaller, but again the data show a fall in real wages.

Height and human capital

The use of anthropometric measures such as height – a common tool widely applied in European economic history – is still highly preliminary at this stage but already making promising and pioneering contributions in quantifying long-term changes in living standards elsewhere. In the absence of accurate height measurements for traditional China, recent studies by Morgan (2006) and Baten and Hira (2008) collect data for Chinese emigrants to Australia and Southeast Asia. These studies allow the reconstruction of height series for Chinese emigrants during the nineteenth century, a period for which other systematic quantitative indicators are sorely lacking. Their preliminary findings confirm that the height of the southern Chinese largely stagnated during the nineteenth century, though with fluctuations. They also point to a drop in average height around the mid-nineteenth century, following the devastation of the Taiping rebellion. Another study of the height of railroad workers by Morgan (2004) shows a slight upward trend in height for the 1900–30 period (0.07 cm per decade), but with large regional variations.

Studies of the height of Indians, summarized in Baten (2006), seem to be available only from the mid-nineteenth century onward and also confirm little change. Guntupalli and Baten (2006) present more detailed data on Indian heights for 1915–44, which reveal no clear upward trend, again with large regional variations. These studies clearly confirm the second divergence apparent in the real wage studies, that occurred with the onset of the Industrial Revolution, and which led to a larger gap in living standards between China and India and the rapidly industrializing western Europe.

One particularly exciting and promising area of anthropometric research measures literacy and numeracy. Joerg Baten and his associates do so using the Whipple index, which is essentially a measure of age heaping. Their studies confirm a strong negative correlation between the incidence of age heaping and indicators of literacy and numeracy rates worldwide. Using Chinese archival documents for the seventeenth and eighteenth centuries and a population census from the 1950s, they reveal strikingly low rates of age heaping and thus high rates of numeracy. In the late-seventeenth- and early-eighteenth-century data, age heaping in China reached a low level that was not attained by most European countries until the late eighteenth century. The high rate of numeracy as measured by age heaping seems to be confirmed for Japan and Taiwan in the nineteenth century (Baten et al., 2010). Crayen and Baten (2008) present preliminary estimates of global trends in numeracy which show east Asian numeracy to have been as high as that in most Western industrialized countries from the early nineteenth century. Meanwhile, age heaping seems to have been fairly prevalent in south Asia, indicating an average low level of numeracy in India (Crayen and Baten, 2008, fig. 3).

It is interesting to compare these preliminary estimates with the traditional historiography on Chinese literacy. Evelyn Rawski's pathbreaking study offered an optimistic estimate of 30–45 percent and 2–10 percent literacy rates for males and females respectively for eighteenth-century China. These estimates are very close to those for Japan (of scholars such as R. P. Dore and Akira Hayami), according to which 43 percent of Japanese males and 19 percent of Japanese females had some schooling. This was reputed to be one of the highest levels of literacy in the early modern world. Rawski's optimistic assessment, as well as more recent studies by Li Bozhong (2003), imply the diffusion of popular education in traditional China, especially the Lower Yangtze, beyond the preparation for the official civil service examination. They point to the rise of a dynamic book-publishing and book-rental service sector, and document the diffusion of the abacus and book-keeping among merchants and households. The more solid data surveyed by Baten et al. (2010) for the 1930s shows 40 percent of people with some schooling, and a literacy rate of about 30 percent. This seems to confirm the findings for the eighteenth century, on the assumption that literacy rates stagnated between these two centuries.

The historiography on India points to very low levels of literacy before the late twentieth century. Literacy was confined to the upper castes, almost exclusively to men, and mainly to certain professions. As Roy (2006) shows, the 1830s data revealed "that instruction was widespread among the priestly, landed, and mercantile castes, but practically unknown among the laboring people and amongst women." One estimate cited in Roy (2008) gives a literacy rate of 11 percent for males and about 1 percent for females for Bengal in 1835–38, which was not very different from estimates in 1901. This seems to be below comparable estimates for China. There seems to have been a unique pattern of relatively high human capital and low per capita income in China and east Asia in the early modern era. This finding has implications that have yet to be explored and may be one of the important strategic factors that contributed to the rapid catch-up, first by Japan and then by East Asia in general. However, far more systematic research is needed to establish comparable estimates across countries.

Beyond living standards: urbanization

Apart from disparities in living standards, major differences in economic structure had already emerged by the early modern era between China and India, on the one hand, and northwest Europe, on the other. The share of agriculture in northwest Europe, and especially in England, began to decline early on, while India and China remained overwhelmingly agricultural.

Urbanization is another related indicator of the level of development. Urban activity appeared to be widespread in seventeenth-century India, from the great towns and cities in the north to the numerous trading centers spread all along the Coromandel Coast in south India and the coastal towns of Gujarat and the west. In 1600, there were thirty-two urban centers in the Mughal empire manufacturing cotton cloth and handicrafts. Estimates of the urban population in Mughal India are based on the notion of the flow of resources from villages to urban centers. More direct evidence comes from the writing of contemporary travellers. Although there were these cities in India, most of the population lived in rural areas. Habib (1999) estimates the share of the urban population in 1600 at 15 percent.[3] This figure declined over the eighteenth and nineteenth centuries, and it was only in the twentieth century that it began to recover.

There is interesting new research on patterns of Chinese urbanization. Li Bozhong (2000) is noteworthy for a systematic account of the growth of cotton textiles, food processing, apparel, tobacco, papermaking, printing, toolmaking, construction and shipbuilding industries in the Lower Yangtze during 1550–1850. But Li argues that the small-scale, skill-intensive, handicraft nature of these industries in the Lower Yangtze did not give rise to megacities, but instead led to the formation of clusters of market towns along the dense and intricate waterways, characterized by extensive geographic specialization in the production and marketing of agricultural and handicraft products, indistinguishable boundaries between urban and rural areas, and the meshing of agricultural, commercial, and industrial activities. Thus standard historical classifications of urbanization applied in the Western context are inadequate and likely seriously to underestimate the degree of urbanization. Nonetheless, the newly revised aggregate estimates of the urbanization rate, even for the most developed parts of the Lower Yangtze, fall below those of England and the Netherlands, which were as high as 20–30 percent in 1800 based on towns of at least 10,000 inhabitants (Chapter 10).

Understanding the Great Divergence: markets and institutions

We believe that institutions and their historical path-dependencies are crucial to an explanation of the Great Divergence between Asia and Europe. However, institutions have figured relatively little in the revisionist literature on Chinese economic history.[4] Our selective survey here draws on specific topics related to this literature.

---

[3] This figure refers to people living in settlements of at least 5,000, in contrast to the estimates of urbanization in Chapter 10 of this volume, which use a threshold of 10,000.

[4] See Pomeranz (2000) on the flexibility of traditional Chinese factor markets.

Markets

Can we explain gaps in living standards in terms of the degrees of market efficiencies across Eurasia? Recent studies on market integration based on regional grain prices have given us a rare glimpse of both the dynamics and comparative degrees of efficiency of interregional trade in China, India, and Europe in the eighteenth and nineteenth centuries. For China, thanks to the elaborate government grain report system, market integration studies based on the statistical correlation of regional grain prices can go back a long way (Wang, 1992; L. Li, 2000; Shiue, 2002; Shiue and Keller, 2007). In particular, Shiue and Keller made a direct comparison of the degrees of market integration in China and Europe based on the strength of the statistical correlation of grain prices. They find no large differences in terms of market integration between China and western Europe in the late eighteenth century. However, they do find that markets were more integrated in England than in either the rest of western Europe or the highly commercialized Yangtze delta markets in China.

A recent study by Roman Studer (2008) suggests that the degree of market integration in parts of India was much lower than in China or western Europe in the eighteenth century, especially over longer distances. Similarly, grain prices in India also displayed greater volatility across time, as revealed in Table 11.5. There is evidence of weak arbitrage and thus large price variation over time and across regions. Supply shocks affected prices and there was great variation across small

Table 11.5 Wheat and rice prices, coefficients of variation

	1764–1794	1870–1910
Wheat prices		
Pune	0.34	0.19
Calcutta	0.79	0.14
Delhi	0.77	0.18
Paris	0.16	0.14
London	0.16	0.14
Berlin	0.19	0.14
Milan	0.15	0.15
Amsterdam	0.17	0.16
Rice prices		
Calcutta	0.38	0.18
Pune	0.29	0.12
Yangtze Valley	0.19	0.18
Osaka	0.20	0.17

Source: Studer, 2008.

geographical areas. Markets became much more integrated with the development of the railways in the last quarter of the nineteenth century, when the spatial price correlation in India improved significantly (Hurd, 1975).

This hierarchy of market integration, based on grain price correlation, with England ahead of Europe and China, followed by India, needs to be interpreted with caution. Is grain price correlation an accurate reflection of market efficiency or something else? How much do geography, technology, or institutions account for the correlation? For China, the relatively high degree of grain price correlation seems to jar with the historiography, which stresses a highly fragmented currency market. In fact, few of these studies on grain prices discussed the complicated problem of Chinese currency in the early modern era. This is not surprising, given that all the grain prices were culled from the government grain reporting system, which aimed at price-smoothing and used the uniform government-sanctioned currency unit, the silver tael, which was rarely used in actual market transactions.

Long-distance trade

The historiography on China and India supports the existence of a large and booming network of commerce and well-established channels of grain trade. Peasants in India and China brought the grain to the market, and the grain merchant organized its transport. There was also a well-established network of trade in manufactured goods. Some artisans worked directly for the nobility or the government, while others sold to the merchants involved in long-distance trade. The system of indigenous credit and banking was well developed. Bills of exchange such as *hundis* in India and various drafts in China were widely used. The local money changer engaged in bill discounting and sometimes deposit banking as well (Raychaudhuri, 1982; Martin, 2008).

Social networks were crucial to this commercialized world. For China, historians identify at least ten distinctive native-place merchant groups. The two most well known are the Hui merchants from around Huizhou city in Anhui province, and the Shanxi bankers from Shanxi province in northern China. Although the bulk of the trading activities of the Hui merchants was along the Yangtze, especially the Lower Yangtze region, their reach extended nationwide and even overseas to Japan by the early twentieth century. The Hui merchants formed their networks mainly through their elaborate and sophisticated lineage system, which, as recent research has argued, possessed some form of "corporate" characteristics, with property ownership lasting beyond the lives of any individual members.

The Shanxi bankers achieved commercial fame possibly even earlier than the Hui, and became most well known through their networks, which established a nationwide money remittance service from the early nineteenth century. Their networks extended into Japan and Korea by the early twentieth century. The Shanxi bankers developed a distinctive set of organizational features in their use of outside managers and staff with minimal or no interference from the owners, and the development of a profit-sharing scheme which aligned the interests of employees with the long-term interests of their firm. But, ultimately, the most predominant feature of the Shanxi bankers was their apprentice system, which recruited staff locally (including those to be sent to branch offices outside Shanxi), carrying out careful background checks and with families or other reliable third parties as guarantors. Any staff member caught and dismissed for fraudulent behavior would be denied future employment opportunities by all Shanxi bankers (Ma, 2004).

Similarly, social networks played an important role in defining the sphere of the Indian merchant. For long-distance trade, Moreland noted the domination of three merchant communities in internal and international trade: Muslim traders overseas, the Hindu *baniyas* in Gujarat, and the Chettis on the Coromandel Coast. The trading world of the Indian merchant has been described in much detail by Ashin Das Gupta.

Indian and Chinese merchants were also involved in long-distance international trade. Indian merchant ships carried goods to Alexandria, Basra, and Baghdad. To the east the ships sailed to Sumatra, but were not sturdy enough to sail the China seas. This was left to Chinese merchants (Das Gupta, 2001). In 1663, Surat merchants alone had fifty ships (Habib, 1969). The commodities traded included primary goods such as rice, pulses, sugar, and raw silk, but also manufactured goods such as textiles. This textile trade was mainly in coarse varieties, unlike the European trade that followed, which was more in fine-quality products. Both China and India imported bullion from outside, spices from Southeast Asia, horses from west Asia, and ivory from eastern Africa. This booming trade in the Indian Ocean and South China Sea was comparable to the European trade.

For India we have other quantitative evidence such as insurance rates, which indicate that interregional trade was widespread. Insurance rates are a good measure of risk and the security of trade. Table 11.6 indicates that rates were fairly moderate for long-distance trade within India as far back as the mid-seventeenth century. The rise in the eighteenth century reflects the political turmoil of the period; however, these rates remained more or less the same in the early nineteenth century. The insurance figures indicate that interregional trade was common, and that the conditions under which it took place did not vary much over the centuries.

Institutions

One explanation of why activities were specific to particular social groups is that informational constraints could be overcome through community ties.

Table 11.6 Insurance rates on interregional trade

Year	Goods insured	Route	Insurance charge (%)
1646	Treasure	Daman–Surat	1
1647	Commercial goods	Ahmedabad–Thatta	1/2
1655	Cash	Masulitatnam–Surat	1
1795	Opium, cloth	Indore–Ahmedabad	2
1795	Coins, bullion	Indore–Ahmedabad	1.25
1795	Money, bullion	Poonah– Malwa	2.00–2.50
1795	Cloth	Nanipur–Malwa	0.5–0.63
1795	Cloth	Jaulnah–Indore	2.00
1795	Cloth	Mirzapur– Indore	1.50–2.0
1820	Opium, cloth	Indore–Ahmedabad	1.00–1.5
1820	Coins, bullion	Indore–Ahmedabad	1.00
1820	Money, bullion	Poonah– Malwa	2.5
1820	Cloth	Nanipur–Malwa	1.0–1.5
1820	Cloth	Jaulnah–Indore	1.25–1.5
1820	Cloth	Mirzapur– Indore	1.75

Source: Seventeenth century – Habib, 1969; eighteenth and nineteenth centuries – Moosvi, 2001.

This is analogous to Avner Greif's influential study of the Maghribi traders in the late medieval Mediterranean. As with the Maghribi traders who operated in the absence of formal legal institutions or codes, Chinese and Indian merchants relied on extensive informal rules in the form of family bylaws, lineage rules, and guild regulations, or caste norms enforced largely through collective mechanisms, to alleviate the pervasive information and commitment problems of the days of premodern transport.

The distinction between what Greif termed private versus public-order institutions raises a much larger set of questions. For China, interesting and controversial research reveals that, in fact, there was no lack of formal legal codes or even legal enforcement institutions. Chinese administrative law, somewhat akin to public law in the West, was possibly one of the most sophisticated and elaborate systems in the early modern world. The crucial distinction is that the Chinese legal apparatus had long been an integral part of the administrative system; the administrative bureaucracy within the hierarchy – from the county level all the way up to the emperor – was the final arbiter in criminal cases. The Ming and Qing penal codes, despite their reputed elaboration and comprehensiveness, were decision rules designed for bureaucrats to mete out punishments proportionate to the extent of criminal violations. Similarly, legal rulings could be reviewed and changed only through the multiple layers of bureaucracy within the administrative hierarchy. Legal statutes or sub-statutes were not open to contestation and interpretation by the litigating parties or independent third parties.

Recent research has overturned the traditional view of a complete absence of civil or commercial law in premodern China. County magistrates ruled on a vast number of civil and commercial cases. However, as legal scholar Shuzo Shiga has pointed out, the decisions of the magistrates were not legal "adjudication" as in the Western legal order. Rather, by invoking general ethical, social, or legal norms as their legal basis, without the citation of legal codes or customs, formal or informal, these rulings were akin to mediation. It is important to note that the absence of formal private laws in commercial and civil matters was not due to the scarcity of customary norms or regulations, which in fact were prevalent in China. Rather, because of the dominance of the Chinese state, whose paramount interest was the maintenance of a largely agrarian-based fiscal base and social stability, customary rules did not evolve into formal laws sanctioned by the state.

Similarly, in pre-colonial India community laws governed the system of trade and commerce, with each trading community adhering to its own moral code. A system of universal law was lacking. When conflict arose in interactions between foreign and local traders, treaties with overseas trading companies became the code used in practice (Moreland, 1923).

What are the efficiency implications of economic regimes based on groups as opposed to rules? One argument, advanced by Greif and others, is that in a relationship- and group-based mechanism, the extent of exchange and the scale of operations may be subject to sharply rising costs of information and coordination, as the group and the extent of trade expands. In contrast, an enforceable legal system with a set of codified and transparent standards and rules, subject to the interpretation and contestation of independent third parties, may be more costly to set up initially but may also exhibit strong scale economies, allowing it to sustain larger volumes of trade, and may thus be conducive to the rise of large-scale impersonal exchange (Greif, 2006).

The question of scale economies carries implications for historical path-dependencies that pertain to the Great Divergence. An interesting starting point is to examine the evolution of capital- and contract-intensive financial and commercial instruments such as paper money, bills of exchange, bills of lading, joint-stock shares, or insurance contracts, as well as forward or futures markets, across Eurasia. We know that almost all these instruments had independently emerged in one form or another in Asia – in some cases, such as paper money, they originated in China. However, most of them remained localized, and their development stagnated in Asia, while the West saw the evolution and elaboration of large-scale, impersonal exchange often backed up with formal legal enforcement and public institutions.

One possible consequence of these different historical paths traced out by institutions is a gap in the level of interest rates across Eurasia. It is beyond doubt that interest rates in India and China were far higher than in Europe, especially northwest Europe, throughout the early modern period. Even the most conservative estimate for Indian interest rates yields a rate of 7.5–9 percent per annum in Surat for 1659, which is twice the rate in England. Interest rates before the mid-seventeenth century were even higher (Habib 1982; Moosvi, 2001). For China, a recent pathbreaking study based on thousands of data points reveals that per annum interest rates for commercial loans in the seventeenth to nineteenth centuries averaged at least 12 percent, with wide variations (Peng et al., 2006).

The significance of this interest rate gap has yet to be fully explored and understood. A large question that needs to be asked is whether the contrast in factor endowments – the much higher capital–labor ratio and thus the lower price of capital relative to labor in Europe than in China and India – was not exogenous, but rather an endogenous outcome of the rise of organized financial intermediaries in western Europe. This might throw fresh light on or call into question the so-called labor-intensive pattern of Asian development, which was really a long-term response to relative capital scarcity, a condition itself created by the insufficiency of public institutions or possibly insecure property rights.[5] Many scholars have pointed to the links between the development of European financial instruments and intermediaries, borrowing by public institutions, and the strengthening of fiscal capacity in modern European states (North and Weingast, 1989). Underlying these important linkages was a host of core institutional developments in the early modern era, such as the rise of incorporated bodies, representative government, and the transition to the rule of law (North, 1981; Rosenberg and Birdzell, 1986).

Colonial rule and the Great Divergence

Did colonization lead to the divergence in the fortunes of Europe and Asia? In the Indian context the political subordination to the rule of the East India Company from the middle of the eighteenth century, followed by the political control of the British crown, had implications for the drain of resources from the colony to the imperial country, the making of economic policy, and changes in the institutional structure. The developmental gains of such changes could come from the introduction of new institutions, such as the land tenure system built on the principle of individual property rights, access to the superior capital market of the imperial country, specialization through links with the global market, and the building of the railway network and the irrigation system. The

---

[5] See Sugihara (2003) for an exposition of the labor-intensive path of development.

dependency school sees the imperial connection as exploitative, and special-ization through trade as the cause of the widening gap in development between Europe and Asia (Frank, 1975). Other literature finds a positive effect through the production of cash crops as the Indian market became integrated into the world economy (Roy, 2006). Per capita national income estimates for 1870 to 1900 show a slightly upward trend as the Indian economy specialized in the production of agricultural products (Heston, 1977). The critique of global-ization comes from the adverse effects of deindustrialization as the Indian textile industry faced competition from Britain's industrial economy (Thorner, 1962).

Whatever the merits of the debate on these issues, the empirical evidence on economic growth in the first half of the twentieth century reveals a widening gap between Europe and India, as European per capita GDP growth was substantial while Indian growth showed a negative trend until the end of the colonial period (Sivasubramonian, 2000). The stagnation of the Indian economy can be attrib-uted to stagnation in Indian agriculture and the failure of the colonial state to avert an ecological crisis as population growth increased. The counterfactual is more difficult to establish – what would have been the path of Indian develop-ment in the absence of colonial exploitation? Investment in agriculture remained limited and the advances in irrigation were limited and failed to increase agricultural productivity. Industrial development was adversely affected in the absence of an independent tariff policy in a period when late industrializers adopted protectionist policies towards their infant industries.

The literature on the gains to Britain from colonial rule suggests that the economic benefits were relatively low. This includes the effect of trade with the empire and returns on investment, as well as the cost of governing and the net drain of resources from India (O'Brien 1988b, Davis and Huttenback, 1988). While colonial rule may have widened the gap between the East and the West, other evidence presented in this chapter suggests that the roots of economic divergence go back to the seventeenth century.

In comparison with India, the impact of Western colonialism on China was far more limited, both in scale and duration. In the mid-eighteenth century, when the East India Company made massive inroads towards the full coloni-zation of the Indian subcontinent, the Qing empire was reaching the peak of its power and prosperity under the capable rule of the Qianlong emperor. It was only by the 1840s that British gunboats reached the Chinese coastline to force open China and east Asia to free trade. Even then, Western imperialism never subjected China to full colonization, but manifested itself through special trading rights, leased territories, and treaty ports with extraterritoriality or spheres of interest. While Western investment and modern enterprise pro-tected by privilege might have crushed or outcompeted indigenous business or

Chinese enterprise, they were also agents of technology transfer and foreign direct investment. Similarly, while Western interests took control of key institutions such as the maritime customs and the imperial postal office, the revenue collected also served the fiscal needs of the Qing empire, and later the Republican government, as well as financing some crucial infrastructure such as railroads in the early twentieth century.

Perhaps the more lasting impact of Western imperialism is that it set off a process of political turmoil that destabilized the empire, culminating in the collapse of the Qing dynasty in 1911 and the subsequent chaotic warlord era. But, even then, the outcome could be mixed. As Ma (2008a, 2008b) shows, treaty port cities such as Shanghai, Tianjin, and Wuhan became the linchpin of economic growth in the first three decades of the twentieth century. One important factor is that the so-called colonial "privileges" in the treaty ports were not just utilized by Western business, but were also exploited, formally or informally, by Chinese business located within the treaty ports. It is important to note that some of these "privileges" happened to coincide with the necessary conditions for growth, such as the maintenance of peace and public order, the security of property rights and contract enforcement, and the freedom from arbitrary taxation or official exaction. It thus comes as no surprise that the so-called golden era of growth in the 1910s and 1920s fell in the period when Western-controlled Shanghai wrested almost complete political and legal autonomy from China: Shanghai in the 1920s became a "city-state."

An even more important effect of Western institutions – if hard to assess – is their intellectual stimulus to long-term economic change in China. One useful benchmark for comparison is the case of Meiji Japan, which took a much more aggressive stance towards the adoption of Western political and economic institutions after 1872. Japan eventually become the first non-Western country to industrialize, and subsequently went down the path of colonization in east Asia. Clearly, the adoption of Western institutions alone is far from sufficient to explain Japanese success in the nineteenth and twentieth centuries; a host of other factors, such as geography or even historical accidents, could have played a role. But without the momentous institutional change during the Tokugawa-Meiji period, it is not inconceivable that Japan could have gone down the path of other Asian empires and states in the wake of Western imperialism.

Conclusion

The survey presented in this chapter takes us closer to the traditional position on comparative living standards across Eurasia than to the revisionists. The evidence we have seen indicates that differences in living standards between

Asia and northwest Europe had already emerged in the early modern era, and only widened further with the onset of the Industrial Revolution. The advanced parts of Asia – India and China – looked more similar to the backward parts of Europe than to the more advanced northwest. The Great Divergence was well under way in the seventeenth century.

Bibliography

Abel, W. 1980. *Agricultural Fluctuations in Europe*. New York: St. Martins Press.

Abū'l-Fazl 1927 [1595]. *The Ā' īn-i-Akbarī*. Delhi: Low Price Publications.

Accominotti, O., and M. Flandreau. 2008. Bilateral Treaties and the Most-Favored-Nation Clause. The Myth of Trade Liberalization in the Nineteenth Century. *World Politics* 60: 147–88.

Acemoglu, D. and S. Johnson. 2005. Unbundling Institutions. *Journal of Political Economy* 113: 949–95.

Acemoglu, D. and J. A. Robinson. 2000. Why Did the West Extend the Franchise? *Quarterly Journal of Economics* 115: 1167–99.

  2005. *Economic Origins of Dictatorship and Democracy*. Cambridge University Press.

  2006. Persistence of Power Elites and Institutions. *American Economic Review* 98: 267–93.

Acemoglu, D., and F. Zilibotti. 1997. Was Prometheus Unbound by Chance? Risk, Diversification, and Growth. *Journal of Political Economy* 105: 709–51.

Acemoglu, D., S. Johnson, and J. A. Robinson. 2001. The Colonial Origins of Comparative Development: An Empirical Investigation. *American Economic Review* 91: 1369–401.

  2005. The Rise of Europe: Atlantic Trade, Institutional Change and Economic Growth. *American Economic Review* 95: 546–79.

Acemoglu, D., D. Cantoni, S. Johnson, and J. A. Robinson. 2008. The Consequences of Radical Reform: The Economic Consequences of the French Revolution, mimeo.

Agren, M., ed. 1998. *Iron-Making Societies: Early Industrial Development in Sweden and Russia, 1600–1900*. Oxford: Berghahn.

A'Hearn, B., J. Baten, and D. Crayen. 2009. Quantifying Quantitative Literacy: Age Heaping and the History of Human Capital. *Journal of Economic History* 69: 783–808.

Alesina, A., S. Ozler, N. Roubini, and P. Swagel. 1996. Political Instability and Economic Growth. *Journal of Economic Growth* 2: 189–213.

Allen R. C. 1981. Entrepreneurship and Technical Progress in the Northeast Coast Pig Iron Industry, 1850–1913. *Research in Economic History* 6: 35–71.

  1992. *Enclosure and the Yeoman*. Oxford: Clarendon Press.

  1994. Agriculture during the Industrial Revolution. In R. Floud and D. N. McCloskey, eds., *The New Economic History of Britain*, Vol. I: 1700–1860, 2nd edn. Cambridge University Press.

  2000. Economic Structure and Agricultural Productivity in Europe, 1300–1800. *European Review of Economic History* 4: 1–26.

  2001. The Great Divergence in European Wages and Prices from the Middle Ages to the First World War. *Explorations in Economic History* 38: 411–47.

2003. Progress and Poverty in Early Modern Europe. *Economic History Review* 56: 403–43.

2004. Agriculture During the Industrial Revolution, 1700–1850. In *The Cambridge Economic History of Modern Britain*, ed. R. Floud and P. Johnson. Cambridge University Press.

2006. The British Industrial Revolution in Global Perspective: How Commerce Created the Industrial Revolution and Modern Economic Growth, mimeo, University of Oxford.

2007. The Industrial Revolution in Miniature: The Spinning Jenny in Britain, France and India, mimeo, University of Oxford.

Allen, R. C., J.-P. Bassino, D. Ma, C. Moll-Murata, and J. L. van Zanden. 2010, forthcoming. Wages, Prices, and Living Standards in China, Japan, and Europe, 1738–1925. *Economic History Review.*

Alter, G. 1992. Theories of Fertility Decline: A Nonspecialist's Guide to the Current Debate. In J. R. Gillis, L. A. Tilly and D. Levine, eds., *The European Experience of Declining Fertility, 1850–1970.* Cambridge, MA: Blackwell.

Álvarez-Nogal, C., and L. Prados de la Escosura, 2007. The Decline of Spain (1500–1850): Conjectural Estimates. *European Review of Economic History* 11: 319–66.

Arasaratnam, S. 1980. Weavers, Merchants and Company: The Handloom Industry in Southeastern India 1750–1790. *Indian Economic and Social History Review* 17: 257–81.

1980. *Merchants, Companies and Commerce on the Coromandel Coast, 1650–1740.* Delhi: Oxford University Press.

Ariès, P. 1960. Interpretation pour une histoire des mentalités. In H. Bergues, ed., *La prévention des naissances dans la famille: ses origines dans les temps modernes.* Paris: Presses Universitaires de France.

Arnould, A. M. 1791. *De la balance du commerce et des relations commerciales extérieures de la France dans toutes les parties du globe particulièrement à la fin du règne de Louis XIV et au moment de la Révolution.* Paris: Buisson.

Ashton, T. S. 1955. *An Economic History of England: The Eighteenth Century.* London: Methuen.

1959. *Economic Fluctuations in England, 1700–1800.* Oxford: Clarendon Press.

Babbage, C. 1830. Reflexions on the Decline of Science in Britain and on Some of Its Causes. *Quarterly Review* 43: 307–42.

Bairoch, P. 1976. *Commerce extérieur et développement économique de l'Europe au XIXe siècle.* Paris: Mouton.

1982. International Industrialization Levels from 1750 to 1980. *Journal of European Economic History* 11: 269–333.

1988. *Cities and Economic Development from the Dawn of History to the Present.* University of Chicago Press.

1989. European Trade Policy, 1815–1914. In P. Mathias and S. Pollard, eds., *The Cambridge Economic History of Europe, Volume VIII, The Industrial Economies: The Development of Economic and Social Policies.* Cambridge University Press.

1990. The Impact of Crop Yields, Agricultural Productivity, and Transport Costs on Urban Growth between 1800 and 1910. In A. Van der Woude, A. Hayami, and J. de Vries, eds., *Urbanization in History. A Process of Dynamic Interactions.* Oxford: Clarendon Press.

1992. *Storia delle città. Dalla proto-urbanizzazione all'esplosione urbana del terzo mondo.* Milan: Jaca Book.

1997. Une nouvelle distribution des populations: villes et campagnes. In J.-P. Bardet and J. Dupâquier, eds., *Histoire des populations de l'Europe.* Paris: Fayard.

Bairoch P., and G. Goertz. 1986. Factors of Urbanization in the Nineteenth Century Developed Countries: A Descriptive and Econometric Analysis. *Urban Studies* 23: 285–305.

Bairoch P., J. Batou, and P. Chèvre. 1988. *La population des villes européennes de 800 à 1850.* Geneva: Droz.

Banerjee, A., and L. Iyer. 2005. History, Institutions, and Economic Performance: The Legacy of Colonial Land Tenure Systems in India. *American Economic Review* 95: 1190–213.

Banken, R. 2005. The Diffusion of Coke Smelting and Puddling in Germany, 1796–1860. In C. Evans and G. Rydén, eds., *The Industrial Revolution in Iron: The Impact of British Coal Technology in Nineteenth-Century Europe.* Aldershot: Ashgate.

Basu, S., and A. M. Taylor. 1999. Business Cycles in International Historical Perspective. *Journal of Economic Perspectives.* 13: 45–68.

Bardet J.-P., and J. Dupâquier, eds. 1997. *Histoire des populations de l'Europe.* Paris: Fayard.

Bassino, J. P., and D. Ma. 2005. Wages and Living Standards of Japanese Unskilled Laborers in 1720–1913: An International Comparison. *Research in Economic History* 23: 229–48.

Baten, J. 2000. Heights and Real Wages in the 18th and 19th Centuries. *Jahrbuch für Wirtschaftsgeschichte* 2000 1: 61–77.

2006. Global Height Trends in Industrial and Developing Countries, 1810–1984: An Overview, mimeo, Tübingen.

Baten, J. and S. Hira. 2008. Anthropometric Trends in Southern China, 1830–1864. *Australian Economic History Review* 48: 209–26.

Baten, J. and Ş. Pamuk. 2007. Inequality in Standards of Living across Europe, 1820–2000, A Preliminary Look. Presented at workshop on Human Capital, Inequality and Living Standards, Measuring Divergence and Convergence in a Globalising Europe, Lund.

Baten, J. and J. L. van Zanden. 2008. Book Production and the Onset of Modern Economic Growth. *Journal of Economic Growth*, 13: 217–35.

Baten, J., D. Ma, S. Morgan and Q. Wang. 2010, forthcoming. Evolution of Living Standards and Human Capital in China in the 18–20th Centuries: Evidences from Real Wages, Age-Heaping, and Anthropometrics. *Explorations in Economic History.*

Beck, L. 1897. *Die Geschichte des Eisens: Dritte Abteilung. Das XVIII. Jahrhundert.* Braunschweig: Friedrich Vieweg.

Becker, G. S. 1960. An Economic Analysis of Fertility. In UNBCFE Research, ed., *Demographic and Economic Change in Developed Countries*. Princeton University Press.

1965. A Theory of the Allocation of Time. *Economic Journal*, 75: 493–517.

Becker, G. S., and R. J. Barro. 1988. A Reformulation of the Economic Theory of Fertility. *Quarterly Journal of Economics* 103: 1–25.

Becker, G. S., Murphy, K., and Tamura, R. 1990. Human Capital, Fertility, and Economic Growth. *Journal of Political Economy* 98: S12–S37.

Beik, W. 2005. Review Article: The Absolutism of Louis XIV as Social Collaboration. *Past and Present* 188: 195–224.

Beloch J. 1937–61. *Bevölkerungsgeschichte Italiens*. Berlin and Leipzig: De Gruyter.

Bengtsson, T., and D. S. Reher. 1998. Short- and Medium-Term Relations between Population and Economy. In C. E. Núñes, ed., *Debates and Controversies in Economic History*. Madrid: Fundación Ramón Areces.

Berelowitch, W., J. Dupâquier, and I. Gieysztor. 1997. L'Europe orientale. In J.-P. Bardet and J. Dupâquier, eds., *Histoire des populations de l'Europe*. Paris: Fayard.

Berg, M. 2007. The Genesis of Useful Knowledge. *History of Science* 45: 123–34.

Beylen, J. Van. 1977. Scheepstypen. In L. M. Akveld, S. Hart, and W. J. Van Hoboken eds., *Maritieme Geschiedenis der Nederlanden*, II. Bussum: De Boer Maritiem.

Bielenberg, A. 1998. The Irish Brewing Industry and the Rise of Guinness, 1790–1914. In R. G. Wilson and T. R. Gourvish, eds., *The Dynamics of the International Brewing Industry since 1800*. London: Routledge.

Blum, A., and I. Troitskaja. 1996. Mortality in Russia during the Eighteenth and Nineteenth Centuries: Local Assessments Based on the Revizii. *Population* 51: 303–28.

Blum, J. 1978. *The End of the Old Order in Rural Europe*. Princeton University Press.

Bogart, D. 2005a. Did Turnpike Trusts Increase Transportation Investment in Eighteenth-Century England? *Journal of Economic History* 65: 439–68.

2005b. Turnpike Trusts and the Transportation Revolution in Eighteenth-Century England. *Explorations in Economic History* 42: 479–508.

2008. Nationalizations and the Development of Transport Systems: Cross-Country Evidence From Railroad Networks, mimeo, Department of Economics, UC Irvine.

Bogart, D. 2009. Nationalizations and the Development of Transport Systems: Cross-Country Evidence from Railroad Networks, 1860–1912. *Journal of Economic History* 69: 202–37.

Bonney, R. 1995. Revenues. In R. Bonney, ed., *Economic Systems and State Finance*. Oxford: Clarendon Press.

1999. France, 1494–1815. In R. Bonney, ed., *The Rise of the Fiscal State in Europe, 1200–1815*. Oxford University Press.

Boonstra, O. W. A. 1993. *De waardij van eene vroege opleiding*. Wageningen: Landbouwuniversiteit.

Boot, H. M. 1995. How Skilled Were Lancashire Cotton Factory Workers in 1833? *Economic History Review* 48: 283–303.

1999. Real Incomes of the British Middle Class, 1760–1850. *Economic History Review* 52: 638–68.

Bordo, M. D., and E. N. White. 1991. A Tale of Two Currencies: British and French Finance during the Napoleonic Wars. *Journal of Economic History* 51: 303–16.

Boserup, E. 1965. *The Conditions of Agricultural Growth: The Economics of Agrarian Change Under Population Pressure.* London: G. Allen & Unwin.

Boucekkine, R., D. de la Croix, and D. Peeters. 2007. Early Literacy Achievements, Population Density and the Transition to Modern Growth. *Journal of the European Economic Association* 5: 183–226.

Bourdelais, P. 2006. *Epidemics Laid Low: a History of What Happened in Rich Countries.* Baltimore: Johns Hopkins University Press.

Bowler, P. J., and I. R. Morus. 2005. *Making Modern Science.* University of Chicago Press.

Boyd, R. and P. J. Richerson. 1985. *Culture and the Evolutionary Process.* University of Chicago Press.

2005. *Not by Genes Alone: How Culture Transformed Human Evolution.* University of Chicago Press.

Brändström, A. 1997. Infant Mortality in Sweden, 1750–1950: Past and Present Research into Its Decline. In C. A. Corsini and P. P. Viazzo, eds., *The Decline of Infant and Child Mortality: The European Experience, 1750–1990.* The Hague and Cambridge, MA: Martinus Nijhoff Publishers/Kluwer Law International.

Brautaset, C., and R. Grafe. 2004. A Long Distance Affair. Shipping and Global Integration in the 19th Century. In Peter Vikström, ed., *Studying Economic Growth. New Tools and Perspectives.* Umeå University Press.

Brennig, J. J. 1986. Textile Producers and Production in Late Seventeenth-Century Coromandel. *Indian Economic and Social History Review* 23: 333–56.

Brewer, J. 1989. *The Sinews of Power: War, Money and the English State.* London: Unwin Hyman.

Briggs, C. 2006. Manor Court Procedures, Debt Litigation Levels, and Rural Credit Provision in England, c.1290–c.1380. *Law and History Review* 24: 519–58.

Broadberry, S. N. 1997. *The Productivity Race: British Manufacturing in International Perspective, 1850–1990.* Cambridge University Press.

2007. Recent Developments in the Theory of Very Long Run Growth: A Historical Appraisal, Warwick Economics Research Paper 818, available at www2.warwick. ac.uk/fac/soc/economics/research/workingpapers/publications/twerp_818.pdf.

Broadberry, S. N., and B. Gupta. 2006. The Early Modern Great Divergence: Wages, Prices and Economic Development in Europe and Asia, 1500–1800. *Economic History Review* 59: 2–31.

2008. Lancashire, India and Shifting Competitive Advantage in Cotton Textiles, 1700–1850: The Neglected Role of Factor Prices. *Economic History Review* 62: 279–305.

Broadberry, S. N. and A. Klein. 2008. Aggregate and per Capita GDP in Europe, 1870–2000: Continental, Regional and National Data with Changing Boundaries, mimeo, University of Warwick.

Brown, J. C., and T. W. Guinnane. 2002. Fertility Transition in a Rural Catholic Population: Bavaria 1880–1910. *Population Studies* 56: 35–50.

2007. Regions and Time in the European Fertility Transition: Problems in the Princeton Project's Statistical Methodology. *Economic History Review* 60: 574–95.

Brunner O. 1968 [1953]. Stadt und Bürgertum in der europäischen Geschichte. In O. Brunner, *Neue Wege der Verfassungs- und Sozialgeschichte.* Göttingen: Vandenhoeck & Ruprecht.

Brunt, L. 2003. Mechanical Innovation in the Industrial Revolution: The Case of Plough Design. *Economic History Review* 56: 444–77.

Brunt, L., and E. Cannon. 2007. Do Banks Generate Financial Market Integration? mimeo, University of Lausanne.

Brunt, L., and A. Fidalgo. 2008. Why Europe and Not Asia? Agricultural Productivity and Industrial Revolution around the World before 1870, mimeo, University of Lausanne.

Brunt, L., J. Lerner, and T. Nicholas. 2008. Inducement Prizes and Innovation, mimeo, Harvard Business School.

Buenstorf, G. 2001. Sequential Production, Dynamic Complementarities and Endogenous Decomposability: A Note on the Microdynamics of Technological Change, mimeo, Max Planck Institute for Research into Economic Systems, Jena.

Bulbeck, D., A. Reid, L. C. Tan, and Y. Wu. 1998. *Southeast Asian Exports since the 14th Century: Cloves, Pepper, Coffee and Sugar.* Leiden: KITLV Press.

Burnette, J. 2006. How Skilled were English Agricultural Labourers in the Early Nineteenth Century? *Economic History Review* 59: 688–716.

Bush, M. L., ed. 1996. *Serfdom and Slavery; Studies in Legal Bondage.* London: Longman.

Butel, P. 1999. *The Atlantic.* London and New York: Routledge.

Butel, P., and F. Crouzet. 1998. Empire and Economic Growth: The Case of 18th Century France. *Revista de Historia Económica* 16: 177–93.

Cameron, R. E., ed. 1967. *Banking in the Early Stages of Industrialization.* New York: Oxford University Press.

Capella Martínez, M., and A. Matilla Tascon. 1957. *Los Cinco Gremios Mayores De Madrid. Estudio Crítico-Histórico.* Madrid: Cámara Oficial de Comercio e Industria.

Capie, F. 1999. Banking in Europe in the Nineteenth Century: The Role of the Central Bank. In R. Sylla, R. Tilly, and G. Tortella, eds., *The State, the Financial System, and Economic Modernization.* Cambridge University Press.

Capra, C. 1995. The Eighteenth Century. I. The Finances of the Austrian Monarchy and the Italian States. In R. Bonney, ed., *Economic Systems and State Finance.* Oxford University Press.

Carreras, A., and X. Tafunell, eds. 2005. *Estadísticas históricas de España (siglos XIX–XX).* Bilbao: Fundación BBVA.

Carter, F. W. 1977. Urban Development in the Western Balkans 1200–1800. In F. Carter, ed., *An Historical Geography of the Balkans.* London: Academic Press.

Cerman M., and S. C. Ogilvie, eds. 1994. *Protoindustrialisierung in Europa. Industrielle Produktion vor dem Fabrikzeitalter*. Vienna: Verlag für Gesellschaftskritik.

Cervellati, M., and U. Sunde. 2005. Human Capital Formation, Life Expectancy, and the Process of Economic Development. *American Economic Review* 95: 153–67.

Chandler, A. 1977. *The Visible Hand: The Managerial Revolution in American Business*. Cambridge, MA: Belknap Press.

Chapman, S. 1984. *The Rise of Merchant Banking*. London: Unwin Hyman.

Chassagne, S. 1991. *Le Coton et ses Patrons: France, 1760–1840*. Paris: EHESS.

    2003. Calico Printing in Europe before 1780. In D. T. Jenkins, ed., *The Cambridge History of Western Textiles*. Cambridge University Press.

Chaudhuri, K. N. 1978. *The Trading World of Asia and the English East India Company, 1660–1760*. Cambridge University Press.

    1985. *Trade and Civilisation in the Indian Ocean: An Economic History from the Rise of Islam to 1750*. Cambridge University Press.

Chesnais, J.-C. 1992. *The Demographic Transition*. Oxford University Press.

Cipolla, C. M. 1972. The So-Called "Price Revolution": Reflections on the Italian Situation. In P. Burke, ed., *Economy and Society in Early Modern Europe*. New York: Harper & Row.

Clapham, J. 1944a. *The Bank of England: A History. Volume 1 1694–1796*. Cambridge University Press.

    1944b. *The Bank of England: A History. Volume 2 1797–1914*. Cambridge University Press.

Clark, G. 1987. Productivity Growth without Technical Change in European Agriculture before 1850. *Journal of Economic History* 47: 419–32.

    1988. The Cost of Capital and Medieval Agricultural Technique. *Explorations in Economic History* 25: 265–94.

    1994. Factory Discipline. *Journal of Economic History* 54: 128–63.

    2005. The Condition of the Working Class in England, 1209–2004. *Journal of Political Economy* 113: 1307–40.

    2007a. *A Farewell to Alms*. Princeton University Press.

    2007b. The Long March of History: Farm Wages, Population, and Economic Growth, England 1209–1869. *Economic History Review* 60: 97–135.

Clark, G., and G. Hamilton, 2006. Survival of the Richest: The Malthusian Mechanism in Pre-industrial England. *Journal of Economic History* 66: 707–36.

Clark, P. 2000. *British Clubs and Societies, 1580–1800: The Origins of an Associational World*. Oxford: Clarendon Press.

Clarkson, L. A. 1985. *Proto-industrialization: The First Phase of Industrialization?* Basingstoke: Macmillan.

    2003. The Linen Industry in Early Modern Europe. In D. T. Jenkins, ed., *The Cambridge History of Western Textiles*. Cambridge University Press.

Cleland, J., and C. Wilson. 1987. Demand Theories of the Fertility Transition: An Iconoclastic View. *Population Studies* 41: 5–30.

Coale, A. J. 1973. *The Demographic Transition Reconsidered*. *International Population Conference*. Liege: International Union for the Scientific Study of Population.

Coale, A., and S. C. Watkins, eds. 1986. *The Decline of Fertility in Europe*. Princeton University Press.

Cole, A. H., and R. Crandall. 1964. The International Scientific Committee on Price History. *Journal of Economic History* 24: 381–88.

Coleman, A. 1999. Storage, Arbitrage and the Law of One Price: New Theory of an Old Problem, mimeo, Princeton University.

Collins, E. J. L. 1969. Labour Supply and Demand in European Agriculture, 1800–1880. In E. L. Jones and S. J. Woolf, eds., *Agrarian Change and Economic Development: The Historical Problems*. London: Methuen.

Collins, M. 1988. *Money and Banking in the UK: a History*. London: Croom Helm.

Condillac, Abbé de. 1776. *Commerce et le gouvernement considéré l'un à l'autre*. Paris: Jombert & Cellot.

Coppens, H. 1992. De financiën van de centrale regering van de Zuidelijke Nederlanden aan het einde van het Spaanse en onder Oostenrijks bewind (*ca. 1680–1788*). Vol. 54/142, *Verhandelingen van de Koninklijke Academie voor Wetenschappen, Letteren en Schone Kunsten van België. Klasse der Letteren*. Brussels: Paleis der Academiën.

Cottrell, P. L., and L. Newton. 1998. Joint-Stock Banking in the English Provinces 1826–1857: To Branch or Not to Branch? *Business and Economic History* 27: 115–28.

——— 1999. Banking Liberalization in England and Wales 1826–1844. In R. Sylla, R. Tilly and G. Tortella, eds., *The State, the Financial System, and Economic Modernization*. Cambridge University Press.

Crafts, N. F. R. 1977. The Industrial Revolution in England and France: Some Thoughts on the Question, Why Was England First? *Economic History Review* 30: 429–41.

——— 1985a. *British Economic Growth During the Industrial Revolution*. Oxford University Press.

——— 1985b. English Workers' Real Wages during the Industrial Revolution: Some Remaining Problems. *Journal of Economic History* 45: 139–44.

——— 1987. British Economic Growth, 1700–1850, Some Difficulties of Interpretation. *Explorations in Economic History* 24: 245–68.

——— 1995. Exogenous or Endogenous Growth? The Industrial Revolution Reconsidered. *Journal of Economic History* 55: 745–72.

——— 1997a. Some Dimensions of the Quality of Life during the Industrial Revolution. *Economic History Review* 50: 617–39.

——— 1997b. The Human Development Index and Changes in Standards of Living: Some Historical Comparisons. *European Review of Economic History* 1: 299–322.

——— 1998. Forging Ahead and Falling Behind: The Rise and Relative Decline of the First Industrial Nation. *Journal of Economic Perspectives* 12: 193–210.

——— 2002. The Human Development Index, 1870–1999: Some Revised Estimates. *European Review of Economic History* 6: 395–405.

——— 2004. Steam as a General Purpose Technology: A Growth Accounting Perspective. *Economic Journal* 114: 338–51.

Crafts, N. F. R., and C. K. Harley. 1992. Output Growth and the British Industrial Revolution: A Restatement of the Crafts–Harley View. *Economic History Review* 45: 703–30.

Crafts, N. F. R., and T. Mills. 2009. From Malthus to Solow: How the Malthusian. Economy Really Evolved. *Journal of Macroeconomics* 31: 68–93.

Craig, L. A., and D. Fisher. 1997. *The Integration of the European Economy, 1850–1913*. London: Macmillan.

 2000. *The European Macroeconomy: Growth, Integration and Cycles 1500–1913*. North Hampton: Edward Elgar.

Craig, L. A., D. Fisher, and T. Spencer. 1995. Inflation and Money Growth under the International Gold Standard, 1850–1913. *Journal of Macroeconomics* 17: 207–26.

Crayen, D., and J. Baten. 2008. Global Trends in Numeracy 1820–1949 and Its Implications for Long-Run Growth, CESifo Working Paper Series No. 2218.

Crouzet, F. 1964. Wars, Blockade, and Economic Change in Europe, 1792–1815. *Journal of Economic History* 24: 567–88.

Cuberes, D., and M. Jerzmanowski. 2007. Growth Cycles and Democracy, mimeo, Clemson University.

Cuenca Esteban, J. 1989. The Markets of Latin American Exports, 1790–1820: A Comparative Analysis of International Prices. In L. L. Johnson and E. Tandeter, eds., *Growth and Integration in the Atlantic Economy*. Albuquerque: University of New Mexico Press.

 1997. The Rising Share of British Industrial Exports in Industrial Output, 1700–1851. *Journal of Economic History* 57: 879–906.

Cullen, L. M. 1993. History, Economic Crises, and Revolution: Understanding Eighteenth-Century France. *Economic History Review* 46: 635–57.

Czap, P., Jr. 1978. Marriage and the Peasant Joint Family in the Era of Serfdom. In D. L. Ransel, ed., *The Family in Imperial Russia: New Lines of Historical Research*. Urbana: University of Illinois Press.

Dam, K. W. 2005. *The Law–Growth Nexus: The Rule of Law and Economic Development*. Washington: Brookings Institution Press.

Das Gupta, A. 2001. *The World of the Indian Ocean Merchant*. New Delhi: Oxford University Press.

Das Gupta A., and M. N. Pearson. 1987. *India and the Indian Ocean*. New Delhi: Oxford University Press.

Dasgupta, P., and P. A. David. 1994. Toward a New Economics of Science. *Research Policy* 23: 487–521.

Daudin, G. 2004. Profitability of Slave and Long Distance Trading in Context: The Case of 18th Century France. *Journal of Economic History* 64: 144–71.

 2005. *Commerce et prospérité: la France au XVIIIe siècle*. Paris: PUPS.

 2006. Do Frontiers Give or Do Frontiers Take? The Case of Intercontinental Trade in France at the end of the Ancien Régime. In O. Pétré-Grenouilleau, P. Emmer, and J. Roitman, eds., *A Deus Ex Machina Revisited. Atlantic Colonial Activities and European Economic Development*. Leiden: Brill.

2007. Traders, Intercontinental Trade, and Growth before the Industrial Revolution, mimeo.

Daunton, M. J. 1995. *Progress and Poverty: An Economic and Social History of Britain, 1700–1850*. Oxford and New York: Oxford University Press.

Davis, L. E., and R. A. S. Huttenback. 1988. *Mammon and the Pursuit of the Empire*. Cambridge University Press.

Davis, R. 1962. English Foreign Trade 1700–1774. *Economic History Review* 15: 285–303.

1969. English Foreign Trade (1700–1774). In W. E. Minchinton, ed., *The Growth of English Overseas Trade in the Seventeenth and Eighteenth Centuries*. London: Methuen.

1978. Maritime History: Progress and Problems. In S. Marriner, ed., *Business and Businessmen: Studies in Business, Economic and Accounting History*. Liverpool University Press.

1979. *The Industrial Revolution and British Overseas Trade*. Leicester University Press.

Deane, P., and W. A. Cole. 1962. *British Economic Growth 1688–1959: Trends and Structure*. Cambridge University Press.

1969. *British Economic Growth, 1688–1959: Trends and structure*, 2nd edn. Cambridge University Press.

De la Croix, D. 2008. Adult Longevity and Economic Take-off: From Malthus to Ben-Porath, mimeo.

DeLong, J. B. 1999. Introduction to the Symposium on Business Cycles. *Journal of Economic Perspectives* 13: 19–22.

DeLong, J. B., and A. Shleifer. 1993. Princes and Merchants: European City Growth before the Industrial Revolution. *Journal of Law and Economics* 36: 671–702.

Dennison, T. K. 2006. Did Serfdom Matter? Russian Rural Society 1750–1860. *Historical Research* 79: 74–89.

Dennison, T. K., and S. Ogilvie, 2007. Serfdom and Social Capital in Bohemia and Russia. *Economic History Review* 60: 513–44.

Dérouet, B. 1980. Une démographie sociale differentielle: clés pour un système auto régulateur des populations rurales d'Ancien Régime. *Annales: Economies, Sociétés, Civilisations* 35: 3–41.

Desai, A. V. 1972. Population and Standards of Living in Akbar's Time. *Indian Economic and Social History Review* 9: 43–62.

1978. Population and Standards of Living in Akbar's Time – A Second Look. *Indian Economic and Social History Review* 15: 53–79.

Desmet, K., and S. L. Parente. 2006. Bigger Is Better: Market Size, Demand Elasticity and Resistance to Technology Adoption, CEPR Discussion Paper 5825.

Dickmann, N. 2003. *Fertility and Family Income on the Move: An International Comparison over Twenty Years*. Syracuse: Maxwell School, Syracuse University.

Dickson, P. G. M. 1967. *The Financial Revolution in England: A Study in the Development of Public Credit, 1688–1756*. London: Macmillan.

1987. *Finance and Government under Maria Theresa 1740–1780*. Oxford University Press.

Dincecco, M. 2006. A Quantitative Analysis of Fiscal Fragmentation and Centralization in Europe, 1700–1871, mimeo, IMT Lucca Institute for Advanced Studies.

2009. Fiscal Centralization, Limited Government, and Public Revenues in Europe, 1650–1913. *Journal of Economic History* 69: 48–103.

Dion, R. 1977. *Histoire de la Vigne et du Vin au France*. Paris: Flammarion.

Doepke, M. 2004. Accounting for Fertility Decline during the Transition to Growth. *Journal of Economic Growth* 9: 347–83.

Doepke, M., and F. Zilibotti. 2005. The Macroeconomics of Child Labor Regulation. *American Economic Review* 95: 1492–524.

2008. Occupational Choice and the Spirit of Capitalism. *Quarterly Journal of Economics* 123: 747–93.

Dormans, E. H. M. 1991. *Het Tekort. Staatsschuld in de tijd der Republiek, NEHA Series III*. Amsterdam: NEHA.

Doveri, A. 2000. Land, Fertility, and Family: A Selected Review of the Literature in Historical Demography. *Genus* 56: 19–59.

Drelichman, M. 2005. The Curse of Moctezuma: American Silver and the Dutch Disease. *Explorations in Economic History* 42: 349–80.

Drelichman, M., and H.-J. Voth. 2008. Debt Sustainability in Historical Perspective: The Role of Fiscal Repression. *Journal of the European Economic Association* 6: 657–67.

Duffy, I. P. H. 1982. The Discount Policy of the Bank of England during the Suspension of Cash Payments, 1797–1821. *Economic History Review* 35: 67–82.

1985. *Bankruptcy and Insolvency in London during the Industrial Revolution*. New York: Garland.

Duranton, G., and D. Puga. 2004. Micro-foundations of Urban Agglomeration Economies. In V. Henderson and J.-F. Thisse, eds., *Handbook of Regional and Urban Economics*, IV. Amsterdam: North-Holland.

Dutton, H. 1984. *The Patent System and Inventive Activity during the Industrial Revolution 1750–1852*. Manchester University Press.

Easterlin, R. A. 1981. Why Isn't the Whole World Developed? *Journal of Economic History* 41: 1–19.

Edwards, M. M. 1967. *The Growth of the British Cotton Trade*, 1780–1815. Manchester University Press.

Ellickson, R. C. 1991. *Order without Law: How Neighbors Settle Disputes*. Cambridge, MA: Harvard University Press.

Elliott, J. H. 1990. The Seizure of Overseas Territories by European Powers. In H. Pohl, ed., *The European Discovery of the World and its Economic Effects on Pre-Industrial Society, 1500–1800, Vierteljahrschrift für Sozial-und Wirstchaftsgeschichte* 89: 43–61.

Engels, F. 1892. *The Condition of the Working Class in England in 1844*. London: Allen & Unwin.

Engerman, S. L. 1972. The Slave Trade and British Capital Formation in the Eighteenth Century: A Comment on the Williams Thesis. *Business History Review* 46: 430–43.

1998. British Imperialism in a Mercantilist Age, 1492–1849: Conceptual Issues and Empirical Problems. *Revista de Historia Económica* 16: 195–233.

Engerman, S., and K. L. Sokoloff. 1997. Factor Endowments: Institutions, and Differential Paths of Growth among New World Economies: A View from Economic Historians of the United States. In S. Haber, ed., *How Latin America Fell Behind: Essays on the Economic Histories of Brazil and Mexico, 1800–1914.* Stanford University Press.

Epstein, S. R. 2000. *Freedom and Growth: Markets and States in Pre-modern Europe.* New York: Routledge.

Ertman, T. 1997. *Birth of the Leviathan: Building States and Regimes in Mediaeval and Early Modern Europe.* Cambridge University Press.

Evans, R. J. 2005. *Death in Hamburg: Society and Politics in the Cholera Years 1830–1910.* New York: Penguin Books.

Fairchilds, C. 1993. The Production and Marketing of Populuxe Goods in Eighteenth-Century Paris. In J. Brewer and R. Porter, eds., *Consumption and the World of Goods.* London and New York: Routledge.

Farnie, D. A. 2003. Cotton, 1780–1914. In D. T. Jenkins, ed., *The Cambridge History of Western Textiles.* Cambridge University Press.

2004. The Role of Merchants as the Prime Movers in the Expansion of the Cotton Industry, 1760–1990. In D. A. Farnie and D. J. Jeremy, eds., *The Fibre that Changed the World: The Cotton Industry in International Perspective, 1600–1990s.* Oxford University Press.

Federico, G. 1997. *An Economic History of the Silk Industry, 1830–1930.* Cambridge University Press.

2003. A Capital Intensive Innovation in a Capital Scarce World: Steam Threshing in 19th-Century Italy. *Advances in Agricultural Economic History* 2: 75–114.

Federico G., and P. Malanima. 2004. Progress, Decline, Growth: Product and Productivity in Italian Agriculture, 1000–2000. *Economic History Review* 57: 437–64.

Federico, G., and K. G. Persson. 2007. Market Integration and Convergence in the World Wheat Market, 1800–2000. In T. J. Hatton, K. H. O'Rourke, and A. M. Taylor, eds., *The New Comparative Economic History: Essays in Honor of Jeffrey G. Williamson.* Cambridge, MA: MIT Press.

Feinstein, C. H. 1972. *National Income, Expenditure and Output of the United Kingdom, 1855–1965.* Cambridge University Press.

1978. Capital Formation in Great Britain. In P. Mathias and M. M. Postan, eds., *The Cambridge Economic History of Europe Vol. 8, Pt. 1, The Industrial Economies: Capital Labour and Enterprise.* Cambridge University Press.

1988. Review: The Rise and Fall of the Williamson Curve. *Journal of Economic History* 48: 699–729.

1998. Pessimism Perpetuated: Real Wages and the Standard of Living in Britain during and after the Industrial Revolution. *Journal of Economic History* 58: 625–58.

Feldbauer P., M. Mitterauer, and W. Schwentker, eds. 2002. *Die vormoderne Stadt. Asien und Europa im Vergleich.* Vienna: Verlag für Geschichte und Politik.

Fenoaltea, S. 2003. Peeking Backward: Regional Aspects of Industrial Growth in Post-unification Italy. *Journal of Economic History* 63: 1059–102.

Ferguson, N. 1998. *The House of Rothschild: Money's Prophets, 1798–1848.* London: Penguin.

Filipczak-Kocur, A. 1999. Poland-Lithuania before Partition. In R. Bonney, ed., *The Rise of the Fiscal State in Europe, 1200–1815.* Oxford University Press.

Finer, S. E. 1997. *The History of Government from the Earliest Times.* Oxford University Press.

Findlay, R. 1990. *The Triangular Trade and the Atlantic Economy of the Eighteenth Century: A Simple General Equilibrium Model.* Essays in International Finance 177. Princeton University Press.

Findlay, R., and K. H. O'Rourke. 2007. *Power and Plenty: Trade, War, and the World Economy in the Second Millennium.* Princeton University Press.

Fink, K. 1991. The Beginnings of Railways in Russia, available at www.fink.com/papers/russia.html.

Fisher, D. 1989. The Price Revolution: A Monetary Interpretation. *Journal of Economic History* 49: 883–902.

Flandreau, M., C. Galimard, C. Jobst, and P. Nogués Marco. 2008. The Bell Jar: Commercial Interest Rates between Two Revolutions, 1688–1789. In J. Atack and L. Neal, eds., *The Origin and Development of Financial Institutions and Markets.* Cambridge University Press.

2009. Monetary Geography before the Industrial Revolution. *Cambridge Journal of Regions, Economy and Society*, 2: 149–71.

Flinn, M. W. 1974. Trends in Real Wages, 1750–1850. *Economic History Review*, 27: 395–413.

1985. *The European Demographic System, 1500–1820.* Baltimore: Johns Hopkins.

Flora, P. 1983. *State, Economy and Society in Western Europe, 1815–1975: A Data Handbook.* Frankfurt, London, and Chicago: Macmillan, St. James Press.

Flora, P., F. Kraus, and W. Pfenning. 1983. *State, Economy and Society in Western Europe 1815–1975*, I. Chicago: St. James Press.

Florén, A. 1998. Iron-Making Societies: The Development of the Iron Industry in Sweden and Russia, 1600–1900. In M. Agren, ed., *Iron-Making Societies, Early Industrial Development in Sweden and Russia, 1600–1900.* Oxford: Berghahn.

Floud, R., and D. N. McCloskey. 1981. *The Economic History of Britain since 1700.* Cambridge University Press.

Floud, R., and P. Johnson, eds. 2004. *The Cambridge Economic History of Modern Britain, Vol. 1, Industrialisation, 1700–1870.* Cambridge University Press.

Fontana, J. 1991. La crisis colonial en la crisis del Antiguo Régimen español. In H. Bonilla, ed., *El sistema colonial en la América española.* Barcelona: Ariel.

Foreman-Peck, J. 2006. Review of Brinley Thomas's *Migration and Economic Growth: A Study of Great Britain and the Atlantic Economy*, EH.Net.

Forsyth, P. J., and S. J. Nicholas. 1983. The Decline of Spanish Industry and the Price Revolution: A Neoclassical Analysis. *Journal of European Economic History* 12: 601–10.

Francis, N., and V. Ramey. 2005. Is the Technology-Driven Real Business Cycle Hypothesis Dead? *Journal of Monetary Economics* 52: 1379–99.

Frank, A. G. 1975. *On Capitalist Underdevelopment*. New York: Oxford University Press.

Freedeman, C. E. 1979. *Joint-Stock Enterprise in France, 1807–1867: From Privileged Company to Modern Corporation*. Chapel Hill: University of North Carolina Press.

Fregert, K., and R. Gustafsson. 2005. Fiscal Statistics for Sweden, 1719–2003, Working Paper No. 40, Department of Economics, Lund University.

Fremdling, R. 1986. *Technologischer Wandel und internationaler Handel im 18. und 19. Jahrhundert, Die Eisenindustrien in Großbritannien, Belgien, Frankreich und Deutschland*. Berlin: Duncker & Humblot.

1989. British Coal on Continental Markets, 1850–1913. In C.-L. Holtfrerich, ed., *Interactions in the World Economy*. New York: Harvester Wheatsheaf.

1996. Anglo-German Rivalry in Coal Markets in France, the Netherlands and Germany 1850–1913. *Journal of European Economic History* 25: 599–646.

2000. Transfer Patterns of British Technology to the Continent: The Case of the Iron Industry. *European Review of Economic History* 4: 195–222.

2004. Continental Response to British Innovations in the Iron Industry during the Eighteenth and Early Nineteenth Centuries. In L. Prados de la Escosura, ed., *Exceptionalism and Industrialisation: Britain and its European Rivals, 1688–1815*. Cambridge University Press.

2005. Foreign Trade – Transfer – Adaptation: British Iron Making Technology on the Continent (Belgium and France). In C. Evans and G. Rydén, eds., *The Industrial Revolution in Iron: The Impact of British Coal Technology in Nineteenth-Century Europe*. Aldershot: Ashgate.

Fremdling, R., and B. P. A. Gales. 1994. Iron Masters and Iron Production During the Belgian Industrial Revolution: The "Enquete" of 1828. In P. Klep and E. van Cauwenberghe, eds., *Entrepreneurship and the Transformation of the Economy*. Leuven University Press.

French, C. J. 1987. Productivity in the Atlantic Shipping Industry: A Quantitative Study. *Journal of Interdisciplinary History* 17: 613–38.

Fritschy, W. 1988. *De patriotten en de financiën van de Bataafse Republiek. Hollands krediet en de smalle marges voor een nieuw beleid (1795–1811)*. The Hague: Stichting Hollandse Historische Reeks.

Fritschy, W. 2003. A "Financial Revolution" Revisited: Public Finance in Holland during the Dutch Revolt, 1568–1648. *Economic History Review* 56: 57–89.

Fritschy, W., and R. Liesker. 2004. *Gewestelijke financiën ten tijde van de Republiek der Verenigde Nederlanden. Deel IV Holland (1572–1795)*. The Hague: Instituut voor Nederlandse Geschiedenis.

Gabaix X., and Y. Ioannides. 2004. The Evolution of City Size Distributions. In V. Enderson and J. F. Thisse, eds., *Handbook of Urban and Regional Economics*. Amsterdam: North-Holland Publishing Company.

Galletti, J. G. A. 1822. *Allgemeines geographische Wörterbuch. Oder alphabetische Darstellung aller Länder, Städte, Flecken, Dörfer, Ortschaften, Meere, Flüsse u.s. w. Mit genauer Angabe ihrer Grösse, Bevölkerung, Producte, Manufacturen, Fabriken, ihres Gewerbes, Handels u.s.w.*, I. Pesth: Hartleben.

Galloway, P. R. 1988. Basic Patterns in Annual Variations in Fertility, Nuptiality, Mortality, and Prices in Pre-industrial Europe. *Population Studies* 42: 275–302.

Galor, O. 2005. From Stagnation to Growth: Unified Growth Theory. In P. Aghion and S. N. Durlauf, eds., *Handbook of Economic Growth Vol. 1A*. Amsterdam: North Holland Press.

Galor, O., and O. Moav. 2002. Natural Selection and the Origins of Economic Growth. *Quarterly Journal of Economics* 117: 1133–91.

2006. Das Human Kapital: A Theory of the Demise of the Class Structure. *Review of Economic Studies* 73: 85–117.

Galor, O., and D. N. Weil. 1996. The Gender Gap, Fertility, and Growth. *American Economic Review* 86: 374–87.

1999. From Malthusian Stagnation to Modern Economic Growth. *American Economic Review* 89: 150–54.

2000. Population, Technology, and Growth: From Malthusian Stagnation to the Demographic Transition and Beyond. *American Economic Review* 90: 806–28.

García-Iglesias, C., and J. K. Kilponen. 2004. Trends, Cycles and Economc Growth in the Nordic Countries during the Classical Gold Standard Period, mimeo, World Congress of Cliometrics.

Garðarsdóttir, Ó. 2002. *Saving the Child: Regional, Cultural and Social Aspects of the Infant Mortality Decline in Iceland, 1770-1920*. Umeå: Demographic Data Base, Umeå University.

Geiger, R. 1994. *Planning the French Canals: Bureaucracy, Politics, and Enterprise under the Restoration*. Newark: Delaware University Press.

Gerhold, D. 1996. Productivity Change in Road Transport before and after Turnpiking, 1690–1840. *Economic History Review* 49: 491–515.

Gerschenkron, A. 1962. *Economic Backwardness in Historical Perspective*. Cambridge, MA: Harvard University Press.

Gervaise, Isaac. 1720. *The System or Theory of the Trade of the World*. London. Available at http://socserv.mcmaster.ca/econ/ugcm/3ll3/gervaise/trade.

Gijsbers, W. M. 1999. *Kapitale ossen: de internationale handel in slachtvee in Noordwest-Europa (1300-1750)*. Hilversum: Verloren.

Gillard, L. 2004. *La Banque d'Amsterdam et le florin européen au temps de la République Néerlandaise (1610-1820)*. Paris: EHESS.

Gillispie, C. C. 1980. *Science and Polity in France at the end of the Old Regime*. Princeton University Press.

Glaeser, E., R. La Porta, F. Lopez-de-Silanes, and A. Shleifer. 2004. Do Institutions Cause Growth? *Journal of Economic Growth* 9: 271–303.

Glass, D. V., and E. Grebenik. 1965. World Population, 1800–1950. In H. J. Habakkuk and M. Postan, eds., *The Cambridge Economic History of Europe, Vol. VI, The Industrial Revolution and After: Incomes, Population and Technological Change, Part I*. Cambridge University Press.

Glete, J. 1993. *Navies and Nations: Warships, Navies and State Building in Europe and America, 1500–1860*. 2 vols. Stockholm: Almqvist and Wiksell International.

Gonzalez de Lara, Y., A. Greif, and S. Jah. 2008. The Administrative Foundations of Self-Enforcing Constitutions. *American Economic Review* 98: 105–09.

Goodman, J. 1993. *Tobacco in History: The Cultures of Dependence*. London: Routledge.

Granger, C. W. J., and C. M. Elliot. 1967. A Fresh Look at Wheat Prices and Markets in the Eighteenth Century. *Economic History Review* 20: 257–65.

Greif, A. 2005. Commitment, Coercion, and Markets: The Nature and Dynamics of Institutions Supporting Exchange. In C. Menard and M. M. Shirley, eds., *Handbook for New Institutional Economics*. Norwell, MA: Kluwer Academic Publishers.

2006. *Institutions and the Path to the Modern Economy: Lessons from Medieval Trade*. Cambridge University Press.

Grigg, D. 1992. *The Transformation of Agriculture in the West*. Oxford: Blackwell.

Grytten, O. H. 2007. Norwegian Wages, 1726–2006. In Ø. Eitrheim, J. T. Klovland and J. F. Qvigstad, eds., Historical Monetary Statistics for Norway, part II, Norges Banks skriftserie/occasional papers 38.

Guinnane, T., R. Harris, N. R. Lamoreaux, and J.-L. Rosenthal. 2007. Putting the Corporation in its Place. *Enterprise and Society* 8: 687–729.

Guiso, L., P. Sapienza, and L. Zingales. 2006. Does Culture affect Economic Outcomes? NBER Working Paper 11999.

Guntupalli, A. M., and J. Baten. 2006. The Development and Inequality of Heights in North, West and East India 1915–44. *Explorations in Economic History* 43: 578–608.

Guy, K. M. 2003 *When Champagne Became French: Wine and the Making of a National Identity*. Baltimore: Johns Hopkins University Press.

Habakkuk, H. J. 1962. *American and British Technology in the Nineteenth Century*. Cambridge University Press.

Habib, I. 1969. Potentialities of Capitalist Development in the Economy of Mughal India. *Journal of Economic History* 29: 32–78.

1982. Monetary System and Prices. In T. Raychaudhuri and I. Habib, eds., *The Cambridge Economic History of India, Volume 1: c.1200–c.1750*. Cambridge University Press.

1999. *The Agrarian System of Mughal India*. Delhi: Oxford University Press.

Hagen, W. 2002. *Ordinary Prussians: Brandenburg Junkers and Villagers, 1580–1840*. Cambridge University Press

Hajnal, J. 1965. European Marriage Pattern in Historical Perspective. In D. V. Glass and D. E. C. Eversley, eds., *Population in History*. London: Arnold.

Hall, R. A. 1974. What Did the Industrial Revolution in Britain Owe to Science? In N. McKendrick, ed., *Historical Perspectives: Studies in English Thought and Society*. London: Europa Publications.

Hall, R. E., and C. I. Jones. 1999. Why Do Some Countries Produce So Much More Output per Worker than Others? *Quarterly Journal of Economics* 114: 83–116.

Hambly, G. R. G., and B. Stein. 1978. Towns and Cities. In T. Raychaudhuri and I. Habib, eds., *The Cambridge Economic History of India, Volume 1: c.1200–c.1750*. Cambridge University Press.

Hamilton, E. J. 1934. *American Treasure and the Price Revolution in Spain, 1501–1650*. Cambridge, MA: Harvard University Press.

Hansen, G. D., and E. C. Prescott. 2002. Malthus to Solow. *American Economic Review* 92: 1205–17.

Hansen, J. 2003. Financial Cycles and Bankruptcies in the Nordic Countries. *Sveriges Riksbank Working Paper Series* 149.

Hansen, S. A. 1970. *Early Industrialisation in Denmark*. Copenhagen: G.E.C. Gads Forlag.

Hansson, G., and O. Olsson. 2006. Country Size and the Rule of Law: Resuscitating Montesquieu, mimeo, Göteborg University.

Harley, C. K. 1971. The Shift from Sailing Ships to Steamships, 1850–1890: A Study in Technological Change and Its Diffusion. In D. N. McCloskey, ed., *Essays on a Mature Economy: Britain after 1840*. Princeton University Press.

    1982. British Industralization before 1841: Evidence of Slower Growth during the Industrial Revolution. *Journal of Economic History* 42: 267–89.

    1988. Ocean Freight Rates and Productivity, 1740–1914: The Primacy of Mechanical Invention Reaffirmed. *Journal of Economic History* 48: 851–76.

    1999. Reassessing the Industrial Revolution: A Macro View. In J. Mokyr, ed., *The British Industrial Revolution: An Economic Perspective*, 2nd edn. Boulder: Westview Press.

Harris, G. R., and M. P. Todaro. 1970. Migration, Unemployment and Development: A Two-Sector Analysis. *American Economic Review* 60: 126–42.

Harris, R. 2000. *Industrializing English Law Entrepreneurship and Business Organization, 1720–1844*. Cambridge University Press.

Hartmann, P. C. 1979. *Das Steuersystem der Europäischen Staaten am Ende des Ancien Regime. Eine offizielle französische Enquete (1763–1768). Dokumente, Analyse und Auswertung England und die Staaten Nord- und Mitteleuropas*. Zurich and Munich: Artemis Verlag.

Hawke, G. R. 1970. *Railways and Economic Growth in England and Wales, 1840–1870*. Oxford: Clarendon.

Heckman, J. J., and Y. Rubinstein. 2001. The Importance of Noncognitive Skills: Lessons from the GED Testing Program. *American Economic Review* 91: 145–49.

Hecksher, E. 1954. *An Economic History of Sweden*. Cambridge, MA: Harvard University Press.

Henry, L. 1956. *Anciennes familles genevoises; étude démographique: XVIe–XXe siècle.* Paris: Presses universitaires de France.

Herlihy, D. 1997. *The Black Death and the Transformation of the West.* Cambridge, MA: Harvard University Press.

Herranz-Loncan, A. 2007. Infrastructure Investment and Spanish Economic Growth, 1850–1935. *Explorations in Economic History* 44: 452–68.

Heston, A. W. 1977. The Standard of Living in Akbar's Time: A Comment. *Indian Economic and Social History Review* 14: 391–96.

Hicks, J. 1969. *A Theory of Economic History.* Oxford: Clarendon.

Hilaire, J. 1986. Introduction, *Historique au droit commercial.* Paris: Presses Universitaires de France.

Hildebrand, K.-G. 1992. *Swedish Iron in the Seventeenth and Eighteenth Centuries: Export Industry before the Industrialization.* Stockholm: Jernkontoret.

Hjerppe, R. 1989. *The Finnish Economy, 1869–1985.* Helsinki: Government Printing Centre.

Hobsbawm, E., and G. Rudé. 1968. *Captain Swing.* Harmondsworth: Penguin.

Hoch, S. L. 1982. Serfs in Imperial Russia – Demographic Insights. *Journal of Interdisciplinary History* 13: 221–46.

Hoffman, P. 1994. Early Modern France, 1450–1700. In P. Hoffman and K. Norberg, eds., *Fiscal Crises, Liberty, and Representative Government.* Stanford: Stanford University Press.

Hoffman, P. 1996. *Growth in a Traditional Society: The French Countryside 1450–1815.* Princeton University Press.

Hoffman, P. T., and J.-L. Rosenthal. 1997. The Political Economy of Warfare and Taxation in Early Modern Europe: Historical Lessons for Economic Development. In J. N. Drobak and J. V. C. Nye, eds., *The Frontiers of the New Institutional Economics.* San Diego: Academic Press.

Hoffman, P. T., G. Postel-Vinay and J.-L. Rosenthal. 2000. *Priceless Markets: The Political Economy of Credit in Paris, 1662–1869.* University of Chicago Press.

Hoffman, P. T., D. S. Jacks, P. Levin, and P. H. Lindert. 2002. Real Inequality in Europe since 1500. *Journal of Economic History* 62: 381–413.

Hoffmann, W. G. 1955. *British Industry 1700–1950.* Oxford: Blackwell.

1965. *Das Wachstum der deutschen Wirtschaft seit der Mitte des 19. Jahrhunderts.* Berlin: Springer.

Hohenberg, P. M., and L. H. Lees. 1985. *The Making of Urban Europe 1000–1950.* Cambridge, MA: Harvard University Press.

Holtfrerich, C.-L. 1973. *Quantitative Wirtschaftsgeschichte des Ruhrkohlenbergbaus im 19. Jahrhundert.* Dortmund: Gesellschaft für Westfälische Wirtschaftsgeschichte.

Homer, S., and R. Sylla. 1991. *A History of Interest Rates.* New Brunswick: Rutgers University Press.

Hoppit, J. 1986. Financial Crises in Eighteenth-Century England, *Economic History Review* 39: 39–58.

1987. *Risk and Failure in English Business, 1700–1800.* Cambridge University Press.

Horrell, S., and J. Humphries 1995. Women's Labour Force Participation and the Transition to the Male-Breadwinner Family, 1790–1865. *Economic History Review* 48: 89–117.

Huck, P. 1995. Infant Mortality and Living Standards of English Workers during the Industrial Revolution. *Journal of Economic History* 55: 528–50.

Humphries, J. 2003. English Apprenticeships: A Neglected Factor in the First Industrial Revolution. In P. A. David and M. Thomas, eds., *The Economic Future in Historical Perspective*. Oxford University Press.

2007. 'Because They Are too Menny...' Children, Mothers and Fertility Decline – The Evidence from Working-Class Autobiographies of the Eighteenth and Nineteenth Centuries. In A. Janssens, ed., *Gendering the Fertility Decline in the Western World*. Bern, New York: Peter Lang.

Hurd, J. 1975. Railways and the Expansion of Markets in India, 1861–1921. *Explorations in Economic History* 12: 263–88.

Hyde, C. K. 1977. *Technological Change and the British Iron Industry, 1700–1870.* Princeton University Press.

Irigoin, M. I., and R. Grafe. 2006. Bargaining for Absolutism: A Spanish Path to Nation State and Empire Building, University of Oxford Discussion Papers in Economic and Social History.

Jacks, D. S. 2004. Market Integration in the North and Baltic Seas, 1500–1800. *Journal of European Economic History* 33: 285–329.

2005. Intra- and International Commodity Market Integration in the Atlantic Economy, 1800–1913. *Explorations in Economic History* 42: 381–413.

2006. What Drove 19th Century Commodity Market Integration? *Explorations in Economic History* 43: 383–412.

Jacob, M. C. 1997. *Scientific Culture and the Making of the Industrial West*, 2nd edn. New York: Oxford University Press.

Jenkins, D. T. 2003. The Western Wool Textile Industry in the Nineteenth Century. In D. T. Jenkins, ed., *The Cambridge History of Western Textiles*. Cambridge University Press.

Jenkins, D. T., and K. G. Ponting 1982. *The British Wool Textile Industry, 1770–1914.* London: Heinemann.

Jeremy, D. J. 1981. *Transatlantic Industrial Revolution*. Oxford: Basil Blackwell.

Jones, C. I. 2001. Was the Industrial Revolution Inevitable? Economic Growth over the Very Long Run. *Advances in Macroeconomics* 1: 1–42.

Jones, E. L. 1981. *The European Miracle*. Cambridge University Press.

2006. *Cultures Merging*. Princeton University Press.

Jonker, J. 1996. *Merchants, Bankers, Middlemen: The Amsterdam Money Market during the First Half of the 19th Century*. Amsterdam: NEHA.

Joslin, D. M. 1954. London Private Bankers, 1720–85. *Economic History Review* 7: 167–86.

Juglar, C. 1967 [1889]. *Des crises commerciales et leur retour periodique en France, en Angleterre, et aux Etats-Unis*. New York: A. M. Kelley.

Justice, Alexander. 1707. *A General Treatise of Monies and Exchanges*. London.

Kahan, A. 1985. *The Plow, the Hammer and the Knout*. University of Chicago Press.

Kanefsky, J. W. 1979. The Diffusion of Power Technology in British Industry. Ph.D. dissertation, University of Exeter.

Kappeler, A. 2002. Stadtluft macht nicht frei! Die russische Stadt in der Vormoderne. In P. Feldbauer, M. Mitterauer, and W. Schwentker, eds., *Die vormoderne Stadt. Asien und Europa im Vergleich*. Vienna: Verlag für Geschichte und Politik.

Kaukiainen, Y. 2001. Shrinking the World: Improvements in the Speed of Information Transmission, c.1820–1870. *European Review of Economic History* 5: 1–28.

Keefer, P. 1996. Protection against a Capricious State: French Investment and Spanish Railroads, 1845–1875. *Journal of Economic History* 56: 170–92.

Kelly, M. 1997. The Dynamics of Smithian Growth. *Quarterly Journal of Economics* 112: 939–64.

  2005. Climate and Pre-Industrial Growth, mimeo, University College Dublin.

Kelly, P. 1821. *The Universal Cambist, and Commercial Instructor*, 2nd edn. London.

Keynes, J. M. 1930. Economic Possibilities for Our Grandchildren. *Nation and Atheneum*.

Khan, B. Z., and K. L. Sokoloff. 1998. Patent Institutions, Industrial Organization, and Early Technological Change: Britain and the United States, 1790–1850. In M. Berg and K. Bruland, eds., *Technological Revolutions in Europe*. Cheltenham: Edward Elgar.

Kindleberger, C. P. 1989. *Manias, Panics, and Crashes: A History of Financial Crises*. New York: Basic Books.

  1993. *A Financial History of Western Europe*, 2nd edn. Oxford University Press.

King, P. 2005. The Production and Consumption of Bar Iron in Early Modern England and Wales. *Economic History Review* 58: 1–33.

  2006. Errata. *Economic History Review* 59: 264.

King, W. T. C. 1936. *The History of the London Discount Market*. London: Routledge.

Kirby, P. 1999. The Historic Viability of Child Labor and the Mines Act of 1842. In M. Lavalette, ed., *A Thing of the Past? Child Labour in Britain in the Nineteenth and Twentieth Centuries*. Liverpool University Press.

Komlos, J. 1983. *The Habsburg Monarchy as a Customs Union*. Princeton University Press.

  1998. Shrinking in a Growing Economy? The Mystery of Physical Stature during the Industrial Revolution. *Journal of Economic History* 58: 779–802.

Kremer, M. 1993. Population Growth and Technological Change: One Million B.C. to 1990. *Quarterly Journal of Economics* 108: 681–716.

Kriedte, P., H. Medick., and J. Schlumbohm. 1981. *Industrialization Before Industrialization: Rural Industry in the Genesis of Capitalism*. Cambridge University Press.

Kuznets, S. 1955. Economic Growth and Income Inequality. *American Economic Review* 45: 1–28.

  1974. *Population, Capital and Economic Growth: Selected Essays*. London: Heinemann, 165–84.

Lains, P. 2003. *Os Progressos do Atraso. Uma Nova Historia Economica de Portugal, 1842–1992*. Lisbon: Imprensa de Ciencias Sociais.

2006. Growth in a Protected Environment: Portugal, 1850–1950. *Research in Economic History* 24: 121–63.

Lamoreaux, N. R., and J.-L. Rosenthal. 2005. Legal Regime and Business's Organizational Choice: A Comparison of France and the United States during the Mid-Nineteenth Century. *American Law and Economic Review* 7: 28–61.

Landes, D. 1969. *The Unbound Prometheus: Technological Change and Industrial Development in Western Europe from 1750 to the Present*. Cambridge University Press.

Lane, F. C., and R. C. Mueller. 1985. *Money and Banking in Medieval and Renaissance Venice*. Baltimore: Johns Hopkins University Press.

Lang, A. W. 1968. *Seekarten der Südlichen Nord- und Ostsee*. Hamburg: Deutsches Hydrographisches Institut.

La Porta, R., F. Lopez de Silanez, A. Shleifer, and R. Vishny. 1997. Legal Determinants of External Finance. *Journal of Finance*: 52: 1131–50.

Laslett, P. 1977. *Family Life and Illicit Love in Earlier Generations: Essays in Historical Sociology*. Cambridge University Press.

Laslett, P., and R. Wall. 1974. *Household and Family in Past Time: Comparative Studies in the Size and Structure of the Domestic Group over the Last Three Centuries in England, France, Serbia, Japan and Colonial North America, with Further Materials from Western Europe*. Cambridge University Press.

Leasure, J. W. 1963. Factors Involved in the Decline of Fertility in Spain 1900–1950. *Population Studies* 16: 71–285.

Lee, J. Z., and C. Campbell. 1997. *Fate and Fortune in Rural China: Social Organisation and Population Behaviour in Liaoning, 1774–1873*. Cambridge University Press.

Lee, J., and F. Wang. 1999. *One Quarter of Humanity, Malthusian Mythology and Chinese Realities, 1700–2000*. Cambridge, MA: Harvard University Press.

Lee, R. D. 1981. Short-term Variation: Vital Rates, Prices, and Weather. In E. A. Wrigley and R. S. Schofield, eds., *The Population History of England, 1541–1871: A Reconstruction*. London: Edward Arnold.

1987. Population Dynamics of Humans and Other Animals. *Demography* 24: 443–65.

2003. The Demographic Transition. Three Centuries of Fundamental Change. *Journal of Economic Perspectives* 17: 167–90.

Lee, R. D., and M. Anderson. 2002. Malthus in State Space: Macroeconomic–Demographic Relations in English History, 1540 to 1870. *Journal of Population Economics* 15: 195–220.

Lee, R. W., and P. Marschalck 2002. Infant Mortality in Bremen in the 19th Century. *History of the Family* 7: 557–83.

Lenoir, T. 1998. Revolution from Above: The Role of the State in Creating the German Research System, 1810–1910. *American Economic Review* 88: 22–27.

Lerner, J., and J. Tirole. 2004. The Economics of Technology Sharing: Open Source and Beyond, NBER Working Paper 10956.

Lescoeur, C. 1877. *Essai historique et critique sur la législation des sociétés commerciales en France et à l'étranger*. Paris: A. Marescq aîné.

Lesthaeghe, R. J. 1977. *The Decline of Belgian Fertility, 1800–1970*. Princeton University Press.

1991. Moral Control, Secularization and Reproduction in Belgium (1600–1900). In Société Belge de Démographie, ed., *Historiens Et Populations: Liber Amicorum Etienne Hélin*. Louvain-la-Neuve: Academia.

1992. Beyond Economic Reductionism: The Transformation of the Reproductive Regimes in France and Belgium in the 18th and 19th Centuries. In C. Goldscheider, ed., *Fertility Transitions, Family Structure, and Population Policy*. Boulder: Westview Press.

Lesthaeghe, R. J., and C. Wilson. 1986. Modes of Production, Secularization, and the Pace of the Fertility Decline in Western Europe, 1870–1930. In A. J. Coale and S. Watkins, eds., *The Decline of Fertility in Europe*. Princeton University Press.

Leunig, T. 2001. Piece Rates and Learning: Understanding Work and Production in the New England Textile Industry a Century Ago, mimeo, London School of Economics.

2006. Time is Money: A Reassessment of the Passenger Social Savings from Victorian British Railways. *Journal of Economic History* 66: 635–73.

Levere, T. H., and G. L' E. Turner. 2002. *Discussing Chemistry and Steam: The Minutes of a Coffee House Philosophical Society 1780–1787*. Oxford University Press.

Lévy-Leboyer, M. 1968. La croissance économique en France au XIXe siècle. *Annales* 23: 788–807.

Lévy-Leboyer, M., and F. Bourguignon. 1990. *The French Economy in the Nineteenth Century*. Cambridge University Press.

Li, B. 1998. *Agricultural Development in Jiangnan, 1620–1850*. New York: St. Martin`s Press.

2000. *Jiangnan de Zaoqi Gongyehua 1550–1850* (Early Industrialization in Jiangnan, 1550–1850). Beijing: Publishing Press of Social Science Materials.

2002. *Lilun, Fangfa, Fazhan Qushi (Theory, Methodology and Developmental Trends)*. Beijing: Tsinghau University Press, 2002.

2003. Bagu zhi wai: Ming Qing Jingnan de jiaoyu ji qi dui jingji de yingxiang (Beyond the Eight-Legged Essay: Education and its impact on Jiangnan Economy in Ming and Qing). *Qing shi yanjiu* (Research in Qing History), 4.

Li, L. 2000. Integration and Disintegration in North China's Grain Markets, 1738–1911. *Journal of Economic History* 60: 665–99.

Lin, J. Y. 1995. The Needham Puzzle: Why the Industrial Revolution Did Not Originate in China. *Economic Development and Cultural Change* 43: 269–92.

Lindert, P. H. 1986. Unequal English Wealth since 1670. *Journal of Political Economy* 94: 1127–62.

2004. *Growing Public: Social Spending and Economic Growth since the 18th Century*. Cambridge University Press.

Lindert, P. H., and J. G. Williamson 1983. English Workers' Living Standards during the Industrial Revolution: A New Look. *Economic History Review* 36: 1–25.

Lipsey, R. G., K. I. Carlaw, and C. T. Bekar, 2005. *Economic Transformations: General Purpose Technologies and Long-Term Economic Growth*. Oxford University Press.

Livi Bacci, M. 1991. *Population and Nutrition: An Essay on European Demographic History*. Cambridge University Press.

2000. *The Population of Europe: A History*. Malden, MA: Blackwell Publishers.

Llopis Agelán E., and M. Gonzáles Mariscal. 2006. La Tasa de Urbanización de Espana a Finales del Siglo XVIII: el Problema de las Agrociudades, Documento de Trabajo de la Asociatión Espanola de Historia Economica DT-AEHE 0601.

Llopis Agelán, E., and M. Jerez Méndez. 2001. El Mercado De Trigo En Castilla y Leon, 1691–1788: Arbitraje Espacial E Intervencion. *Historia Agraria* 25: 13–68.

Long, J. 2006. The Socioeconomic Return to Primary Schooling in Victorian England. *Journal of Economic History* 66: 1026–53.

Long, J. B., Jr., and C. I. Plosser. 1983. Real Business Cycles. *Journal of Political Economy* 91: 39–69.

Lucas, R. E. 1988. On the Mechanics of Economic Development. *Journal of Monetary Economics* 22: 3–42.

2002. The Industrial Revolution: Past and Future. In R. E. Lucas, *Lectures on Economic Growth*. Cambridge, MA: Harvard University Press.

Lucassen, J., and R. Unger. 2000. Labour Productivity in Ocean Shipping, 1500–1850. *International Journal of Maritime History* 12: 127–41.

Ma, D. 2004. Growth, Institutions and Knowledge: A Review and Reflection on the Historiography of 18th–20th Century China. *Australian Economic History Review* 44: 259–77.

2006. Law and Commerce in Traditional China, an Institutional Perspective on the "Great Divergence." *Keizai-Shirin* 73.

2007. Law and Economic Growth: The Case of Traditional China – a Review with some Preliminary Hypotheses, mimeo.

2008a. Economic Growth in the Lower Yangzi Region of China in 1911–1937: A Quantitative and Historical Perspective. *Journal of Economic History* 68: 385–92.

2008b. Shanghai-based Industrialization in the Early 20th Century: A Quantitative and Institutional Analysis, mimeo.

Maddison, A. 2001. *The World Economy: A Millenial Perspective*. Paris: OECD.

2003a. *The World Economy: Historical Statistics*. Paris: OECD.

2003b. Growth Accounts, Technological Change, and the Role of Energy in Western Growth. In S. Cavaciocchi, ed., *Economia e Energia Secc. XIII-XVIII: Atti della "Trentaquattresima Settimana di Studi 15–19 aprile 2002*. Prato: Le Monnier.

2007. *Chinese Economic Performance in the Long Run*. Paris: OECD.

Mak, J., and G. M. Walton. 1972. Steamboats and the Great Productivity Surge in River Transportation. *Journal of Economic History* 32: 619–40.

Malanima, P. 1998. Italian Cities 1300–1800. A Quantitative Approach. *Rivista di Storia Economica* 14: 91–126.

2002. *L'economia italiana. Dalla crescita medievale alla crescita contemporanea*. Bologna: Il Mulino.

2005. Urbanisation and the Italian Economy during the last Millennium. *European Review of Economic History* 9: 97–122.

2006a. Pre-modern Equality: Income Distribution in the Kingdom of Naples (1811), presented at "A Global History of Income Distribution in the Long 20th century," XIV International Congress of Economic History, Helsinki.

2006b. An Age of Decline. Product and Income in Eighteenth–Nineteenth-Century Italy. *Rivista di Storia Economica* 21: 91–133.

Malthus, T. R. 1970 [1798]. *An Essay on the Principle of Population as it Affects the Future Improvement of Society with Remarks on the Speculations of Mr Godwin, M. Condorcet, and Other Writers*. London: Penguin.

Mankiw, N. G. 1989. Real Business Cycles: A New Keynesian Perspective. *Journal of Economic Perspectives* 3: 79–90.

Marczewski, J. 1961. Some Aspects of the Economic Growth of France, 1660–1958. *Economic Development and Cultural Change* 9: 369–86.

Marmocchi, F. C. 1854–62. *Dizionario Geografico Universale*. Turin: Sebastiano.

Marshall, J. 1833. *A Digest of All Accounts*. London.

Martin, M. 2008. Hundi/Hawala: The Problem of Definition. *Modern Asian Studies* 43: 909–37.

Mathias, P. 1979. *The Transformation of England*. New York: Columbia University Press.

Mathias, P., and P. K. O' Brien. 1976. Taxation in Britain and France, 1715–1810. *Journal of European Economic History* 5: 601–50.

Marx, K. 1967 [1867]. *Das Kapital*. English translation, *Capital*, by S. Moore and E. Aveling, 2 vols. New York: International Publishers.

Maynes, M. J. 2002. Class Cultures and Images of Proper Family Life. In D. I. Kertzer and M. Barbagli, eds., *Family Life in the Long Nineteenth Century 1780–1913*. New Haven: Yale University Press.

McArdle, F. 1978. *Altopascio: A Study in Tuscan Rural Society 1587–1784*. Cambridge University Press.

McCallum, B. 1989. Real Business Cycle Models. In R. J. Barro, ed., *Modern Business Cycle Theory*. Cambridge, MA: Harvard University Press.

McCloskey, D. N. 1981. The Industrial Revolution, 1780–1860: A Survey. In R. Floud and D. McCloskey, eds., *The Economic History of Britain since 1700, Volume 1: 1700–1860*. Cambridge University Press.

McCusker, J. J. 1978. *Money and Exchange in Europe and America, 1650–1775: A Handbook*. Chapel Hill: University of North Carolina Press.

McEvedy, C., and R. Jones. 1978. *Atlas of World Population History*. New York: Viking Penguin.

Macfarlane, A. 1979. *The Origins of English Individualism: The Family, Property, and Social Transition*. Cambridge University Press.

1987. *The Culture of Capitalism*. Oxford: Blackwell.

McGowan, B. 1981. *Economic Life in Ottoman Europe, Trade and the Struggle for Land, 1600–1800*. Cambridge University Press.

McKeown, T. 1976. The *Modern Rise of Population*. New York: Academic Press.

McKeown, T., and R. G. Record. 1962. Reasons for the Decline of Mortality in England and Wales during the Nineteenth Century. *Population Studies* 16: 94–122.

MacLeod, C. 1988. *Inventing the Industrial Revolution: The English Patent System, 1660–1800.* Cambridge University Press.

MacLeod, C., and A. Nuvolari. 2007. Inventive Activities, Patents, and Early Industrialization: A Synthesis of Research Issues, mimeo.

Menard, R. R. 1991. Transport Costs and Long-Range Trade, 1300–1800: Was There a European Transport Revolution in the Early Modern Era? In J. D. Tracy, ed., *The Political Economy of Merchant Empires.* Cambridge University Press.

Mendels, F. F. 1972. Proto-Industrialization: The First Phase of the Industrialization Process. *Journal of Economic History* 32: 241–61.

Mercer, A. 1990. *Disease, Mortality, and Population in Transition.* Leicester University Press.

Metzger, E. 1888. *Geographisch-statistisches Welt-Lexikon.* Stuttgart: Krais.

Meyers Konversations-Lexikon. Eine Encyklopädie des allgemeinen Wissens (1885–90), 4., gänzlich umgearbeitete Auflage. Leipzig: Bibliographisches Institut.

Michie, R. C. 1999. *The London Stock Exchange: A History.* Oxford University Press.

2000. *The Development of London as a Financial Centre.* London: Tauris.

Milward, A. S., and S. B. Saul. 1973. *The Economic Development of Continental Europe 1780–1870.* Totowa, NJ: Rowman & Littlefield.

Millward, R. 2005. *Private and Public Enterprise in Europe: Energy Telecommunications and Transport, 1830–1990.* Cambridge University Press.

Mingay, G. E., ed. 1989. *The Agrarian History of England and Wales, Volume VI, 1750–1850.* Cambridge University Press.

Mironov, B. N. 2004. Real Wages in St. Petersburg for Three Centuries, 1703–2003, presented at "Towards a Global History of Prices and Wages," Utrecht.

Mironov, B. N., and B. Eklof. 2000. *A Social History of Imperial Russia, 1700–1917.* Boulder: Westview Press.

Mitch, D. F. 1984. Underinvestment in Literacy: The Potential Contribution of Government Involvement in Elementary Education to Economic Growth in 19th-Century England. *Journal of Economic History* 44: 557–66.

1991. *The Rise of Popular Literacy in Victorian England: The Influence of Private Choice and Public Policy.* Philadelphia: University of Pennsylvania Press.

1993. The Role of Human Capital in the First Industrial Revolution. In J. Mokyr, ed., *The British Industrial Revolution: An Economic Perspective.* Boulder: Westview.

1999. The Role of Education and Skill in the First Industrial Revolution. In J. Mokyr, ed., *The British Industrial Revolution: An Economic Perspective.* Boulder: Westview.

2004. Education and the Skill of the British Labour Force. In R. Floud and P. Johnson, eds., *The Cambridge Economic History of Modern Britain, Volume 1: Industrialisation, 1700–1860.* Cambridge University Press.

Mitchell, B. R. 1975. *European Historical Statistics, 1750–1970.* London: Macmillan.

1978. *European Historical Statistics, 1750–1970.* New York: Columbia University Press.

1988. *British Historical Statistics.* Cambridge University Press.

1992. *International Historical Statistics: Europe, 1759–1988.* New York: Stockton Press.

2003. *International Historical Statistics. Europe 1750–2000*. Basingstoke and New York: Palgrave Macmillan.

Moav, O. 2005. Cheap Children and the Persistence of Poverty. *Economic Journal* 115: 88–110.

Moch, L. P. 1992. *Moving Europeans: Migrations in Western Europe since 1650*. Bloomington and Indianapolis: Indiana University Press.

Moehling, C. M. 1999. State Child Labor Laws and the Decline of Child Labor. *Explorations in Economic History* 36: 72–106.

Mokyr, J. 1977. Demand vs. Supply in the Industrial Revolution. *Journal of Economic History* 37: 981–1008.

1985. *Why Ireland Starved*, rev. edn. London: Allen and Unwin.

1987. Has the Industrial Revolution Been Crowded Out? *Explorations in Economic History* 24: 293–319.

1990. *The Lever of Riches: Technological Creativity and Economic Progress*. New York: Oxford University Press.

1993. Editor's Introduction: The New Economic History and the Industrial Revolution. In J. Mokyr, ed., *The British Industrial Revolution: An Economic Perspective*. Boulder: Westview.

1994. Technological Change, 1700–1830. In R. Floud and D. McCloskey, eds., *The Economic History of Britain Since 1700, Second Edition, Volume 1: 1700–1860*, Cambridge University Press.

2002. *The Gifts of Athena: Historical Origins of the Knowledge Economy*. Princeton University Press.

2006. The Great Synergy: The European Enlightenment as a Factor in Modern Economic Growth. In W. Dolfsma and L. Soete, eds., *Understanding the Dynamics of a Knowledge Economy*. Cheltenham: Edward Elgar.

2008. The Institutional Origins of the Industrial Revolution. In E. Helpman, ed., *Institutions and Economic Performance*. Cambridge, MA: Harvard University Press.

Mokyr, J., and J. Nye. 2007. Distributional Coalitions, the Industrial Revolution, and the Origins of Economic Growth in Britain. *Southern Economic Journal* 74: 50–70.

Moon, D. 1999. *The Russian Peasantry 1600–1930: The World the Peasants Made*. London and New York: Longman.

Moor, M. de, L. Shaw-Taylor, and P. Warde, eds. 2002. *The Management of Common Land in North West Europe, c. 1500–1850*. Turnhout: Brepols.

Moosvi, S. 1973. Production, Consumption and Population in Akbar's Time. *Indian Economic and Social History Review* 10: 181–95.

1977. Note on Professor Heston's "Standard of Living in Akbar's Time – A Comment. *Indian Economic and Social History Review* 14: 397–401.

1987. *The Economy of the Mughal Empire c.1595*. Delhi: Oxford University Press.

Moosvi, S. 2001. The Indian Economic Experience 1600–1900: A Quantitative Study. In K. N. Panikkar, T. J. Byres, and U. Patnaik, eds., *The Making of History: Essays Presented to Irfan Habib*. New Delhi: Tulika.

Moreland, W. H. 1923. *From Akbar to Aurangzeb: A Study in Indian Economic History*. London: Macmillan.

Morgan, S. 2004. Economic Growth and the Biological Standard of Living in China, 1880–1930. *Economic and Human Biology* 2: 197–218.

———. 2006. The Biological Standard of Living in South China during the 19th Century: Estimates Using Data from Australian Immigration and Prison Records, Asia-Pacific Economic and Business History Conference, Queensland University of Technology, Brisbane, 16–18 February, available at www.uow.edu.au/commerce/econ/ehsanz/pdfs/Morgan1.pdf.

———. 2008. The Biological Standard of Living in South China during the 19th century: Estimates Using Data from Australian Immigration and Prison Records. *Explorations in Economic History* 16: 363–80.

Moser, P. 2005. How Do Patent Laws Influence Innovation? Evidence from Nineteenth-Century World's Fairs. *American Economic Review* 95: 1214–36.

Mousnier, R. 1974. *Les institutions de la France sous la monarchie absolue: 1598–1789*. Paris: Presses Universitaires de France.

———. 1970. French Institutions and Society, 1610–1661. In J. P. Cooper, ed., *The New Cambridge Modern History, Volume 4: The Decline of Spain and the Thirty Year's War*. Cambridge University Press.

Muhleman, M. L. 1896. *Monetary Systems of the World*. New York: Charles H. Nicoll.

Murphy, K. M., A. Shleifer, and R. Vishny. 1989. Industrialization and the Big Push. *Journal of Political Economy* 97: 1003–26.

Musson, A. E., and E. Robinson. 1960. The Origins of Engineering in Lancashire. *Journal of Economic History* 20: 209–33.

———. 1969. *Science and Technology in the Industrial Revolution*. Manchester University Press.

Murphy, A. E. 1986. *Richard Cantillon: Entrepreneur and Economist*. Oxford: Clarendon Press.

———. 1997. *John Law: Economic Theorist and Policy-Maker*. Oxford: Clarendon Press.

Muzzi, S. 1854. *Dizionario Geografico Universale*. Bologna: Monti.

Nardinelli, C. 1980. Child Labor and the Factory Acts. *Journal of Economic History* 40: 739–55.

Neal, L. 1990. *The Rise of Financial Capitalism: International Capital Markets in the Age of Reason*. New York: Cambridge University Press.

———. 1991. A Tale of Two Revolutions: International Capital Flows 1789–1819. *Bulletin of Economic Research* 43: 57–92.

———. 1994. The Finance of Business during the Industrial Revolution. In R. Floud and D. McCloskey, eds., *The Economic History of Britain Since 1700, Second Edition, Volume 1: 1700–1860*. Cambridge University Press.

———. 1998. The Financial Crisis of 1825 and the Restructuring of the British Financial System. *Federal Reserve Bank of St. Louis Review* 80: 53–76.

———. 2000. How It All Began: The Monetary and Financial Architecture of Europe from 1648 to 1815. *Financial History Review* 7: 117–40.

Ngai, L. R. 2004. Barriers and the Transition to Modern Growth. *Journal of Monetary Economics* 51: 1353–83.

Nicolini, E. 2007. Was Malthus Right? A VAR Analysis of Economic and Demographic Interactions in Pre-industrial England. *European Review of Economic History* 11: 99–121.

Nitsch, V. 2005. Zipf Zipped. *Journal of Urban Economics* 57: 86–100.

Norberg, K. 1994. The French Fiscal Crisis of 1788 and the Financial Origins of the Revolution of 1789. In K. Norberg and P. Hoffman, eds., *Fiscal Crises, Liberty, and Representative Government*. Stanford University Press.

Nordhaus, W. D. 2004. Schumpeterian Profits in the American Economy: Theory and Measurement, Cowles Foundation Discussion Paper 1457.

North, D. C. 1981. *Structure and Change in Economic History*. New York: Norton.
    2005. *Understanding the Process of Economic Change*. Princeton University Press.

North, D. C., and B. Weingast. 1989. Constitutions and Commitment: The Evolution of Institutions Governing Public Choice in Seventeenth-Century England. *Journal of Economic History* 49: 803–32.

Nugent, J. B., and N. Sanchez. 1989. The Efficiency of the Mesta Reconsidered: A Parable. *Explorations in Economic History* 26: 261–84.

O'Brien, P. K. 1982. European Economic Development: The Contribution of the Periphery. *Economic History Review* 35: 1–18.
    1988a. The Political Economy of British Taxation, 1660–1815. *Economic History Review* 41: 1–32.
    1988b. The costs and Benefits of British Imperialism, 1846–1914. *Past and Present* 120: 163–200.
    2001. Fiscal Exceptionalism: Great Britain and its European Rivals. From Civil War to Triumph at Trafalgar and Waterloo, mimeo, London School of Economics.

O'Brien, P. K., and S. L. Engerman. 1991. Exports and Growth of the British Economy from the Glorious Revolution to the Peace of Amiens. In B. L. Solow, ed., *Slavery and the Rise of the Atlantic System*. Cambridge University Press.

O'Brien, P. K., and C. Keyder. 1978. *Economic Growth in Britain and France 1780–1914: Two Paths to the Twentieth Century*. London: Allen & Unwin.

O'Brien, P. K., and L. Prados de la Escosura. 1998. The Costs and Benefits for Europeans from their Empires Overseas. *Revista de Historia Económica* 16: 29–89.
    1992. Agricultural Productivity and European Industrialization, 1890–1980. *Economic History Review* 45: 514–36.

O'Brien, P. K., T. Griffiths, and P. Hunt 1991. Political Components of the Industrial Revolution: Parliament and the English Cotton Textile Industry, 1660–1774. *Economic History Review* 44: 395–423.

Officer, L. H. 2001. Comparing the Purchasing Power of Money in Great Britain from 1264 to Any Other Year Including the Present, available at www.eh.net/hmit/ppowerbp/.

Ogilvie, S. 1997. *State Corporatism and Proto-Industry: The Württemberg Black Forest, 1580–1797*. Cambridge University Press.
    2001. The Economic World of the Bohemian Serf: Economic Concepts, Preferences and Constraints on the Estate of Friedland 1583–1692. *Economic History Review* 54: 430–53.

2005. Communities and the "Second Serfdom" in Early Modern Bohemia. *Past and Present* 187: 69–119.

Ogilvie, S., and K. Cerman. 1996. The Theories of Proto-Industrialization. In S. Ogilvie and M. Cerman, eds. *European Proto-Industrialization.* Cambridge University Press.

Ogilvie, S., and J. Edwards. 2000. Women and the "Second Serfdom": Evidence from Bohemia. *Journal of Economic History* 60: 961–94.

Ó Gráda, C. 1988. *Ireland before and after the Famine.* Manchester University Press.

2007. Making Famine History. *Journal of Economic Literature* 45: 5–38.

Oliner, S. D., and D. E. Sichel. 2000. The Resurgence of Growth in the Late 1990s: Is Information Technology the Story? *Journal of Economic Perspectives* 14: 3–22.

O'Rourke, K. H. 1997. The European Grain Invasion, 1870–1913. *Journal of Economic History* 57: 775–801.

2006. The Worldwide Economic Impact of the French Revolutionary and Napoleonic Wars, 1793–1815. *Journal of Global History* 1: 123–49.

O'Rourke, K. H., and J. G. Williamson. 1999. *Globalization and History: The Evolution of a Nineteenth-Century Atlantic Economy.* Cambridge, MA: MIT Press.

2002a. After Columbus: Explaining the Global Trade Boom 1500–1800. *Journal of Economic History* 62: 417–56.

2002b. When did Globalization Begin? *European Review of Economic History* 6: 23–50.

2005. From Malthus to Ohlin: Trade, Industrialisation and Distribution since 1500. *Journal of Economic Growth* 10: 5–34.

O'Rourke, K. H., A. Rahman, and A. M. Taylor. 2008. Luddites and the Demographic Transition, mimeo.

O'Sullivan, A. 2003. *Urban Economics.* Irwin: McGraw-Hill.

Owen, T. 1991. *The Corporation under Russian Law; A Study in Tsarist Economic Policy.* Cambridge University Press.

Ozmucur, S., and Ş. Pamuk 2002. Real Wages and Standards of Living in the Ottoman Empire, 1489–1914. *Journal of Economic History* 62: 292–321.

Palairet, M. 1997. *The Balkan Economies c. 1800–1914. Evolution Without Development.* Cambridge University Press.

Pamuk, Ş. 2006. Estimating Economic Growth in the Middle East since 1820. *Journal of Economic History* 66: 809–28.

Parry, J. H. 1971. *Trade and Dominion: The European Oversea Empires in the Eighteenth Century.* London: Weidenfeld & Nicolson.

Parthasarathi, P. 1998. Rethinking Wages and Competitiveness in the Eighteenth Century: Britain and South India. *Past and Present* 158: 79–109.

2001. *The Transition to a Colonial Economy: Weavers, Merchants and Kings in South India, 1720–1800.* Cambridge University Press.

Paulinyi, A. 2005. Good Ore but no Coal, or Coal but Bad Ore: Responses to the British Challenge in the Habsburg Monarchy. In C. Evans and G. Rydén, eds., *The Industrial Revolution in Iron: The Impact of British Coal Technology in Nineteenth-Century Europe.* Aldershot: Ashgate.

Pearson, R., and D. Richardson. 2001. Business Networking in the Industrial Revolution. *Economic History Review* 54: 657–79.

Pedreira, J. M. 1993. La economía portuguesa y el fin del imperio luso-brasileño. In L. Prados de la Escosura and S. Amaral, eds., *La independencia americana: consecuencias económicas*. Madrid: Alianza.

Peng, K., et al. 2006. A Research Report: Chinese Interest Rates in the Early and Modern Eras, mimeo.

Perkins, D. H. 1969. *Agricultural Development in China, 1368–1968*. Chicago: Aldine Publishing Co.

Persson, K. G. 1999. *Grain Markets in Europe, 1500–1900: Integration and Deregulation*. Cambridge University Press.

Piketty, T., G. Postel-Vinay, and J.-L. Rosenthal. 2006. Wealth Concentration in a Developing Economy: Paris and France, 1807–1994. *American Economic Review* 96: 236–56.

Pinto, Isaac De. 1771. *Traité de la circulation et du crédit. Contenant une analyse raisonné des fonds d'Angleterre, & de ce qu'on appelle commerce ou jeu d'actions*. Amsterdam: Chez Marc Michel Rey.

Plosser, C. I. 1989. Understanding Real Business Cycles. *Journal of Economic Perspectives* 3: 51–77.

Poell, T. 2008. Local Particularism Challenged (1795–1813). In O. Gelderblom, ed., *The Political Economy of the Dutch Republic*. Aldershot: Ashgate.

Pollard, S. 1964. Fixed Capital in the Industrial Revolution in Britain. *Journal of Economic History* 24: 299–314.

  1965. *The Genesis of Modern Management*. London: Penguin.

  1981. *Peaceful Conquest: The Industrialization of Europe, 1760–1970*. Oxford University Press.

Pomeranz, K. 2000. *The Great Divergence: Europe, China, and the Making of the Modern World Economy*. Princeton University Press.

Posner, E. A. 2000. *Law and Social Norms*. Cambridge, MA: Harvard University Press.

Post, J. D. 1988. The Mortality Crises of the Early 1770s and European Demographic Trends. *Journal of Interdisciplinary History*. 21: 29–62.

Pounds, N. J. G. 1990. *An Historical Geography of Europe*. Cambridge University Press.

Poussou, J.-P. 1997. Migrations et mobilité de la population en Europe à l' époque de la révolution industrielle. In J.-P. Bardet and J. Dupâquier, eds., *Histoire des populations de l' Europe*. Paris: Fayard.

Prados de la Escosura, L. 1988. *De imperio a nación: Crecimiento y astraso económico en España (1780–1930)*. Madrid: Alianza.

  1993. La pérdida del imperio y sus consecuencias económicas. In L. Prados de la Escosura and S. Amaral, eds., *La independencia americana: consecuencias económicas*, Madrid: Alianza.

  1994. Terms of Trade between Spain and Britain, 1714–1913: Testing the Prebisch Hypothesis during the Industrial Revolution, working paper in economic history, Universidad Carlos III.

2000. International Comparisons of Real Product, 1820–1990: An Alternative Dataset. *Explorations in Economic History*, 37: 1–41.

2003. *El progreso económico de España, 1850–2000*. Madrid: Fundación BBVA.

Prak, M., and J. L. van Zanden. 2006. Towards an Economic Interpretation of Citizenship: The Dutch Republic between Mediaeval Communes and Modern Nation-States. *European Review of Economic History* 10: 111–46.

Predari, F. 1871. *Dizionario di Geografia Antica e Moderna*. Milan: M. Guigoni.

Pressnell, L. 1956. *Country Banking in the Industrial Revolution*. Oxford: Clarendon Press.

Price, J. M. 1980. *Capital and Credit in British Overseas Trade: The View from the Chesapeake, 1770–1776*. Cambridge, MA: Harvard University Press.

Price, R. 1983. *The Modernization of Rural France: Communication Networks and Agricultural Market Structures in Nineteenth-Century France*. New York: St. Martin's Press.

Quinn, S. 2004. Money, Finance and Capital Markets. In R. Floud and P. Johnson, eds., *The Cambridge Economic History of Modern Britain*. Cambridge University Press.

Ramaswamy, V. 1985. *Textile Weavers in Medieval South India*. Delhi: Oxford University Press.

Ramirez, F. O., and J. Boli. 1987. The Political Construction of Mass Schooling – European Origins and Worldwide Institutionalization. *Sociology of Education* 60: 2–17.

Ransel, D. L. 2000. *Village Mothers: Three Generations of Change in Russia and Tataria*. Bloomington: Indiana University Press.

Rao, D. D. P. 1993. Intercountry Comparisons of Agricultural Output and Productivity, Food and Agriculture Organization Economic Development Paper 12, Rome.

Rawski, T. G., and L. M. Li, eds. 1992. *Chinese History in Economic Perspective*. Berkeley: University of California Press.

Raychaudhuri, T. 1982. The State and the Economy: The Mughal Empire. In T. Raychaudhuri and I. Habib, eds., *The Cambridge Economic History of India, Volume 1, c.1200–c.1750*. Cambridge University Press.

Redish, A. 1990. The Evolution of the Gold Standard in England. *Journal of Economic History* 50: 789–805.

Reinhard, M., A. Armengaud, and J. Dupâquier. 1968. *Histoire générale de la population mondiale*. Paris: Montchrestien.

Reis, J. 2005. Economic Growth, Human Capital Formation and Consumption in Western Europe before 1800. In R. C. Allen, T. Bengtsson, and M. Dribe, eds., *Living Standards in the Past: New Perspectives on Well-being in Asia and Europe*. Oxford University Press.

Reuss, C., E. Koutny, and L. Tychon. 1960. *Le progrès économique en sidérurgie, Belgique, Luxembourg, Pays-Bas 1830–1955*. Louvain: Nauwelaerts.

Riley, J. C. 1986a. Insects and the European Mortality Decline. *American Historical Review* 91: 833–58.

1986b. *The Seven Years War and the Old Regime in France: The Economic and Financial Toll*. Princeton University Press.

2001. *Rising Life Expectancy: A Global History*. Cambridge University Press.

2005. Estimates of Regional and Global Life Expectancy, 1800–2001. *Population and Development Review* 31: 537–43.

Ringrose, D. R. 1996. *Spain, Europe, and The "Spanish Miracle," 1700–1900*. Cambridge University Press.

Roche, D. 2000. *A History of Everyday Things: The Birth of Consumption in France, 1600–1800*. Cambridge University Press.

Rodrik, D., A. Subramanian, and F. Trebbi. 2004. Institutions Rule: The Primacy of Institutions over Geography and Integration in Economic Development. *Journal of Economic Growth* 9: 131–65.

Rogers, J. 1995. *The Early History of the Law of Bills and Notes*. Cambridge University Press.

Romano, R. 1962. Per una valutazione della flotta mercantile europea alla fine del secolo XVIII. In A. Giuffé, ed., *Studi in onore di Amintore Fanfari*. Milan: A. Giuffrè.

Romer, Christina D. 1999. Changes in Business Cycles: Evidence and Explanations. *Journal of Economic Perspectives* 13: 23–44.

Rosenberg, M. 1972. Factors Affecting the Diffusion of Technology. *Explorations in Economic History* 10: 3–34.

Rosenberg, N., and L. E. Birdzell. 1986. *How the West Grew Rich*. London: I.B. Tauris.

Rosenberg, N., and M. Trajtenberg. 2004. A General-Purpose Technology at Work: The Corliss Steam Engine in the Late-Nineteenth-Century United States. *Journal of Economic History* 64: 61–99.

Rosenthal, J.-L. 1992. *The Fruits of Revolution, Property Rights, Litigation and French Agriculture (1700–1860)*. New York: Cambridge University Press.

Rosés, J. R., K. H. O'Rourke, and J. G. Williamson. 2007. Globalization, Growth and Distribution in Spain 1500–1913, NBER Working Paper 13055.

Roseveare, H. 1991. *The Financial Revolution 1660–1760*. London: Longman.

Rostow, W. W. 1975. *How It All Began: Origins of the Modern Economy*. New York: McGraw-Hill.

Rothenbacher, F. 2002. *The European Population, 1850–1945*. The Societies of Europe. Houndmills and New York: Palgrave Macmillan.

Roy, T. 2006. *The Economic History of India 1857–1947*, 2nd edn. Oxford University Press.

2008. Knowledge and Divergence from the Perspective of Early Modern India. *Journal of Global History* 3: 361–87.

Russell, J. C. 1972. *Medieval Regions and their Markets*. Newton Abbot: David & Charles.

Rydén, G. 2005. Responses to Coal Technology without Coal: Swedish Iron Making in the Nineteenth Century. In C. Evans and G. Rydén, eds., *The Industrial Revolution in Iron: The Impact of British Coal Technology in Nineteenth-Century Europe*. Aldershot: Ashgate.

Sandberg, L. G. 1979. Case of the Impoverished Sophisticate – Human Capital and Swedish Economic Growth before World War I. *Journal of Economic History* 39: 225–41.

Sanderson, W. C. 1976. On Two Schools of the Economics of Fertility. *Population and Development Review* 2: 469–77.

Sargent, T. J., and F. R. Velde 1995. Macroeconomic Features of the French Revolution. *Journal of Political Economy* 103: 474–518.

Sauerbeck, A. 1878. *Production and Consumption of Wool*. London: J. J. Metcalfe.

Schofield, R. 1973. Dimensions of Illiteracy, 1750–1850. *Explorations in Economic History* 10: 437–54.

Schön, L. 1988. *Historiska Nationalräkenskaper för Sverige: Industri och Hantverk 1800–1980*. Lund: Ekonomisk-historiska föreningen.

Schulze, M. S. 2000. Patterns of Growth and Stagnation in the Late Nineteenth Century Habsburg Economy. *European Review of Economic History* 4: 311–40.

Schumpeter, J. A. 1939. *Business Cycles: A Theoretical, Historical, and Statistical Analysis of the Capitalist Process*. New York: McGraw-Hill.

Sen, A. K. 1981 *Poverty and Famines*. Oxford University Press.

Serruys, M. W. 2008. Urban Networks on the Move. The Austrian Netherlands' Transit Policy and the Influence on the Commercial Flows between the Southern Netherlands and the Dutch Republic (1713–1789), paper given at the Seventh European Social Science History Conference.

Sewell, W. H., Jr. 1988. Uneven Development, the Autonomy of Politics, and the Dockworkers of Nineteenth-Century Marseille. *American Historical Review* 93: 604–37.

Shaw-Taylor, L., and E. A. Wrigley. 2008. *The Occupational Structure of England, c.1750–1851: A Preliminary Report*, mimeo, University of Cambridge.

Shepherd, J. F., and G. M. Walton. 1972. *Shipping, Maritime Trade, and the Economic Development of Colonial North America*. Cambridge University Press.

Shepherd, J. F., and G. M. Walton. 1976. Economic Change after the American Revolution. *Explorations in Economic History* 13: 397–422.

Shiue, C. 2002. Transport Costs and the Geography of Arbitrage in Eighteenth-Century China. *American Economic Review* 92: 1406–19.

  2005. From Political Fragmentation towards Customs Union: Border Effects of the German Zollverein, 1815–1855. *European Review of Economic History* 9: 129–62.

Shiue, C., and W. Keller. 2007. Markets in China and Europe on the Eve of the Industrial Revolution. *American Economic Review* 97: 1189–216.

Simpson, J. 1995. *Spanish Agriculture: The Long Siesta, 1765–1965*. Cambridge University Press.

Sivasubramonian, S. 2000. *The National Income of India in the Twentieth Century*. New Delhi: Oxford University Press.

Skinner, G. W. 1997. Family Systems and Demographic Processes. In D. I. Kertzer and T. E. Fricke, eds., *Anthropological Demography: Toward a New Synthesis*. University of Chicago Press.

Smets, F., and R. Wouters. 2007. Shocks and Frictions in US Business Cycles. *American Economic Review* 97: 586–606.

Smith, A. 1966 [1776]. *The Wealth of Nations*. New York: Augustus M. Kelley. 1976. *The Wealth of Nations*. University of Chicago Press.

Smith, B. G. 1981. *Ladies of the Leisure Class: The Bourgeoises of Northern France in the 19th Century*. Princeton University Press.

Smith, T. C., R. Y. Eng, and R. T. Lundy. 1977. *Nakahara: Family Farming and Population in a Japanese Village, 1717–1830*. Stanford University Press.

Smits, J.-P., E. Horlings and J. L. van Zanden. 2000. Dutch GDP and its Components, 1800–1913, Groningen Growth and Development Centre, available at http://www.ggdc.net/index-dseries.html#top.

Solar, P. M. 1990. The Irish Linen Trade, 1820–1852. *Textile History* 21: 54–85. 2003. The Linen Industry in the Nineteenth Century. In D. T. Jenkins, ed., *The Cambridge History of Western Textiles*. Cambridge University Press.

Sombart, W. 1928. *Der moderne Kapitalismus*, XXII. Munich: Duncker & Humblot.

Sommer, J. G. 1839. *Das Kaiserthum Oesterreich, geographisch-statistisch dargestellt*. Prague: J. G. Calve'sche Buchhandlung.

Soo, K. T. 2003. *Zipf's Law for Cities: A Cross-Country Investigation*, mimeo, Centre for Economic Performance, London School of Economics.

Soysal, Y. N., and D. Strang. 1989. Construction of the First Mass Education Systems in 19th-Century Europe. *Sociology of Education* 62: 277–88.

Sperling, J. 1962. The International Payments Mechanism in the Seventeenth and Eighteenth Centuries. *Economic History Review* 14: 446–68.

Stabel, P., B. Blondéé, and A. Greve, eds. 2000. *International Trade in the Low Countries (14th–16th Centuries): Merchants, Organisation, Infrastructure, Studies in Urban, Social, Economic, and Political History of the Medieval and Early Modern Low Countries* (Marc Boone, general editor), no. 10. Leuven: Apeldoorn.

Statistik des Deutschen Reichs. 1969 [1877]. *A.F. Band 25, zweiter Teil: Monatshefte zur Statistik des Deutschen Reichs fuer das Jahr, Repr*. Osnabrueck: Otto Zeller.

Stern, W. M. 1960. *The Porters of London*. London: Longman.

Studer, R. 2008. India and the Great Divergence: Assessing the Efficiency of Grain Markets in Eighteenth- and Nineteenth-Century India. *Journal of Economic History* 68: 393–437.

Sugihara, K. 2003. The East Asian Path of Economic Development: A Long-Term Perspective. In G. Arrighi, T. Hamashita, and M. Selden, eds., *The Resurgence of East Asia: 500-, 150- and 50-Year Perspectives*. London: Routledge.

Sullivan, R. J. 1989. England's "Age of Invention": The Acceleration of Patents and Patentable Invention during the Industrial Revolution. *Explorations in Economic History* 26: 424–52.

Sundbärg, A. G. 1968. *Aperçus statistiques internationaux*. New York: Gordon & Breach Science Pub.

Sylla, R., R. Tilly, and G. Tortella, eds. 1999. *The State, the Financial System, and Economic Modernization*. Cambridge University Press.

Szreter, S. 1988. The Importance of Social Intervention in Britain's Mortality Decline c. 1850–1914: A Re-interpretation of the Role of Public Health. *Social History of Medicine* 1: 1–37.

    1996. *Fertility, Class and Gender in Britain, 1860–1940*. Cambridge University Press.

    1997 Economic Growth, Disruption, Deprivation, Disease, and Death: On the Importance of the Politics of Public Health for Development. *Population and Development Review* 23: 693–728.

Tabellini, G. 2006. Culture and Institutions: Economic Development in the Regions of Europe, mimeo, Bocconi.

Tarkka, J. 1993. *Raha ja rahapolitiikka*. Jyväskylä: Gaudeamus.

Temin, P. 1997. Is it Kosher to Talk about Culture? *Journal of Economic History* 57: 267–87.

Temin, P., and H.-J. Voth. 2008. Interest Rate Restrictions in a Natural Experiment: Loan Allocation and the Change in the Usury Laws in 1714. *Economic Journal* 118: 743–58.

t'Hart, M., J. Jonker, and J. L. van Zanden, eds. 1997. *A Financial History of the Netherlands*. Cambridge University Press.

Thomas, B. 1973. *Migration and Economic Growth: A Study of Great Britain and the Atlantic Economy*. Cambridge University Press.

Thomas, R. P., and D. N. McCloskey. 1981. Overseas Trade and Empire, 1700–1860. In R. Floud and D. McCloskey, eds., *The Economic History of Britain since 1700, Volume 1: 1700–1860*. Cambridge University Press.

Thompson, E. P. 1967. Time, Work-Discipline, and Industrial Capitalism. *Past and Present* 38: 56–97.

Thorner, D., and A. Thorner. 1962. *Land and Labour in India*. Bombay: Asia Publishing House.

Tielhof, M. van. 2002. *The "Mother of All Trades." The Baltic Grain Trade in Amsterdam from the Late 16th to the Early 19th Century*. Leiden: Brill.

Tilly, C. 1992. *Coercion, Capital, and European States, ad 990–1992*. Oxford: Blackwell.

Tinbergen, J. 1975. *Income Distribution: Analysis and Policies*. Amsterdam: North-Holland.

Todorov, N. 1983. *The Balkan City, 1400–1900*. Seattle and London: University of Washington Press.

Tortella, G., and F. Comín. 2001. Fiscal and Monetary Institutions in Spain (1600–1900). In M. D. Bordo and R. Cortés Conde, eds., *Transferring Wealth and Power from the Old to the New World. Monetary and Fiscal Institutions in the 17th through the 19th Centuries*. Cambridge University Press.

Toutain, J.-C. 1987. Le Produit interieur brut de la France de 1789 à 1982. *Économies et Sociétés* 15: 1–237.

Tracy, J. D., ed. 1990. *The Rise of the Merchant Empires. Long-Distance Trade in the Early Modern World, 1350–1750*. Cambridge University Press.

    1991. *The Political Economy of Merchant Empires*. Cambridge University Press.

Trebilcock, C. 1981. *The Industrialization of the Continental Powers 1780–1914*. New York: Longman.

Tunzelmann, G. N. von. 1978. *Steam Power and British Industrialization to 1860*. Oxford University Press.

1981. Technical Progress during the Industrial Revolution. In R. Floud and D. McCloskey, eds., *The Economic History of Britain since 1700, Volume 1: 1700–1860*. Cambridge University Press.

Unger, R. W. 1992. The Tonnage of Europe's Merchant Fleets 1300–1800. *The American Neptune* 52: 247–61.

2006a. Investment and Risk: Ship Design and Investment in Port Infrastructure, 1200–1800. In S. Cavaciocchi, ed., *Ricchezza del mare. Ricchezza dal mare. Secc. XIII-XVIII-Atti delle "Settimane di Studi" 11–15 aprile 2005*. Prato: Le Monnier.

2006b. Warships, Cargo Ships and Adam Smith: Trade and Government in the 18th Century. *The Mariner's Mirror* 92: 41–59.

United Kingdom Board of Trade. Various years. *Abstract of Foreign Statistics*.

United Kingdom House of Commons. 1968 [1831]. *Population: Comparative Account of the Population of Great Britain in the Years 1801, 1811, 1821, and 1831*. Shannon: Irish University Press.

United Kingdom Parliamentary Papers. 1841. *Report on Roads* 27: 79.

Urlanis, B. T. 1941. *Rost Naselenie v Europe*. Moscow: Ogiz.

Valerio, N., ed. 2001. *Portuguese Historical Statistics*. Lisbon: Instituto Nacional de Estatistica.

Van Bavel, J. 2004. Diffusion Effects in the European Fertility Transition: Historical Evidence from within a Belgian Town (1846–1910). *European Journal of Population/Revue europeenne de demographie* 20: 63–85.

Vandenbroeke, C. 1985. *Sociale Geschiedenis van het Vlaamse Volk*. Leuven: Kritak.

Veenendaal, A. J. 1995. State versus Private Enterprise in Railway Building in the Netherlands, 1838–1938. *Business and Economic History* 24: 186–93.

Velde, F. R. 2003. Government Equity and Money: John Law's System in 1720 France, Federal Reserve Bank of Chicago working paper.

Vial, J. 1967. *L'industrialisation de la sidérurgie Française 1814–1864*. Paris: Mouton.

Ville, S. 1986. Total Factor Productivity in the English Shipping Industry: The North-East Coal Trade, 1700–1850. *Economic History Review* 39: 355–70.

1990. *Transport and the Development of the European Economy, 1750–1918*. Basingstoke: Macmillan.

Viner, J. 1948. Power versus Plenty as Objectives of Foreign Policy in the Seventeenth and Eighteenth Centuries. *World Politics* 1: 1–29.

Vivien de Saint-Martin, M. 1879–95. *Nouveau dictionnaire de géographie universelle*. Paris: Hachette.

Voigtländer, N., and H.-J. Voth. 2006. Why England? Demographic Factors, Structural Change and Physical Capital Accumulation during the Industrial Revolution. *Journal of Economic Growth* 11: 319–61.

2008. The Horsemen of Growth: Plague, War and Urbanization in Early Modern Europe, mimeo, Pompeu Fabra.

Voth, H.-J. 1998. Time and Work in Eighteenth-Century London. *Journal of Economic History* 58: 29–58.

2001a. *Time and Work in England 1750–1830*. Oxford University Press.

2001b. The Longest Years: New Estimates of Labor Input in England, 1760–1830. *Journal of Economic History* 61: 1065–82.

2003. Living Standards during the Industrial Revolution: An Economist's Guide. *American Economic Review* 93: 221–26.

2004. Living Standards and the Urban Environment. In R. Floud and P. Johnson, eds., *The Cambridge Economic History of Modern Britain, Volume 1, Industrialisation, 1700–1860*. Cambridge University Press..

Vries, J. de. 1978. *Barges and Capitalism: Passenger Transportation in the Dutch Economy 1632–1839*. Wageningen: A. A. G. Bijdragen.

1981. *Barges and Capitalism: Passenger Transportation in the Dutch Economy, 1632–1839*, 2nd edn. Utrecht: HES.

1984 *European Urbanization 1500–1800*. Cambridge, MA: Harvard University Press.

1990. Problems in the Measurement, Description, and Analysis of Historical Urbanization. In A. Van der Woude, A. Hayami, and J. De Vries, eds., *Urbanization in History. A Process of Dynamic Interactions*. Oxford: Clarendon Press.

1994. The Industrial Revolution and the Industrious Revolution. *Journal of Economic History* 54: 249–70.

2001. Economic Growth before and after the Industrial Revolution: A Modest Proposal. In M. Prak, ed., *Early Modern Capitalism: Economic and Social Change in Europe, 1400–1800*. London: Routledge.

2003. Connecting Europe and Asia: A Quantitative Analysis of the Cape-Route Trade, 1497–1795. In D. O. Flynn, A. Giráldez and R. von Glahn, eds., *Global Connections and Monetary History, 1470–1800*. Aldershot: Ashgate.

2008. *The Industrious Revolution*. Cambridge University Press.

Vries, J. de, and A. van der Woude. 1997. *The First Modern Economy: Success, Failure, and Perseverance of the Dutch Economy, 1500–1815*. Cambridge University Press.

Wall, R., J. Robin, and P. Laslett. 1982. *Family Forms in Historic Europe*. Cambridge University Press.

Wang, Y.-C. 1992. Secular Trends of Rice Prices in the Yangzi Delta, 1638–1935. In T. Rawski and L. Li, eds., *Chinese History in Economic Perspective*. Berkeley: University of California Press.

Warde, P. 2006. *Ecology, Economy and State Formation in Early Modern Germany*. Cambridge University Press.

Waterways Association. 1913. *Digest of the Report and Recommendations of the Royal Commission on Canals*. Birmingham.

Watkins, S., and J. Menken. 1985. Famines in Historical Perspective. *Population and Development Review* 11: 647–75.

Watkins, S., and E. van de Walle. 1985. Nutrition, Mortality, and Population Size: Malthus' Court of Last Resort. In R. I. Rotberg and T. K. Rabb, eds., *Hunger and History*. Cambridge University Press.

Weber, M. 1921. *Wirtschaft und Gesellschaft*. Tübingen: Mohr.

Wee, H. van der. 1977. Monetary, Credit and Banking Systems. In E. E. Rich and C. H. Wilson, eds., *The Cambridge Economic History of Europe, Volume V, The Economic Organization of Early Modern Europe*. Cambridge University Press.

2003. The Western European Woollen Industries, 1500–1750. In D. T. Jenkins, ed., *The Cambridge History of Western Textiles*. Cambridge University Press.

Weir, R. B. 1977. The Patent Still Distillers and the Role of Competition. In L. M. Cullen and T. C. Smout, eds., *Comparative Aspects of Scottish and Irish Economic and Social History 1600–1900*. Edinburgh: Donald.

Wells, H. G. 2005 [1905]. *A Modern Utopia*. New York: Penguin.

Wertime, T. A. 1962. *The Coming of the Age of Steel*. University of Chicago Press.

White, E. N. 1989. Was There a Solution to the *Ancien Régime*'s Financial Dilemma? *Journal of Economic History* 49: 545–68.

1995. The French Revolution and the Politics of Government Finance, 1770–1815. *Journal of Economic History* 55: 227–55.

2001. France and the Failure to Modernize Macroeconomic Institutions. In M. D. Bordo and R. Cortés Conde, eds., *Transferring Wealth and Power from the Old to the New World. Monetary and Fiscal Institutions in the 17th through the 19th Centuries*. Cambridge University Press.

Willan, T. S. 1964. *River Navigation in England, 1600–1750*. Cambridge University Press.

Willcox, W. F. 1929. *International Migrations*. New York: National Bureau of Economic Research.

Williams, E. E. 1966. *Capitalism and Slavery*. New York: Capricorn.

Williamson, J. G. 1982. The Structure of Pay in Britain, 1710–1911. *Research in Economic History* 7: 1–45.

1985. *Did British Capitalism Breed Inequality?* London: Allen and Unwin.

1987a. Has Crowding Out Really Been Given a Fair Test? A Comment. *Journal of Economic History* 47: 214–16.

1987b. Debating the Industrial Revolution. *Explorations in Economic History* 24: 269–92.

1987c. Did English Factor Markets Fail During the Industrial Revolution? *Oxford Economic Papers* 39: 641–48.

1991. *Inequality, Poverty and History*. Cambridge, MA: Blackwell.

2006. *Globalization and the Poor Periphery before 1950*. Cambridge, MA: MIT Press.

Wilson, C., and G. Parker G., eds. 1977. *An Introduction to the Sources of European Economic History 1500–1800, 1, Western Europe*. London: Weidenfeld & Nicolson.

Wirth, L. 1938. Urbanism as a Way of Life. *American Journal of Sociology* 44: 1–24.

Woloch, I. 1994. *The New Regime: Transformations of the French Civic Order, 1789–1820s*. New York: Norton.

Woodford, M. 2003. *Interest and Prices: Foundations of a Theory of Monetary Policy*. Princeton University Press.

Woods, R. 1989. Population Growth and Economic Change in the Eighteenth and Nineteenth Centuries. In P. Mathias and J. A. Davis, eds., *The First Industrial Revolutions*. Oxford: Blackwell.

2000. *The Demography of Victorian England and Wales.* New York: Cambridge University Press.

2003. Urban–Rural Mortality Differentials: An Unresolved Debate. *Population and Development Review* 29: 29–46.

Wrigley, E. A. 1967. A Simple Model of London's Importance in Changing English Society and Economy 1650–1750. *Past and Present* 37: 44–70.

1983. The Growth of Population in Eighteenth-Century Britain: A Conundrum Resolved. *Past and Present* 98: 121–50.

1991. Energy Availability and Agricultural Productivity. In B. M. S. Campbell and M. Overton, eds., *Land, Labour and Livestock.* Manchester University Press.

2004a. British Population during the "Long" Eighteenth Century, 1680–1840. In R. Floud and P. Johnson, eds., *The Cambridge Economic History of Modern Britain.* Cambridge University Press.

2004b. *Poverty, Progress, and Population.* Cambridge University Press.

2006. The Transition to an Advanced Organic Economy: Half a Millennium of English Agriculture. *Economic History Review* 59: 435–80.

Wrigley, E. A., and R. S. Schofield. 1989. *The Population History of England 1541–1871: A Reconstruction,* 2nd edn. Cambridge University Press.

Wrigley, E. A., R. S. Davies, J. E. Oeppen, and R. S. Schofield. 1997. *English Population History from Family Reconstitution, 1580–1837.* Cambridge University Press.

Zanden, J. L. van. 1995. Tracing the Beginning of the Kuznets Curve: Western Europe during the Early Modern Period. *Economic History Review* 48: 643–64.

2001. Early Modern Economic Growth: A Survey of the European Economy, 1500–1800. In M. Prak, ed., *Early Modern Capitalism Economic and Social Change in Europe, 1400–1800.* London and New York: Routledge.

2005a. Cobb-Douglas in Pre-modern Europe: Simulating Early Modern Growth, IISH working paper.

2005b. Una estimacion del crecimiento económico en la edad moderna. *Investigaciones de Historia Economica* 1: 9–38.

2009. *The Road to the Industrial Revolution: Institutions and Human Capital Formation in Europe in Global Perspective, 1000–1800.* Leiden: Brill.

Zanden, J. L. van, and T. de Moor. 2010. Girl Power: The European Marriage Pattern and Labour Markets in the North Sea Region in the Late Medieval and Early Modern Period. *Economic History Review* 63: 1–33.

Zanden, J. L. van, and A. van Riel. 2004. *The Strictures of Inheritance: The Dutch Economy in the Nineteenth Century.* Princeton University Press.

Zarnowitz, V. 1999. Theory and History behind Business Cycles: Are the 1990s the Onset of a Golden Age? *Journal of Economic Perspectives* 13: 69–90.

Index